The **Rough Guide** to

First-Time
Latin America

written and researched by

Polly Rodger Brown and James Read

Contents

Colour section   1

Introduction 6
Preparing for your
    big adventure......................... 9
Reasons to go.......................... 11

The big adventure   17

1 Planning your route............. 19
2 Visas, tickets and
    insurance 45
3 Studying, volunteering and
    working 55
4 When to go 65
5 How much will it cost?........ 74
6 Guidebooks and other
    resources 82
7 What to take 93
8 Your first night.................. 104
9 Culture shock.................... 111
10 Getting around 127
11 Accommodation................ 145
12 Staying healthy 157
13 Keeping in touch 173
14 Crime and safety............... 179
15 Coming home 194

Where to go   199

Mexico & Central America
Mexico.................................... 201
Belize..................................... 207
Costa Rica 211
El Salvador............................. 216
Guatemala 220

Honduras 224
Nicaragua 228
Panama................................... 232

South America
Argentina 237
Bolivia.................................... 243
Brazil...................................... 248
Chile 255
Colombia 261
Ecuador 266
The Guianas........................... 271
Paraguay................................. 276
Peru 280
Uruguay 286
Venezuela 290

Directory   295

Discount travel agents 297
Online booking agents 297
Specialist tour operators........ 298
Volunteer organizations.......... 301
Health 301
Official advice on international
    trouble spots..................... 302
Responsible tourism 303
Travel book and map stores... 303
Online travel resources 304
Specialist Latin American
    resource centres 304
Travel equipment suppliers 305

Travel store   309

Small print & Index   311

◀◀ Whitewater rafting, Chile ◀ Woman wearing traditional clothes, Cusco, Peru

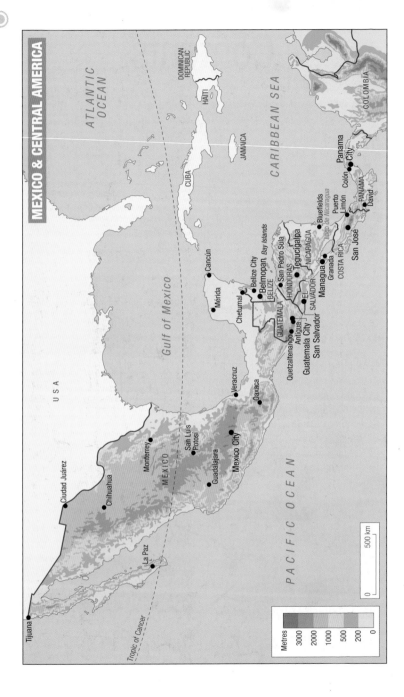

MEXICO & CENTRAL AMERICA

USA

Gulf of Mexico

ATLANTIC OCEAN

CUBA

JAMAICA

CARIBBEAN SEA

HAITI

DOMINICAN REPUBLIC

COLOMBIA

Tijuana

Ciudad Juárez

Chihuahua

Monterrey

La Paz

Guadalajara

San Luis Potosí

Mexico City

MÉXICO

Veracruz

Oaxaca

Mérida

Cancún

Chetumal

Bay Islands

Belize City

Belmopan

BELIZE

San Pedro Sula

HONDURAS

GUATEMALA

Quetzaltenango

Antigua

Guatemala City

San Salvador

EL SALVADOR

Tegucigalpa

Bluefields

Lago de Nicaragua

NICARAGUA

Managua

Granada

COSTA RICA

Puerto Limón

San José

Colón

Panama City

PANAMA

David

PACIFIC OCEAN

Tropic of Cancer

Metres

3000
2000
1000
500
200
0

0   500 km

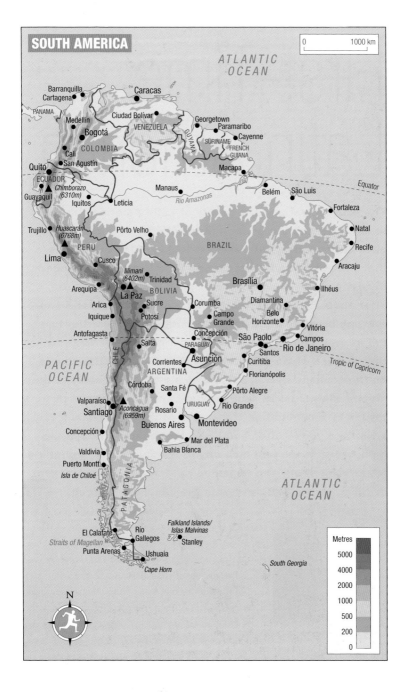

SOUTH AMERICA

0   1000 km

ATLANTIC
OCEAN

Barranquilla
Cartagena
PANAMA
Medellín   Ciudad Bolívar
Caracas
Bogotá   VENEZUELA   Georgetown
Cali   COLOMBIA   Paramaribo
San Agustín   SURINAME   Cayenne
Quito   FRENCH
ECUADOR   GUIANA
Chimborazo   Macapa
(6310m)   Equator
Guayaquil   Manaus
Iquitos   Leticia   Rio Amazonas   Belém   São Luis
Trujillo   Huascarán   Fortaleza
(6768m)   Pôrto Velho   Natal
PERU   BRAZIL   Recife
Lima   Cusco   Aracaju
Illimani   Brasília
Arequipa   (6402m)   Trinidad   Ilhéus
La Paz   BOLIVIA   Diamantina
Arica   Sucre   Corumba
Iquique   Potosí   Campo   Belo
Grande   Horizonte   Vitória
Antofagasta   Concepción   Campos
Salta   São Paolo   Rio de Janeiro
PARAGUAY   Santos
Corrientes   Asunción   Curitiba   Tropic of Capricorn
PACIFIC   ARGENTINA   Florianópolis
OCEAN   Córdoba   Pôrto Alegre
Santa Fé
Valparaíso   Aconcagua   URUGUAY   Río Grande
Santiago   (6959m)   Rosario
Buenos Aires   Montevideo
Concepción
Mar del Plata
Valdivia   Bahia Blanca
Puerto Montt
Isla de Chiloé   ATLANTIC
OCEAN
PATAGONIA

Falkland Islands/
El Calafate   Río   Islas Malvinas
Gallegos   Stanley
Straits of Magellan   South Georgia
Punta Arenas   Ushuaia
Cape Horn

Metres	
5000	
4000	
2000	
1000	
500	
200	
0	

N

Introduction to

First-Time Latin America

The extreme variety and beauty of Latin America's landscapes and the extraordinary vitality of its people have always attracted travellers looking for experiences that will enrich and even change their lives. And the sheer diversity of the region is such that it has something to offer almost every taste, whether you're looking for a short relaxing break to get away from it all, or a long adventure full of exciting challenges and new encounters. You may find yourself sipping caipirinhas with the beautiful people on Copacabana beach; salsa-dancing the night away in the steamy nightclubs of Cali; or searching for leatherback turtles by moonlight on the shores of the Caribbean. If it's adventure you're after, you could be trekking through the high Andes to the lost Inca city of Machu Picchu; searching for rare wildlife in the immense rainforests of the Amazon; or riding on a cattle drive with the gauchos of Argentina.

Nearly all these activities are affordable even for travellers on a tight budget, because most of Latin America is inexpensive compared to Europe or the United States (though generally a more expensive place to travel than Africa or Asia). Managed carefully, your money will go much further than it does back home. Unsurprisingly, a growing number of adventurers from all over the world are visiting the region, and there's now a well-established "Gringo Trail" linking the main attractions in each country, with many cities and towns home to a lively travellers' scene. This is nowhere near as intense as on the backpackers'

▲ Lapa, Rio de Janeiro, Brazil

trail in Asia, however, and one of the joys of travel in Latin America is that it's refreshingly easy to get off the beaten track and visit places that as yet see few or no tourists. This becomes even easier if you learn a little Spanish - the one language that links the overwhelming majority of the region (pick up some Portuguese if you're travelling in Brazil). You'll be able to speak to and understand almost everyone you meet, making it possible to engage the local culture and people in a way that (unless you are a brilliant linguist) you just can't do on a trip to other continents.

It's the people themselves, and their diverse and compelling lifestyles, that are perhaps the greatest attractions of Latin America. For though the region may initially appear to have a relatively uniform culture, in fact each country is made up of a diverse and compelling blend of indigenous, European and African influences; the product of Latin America's complex and extraordinary history. Even within individual countries, regional differences in human experience can be remarkable, ranging from bankers working in gleaming high-rises to semi-nomadic tribes hunting for their next meal with bows and arrows. The sheer exuberance of daily

▲ Indigenous people, Ecuador

The Amazon

Of all the natural wonders of Latin America, none has captured the world's imagination more than the Amazon Basin. Almost as large as Australia and extending from its heart in Brazil across the border to cover great expanses of Colombia, Peru, Bolivia, Venezuela and the Guianas, the Amazon is the largest tropical rainforest and by far the most biologically diverse ecosystem on earth, home to a staggering variety of plant and animal life. Through this immense forest habitat, fed by innumerable tributaries, flows the mighty River Amazon itself, a vast river-sea that carries about a fifth of the world's running fresh water. You can experience the astonishing natural beauty of the rainforest first

▲ Jaguar

hand by visiting one of the numerous national parks in the Amazon. Travelling by dugout canoe, you can see an extraordinary range of wildlife: macaws and toucans flying overhead; monkeys chattering in the treetops; turtles and cayman crocodiles basking on sandbanks; pink river dolphins hunting piranha fish in the river. With luck, you may even see an elusive jaguar, tapir or giant anteater. Despite its immense size, the Amazon rainforest is disappearing at an alarming rate. If current rates of deforestation continue, scientists fear it could be completely destroyed within the next few decades, fuelling global climate change and representing the loss of a vast and irreplaceable repository of genetic resources. By visiting the rainforest, you may be contributing to its conservation, as ecotourism can help local people earn a living without destroying the ecosystem.

life is exemplified by music that will accompany you like a soundtrack wherever you go, from the pulsating samba of Brazil and reggaeton in the Caribbean to the haunting panpipes of the high Andes. And that Latin spirit is reflected in the food: the fiery heat of Mexican chillies; the intensity of Colombian coffee; the exquisite beef of Argentina; the sensational seafood of Peru; and the delicious tropical fruit juices you can sample almost everywhere you go.

Of course, travel in Latin America can also be a disquieting experience. It's not unusual to be shocked by your first sight of a sprawling slum and upset by your first encounter with a malnourished child begging for change. Many first-timers are distressed by the chaos and squalor of some Latin American cities and by the often desperate poverty. Some get frustrated by the sometimes labyrinthine bureaucracy that can complicate even the simplest transaction, and by the locals' flagrant disregard for punctuality. Others feel unnerved by suddenly being a relatively wealthy person in a poor country and paranoid about the risks of rip-offs and violent crime that await the unwary. And then there are climatic factors like oppressive heat or extreme altitude to deal with, not to mention the strange local customs and attitudes. The truth is, every trip involves a

▲ Painted buildings, Buenos Aires, Argentina

degree of hassle, and travel would be rather dull if everything always went as planned. Adventures are by definition unpredictable affairs, and it's often the dramas and surprises that make for the most memorable experiences.

Preparing for your big adventure

This book is intended to prepare you for your trip, whether it's a couple of weeks on the beach in Cancún or a twelve-month journey from Mexico down to Tierra del Fuego. It's a book to read before you go rather than an on-the-road guide, a planning handbook to help you decide on the kind of trip you'd like to make and prepare you for that journey. The opening section of the book, **The big adventure**, gives all the practical information you need to turn your dream of travel in Latin America into a reality. You'll find chapters on what to take, when to go and how to cope when you arrive, as well as detailed advice on choosing the right ticket, sorting out visas and insurance, and keeping in touch with home. We also

▲ Chorizo stand, Buenos Aires, Argentina

look at life on the road in Latin America, giving you an idea of what to expect in terms of transport and accommodation, advice on how to stay safe and healthy while you're away, and tips on how to avoid the potential hassles and hazards that await the unwary traveller.

The lure of El Dorado

Among the most fascinating and mysterious sights in Latin America are the ruined cities and temples of the great indigenous civilizations that existed before the first Spanish and Portuguese conquistadors arrived. The dream of El Dorado, a lost city of gold hidden in the wilderness, has entranced and obsessed travellers for

▲ El Castillo Pyramid, Chichén Itzá, Mexico

centuries. In southern Mexico, Guatemala and Honduras, the mighty stone pyramids of the ancient Maya at sites like Tikal, Palenque and Chichén Itzá are an astonishing testimony to the sophistication of a culture that reached its peak more than a thousand years ago. Mexico City itself is built on the ruins of the Aztec metropolis of Tenochtitlan, and the remains of the temple complex where humans were sacrificed to bloodthirsty gods can still be explored.

In South America, the Andes are dotted with extraordinary cities and temples built by the Incas, whose vast empire stretched north to Colombia and south to Chile from its heartland in Peru. The most famous of these is Machu Picchu, the original Lost City of the Incas, a magical citadel with a stunning setting in jungle-covered mountains that roads have still not penetrated. Reached by train or on foot along the Inca Trail, Machu Picchu is just one of many ruins close to Cusco, the Inca capital. And the Incas were just the last in a series of civilizations whose ancient ruins can be explored in Peru. The country is dotted with remarkable archeological sites – the Nazca Lines, the pyramids of the desert coast, the stone citadel of Kuelap, the underground labyrinth at Chavin – each one more mysterious than the last. What's more, the dream of El Dorado is still alive, as new sites are being discovered all the time, and would-be Indiana Joneses continue to set off into the jungle in search of that mythical city of gold.

The first thing you'll need to decide is which countries and regions in Latin America you want to visit and which places to skip. The middle section of the book, **Where to go**, outlines the possibilities with a profile on each country in Central and South America plus Mexico, including a roundup of the main highlights, as well as a selection of personal recommendations.

Finally, the **Directory** is packed with useful addresses, websites and phone numbers for further information on everything from discount flight agents and specialist tour operators to jungle equipment suppliers and volunteer work opportunities.

reasons to go

Latin America embraces such a range of cultures, climates and landscapes that the very diversity that makes it so appealing can also make it seem a daunting place to visit. The trick is to decide on what kinds of experiences you hope to have, rather than setting up a whirlwind tour of the major sights. What follows is a selective taste of things you could do on your adventure.

01 Celebrate Carnaval Page **254** • The world's wildest and most extravagant party is held in Rio de Janeiro every year, and carnaval is celebrated throughout Brazil and the rest of Latin America.

04 Explore a lost city From Chichén Itzá in Mexico (Page **202**) to Machu Picchu in Peru (Page **284**), the great stone cities built by civilizations like the Maya and Inca long before Europeans conquered Latin America are among the most beautiful and mysterious sites the region has to offer.

02 Ride with the gauchos on an estancia Page **148**
• By staying on a working cattle ranch or estancia you sample the free-roaming lifestyle of South America's cowboys.

03 Spot wildlife in the rainforest Page **31** • The tropical rainforests of Latin America are the most biodiverse environments on earth, home to an astonishing variety of wildlife including monkeys, toucans, dolphins and jaguars.

05 Ride a train Page **134** • Latin America's few remaining railway lines allow you to travel in style through some of the most rugged and remote landscapes in the region.

06 **Ride the rapids** Page **28** • The mighty rivers that plunge down from the Andes in Peru, Chile and Ecuador offer some of the most exhilarating whitewater rafting anywhere in the world.

07 **Listen to Andean music** With their panpipes, drums and twelve-stringed *charangos*, musicians in the Andes are liable to strike up a lively tune at any social gathering, with haunting tunes that seem inseparable from the mighty mountains they inhabit.

08 Explore the colonial past The legacy of Portugal and Spain is most evident in the elaborate colonial architecture that graces towns and cities such as Quito (Page **270**) and Antigua (Page **220**).

09 Go whale watching Page **205** • From the Pacific Ocean off Baja California in Mexico to Peninsula Valdés in Argentina, excellent opportunities abound to spot majestic whales and other marine mammals.

10 Shop in an indigenous market Page **221** • The unique cultural heritage of Latin America's many indigenous peoples is often on display at markets like this one in Ecuador, where farmers sell and trade crops, livestock, weavings and other handicrafts.

11 Hang loose in a hammock Page **154** • Arguably Latin America's greatest gift to the world, the hammock is a perfect place to adjust to the local pace of life and chill out on the idyllic beaches of Brazil or the Caribbean.

12 Learn to dance the tango

Page **59** • Master the sensuous, melancholy moves of the tango and you're halfway to being accepted as an Argentine. And if you don't fancy the tango, there's always salsa, cumbia or merengue.

13 Get wet in a waterfall Whether you take a dip at the foot of one of Central America's countless cascades or just feel the spray of mighty Iguazú Falls (Page **240**), Latin America's waterfalls are eminently refreshing after a long day in the sun.

14 Climb a volcano Page **268** • From Mexico to Chile, lava-spewing volcanoes offer a dramatic encounter with nature's most powerful forces.

15 **Take a slow boat down the Amazon** Page 136 • A boat trip down the world's mightiest river is a quintessential Latin American experience – even though it's so big that at times you can't see either bank.

16 **See icebergs up close** Page 259 • In the wild, austral region of Patagonia – a land much closer to Antarctica than the Amazon – some of the world's mightiest glaciers can be seen (and heard).

17 **Scuba dive in the Caribbean** Page 28 • The world's second largest barrier reef and a string of coral atolls make the Caribbean coast and islands of Mexico and Central America world-class scuba-diving and snorkelling destinations.

18 **Experience a football game** Page 255 • In most of Latin America football is closer to a religion than a game, and the atmosphere for big matches in stadiums like the Maracanã in Brazil is electrifying.

First-Time Latin America

The big adventure

1	Planning your route	19
2	Visas, tickets and insurance	45
3	Studying, volunteering and working	55
4	When to go	65
5	How much will it cost?	74
6	Guidebooks and other resources	82
7	What to take	93
8	Your first night	104
9	Culture shock	111
10	Getting around	127
11	Accommodation	145
12	Staying healthy	157
13	Keeping in touch	173
14	Crime and safety	179
15	Coming home	194

1

Planning your route

L atin America is a vast area, encompassing **twenty-one countries**, two ocean coastlines, one of the world's mightiest rivers, the Amazon, and a mountain range, the Andes, which stretches well over 4000 miles. With an incredible multitude of different landscapes and cultures – including Amerindian, colonial European and African – to experience, choosing exactly where to go is no easy decision.

Built-in constraints like **time** and **budget** will help you to whittle down the myriad possibilities, but there are other factors to consider. Think about making your itinerary as varied as possible: spend time in the mountains, the rainforest and by the sea, as well as mixing the experience of rural indigenous life with peaceful colonial towns and big-city bustle. On the other hand, don't make the mistake of trying to see too much in a limited time – you'll return home with very little impression of your travels.

Try to be as **flexible** as possible when planning your route. Until you arrive you won't really know how much you're going to like (or dislike) the places you're visiting, so build enough time into your itinerary so that you're able to extend your stay if somewhere particularly takes your fancy.

See "**When to go**" (p.65) for more detailed information on climate and specific holiday seasons.

Itineraries

The following itineraries describe some classic Latin American **journeys** and are intended to provide inspiration on how to structure your trip,

www.roughguides.com

whether you want to hike up Andean peaks, explore the ruined cities of the Maya or Inca, or simply lounge around on a Caribbean beach.

Ruta Maya

One of the world's most fascinating ancient cultures, the **Maya** civilization's most remarkable legacy is the often spectacular remains of hundreds of cities – the majority still unexcavated – across southern Mexico, Belize, Guatemala, Honduras and El Salvador. While the Ruta Maya (or Mayan Route) is essentially a tourist-board invention, it makes an excellent itinerary for exploring parts of **Mexico** and **Central America**. The most important – and magnificent – sites are at Palenque, Uxmal and Chichén Itzá in Mexico, Tikal in Guatemala and Copán in Honduras; it's possible to see all five in three or four weeks, as well as explore the surrounding region, which includes the gorgeous Caribbean coast of the Yucatán Peninsula in Mexico, the coral reefs and islands of Belize and Honduras, and the dense jungle surrounding Palenque and Tikal.

A good starting point for visiting the Maya region is **Cancún**, on the northeastern tip of Mexico's Yucatán Peninsula, partly because you can fly there direct from the US and partly because it's close to two of the most significant Maya sites – **Uxmal** and **Chichén Itzá**. A short detour south from the Yucatán to the Mexican state of Chiapas takes in the wonderfully atmospheric site of Palenque. Back in the Yucatán, you can cross the border at Chetumal into Belize, whose Caribbean cayes make an idyllic spot for some welcome relaxation after exploring a few ruins, before continuing on to **Tikal** in northern Guatemala, perhaps the most impressive of all Maya sites. From Tikal, head southwest into the highlands of Guatemala, still largely inhabited by pure-blooded descendants of the ancient Maya, who preserve their traditional customs and colourful costumes. From Guatemala, it's easy to reach neighbouring Honduras and **Copán**, the last of the big five Maya sites, renowned for its carvings. Finally, if you'd rather venture off the well-trodden trail, there are plenty of less-touristed but rewarding Maya sites to visit, such as Caracol, Lamanai and Xunantunich in Belize, Ceibal and El Mirador in Guatemala's Petén region, San Andrés in El Salvador, or the vast site of Calakmul in Mexico.

Central America

The seven compact countries that make up Central America are conveniently linked in a long narrow isthmus, and form an easily negotiated, ready-made itinerary. Essentially a bridge between the temperate climate of North America and tropical South America, Central America is blessed with a geographical diversity that belies its tidy proportions.

With terrain ranging from the cloudforests of Costa Rica and Panama to the swampy flatlands of Mosquitía in Honduras and Nicaragua and the Caribbean coral atolls of Belize, linked by a central chain of volcanoes – over 250 in all, a number of them active – running the length of the isthmus, this region has much to offer outdoor enthusiasts. Culturally, too, Central America is rich in diversity, its peoples ranging from the deeply traditional Maya groups of the Guatemalan highlands to the English-speaking African-descended population of the Caribbean coast.

It's possible to travel through the whole of Central America, north to south, in two or three months. **Belize** is a good starting point, especially since it's easy to reach overland from Cancún in Mexico, which has direct flights from the US and Europe. From Belize City, you can head out to **Caye Caulker** in the Caribbean for some great snorkelling and then move down the coast to the Garífuna communities (black descendants of African slaves with their own language and culture) of Dangriga and Hopkins to listen to some distinctive local drumming and music. Then cross the country westwards towards Guatemala and the magnificent Maya site of **Tikal**, before heading southwest into Guatemala's **Western Highlands**. Spend some time exploring the indigenous lakeside villages of **Lake Atitlán** and their colourful markets before crossing the border into tiny **El Salvador**. Then travel on to Honduras, where there's superb snorkelling and diving in the **Bay Islands**, before crossing the border to visit **Lago de Nicaragua**. From Nicaragua, head into **Costa Rica**, the most developed of the Central American countries, with a range of ecotourism opportunities and over 850 species of birds. Finish your journey off in **Panama**, which has a similar wealth of natural attractions but fewer tourists and an enticing capital city. **Panama City** is one of the most vibrant of Central American capitals, a melting pot of different immigrant and domestic cultures situated on one of the great crossroads of the world.

The Caribbean coast

From the **Yucatán Peninsula** of Mexico south through Central America and curving east along the northern edge of South America, Latin America forms the western edge of the **Caribbean Sea**. If you're looking for palm-fringed beaches or coral-fringed islands, this is the place to come. With clear aquamarine waters and a barrier reef extending from Mexico's Yucatán Peninsula to the Bay Islands of Honduras, the scuba diving and snorkelling are excellent; for those who'd rather just lie in the sun, there are endless little beach communities. In terms of culture, Latin America's Caribbean stretch has its own distinctive feel – thanks to a mixture of the Afro-Caribbean (descendants of slaves brought in by the Spanish to work on plantations) and mestizo (European-Amerindian) populations of the interior. You're as likely to hear reggae and soca rhythms as Latin American salsa, English is widely spoken in some places, and the region's cuisine is often spiced up with ingredients like coconut milk and chilli.

There are two strands to this itinerary, which can be joined together if you have several months' travelling time. The first is to fly to **Caracas** in Venezuela, a major air-hub with direct connections to the US and Europe, and then make your way along a stretch of Venezuela's 2800-metre coastline (the longest in the Caribbean) to Colombia. Heading west from Caracas brings you to the travellers' hot spot of **Choroní**, a pretty beach resort reached via a spectacular bus ride through the cloudforest of the **Parque Nacional de Henri Pittier**. Other highlights of this coastline include the paradisical islands of the **Parque Nacional de Morrocoy** – you can charter a boat here without breaking the bank and even camp overnight on some islands.

Once over the border in Colombia, most travellers head to the city of **Cartagena** via the popular Parque Nacional Tayrona, a collection of white sandy beaches where you can hang a hammock or camp. From here consider embarking on the spectacular five-day trek to the **Cuidad Perdida** in the Sierra Nevada de Santa Marta mountain range. Cartagena itself is one of the loveliest colonial cities in Latin America and probably the most interesting destination on the coast, with a massive defensive wall and several fortresses remaining from its past as the biggest port in northern South America. From Cartagena either head south into Colombia towards Ecuador, or fly to Colón in Panama to explore Central America.

The second strand of the itinerary encompasses the Caribbean coast of Central America and especially its offshore islands. These include the **San Blas archipelago** of Panama, home to the indigenous Kuna tribe; the **Bay Islands** of Honduras, one of the cheapest and most popular spots to learn to scuba dive; and the **cayes of Belize**, which lie right on the edge of a lengthy coral reef. It's not possible to hop from one chain of islands to another, though – you'll have to return to the mainland and travel to the next departure point (see p.20 for details of the Central America itinerary). Highlights inland are Costa Rica's **Parque Nacional Tortuguero**, especially in turtle-hatching season, and surfing spot Puerto Viejo; the wild swamplands of the **Mosquitía region** in Nicaragua; and the Afro-Caribbean Garífuna villages of **Honduras**.

The Amazon

Covering over half of Brazil and significant parts of The Guianas, Venezuela, Colombia, Ecuador, Peru and Bolivia, the **Amazon basin** is one of the world's defining landscapes. It's the largest tropical rainforest on earth with the greatest biodiversity: more than 6000 known species of plant (and doubtless many more unknown), 15,000 animal species and a fifth of the planet's birds can be found in the Amazon; the river itself extends 6500km from source to mouth and has over a thousand tributaries. The basin also supports hundreds of thousands of indigenous peoples, living deep within the forest with most groups integrated into the mainstream though others remain largely undisturbed by outside influence. That said, it's not easy to penetrate the jungle – your best bet is to visit the region as part of a guided tour or on a boat trip along the river.

Popular starting points for organized trips into the Amazon are **Iquitos** in Peru, **Tena** and **Misahuallí** in eastern Ecuador, and **Rurrenabaque** in Bolivia – the last is the base for the cheapest trips into the Amazon (from US$30 a day). All these towns are easily reached by land, offer accommodation in jungle lodges and established routes down rivers and into the forest. With less infrastructure and fewer tourists but similar environments are **Leticia** in Colombia (which you'll have to fly to within Colombia – there's no road access), **Puerto Ayacucho** on the Venezuelan border with Colombia and **Puerto Maldonado** in Peru. Several national parks close to Puerto Maldonado, the **Tambopata-Candamo Reserved Zone** and the **Manu Biosphere Reserve**, are in a region which is arguably the most biodiverse on Earth and the absence of city noise and light make them perfect places to experience the unique fauna, flora and atmosphere of the jungle.

A quintessential Amazon journey is the Brazilian trip from the mouth of the Amazon River at **Belém** to **Manaus**, right in the heart of the rainforest, a boat journey of five days. Because of the massive width of the river between these points (you can't see both its banks when you're on it), you won't see a lot of wildlife, but it's a classic adventure all the same, with accommodation in hammocks, river dolphins playing in the boat's wake (if you're lucky), and local people paddling past in canoes, selling jungle fruit. From Manaus, which you can fly directly to if you'd rather miss out the main river ride, it's possible to make shorter boat trips on the Amazon's tributaries – such as the **Río Negro**, which winds northwards to Colombia, or the **Río Madeira**, which makes its way down towards Brazil's border with Bolivia – many of which are sizeable rivers in their own right and offer better opportunities for spotting river wildlife.

The Andes

The longest chain of mountains in the world at 7200km, the **Andes** run the length of western South America, from the southern tip of Chile to Venezuela in the north, and include some of the highest peaks outside the Himalayas. Made up of dozens of parallel mountain ranges or cordilleras,

www.roughguides.com

the Andes provide some of the most spectacular scenery in Latin America. These mountains were home to the great Inca race and to others before them – Chavín, Nazca and Tiahuanuco, to name three – who left behind a string of dramatic ruined cities and trading routes that now form memorable hiking trails. Today, the rural highlands are still inhabited by indigenous peoples, principally the Quechua and Aymara, who wear traditional costume, farm the terraced slopes much as their ancestors did, and come together to trade in colourful weekly markets.

The classic Andean itinerary runs between Quito in Ecuador and La Paz in Bolivia via Peru – this is the most visited region in Latin America and not without reason known as the "**Gringo Trail**". It's easy to escape other travellers, though – apart from the resorts and attractions on the well-worn route (listed below), the Andean region is still largely overlooked by tourists and some less touristy destinations are also listed in this itinerary.

Quito, capital of Ecuador, is an attractive colonial city; its Old Town or *El Centro Histórico* is packed with churches, monasteries and a wealth of seventeenth- and eighteenth-century religious paintings. With its easy-going charm, spring-like climate and good tourist facilities, the city makes an excellent starting point. The country's central sierra, site of the so-called **Avenue of the Volcanoes**, has some spectacular trekking and climbing opportunities and is also the indigenous heart of Ecuador. Heading south towards Peru, highlights include **Baños**, a small thermal spa town with a subtropical climate; **Cuenca**, an even finer example of colonial architecture than Quito – and without the capital's noise and traffic; and **Vilcabamba**, a gringo hangout set in a beautiful valley and close to the cloudforests of **Parque Nacional Podocarpus**. Crossing into Peru, head for the **Cordillera Blanca**, the highest tropical mountain range in the world with spectacular scenery, glacial lakes and pre-Inca ruins, before making for Cusco. A delightful colonial city with a lively backpacker scene, **Cusco** is the gateway to the Inca ruins of **Machu Picchu**, Latin America's biggest tourist attraction, set on a terraced plateau between two prominent mountain peaks; one of the most popular ways of reaching it is the **Inca Trail**, a strenuous three- to five-day hike. Bolivia's Andean highlights include the clear blue waters of **Lago Titicaca**, which straddles the border between Bolivia and Peru, the legendary silver-mining city of **Potosí**, and **La Paz**, Bolivia's de facto capital and a bustling cultural melting pot situated at an altitude of over 3500m. Close to the city, **Huayna Potosí** is one of the few peaks in South America over 6000m that can be climbed by people with no mountaineering experience. To cover this stretch of South America, you should allow two to three months.

If you have more time to spare – at least a fortnight, though ideally a month – you ought to consider exploring the dramatic and awe-inspiring mountain regions of Chile and Argentina. Moving south from Bolivia, you'll cross into the **Chilean Altiplano**, a high mountain plain with starkly beautiful scenery punctured by turquoise lakes and snowcapped Andean volcanoes. The main tourist centre of the region is **San Pedro de Atacama**, a friendly village with adobe houses and a large backpacker scene, sitting at 2400m between the desert and the Altiplano. Trips can be arranged from the village to the eerie lunar landscape of the **Valle de la Luna**, the salt flats of the **Salar de Atacama** and the fuming geysers of **El Tatio**. Another attractive settlement in the Chilean Altiplano is **Parinacota**, a typical *pueblo altiplánico* with a bright, whitewashed church. Parinacota is headquarters for the **Parque Nacional Lauca**, a starkly beautiful place where herds of vicuña (a llama relative) roam near the shores of the wide **Lago Chungará** and nearby stands one of the highest peaks in Chile, **Volcán Parinacota**.

Chile's eastern border with Argentina is a natural one, formed by a 5000m-long cordillera of the Andes, and it's on the Argentine side of this border that **Aconcagua**, the highest mountain outside the Himalayas (6959m), juts above an array of impressive neighbouring peaks. Although you shouldn't trek to its summit unless you're an experienced mountain climber, the region around the peak, **Alta Montaña**, is very picturesque with good skiing and hiking opportunities. From here

▲ Driving in the Chilean Altiplano

you could head into Argentina's **Lake District** and on to **Patagonia** (see below) or loop back into Chile and head south to explore the **Carretera Austral**, a 1000m road that winds through a lush green wilderness laced with national parks.

Patagonia and Tierra del Fuego

Patagonia, a huge and remote wilderness in the far south of South America, encompasses more than a third of Argentina along with the southern tip of Chile. Its main attractions lie in the west and south where huge Andean peaks, glaciers and lakes puncture dramatic mountain terrain. At its tip lies the isolated archipelago of **Tierra del Fuego**, again split between Argentina and Chile and quite literally the end of the continent. With its world-class trekking, mountains and national parks – Patagonia will satiate even the hardiest of outdoor types.

An exhaustive trip starts with flying into **Buenos Aires**, then heading south to **Chile**, a journey of over 1500km. Most travellers skip the vast dry steppe of Central Patagonia and head west and/or south. In this scarcely populated region, distances between areas of interest are immense – you'll either have to fly from place to place (both El Calafate, close to the Perito Moreno glacier and Tierra del Fuego's capital Ushuaia have several scheduled flights a day from Buenos Aires) or be prepared to spend days in either a bus or rental car.

The region has many memorable highlights, including (from north to south) the **Península Valdés**, with its colonies of penguins, killer whales and other marine wildlife; the forested hills of the **Lake District** region with the attractive resort of **Bariloche** at its centre; 10,000-year-old handprints on the walls of the **Cueva de los Manos Pintadas**; and the **Perito Moreno Glacier**, with its sixty-metre cliffs of ice. Close to the glacier is **El Chaltén**, a small town with well-signed treks into the dramatic **Parque Nacional de los Glaciers**. Furthest south is **Tierra del Fuego**, boasting an incredible location for its capital, **Ushuaia**, which sits on the Beagle Channel, wedged between the mountains and the sea.

From Ushuaia it's easy to cross the border into Chile and take the two-day ferry ride from Puerto Natales, conveniently near to **Parque Nacional Torres del Paine**, through the Chilean fjords to **Puerto Montt** and on up the scenic **Carretera Austral** to points north in Chile and the other Andean countries.

You'll need several weeks to fully explore the region. Bear in mind that roads here are often not in the best of conditions – particularly large stretches of the **RN-40**, fabled for its beauty, in Argentina – and that during the winter months of June and July temperatures drop to as low as -25°C/-13°F. Additionally Patagonia is one of the most expensive regions to tour in Latin America; it is also increasingly popular (with Latin Americans as well as foreigners) and in the summer you will need to book accommodation and transport well in advance.

Themed trips

If you've a particular interest, be it wildlife, or ancient civilizations, or activities such as whitewater rafting, trekking or scuba diving, your Latin American trip can certainly be planned around a **theme**.

Adventure sports

Latin America, with its diverse, grand and unspoilt landscapes, has an extremely impressive range of **adventure sports** on offer, many of which are very reasonably priced; bear in mind, though, that safety standards are often questionable. If you have your own **equipment**, consider bringing it along, in case the quality of gear available isn't up to scratch.

● **Mountaineering and rock climbing** There are superb climbing opportunities in the Andean countries of South America, ranging from some of the world's most challenging ascents to relatively easy ones that can be tackled by anyone with a reasonable level of fitness (remember, though, that you'll need to be properly acclimatized, or you risk developing the potentially fatal acute mountain sickness – see p.167). John Biggar's *The Andes: A Guide for Climbers* (Andes) is an excellent, comprehensive climbing guide to the region.

Bolivia's spectacular Cordillera Real, close to La Paz, has six peaks over 6000m and is one of the region's best destinations for mountaineering. Huayna Potosí (6088m), one of the Real's biggest peaks, can be climbed by people with absolutely no mountaineering experience. For experienced climbers, *Bolivia: A Climbing Guide* by Yossi Brain (Mountaineers Books), is an essential read. Ecuador's Avenue of the Volcanoes, south of Quito, also offers a wealth of climbing opportunities (see *Climbing and Hiking in Ecuador* by Rob Rachowiecki, Mark Thurber and Betsy Wagenhauser (Bradt Travel Guides) for further details). The *departamento* of Ancash in Peru, particularly the Huarez valley of the Cordillera Blanca, has some of the best mountaineering in the Americas. Huascarán (6768m) is Peru's tallest peak and the climb to the top is challenging and for serious mountaineers only. Less difficult peaks to scale are Pisco and Urus; for all these climbs you'll need local guides. In Argentina, the main climbing centres are the city of Mendoza, close to South America's highest peak, Aconcagua (6962m); the holiday resort of Bariloche in the Patagonian Lake District; and western Patagonia, particularly the Fitz Roy Massif in the Parque Nacional Los Glaciares and the Volcán Lanin (3776m).

● **Skiing** Argentina's main resort is Las Lenas in the southwest of Mendoza province, which attracts a chic South American crowd as well as northern hemisphere skiers looking for some summer (June–Oct) action. If you fancy skiing at the "end of the earth" there is also a modest ski resort close to Ushuaia in Tierra del Fuego as well as scenic Nordic (or cross-country) skiing trails around town. Chile has the best skiing in South America, with very dry powder snow; the main resorts – El Colorado, La Parva and Valle Nevado – are all roughly 40km from Santiago.

● **Whitewater rafting and river kayaking** Latin America has some championship-level locations for whitewater rafting and river kayaking. In Chile there are two world-class rafting rivers (graded III–IV) in spectacular settings, with backdrops of volcanoes, waterfalls and lush forest: the Bío Bío on the southern edge of the Central Valley; and the Futaleufu down by the southern Carretera Austral, occasional venue of the Rafting World Championships. Gentler waters can be found on the Río Maipo near Santiago, the Río Trancura near Pucon and Río Petrohue near Puerto Varas. Peru also offers some of the best whitewater rafting in the world, the main centre being Cusco, from where you can organize trips to the Urubamba and Vilcanota rivers; the Cotahuasi and Colca river canyons close to Arequipa are also popular. For a thrilling account of a 1986 journey by kayak from the Amazon's source to its mouth (2500km later), read *Running the Amazon* by Joe Kane (Vintage).

● **Other adrenaline highs** Thrill-seekers might enjoy **bungee jumping** in Costa Rica, from a bridge over the Río Colorado in the Central Valley, and also in Guatemala, over one of the ravines near Guatemala City or on the Río Dulce; **hang-gliding** from the Parque Nacional de Tijuca in Rio de Janeiro, where a spectacular tandem flight takes you 520m down to the beach at São Conrado; and **mountain biking** on the road which runs dramatically from the mountains of La Paz to the jungle lowlands around Coroico in Bolivia (see p.247).

Scuba diving and snorkelling

The Caribbean coast and islands offer the best **scuba diving** and **snorkelling** in Latin America, with great visibility. The year-round warmth and calm waters of the **Caribbean Sea**, make this a particularly good place for beginners and those keen to learn to scuba dive. There is a wealth of marine life including the world's largest fish, the whale shark; parrotfish; eagle rays and stingrays; barracuda, hammerhead and nurse sharks. **Courses** range in price – from fairly expensive in Mexico to very cheap in Honduras. There are various isolated snorkelling and diving spots in South America, too, principally the **Galápagos Islands**.

- **Mexico, Belize and Honduras** Lying offshore from the Caribbean coast of the Yucatán Peninsula in Mexico is a huge coral reef which offers some world-class scuba diving, particularly around the island of Cozumel and further south around the pristine Banco Chincorro. The cayes of Belize and Bay Islands of Honduras, set on the same 290-kilometre-long coral reef that begins in Mexico, also have wonderful diving, along with idyllic island settings. There are three atolls in Belize alone and the renowned Great Blue Hole, a vast collapsed cave made famous by Jacques Cousteau. The Bay Islands are especially popular with backpackers – Utila has the cheapest diving courses in Latin America. Recommended specialist guidebooks are: *Diving and Snorkeling Guide to Cozumel* by George S. Lewbel (Lonely Planet), *Diving in Belize* by Ned Middleton (Aqua Quest Publications), and Cindy Garoute's *Diving the Bay Islands* (Aqua Quest Publications).
- **Colombia** The tiny coral islets called the Islas del Rosario, just off the Caribbean coast at Cartagena, are teeming with brightly coloured fish – dive operators in Cartagena take trips out to the islands. Further out in the Caribbean, the island of Providencia also has wonderful scuba diving and snorkelling in a pristine turquoise sea.
- **Ecuador** The waters off the Galápagos Islands are home to unique marine species including marine iguanas, the Galápagos fur seal and the stalkeye scorpion fish, and offer some of the world's best diving (and snorkelling), although colder temperatures, strong swirling currents and low visibility mean that this is for experienced divers only, and rates are not cheap.
- **Brazil** The Atlantic coast of South America has crystal-clear waters and good scuba diving around the marine park island of Fernando de Noronha in northeastern Brazil. Its position, 340km from the mainland, means that abundant marine life is largely undisturbed and includes turtles, stingrays and spinner dolphins. There are numerous caverns, submerged rocks and several shipwrecks including the *Corveta V17*, a cargo ship with structure intact. Other notable places to scuba dive are Abrolhos, an archipelago off the coast of Bahia with one of the largest

www.roughguides.com

THE BIG ADVENTURE

and healthiest coral reefs in the South Atlantic and visited by humpback whales between June and December and Arrail do Cabo Marine Reserve near Rio de Janeiro where divers can spot seahorses, moray eels and Queen Angelfish.

- **Argentina** Scuba diving in Argentina is not for the faint-hearted – water temperatures are never warm and divers will need to use dry suits. However, the seas around Península Valdés teem with sea lions, dolphins and whales whose mournful call often penetrates the underwater world. In Ushuaia one of the main attractions is the recently discovered shipwreck of the *Montes Cervantes* vessel lying at the bottom of the Beagle Channel.

Surfing

The entire Pacific coast of Latin America is dotted with **surfer communities**, with a high concentration in Mexico and Costa Rica, and several in El Salvador and Nicaragua – these are populated mostly by well-organized and friendly American expats. In South America the scene is much more homegrown, with large domestic surf spots in Peru and Brazil. **Renting** reasonably priced boards and equipment is possible in all these places. Check ⓦwww.surfline.com and ⓦwww .surflink.com for detailed reports on the best breaks.

- **Mexico** The Pacific coast has the best waves and the most established surfer communities, notably the laid-back town of San Blas and the larger resort of Puerto Escondido. The Baja California peninsula also has lots of more remote surfing beaches including Punta El Conejo and El Martillo (The Hammer) on the Islas de Todos Santos.
- **El Salvador** The friendliness of the locals, the cheap cost of living and the relatively small number of surfers attracts mainly North Americans to several bays on the central Pacific coast. La Libertad is the capital of Salvadoreño surfing and home to the Punta Roca, one of the best right-handed point breaks in the world. With some famous breaks on both coasts, Costa Rica has a big surfing scene. The Pacific side attracts more visitors – with top spots including Boca Barranca, Jaco and Dominical – while Puerto Viejo on the Caribbean is home to the salsa brava, one of the country's few really big waves.
- **Peru** Peru has some of the longest waves in the world, with quality surf spots around Lima, particularly Punta Hermosa, 50km south of the city. The far north of the country receives consistent swell and is much less crowded.
- **Brazil** The best surfing in South America is on the southern beaches, such as Barra de Tijuca in Rio de Janeiro and Ubatuba in

São Paulo state, though Brazilian surfers have a terrible reputation for aggressive riding and stealing waves. The island of Santa Catarina in the state of the same name is famous for its waves and hosts the Brazilian national championships every January.

Wildlife

With an incredible variety of **flora** and **fauna** and a rich diversity of habitats, largely undeveloped and unspoilt by mass tourism, Latin America is one of the world's leading destinations for ecotourists and wildlife enthusiasts. Of course, the **Amazon** rainforest has no equal in terms of its profusion of animal and plant species, but the region holds numerous other habitats – such as flat grasslands, mountain forests, alpine lakes and seas – which are also strikingly fertile. Indeed, every Latin American country offers good opportunities for spotting wildlife, but some – notably Belize, Costa Rica and Argentina – have better organized networks of **national parks** and **reserves**, which can make a wildlife-themed trip a lot easier and more rewarding. Animals you might see include anteaters, tapirs, pumas and jaguars; howler monkeys and sloths; giant turtles, caymans and anacondas; poison dart frogs and leafcutter ants. The region is also a paradise for **birdwatchers**, both in terms of quantity – there are more species of bird in Brazil and Colombia than in any other country in the world, while Guatemala and Costa Rica aren't far behind – and celebrated species – condors, scarlet and hyacinth macaws, toucans and quetzals all reside here.

There are a few books which are a great introduction to Latin American wildlife: *Andes to Amazon: A Guide to Wild South America* by Michael Bright (BBC Books) and John C. Kricher's *A Neotropical Companion: An Introduction to the Animals, Plants and Ecosystems of the New World Tropics* (Princeton University Press) are recommended guidebooks to the flora and fauna of Latin America. There are also dozens of specialist books on birds – *A Field Guide to the Birds of Mexico and Central America* by Meyer de Schauensee (University of Texas Press) and L.I. Davis's *A Guide to the Birds of South America* (Museum of Natural History Press) are the most comprehensive.

Below are just a few of the best destinations – other than the Amazon (covered on pp.22–23) – for spotting wildlife in Latin America.

- **The Petén** In northern Guatemala, the Petén comprises a mixture of low-lying swamp, savannah and rainforest, and includes the Maya Biosphere Reserve, the largest tropical forest reserve in Central America. The most accessible area is that surrounding the Maya site at Tikal, a wonderfully atmospheric place alive with the screeching of monkeys and noisy flocks of scarlet macaws.

www.roughguides.com

- **The Darién Gap** Straddling the border between Panama and Colombia, much of the Darién Gap is currently off-limits thanks to the activities of guerrillas and drug runners (see p.42). However, parts of this great, untouched natural wilderness can be explored from the Panamanian side, where large tracts of forest are protected by the Parque Nacional Darién.

- **Los Llanos** A vast area of plains between the Andes and the Río Orinoco basin in Venezuela, Los Llanos is flooded annually in October and November, when wildlife spotting is at its best – species include river dolphins, alligators, puma and howler monkeys.

- **The Pantanal** The open swampland of the Pantanal in western Brazil is not easily reached independently, but there are dozens of tour operators in Corumba running trips into the area. The flatness of the Pantanal (and its lack of inhabitants) means that sighting wildlife is more likely than almost anywhere else in Latin America – with luck you might see anteaters, armadillos, rare blue macaws, toucans, jaguars and anacondas.

- **The Galápagos Islands** Though the cost of reaching the famous Galápagos Islands, 950km off the coast of Ecuador, is enough to put a sizeable hole in all but the deepest of budgets – there can be little doubt that it is money well spent. The abundant marine fauna of one the world's pre-eminent wildlife destinations leaves an unforgettable impression, not to mention the rare chance to glimpse a venerable giant tortoise. The waters off the islands are home to unique species including marine iguanas, the Galápagos fur seal and the stalkeye scorpion fish,

- **Península Valdés** One of the most important marine reserves on earth, the waters around the arid Península Valdés in Argentine Patagonia are home to an array of dramatic mammals – from southern right whales to pods of killer whales known to momentarily strand themselves as they hunt for young sea lions and elephant seals idling at the foot of the peninsula's cliffs.

Trekking

Even if walking and outdoor activities are normally anathema to you, the dramatic beauty of Latin America's mountains, rainforests and Inca trails is likely to tempt you to do some trekking on your trip. Try always to stick to **established paths** and, if you're walking in an area with a guerrilla or paramilitary presence (such as Colombia or Chiapas in Mexico), check first with the locals about the current situation and err on the side of caution. Never go trekking alone – even a sprained ankle could prove hazardous if you're stuck on your own in a remote region.

If you're planning on doing several long treks (three or more days), consider taking your own camping and water filtration **equipment**. Detailed topographical **maps** can be purchased from the relevant Instituto Nacional Geográfico/Militar (normally located in capital cities). Several well-worn routes in Latin America (notably the Inca Trail, see p.284) can only be undertaken in organized groups with registered guides – these regulations are to protect you as well as the landscape and should be respected. Even if a **guide** is not strictly necessary, you should always consider the option when trekking in lesser known areas and particularly in the jungle, where dense vegetation makes getting lost a real possibility. If your plans entail hiking for several days in a national park you may have to book your place well in advance. And finally, if you're trekking in the Andes, bear in mind that at **high altitudes** there's an enormous difference in temperature between sunny and shady areas during the daytime – and once the sun sets it gets very cold indeed.

Guidebook publishers Bradt are experts in trekking and have some excellent guides to climbing and trekking in Latin America. There are spectacular opportunities for trekking in every country in Latin America – listed below are just a few of the best.

- **Guatemala** The Western Highlands of Guatemala provide a variety of trekking experiences through lush green hills dotted with volcanoes and traditional Maya villages. The Ixil triangle in the Cuchumatanes mountains is another of the region's picturesque walking areas, while the northern Petén region offers an arduous two-day trek with packhorses through remote jungle to the remote Maya ruin of El Mirador.
- **Costa Rica** Costa Rica's many national parks and nature reserves are home to numerous excellent, well-organized walking trails. Some of the most popular include those in the famous Monteverde Cloudforest Reserve (and in the less-touristed Santa Elena Reserve nearby), the trek along the coast of the pristine Osa peninsula in the Parque Nacional de Corcovado, and the challenging climb to Costa Rica's highest point at 3819m in the Parque Nacional Chirripó.
- **Colombia** Starting from the Caribbean coast, the five- or six-day trek to the Cuidad Perdida of the Tayrona Indians in the Sierra Nevada de Santa Marta is one of the country's highlights, while the mountainous Parque Nacional de Puracé, in southern Colombia, offers a rewarding day's trek up Volcán Puracé, with the possibility of spotting condors, bears and tapirs.
- **Venezuela** Climbing the *tepui* or flat-topped mountain of Roraima at the eastern edge of the Gran Sabana is strenuous and

takes at least five days, but the eerie landscape at its summit, with a black craggy surface split by fissures and weirdly shaped rocks, makes the climb well worth it.

- **Bolivia** Bolivia's most popular trekking region is the Cordillera Real, which is blessed with high Andean scenery and easily reached from La Paz. Three different Inca trails run from close by La Paz across the mountains and down to the tropical valleys of the Yungas – the most spectacular, the Takesi Trail, takes two to three days and is easily done by less experienced hikers without a guide.

- **Peru** The Peruvian Andes are home to Latin America's most popular trek, the three- to five-day Inca Trail to the legendary ruined city of Machu Picchu. There are many other good trekking opportunities in the surrounding Sacred Valley, while Huaraz in the Cordillera Blanca, north of Lima, is the starting point for serious mountain-hiking.

- **Brazil** Parque Nacional de Chapada Diamantina in Bahia, northeastern Brazil, is laced with caves, waterfalls and dramatic rock formations rising from flat grasslands. The full day's trek from the colonial mining town of Lençois to the hamlet of Capão is one of many spectacular walks in the park.

- **Argentina** Most visitors to Argentina head to Patagonia to trek and particularly the Fitz Roy region around El Chaltén. Other popular trekking areas include Parque Nacional Nahuel Huapí Park, just south of Bariloche. In the north of Argentina both Jujuy and Salta provinces offer a wide range of walking terrains, from subtropical to cloudforest and high mountain valleys.

- **Chile** The meadows, lakes and forests of the Chilean Lake District make it the most popular trekking region of the country, along with the spectacular mountain peaks of the Parque Nacional Torres del Paine in Chilean Patagonia.

Ancient civilizations

Long before the Spanish and Portuguese colonizers arrived in the Americas in the sixteenth century, much of Latin America's **Amerindian** population had organized itself into a series of complex and fascinating societies with their own languages, culture and political and belief systems. Although much of what these ancient civilizations – such as the Maya, Inca and Aztec – created was razed to the ground by tribal wars and systematically destroyed by the European invaders, some surprisingly intact remnants – including cities, temples and burial grounds – are scattered across Latin America. With new **archeological discoveries** still being made, these civilizations and their enduring cultural heritage together are one of the region's defining attractions.

Good sources of background information, current news and essays on the pre-Hispanic civilizations of Latin America are Mesoweb (ⓦwww .mesoweb.com), Archnet (ⓦarchnet.asu.edu) and the Archaeological Institute of America (ⓦwww.archaeological.org) which organizes pricey but very professional archeological tours of Latin America. The Lanic (Latin American Network Information) website (ⓦlanic .utexas.edu) has dozens of links to relevant societies, online magazines and websites.

● **The Maya** Perhaps the best known of Latin America's ancient civilizations is the Maya. Over three thousand years ago nomadic tribes began to settle in the rainforests of middle (or *meso*) America, over a landmass that includes the countries now known as Mexico, Guatemala, Belize, Honduras and El Salvador. They established the most sophisticated pre-Hispanic civilization in Latin America, one that, with its complex structures and incredible prowess in engineering, architecture, mathematics and astronomy, rivalled those of contemporary Europe. Even though all their cities had been mysteriously abandoned by 1200 AD, Maya culture lives on, particularly in Guatemala which has a majority population of pure-blooded Maya. The villages around Lake Atitlán and in the Western Highlands are particularly rich in tradition with colourful markets and fiestas. A detailed itinerary, covering the major sites of the Maya world, is listed on p.20.

For some pre-trip inspiration, both Michael Coe's *The Maya* (Thames and Hudson) and Robert J. Sharer's *The Ancient Maya* (Stanford University) should be considered required reading. *Sastun: One Woman's Apprenticeship with a Maya Healer* by Rosita Arvigo (Harper) is a more modern take on the traditions of Maya culture.

● **The Inca Empire** The Inca Empire was once the largest in the world. Much later in formation than the Maya civilization and much shorter in length (three hundred years rather than two thousand), it began in 1200 AD and was centred in the valleys around Cusco in the Peruvian Andes. At its height the Inca Empire covered around 980,000 square kilometres linked by 30,000km of roads and stretched from southern Colombia down to northern Chile. These days the remains of Inca sites, still spectacularly impressive, are the most visited places in the whole of Latin America.

To read up on the Incas before exploring their enduring sites, *The Conquest of the Incas* (Papermac) by John Hemming is a must-read, widely considered to be the authoritative account of the end of the Inca Empire. Michael E. Moseley's *The Incas and Their Ancestors* (Thames and Hudson) is a good overview of the civilization.

Most visitors to Latin America explore Inca culture as part of a trip to the high Andes of South America. The Andes itinerary (see p.23) joins together various places of interest in this area though you may want to concentrate your time on Peru where all the major Inca sites are located, most notably Machu Picchu, a three- to five-day hike from the Inca capital of Cusco. Around Cusco there are several other impressive Inca sites including the megalithic fortress of Sacsayhuaman and the sacred spots of Qenko and Salapunco, both marked by rocks carved with Inca patterns, pumas and snakes. Close to Machu Picchu are the ruins of Pisac and Ollantaytambo and hundreds of lesser known Inca trails which wind through the mountain scenery. Further north, close to Lima in the Rimac valley, are the impressive Inca remains of Pachacamac, once one of the most famous shrines in the Inca Empire. On the shores of Lago Titicaca is the Incan Templo de Fertilidad which has a hundred stone phalluses jammed within its walls, and on the Bolivian side of the lake is the Isla de Sol, the birthplace of the sun, the mythical father of the Inca race. In Ecuador, Ingapirca, a city in the southern sierra, is the country's only notable Inca ruin with a striking temple forming the centrepiece of the site.

- **The Aztecs** Like the Incas, the Aztec civilization arose late and was short-lived (1200–1521 AD), and in Mexico is overshadowed by the more lasting legacy of the Maya. Still, the Aztecs, or Mexica, gave Mexico its name and were in their time the most formidable of all Mexican empires, dominating the whole of central and southern Mexico in less than a hundred years. Their capital city, Tenochtitlán, was vast and so impressed Cortés and his Spanish army when they arrived to conquer the country that some of them thought it a mirage. The modern-day Mexico City sits above the Aztec's capital and remains, albeit small, can be found dotted all round the city. Beneath the main square or *zocaló* is an Aztec temple, Templo Major, and on the outskirts of the city are the ruins of Tlatelolco where the beleaguered Aztecs made their last stand against Cortés in 1521. Aztec culture didn't expand beyond Mexico – those interested in exploring it in depth would be best served by basing themselves in Mexico City.

Essential reading on the Aztecs includes *The Aztecs* (Thames and Hudson) by Richard F. Townsend and Warwick Bray's *Everyday Life of the Aztecs* (P Bedrick).

Other ancient civilizations

There are dozens of ancient civilizations in Latin America, aside from the Maya, the Incas and the Aztecs, that have also left fascinating marks on the landscape. Listed below are the countries where you will find the most fascinating legacies.

- **Mexico** Mexico has, by a large margin, the richest cultural history in Latin America. Apart from the legacies of the Mayans and Aztecs, there are remains throughout the country left by the Olmec, Zapotec, Mixtec, Toltec and Teotihuacán cultures, among others. A good starting point for exploring these civilizations is in the well-laid-out rooms of the Museo Nacional de Antropología in Mexico City, one of the world's foremost museums. Major sites include the great pyramids of Teotihuacán just outside Mexico City and also at Cholula; the Toltec city of Tula, also near Mexico City, with its famous atlantes, five-metre statues of fabled warrior prince Quetzalcoatl; El Tajín, close to Veracruz on the Gulf of Mexico, one of the most enigmatic of ruined cities with an unknown provenance and seventeen ball courts; Monte Alban in Oaxaca state, built by the Zapotecs and a masterpiece of engineering with a mountaintop flattened by hand to create a massive plateau on which the Zapotecs built palaces, pyramids and astronomical observatories. Nigel Davies' book *The Ancient Kingdoms of Mexico* (Viking) is an excellent introduction to the "other" ancient cultures of Mexico.
- **Colombia** There are two ancient cultural sites in Colombia that warrant a visit: San Agustín and Tierradentro. Both are in the far south of the country, and are difficult to get to, involving several bus journeys from the nearest town. Still, the trip is well worth the effort – San Agustín is an attractive place and its Parque Archaeológico is home to over a hundred standing statues, many zoomorphic, of mysterious origin. There are hundreds more statues dotted across the neighbouring hillsides – you could easily spend a week visiting them. Tierradentro consists of a series of circular burial caverns, some as deep as seven metres and decorated with unusual geometric designs. The surrounding countryside is a walker's paradise with hiking trails to Indian villages and waterfalls in the hills.
- **Peru** Like Mexico, Peru has been host to many important ancient civilizations other than its greatest, the Inca, though we still know very little about them. Perhaps the most important archeological site in the country is a fairly recent discovery – the pyramids of Caral. The oldest pyramids in the world, which

date from 2600 BC and were functioning 100 years before the Great Pyramid at Giza, Caral is situated just north of Lima and is still being excavated. Visitors need special permission to visit from INRENA – Peru's main conservation agency – in Lima. In Lima itself are the ruins of Huaca Pucllana, a vast pre-Inca adobe mound and one of thousands of *huacas* (sacred places) in Peru. South of the capital is the consecrated citadel Pachacamac ("the Earth's creator") which was occupied well before 500 AD and later used by the Incas as a shrine. Other major sites in Peru include the world-famous Nazca Lines, a series of geometric shapes and animal figures, some 200m in length, drawn in the desert landscape of Pampa de San José; Chavín de Huantar, a temple complex in the Cordillera Blanca which had over three thousand resident priests and temple attendants in its heyday of 300 BC; Chan Chan, the capital city of the Chimu Empire, an urban civilization which appeared on the Peruvian coast around 1100 AD; and Kuelap in the north of Peru, a ruined city with 20m limestone walls and round stone houses decorated with a distinctive zigzag pattern.

Both Richard Keatinge's *Peruvian Prehistory* (Cambridge University Press) and *Ancient Civilizations of Peru* by J. Alden Mason (Penguin) are recommended reading if you're interested in learning more about the pre-Hispanic history of Peru.

● **Chile** Although tiny Easter Island, or Rapa Nui, is part of Chilean territory, it is actually located almost 4000km from the Chilean coast (a five-hour flight from Santiago) in the Pacific Ocean. Its isolation has given it a unique atmosphere – much more South Pacific than Latin American – which is augmented by the famous standing stones or *moai* which line the island's shores. The source of endless speculation – Who built them? And why? – the stones are discussed in several scholarly books, the best of which are *Easter Island* (André Deutsch) by Belgian anthropologist Alfred Métraux – though it's currently out of print – and *The Mystery of Easter Island* by Katherine Routledge (Cosimo Classics).

Indigenous culture

Long before the earliest classic civilizations of Latin America began to organize themselves into empires, its original inhabitants, now known as **Amerindians**, migrated to the continent from Asia. It is widely – though not universally – believed that the ancestors of Latin America's present-day indigenous population crossed the Bering Strait from Siberia to America during the last Ice Age (11,000 to 17,000 years ago) and then filtered its way down through the American landmass.

While in some regions these people developed advanced civilizations, many groups remained **semi-nomadic**, hunter-gatherers living in the rainforest or other wildernesses. Although the Spanish and Portuguese colonizers wiped out much of the indigenous population, vibrant Amerindian communities remain, some living in much the same way as their migrant ancestors. Appallingly treated by past – and present – governments, indigenous Latin Americans are engaged in a constant struggle for land and human rights.

The growing trend of **responsible tourism** (see Chapter 9), which encourages tourists to contribute positively to the places and people they're visiting, makes it increasingly possible to catch more than a cursory glimpse of the indigenous culture of Latin America. This obviously requires some sensitivity since many of the existing tribes or groups of Amerindians are traditionally wary of outsiders. If you are interested, it's best to seek out eco- or **community-based tourism** or **volunteer projects**, either from home or on the ground once you arrive. These will encourage you to get involved and learn from your experience rather than just taking a tour to "gawp at Indians", a hideous practice which should be avoided at all costs. Taking photographs and any kind of unwelcome intrusiveness is often a no-no – always ask first and accept the answer "no" with good grace.

Good web resources on indigenous Amerindians include ⓦwww .nativeweb.org, ⓦwww.cs.org and ⓦwww.survival-international.org. Recommended books are *Fate of the Forest: Developers, Destroyers and Defenders of the Amazon* by Susanna Hecht and Alexander Cockburn (Penguin); *Tristes Tropiques* by Claude Lévi-Strauss (Penguin): *One River* by Wade Davis (Simon and Schuster); *Savages* by Joe Kane (Pan/Vintage) and *Indians of the Paraguayan Chaco* by John Renshaw (University of Nebraska).

There are groups of surviving indigenous people in almost every country in Latin America. Listed below are just some of the places where there are well-conceived opportunities to explore indigenous culture. A decent guidebook will also detail these places as well as the best way to visit them.

● **Mexico** The Huichol, numbering 100,000, live in the isolated mountain regions just north of Guadalajara, and are possibly the indigenous group least affected by colonization and the modern world in Mexico. Although you need permission to visit their lands and there are no facilities for visitors, the Huichol Centre for Cultural Survival in nearby Santiago Ixcuintla is a cooperative enterprise selling distinctive Huichol woven paintings which depict animals, suns, moons, fertility and birth. It also has an extensive ethnographic archive with photos and taped interviews of Huichol leaders and particularly shaman, who use the hallucinogenic cactus *peyote* to reach the spirits. On the shores of Lago Zirahuen in Michoacán there is an eco-cultural village where Huichols run workshops in traditional crafts and natural medicine.

Much further south in Chiapas, the Lacandón Maya (also known as the "Hach Winik" or "True People"), distinguished by their long white robes and pageboy haircuts, are another of the most isolated groups of Amerindians. Close to the Maya ruin of Bonampak, Lacanhá Chansayab is a Lacandón village with campsites and local guides who will show you the waterfalls and rivers in the area and sell you well-crafted artesanía (clay and wood figurines, wooden bow and arrow sets). The best place to visit to learn about the Lacandón is Casa na-Bolom in San Cristóbal de las Casas. Once the home of Danish/Swiss anthropologists Frans and Gertrude Blom, it is now renowned as a centre for the study of the region's indigenous cultures, particularly the Lacandón.

- **Costa Rica** Close to Puerto Viejo de Talamanca on Costa Rica's Caribbean coast, is the KéköLdi Indigenous Reserve, home to two hundred Bríbrí and Cabécar people. The best way to visit the reserve is on one of the tours offered by the Asociación Talamaqueña de Ecoturismo y Conservación (ATEC; ⓦwww .ateccr.org). Tours usually consist of guided treks in the Talamanca mountains on Bríbrí trails with traditional medicinal plants pointed out along the way and folklore explained by indigenous guides.

- **Panama** Stretching some 375km along the northeastern Caribbean coast of Panama, Kuna Yala is the autonomous home of the Kuna (or Dúle), and one of the only regions in Latin America populated and governed exclusively by indigenous people. Living mostly on 40 of the islands of the San Blas archipelago, the Kuna survive on fishing and selling brightly coloured fabric pictures in reverse-appliqué known as *molas*. It is possible to visit the islands, either independently or on a tour although all visitors are expected to abide by strict codes of conduct. Homestays with local families are popular, and once you've arrived on an island and asked permission to stay from the village elder or *sahila*, a guide will usually be assigned to you and a place to stay arranged.

- **Venezuela** In the Orinoco Delta of Venezuela there are numerous river lodges close to the isolated communities of the Warao. Activities whilst staying there include visiting Warao villages, canoeing and even piranha fishing. Website ⓦwww.waroa.org details some of the hardships currently faced by the Warao in battling diseases and oil drilling on their lands.

- **Ecuador** The Oriente, or Ecuador's slice of the Amazon basin, hosts one of the fastest-growing "ethnotourism" scenes with plenty of well-organized opportunities to explore indigenous communities. One of the most attractive is in the village of Añangu, on the south shore of the Río Napo, where the Quichua people have built their own visitors' lodge. Jungle walks and canoe rides are led by expert guides, and there are visits to parrot licks where a wide variety of parrots and parakeets come, in a frenzy of sound and colour, to feed. For more context, *Defending Our Rainforest: A Guide to Community-Based Ecotourism in the Ecuadorian Amazon* by Rolf Wesche and Andy Drumm is packed with useful information.

Where shall I go first?

Once you've thought about which part of Latin America you'd like to go to, it's time to decide exactly where to begin your trip so that you can start booking tickets and buying guidebooks.

Bear in mind that if you fly in on a long-haul flight you'll be suffering from jet lag and may not be ready to face the full force of culture shock. To ease yourself into your trip gently, choose a relatively safe and easy-going city or a well-established resort town to arrive and acclimatize in: good starting points include **Cancún** in Mexico, **San José** in Costa Rica, **Santiago** in Chile and **Buenos Aires** in Argentina. **Quito** in Ecuador is also relatively small and trouble-free, although its high altitude may mean that you suffer from headaches and nausea for your first few days. Flying directly into **La Paz** in Bolivia, the world's highest capital city at 3500m above sea level, is also highly likely to give you a bout of altitude sickness (see "Staying Healthy" for more details). You might want to consider flying into Bolivia's second city, low-lying **Santa Cruz** or (since flights to Bolivia from Europe are the most expensive in Latin America) coming overland from Peru, Chile or Argentina.

If you're thinking of starting your trip in **Rio de Janeiro**, **Bogotá**, **Caracas** or **Mexico City**, take heed that while these cities are undeniably exciting they are also large, noisy and not always safe (in Mexico's case, there are many smaller and safer cities which are accessible from the US by plane). The capital cities of Central America – with the exception of San José in Costa Rica are equally daunting places to arrive in with dangerous downtown streets and chaotic transport systems. Many tourists choose to enter Central America from the **Yucatán** region of Mexico.

For more general information on helping you to plan where to go and in what order, see the itineraries and themed trips listed in this chapter.

Getting there

By air

There are plenty of options when it comes to flying into Latin America – **major gateway cities** include Mexico City and Cancún in Mexico, San José in Costa Rica, Lima in Peru, Santiago in Chile, Buenos Aires in Argentina, and São Paulo and Rio de Janeiro in Brazil. Major cities across the US – notably New York, Miami, Houston and Los Angeles – have a wide range of connections to Latin America; Miami offers the greatest choice, with several daily flights not just to capital cities, but to smaller destinations as well, and Houston has almost as many.

In Europe, there are **direct flights** to most Latin American capitals from Madrid and to a much lesser extent from Paris, Amsterdam and Frankfurt. Flights from London now only go directly to Mexico City, Cancún (with Dutch carrier KLM), Buenos Aires and both São Paulo and Rio de Janeiro in Brazil. For other destinations it's best to head first to the US (see above) or fly via Madrid.

From South Africa (Johannesburg and Cape Town) there are direct flights with the national airline South African Airways to São Paulo and Buenos Aires. From Australia (Sydney) and New Zealand (Auckland) there are currently direct flights to Santiago and Buenos Aires. For other destinations Australasians will have to fly first to Los Angeles and connect onwards from there. For more advice on buying a **plane ticket** to Latin America, see pp.48–52.

Crossing the Darién Gap

Connecting Central and South America, the **Darién Gap** is the name given to the region of jungle wilderness that straddles the border between Panama and Colombia. There are no roads across it – the Pan-American Highway, which runs the length of the Americas from Alaska to Tierra del Fuego – suffers its one and only interruption (hence the "gap" here, meaning that travel from Panama to Colombia is by plane, boat or on foot only. Previously, the overland crossing of the Darién Gap was one of the classic Latin American adventures (although risky at the best of times), whereas these days the presence of Colombian guerrillas, paramilitaries and drug traffickers means it's now extremely dangerous, with a significant risk of kidnap or murder, and should on no account be contemplated. Accordingly it seems that Panamanian border guards are currently forbidding foreigners to undertake the journey. Nowadays, most visitors cross the gap by **plane** – you can fly from Panama City to various cities in Colombia, with Cartagena being the most popular option. A more adventurous crossing is by **sea**, most easily done by travelling on one of the private yachts that sail regularly between Colón and Cartagena, a three- to four-day trip. Ask around at the yacht clubs in Colón or Panama City for up-to-date information on which yachts are carrying passengers on this route.

Overland from the US

If your home country is the US (or Canada, though this is less practical given the vast distances involved), you might consider travelling overland to **Mexico** and beyond – though there aren't as many advantages to this as you might think. **Greyhound bus services** (@www.greyhound.com) run to all the main **border crossings** (there are more than twenty in total between the US and Mexico) and some of these will take you right into Mexico and drop you conveniently at the local bus station for onward routes. Additionally many Mexican bus companies cross the border into the US, so that you can now pick up a bus back into Mexico as far north as Houston or Los Angeles. Distances can be huge, though – 60 hours travel time from New York to the Texas–Mexico border and 15 hours from San Francisco to the Baja California border – and you'll need a further day to get from the border to Mexico City. You might save some money travelling overland since bus journeys are generally cheaper than flights (New York to border town El Paso in Texas, for example, costs from US$190 round-trip by bus and around US$300 by plane), you'll get to see a lot of both countries from the bus window, and have plenty of time to **acclimatize** to your new surroundings.

Another overland option is to travel by **car**. This gives you complete freedom of movement and means that you have access to those off-the-beaten track places you might otherwise never find. If you're planning on camping or carrying a lot of gear, taking your own car or van removes the stress of lugging all your stuff around on public transport. Taking a car into Mexico, however, is a complicated process. You'll need to buy a temporary importation permit (approx US$27 and only valid for six months) at the border and show your registration and title for the car as well as your **driving licence** (US, Canadian, British, Irish, Australian, New Zealand, South African and most European driving licences are valid in Mexico) and passport. You'll also need to leave a credit card imprint to stop you selling the car in Mexico or a neighbouring country. Additionally US/Canadian car insurance isn't valid in Mexico so you'll need to take out Mexican insurance from one of the numerous agencies who line either side of every border crossing. And all this before you deal with the state of the roads, Mexican and Central America driving, corrupt traffic cops and the possibility of car theft.

If you do decide to travel overland by car, make sure that everything is in order before you leave, that you have all the relevant paperwork and a good set of **road maps** (the American and Canadian Automobile Associations produce maps and route planners specifically for travel to Mexico; @www.aaa.com, @www.caa.ca). The *Rough Guide to Mexico* has more detailed information on red tape and crossing the border with a vehicle.

www.roughguides.com

Border crossings

Unless you're planning to visit just one country or to fly everywhere, you will find yourself at some point experiencing a **land border crossing**. These vary enormously from country to country. Some of them, like the main ones from the US into Mexico, are highly organized with clear procedures, officials in uniforms and surrounding communities designed to service the traveller's every need with money-changing facilities, onward transport hubs and tourist information. Others, like Punta Gorda in Belize, consist of a ramshackle hut and a sleepy immigration officer. Some are scruffy, confusing and down at heel, like that at Tumbes between Peru and Ecuador – and others, like Sixaola, between Costa Rica and Panama, which involves crossing a long rickety bridge over the river are dramatic and picturesque. There are several border crossings in Latin America on the water – rivers or lakes (like LagoTiticaca which divides Peru and Bolivia, the Río San Juan between Nicaragua and Costa Rica or the Cruce Internacional de los Lagos which connects Chile and Argentina).

However informal the border, you should always have your wits about you – and your manners. As with **immigration** at airports, border guards have the right to refuse you entry to their country for any reason. Be polite and have your passport and all documents (plane tickets, proof of funds and any visas necessary) ready for inspection.

Also do your homework in advance – some border crossings don't have the right paperwork to permit entry and you'll need to pick up entry cards or immigration forms in the nearest big town – or even capital city – to the border before you arrive. Many smaller border crossings close at night so make sure you arrive in daylight. Others have idiosyncrasies – while you won't need a visa for Venezuela if you fly in, for example, crossing its land borders may require an entry card which you'll have to get in a Venezuelan consulate in the country you're leaving. See individual country profiles in the "Where to go" section for details on all the main border crossings.

By sea

Travelling to Latin America by **sea** may sound exciting, but in reality it's usually expensive (costing at least three times as much as flying) and time-consuming – if you're coming from Europe, voyages across the Atlantic take three weeks or more. Cargo ships take a limited number of passengers, while the fares are high and the journey long.

It might also be possible to reach Latin America across the Atlantic for free by working your passage as a **crew member**. In Europe the best place to hitch a ride is Gran Canaria in the Canary Islands, where lots of commercial shipping stops en route to the Caribbean islands or the Venezuelan coast. Once in the Caribbean, there are plenty of boats between islands and over to Central America (particularly Panama, a good place to find onward rides and yachting work in general: visit the Panama Canal Yacht Club in Colón) and the coasts of Colombia and Venezuela. Ask around at any major port or large marinas. If you're keen on setting up lifts before you set off, you could check the classified ads sections of boating magazines or one of a number of crew-finding websites (@www.crewfinders.com, for example).

Visas, tickets and insurance

Once you've decided where you're going, there are several essential documents you'll have to organize, including a **plane ticket**, **insurance**, and any **visas** you might require. You'll also need to make sure your **passport** remains valid for the entire length of your stay and beyond – officially, all countries in Latin America require you to hold a passport which still has at least six months before it expires. Renewing your passport is fairly straightforward – in most cases you can apply for a new one at your local post office or online. Don't leave it to the last minute, though, or you may have to pay much more than the standard fee for rapid processing.

Visas

Very few Latin American countries now require visitors to get a visa before arrival. Current **entry regulations** are given in the box on p.46, but bear in mind they change occasionally - if you're arriving by air your travel agent should inform you in advance of any visa requirement. The World Travel Guide online (Ⓦ www.worldtravelguide .net) has up-to-date details in its country guides as do any number of travel websites. If you do need a visa, you'll have to apply to the relevant **embassy** or consulate in your country – which can mean hours of queuing, armed with photos, a return air ticket and proof of funds. Don't leave this until the last minute: find out how long your visa will take to process well before you set off (although it rarely takes longer than two weeks). In some cases there won't be a consulate in your

www.roughguides.com

country, so you may have to write to one abroad – the only European consulates for Suriname, for example, are in Holland and Germany.

Visas usually have a **time limit**: you'll have to use them within three to six months of their being issued. If you're planning a long trip, this might make it impossible to collect all your visas in advance, in which case you'll have to wait until you arrive in a neighbouring country and apply for a visa there (take all the necessary documents with you, including **passport photos**). If you do have to do this, remember that Latin American bureaucracy is notoriously inefficient and frequently corrupt. You might be given incorrect information, the office may have run out of the relevant pieces of paper, or its staff might not know how to deal with you. Always give yourself plenty of time to cope with any problems that might arise. It's also probably worth applying for a **multiple-entry visa** if you think you might want to leave and re-enter a particular country; though this usually costs more than a single-entry visa, you could save yourself a lot of time and paperwork.

Entry cards and stamps

On arrival, your passport will be stamped and you may also be given an **entry card** – known variously as a *tarjeta de turismo* (tourist card), *tarjeta de embarque* (embarkation card), *tarjeta de entrada* (entrance card) or *tarjeta de ingreso* (entry card). To obtain your entry card, you'll have to fill out a form. Although you may not know where you'll be staying it's always best to fill in the destination address box on the form (a blank space can make officials nervous) – if you don't have a hotel, pick one, preferably well known, from your guidebook; no one will check whether or not you actually stay there.

On arrival you'll have to present your completed form to an immigration official who, all being well, will stamp your passport and give you one half of the entry card, if you're being issued one (he'll keep the other half). In several Central American countries you'll have to pay a **fee on arrival**; this will be in dollars, so keep at least US$10 to hand. Take special care of your entry card – it's regarded as being as important as your passport, and officials will not take kindly to you being without

Visa requirements for Latin America

At present, the following countries require certain visitors to hold a visa:
Bolivia citizens of the US and South Africa
Brazil citizens of the US, Canada, Australia, New Zealand
Paraguay citizens of the US, Canada, Australia, New Zealand
Suriname citizens of the UK and Ireland, US, Canada, Australia, New Zealand and South Africa
Venezuela anyone entering via a land border

it if you're asked to show your documents whilst in the country. You may have to surrender it on departure, so have it ready when leaving.

Although in theory there are complicated regulations regarding the length of your stay according to your nationality, in practice the decision is left to individual officials. It's always worth asking, as politely as you can, for the standard maximum of ninety days (note: this is theoretically limited to 30 days for citizens of particular countries – check with the relevant embassy before you plan your trip), although you may not get it – it's infinitely preferable to have more days than you'll need rather than to have to extend your stay, which is generally a costly and time-consuming procedure.

Extending your stay

In theory, it's almost always possible to **renew** your entry stamp if you decide to stay longer. The procedure involves going to the nearest immigration office (*inmigración*) or police station (*policía*) with your documents – passport, return ticket, proof of funds – and asking for a *prórroga* (extension) *de turista*. Bear in mind that although extensions are nearly always granted, you're not guaranteed to be given one – dress smartly and be polite. In many cases, it's possible to add an extra ninety days to your original ninety (though you'll never get more than 180 days in total); however, you may only be given another month or two. Extensions **cost** anything from a few dollars (US$15 in Panama, US$30 in Peru, US$40 in Brazil) up to US$100 in Chile.

An alternative way of prolonging your stay – especially in Central America, where distances are relatively small – is simply to cross briefly into a neighbouring country and then return over the border, where you'll be given a brand-new entry stamp.

Overstaying

If you stay beyond the date stamped in your passport or written on your tourist card, you'll have to pay a **fine** when you leave the country. This is usually calculated on a daily basis of a few dollars per day, though some countries operate a fixed fine (US$30 in Argentina, US$40 in Chile, US$45 in Mexico for example) irrespective of how long you've overstayed. If you know you're going to overstay your visa, make sure it's not going to cost an arm or a leg first – if the fine is cheap it may be worth paying it rather than going through a costly extension process or having to leave and re-enter the country. But remember that overstaying your welcome is a **risk** – although most Latin American countries will just fine you and let you go with no problems at all, there's always the possibility that you might be refused entry to that country in the future.

Tickets

In all likelihood, your biggest single expense will be your **airline ticket** to Latin America. Whichever country you're planning to fly into, there will be a variety of routes and fares, so give yourself plenty of time to shop around and make sure you do your homework: a few hours' research should give you a good idea of current prices and routings. It's also best to adopt a **flexible** approach so that you're able to take advantage of any special deals which crop up, even if this means, say, starting your trip in a city or country other than the one you had in mind – for example, there are cheaper and more frequent connections to Lima in Peru or Santiago in Chile than to La Paz in Bolivia. As a rule of thumb, more affluent cities with well-established tourist attractions or business links with Europe, North America and Australasia will have better plane services and therefore potentially cheaper deals. These include Mexico City, São Paulo and Rio de Janeiro, Buenos Aires and Santiago.

Fares vary according to the **season**. High season in Latin America runs from mid-November to mid-January (fares are particularly high over Christmas), Easter, July and August. If you're determined to fly at Christmas or Easter, be prepared to pay premium prices and book months in advance. By contrast, flying in low season can knock several hundred dollars off the cost of your flight. The most direct flights are faster but usually more expensive, and you can save cash by taking an indirect flight.

In recent years, paper airline tickets have been largely replaced by **electronic tickets**. This means that when you book your ticket you'll be sent an invoice or voucher (usually online) with all the relevant flight details as well as a reference number. Though not strictly necessary it's best to print out this document; you should, at the very least, make a note of your reference number and keep it with you while you travel. In normal circumstances you'll be able to turn up at the airport and hand over your passport at the check-in desk - this is usually sufficient for you to be checked in. It won't hurt, however, to have all your flight details in a paper format which you can flourish at the relevant person, just in case.

One-way tickets

Purchasing a **one-way** or single ticket to Latin America is impractical and ill-advised. Though many airlines now sell scheduled flights in single portions (which does give you the benefit of complete freedom of movement) these are often at much higher rates than buying a return ticket through a travel agent. More importantly you'll have to deal with immigration on arrival: without an onward or return ticket, proving that your stay is temporary will be virtually impossible, and you might even

Arriving at night

When booking your ticket, remember that it's best to avoid arriving in Latin America at night. Banks, bureaux de change and tourist information desks may well be closed, and if you don't have a hotel or hostel booked you won't want to start wandering through a strange city in the dark.

be refused entry. Then you'll have to go to the trouble of buying a flight home if and when you decide to return; you'll also be liable for steep airport departure taxes which are usually included in a return ticket.

Returns, open-jaw returns and circle tickets

Mile for mile, **return** tickets are a much more **economical** option than one-way fares. However flying in and out of the same city does restrict your movements, and you may find yourself either having to take a local flight to get back to where you started or wasting valuable days retracing your steps. A useful alternative is an **open-jaw** return, which allows you to fly into one city and return from another – ticket prices aren't much more than a standard return. A slight variation on an open jaw is a **circle ticket**, which involves flights linking more than one destination – for example London–Caracas–Bogotá–London. This may sound ideal if you want to travel large distances and on specific stopover routes, but choosing several cities to fly between months in advance really does set your itinerary in stone, and a certain amount of backtracking is required on each leg, since you'll have to return to the city you arrived in to fly on to the next.

Round-the-world (RTW) tickets

If Latin America is part of a longer trip, you might consider a **round-the-world (RTW) ticket**, which is often excellent value for money (prices start at £800/US$1000 for half a dozen stops). However the countries of Latin America still aren't included on many standard RTW itineraries – which tend to focus on Asia and Australasia – and where they are, they tend to be on the more expensive routings. Nevertheless RTW itineraries can almost always be customized to your preference; the most frequently featured Latin American cities are Mexico City, Lima, Santiago, Buenos Aires and Rio de Janeiro. The BootsnAll website (ⓦwww.bootsnall.com) has an excellent section on RTW tickets as does ⓦwww.roundtheworldticket.com and most of the online student travel agencies and **gap year websites**. Star Alliance (ⓦwww.star alliance.com), One World (ⓦwww.oneworldalliance.com) and Circle the Planet (ⓦwww.circletheplanet.com) are all recommended companies which will help you to find the right routings and fare. On offer at the

www.roughguides.com

Sample return fares

The following sample fares are for flights during low season.

To Mexico City

From London	£520–670
From Los Angeles	US$270–410
From New York	US$320–430
From Toronto	Can$530–660
From Sydney	Aus$1390–2600
From Auckland	NZ$2610–3320
From Johannesburg	ZAR5490

To Lima

From London	£660–740
From Los Angeles	US$520–670
From New York	US$450–590
From Toronto	Can$570–710
From Sydney	Aus$1800–2160
From Auckland	NZ$1620–2150
From Johannesburg	ZAR–4980

To Buenos Aires

From London	£650–840
From Los Angeles	US$670–910
From New York	US$850–920
From Toronto	Can$820–980
From Sydney	Aus$1070–1840
From Auckland	NZ$1110–2040
From Johannesburg	ZAR3500

time of writing was a tour starting in the States: Miami–Rio de Janeiro–Buenos Aires–Santiago–Lima–Cusco–Quito–San José–Guatemala City–Miami at US$1749 (Ⓦwww.airtreks.com); the Conquistador trip, Dallas–Guatemala–Costa Rica–Panama–Dallas at US$1099 (Ⓦwww .circletheplanet.com) and, more comprehensively, a World Classic Trip, London–Buenos Aires–Santiago–Lima–Santiago–Sydney–Tokyo–Hong Kong–London at £2189 (Ⓦwww.roundtheworldexperts.co.uk).

Charter flights

There are now a number of tour operators offering **charter flights** to Latin America from the UK and many more from North America. Virtually all charters go to tourist resorts in Mexico, Costa Rica or Brazil; although they're often much cheaper than scheduled flights, tickets are only valid for a maximum of **three weeks**. One possibility, if you can manage to find a charter return which is less than half the price of the standard fare (not as unlikely as you'd imagine), is to buy two and ditch the half of each you won't be using – your local **travel**

agent may be able to come up with a good deal. Check out website Ⓦwww.charterflights.co.uk for useful information.

Airpasses

Given the size of Latin America, at some point you might want to take an **internal flight**. If you're planning a series of short flights within a country or several neighbouring countries of Latin America it's more economical to buy an **airpass** in advance from a Latin American airline: it's best to contact a specialist travel agency if you want to buy one (see Directory for details) because there are many options which change frequently and the regulations regarding each airpass are varied and complex.

Currently, only Brazilian airline TAM (Ⓦwww.tam.com) offers a single-country airpass. It costs from US$551 for 4 flights up to US$2000 for the maximum of 9 stops within Brazil. More widely available and more useful are regional airpasses. The All America Airpass (Ⓦwww.allairpass.com) is the most comprehensive deal, linking the destinations of 21 North, Central and South American airlines and costs from US$111 per flight. The Hop Over Pass is offered by Copa Airlines, Panama's national carrier, and is almost as wide-reaching. In South America, the Mercosur airpass covers Argentina, Brazil, Uruguay, Paraguay and Chile, as do South America airpasses from TAM and Aerolineas Argentina. Chile's national airline LAN has a more extensive South America airpass which also includes Peru, Ecuador and Venezuela. The Mexipass takes in all the Latin American cities served by the domestic Mexican airlines AeroMéxico and Mexicana as well as North American cities.

Discount and specialist travel agencies

The most obvious, though often also the most expensive, way of buying a plane ticket is to contact the relevant **airline** directly. In most cases the airline will just quote you their standard scheduled fares, although they do occasionally have special offers which are worth checking for. In general, however, it's cheaper to go via a discount ticket agent – known as "**bucket shops**" in the UK and **flight consolidators** in North America.

Discount agencies are often listed in the **classified ads** of newspapers' travel sections, and in free or listings magazines. These include, in the UK, the *Sunday Times* travel section, the *Evening Standard* or, best of all, London's *Time Out*; in the US, there's the *Village Voice* in New York, the *Chicago Tribune* and the *Los Angeles Times*; in Australia, try the *Sydney Morning Herald* or *TNT* magazine. Ring around as many as you can and compare prices, which can vary dramatically. If you do decide to buy your ticket from a bucket shop, check that they're

www.roughguides.com

bonded with ATOL (⊛www.atoldata.org.uk) or ABTA (⊛www.abta
.com) in the UK, or with AFTA (⊛www.afta.com.au) in Australia. This
means that if the company goes bust you'll be refunded in full – it also
tends to indicate a decently run and professional operation. There is no
such organization in the US though travel agents registered with ASTA
– the American Society of Travel Agents (⊛www.asta.org) adhere to a
strong ethical and consumer code. All travellers can protect themselves
by paying with a **credit card;** again, you'll be refunded in full if your
ticket agent goes bust.

Best of all and strongly recommended is to find a **specialist travel
agency** with expertise in Latin America (see the list in Directory on
p.300). Most of these have expert staff with first-hand experience of the
region, and they can often match the cheapest flights found in bucket
shops – as well as giving you the lowdown on air passes, visas and
perhaps even inoculation requirements.

The internet

Booking airline tickets on the **internet** cuts out the travel agent or mid-
dleman, and if you search thoroughly you may find some great bargains.
The Cheap Flights series of websites (in the US, UK, Canada and Australia)
compares prices on a wide range of airlines, and is particularly competitive.
However, booking online has the disadvantage that you'll usually need to
specify both outward and return dates (with no option to purchase an
open ticket) and you won't get the specialist knowledge a decent travel
agent can offer. See p.299 for a list of online discount travel agents.

Insurance

Having some form of **travel insurance** is absolutely essential. Although
the vast majority of travellers to Latin America return home safe and
sound, accidents do happen, and without insurance you could be faced
with huge medical or legal bills that you can't possibly pay for. As with
airfares, it's worth doing a little research on travel insurance before you
buy a policy.

Insurance is a very lucrative – and hence highly competitive –
business, which helps keep prices low. Premiums vary depending on
the level of coverage selected, ranging from around £30/US$50 to
£70/US$115 for six weeks, and approximately £60/US$85 to £185/
US$250 for six months. It might be cheaper to buy **annual travel
insurance** which covers all travel you may do in a year. Some travel
agents will try and sell you their own insurance policy when you buy
your ticket – these are usually as good as any you can find yourself, but
check the details before you sign up. The specialist travel agencies listed

in Directory (see p.300) also offer insurance. Other insurers advertise in the travel sections of the publications listed in "Buying a ticket" on pp.48–51, and on the internet.

Choosing a policy

All insurance policies provide slightly different types of cover, though all include some form of **medical coverage** and some protection against loss of **personal effects** (unless you choose to go without this part of the policy – see below). Other eventualities usually covered by travel insurance policies are unavoidable missed flights or cancelled trips, legal expenses, hijack and kidnap, though you won't be covered in the event of a natural disaster or the outbreak of war. Consider the following before you buy your travel insurance:

- Every policy is slightly different, both in the cover it offers and the way it's written, and it's important to read every last detail. The small print (usually "conditions and exclusions") will tell you exactly what you can and can't claim for – there are virtually as many exclusions as inclusions on most insurance policies.
- Almost all travel insurance policies are one hundred percent refundable within a week of purchase, provided you haven't set off yet. If you decide you're not happy with yours, send it back.
- Dangerous sports, such as rock climbing, skiing, scuba diving and whitewater rafting, often aren't covered by insurance policies unless you pay an additional premium – even fairly innocuous activities like horse-trekking are sometimes not covered. Pay particular attention to the small print in this section to see what's included and what's not.
- Check that you're able to extend your policy from abroad if you decide to extend your trip – this usually just takes a phone call.

Once you've bought insurance, it's essential to make a note of your **policy number** and the emergency 24-hour telephone **helpline** (most travellers take their insurance certificates with them, although this isn't usually strictly necessary). You'll have to quote your policy number in any contact you have with your insurance company. If something does happen to you, hold on to copies of all medical bills, receipts or other official documents – without them you won't have a claim.

Medical coverage

By far the most important part of your travel insurance is the **medical coverage**. In a worst-case scenario, you may have to be airlifted to hospital and perhaps even repatriated with a trained medical team. Very few people could afford the vast cost of doing this, which is where your insurance company steps in. Less dramatic expenses – medicine and doctor's fees – are also covered. The exception is if you have any exist-ing medical condition which leads to you being treated or hospitalized abroad, in which case you will not be able to make a claim.

Check what the procedure is should you need **emergency medical treatment**: some companies require you to pay first and then reclaim the costs on your return; others will pay your bill directly to the relevant hospital or doctor. You may also be required to phone (collect call) first to speak to a company-approved doctor to check that you're being offered the correct treatment.

Personal effects

Although the medical component of your insurance is the most impor-tant part, the most common cause of insurance claims is **theft** – most insurers now offer a discount of around twenty percent if you choose to leave out this area of cover and take your chances. Coverage for personal effects usually includes the loss of a certain amount of cash, passports and other essential documents, but there's usually a maximum amount you can claim for any one item – roughly £250/US$410 – mean-ing that you may not be able to claim for the full value of expensive items like cameras which exceed this limit. You might need to invest in a household insurance policy which covers them outside the home or get **specialist insurance** – camera insurers sometimes advertise in photographic magazines.

3

Studying, volunteering and working

While many visitors to Latin America will be dreaming of gathering thrilling experiences, seeing new and exotic places, or even just enjoying an extended holiday, you might want to immerse yourself in Latin American **culture** in a more long-lasting manner. There are several ways of doing this – learn the **language** of the countries you're visiting, **study** a subject like conservation or archeology, work as a **volunteer** or even find **paid work** to subsidize your trip while you're there. With the growing trend of "gap year" and career break travels, there are dozens of websites which specialize in helping people to find courses and work – unpaid or paid – abroad: ⓦ www.gapyear.com, ⓦ www.gapyear directory.co.uk, ⓦ www.workingabroad.com, ⓦ www.ciee.org and ⓦ www.transitionsabroad.com are just some of the best.

Learning a language

One of the strongest bonds between the countries of Latin America is their shared linguistic inheritance, with **Spanish** being the principal language in all but five of the region's nations. If you don't already speak Spanish and haven't attempted to learn it at home (see "Guidebooks and other resources", p.82–92, for details), you could arrange your trip around taking a **language course** in Latin America itself. This has long been a popular way to begin travelling in Latin America, and most towns on the Gringo Trail have at least one language school, while some have become specialist centres with dozens of establishments to choose from.

In large Latin American tourist resorts and throughout cosmopolitan countries like Argentina or Costa Rica, many people you'll encounter speak basic English. However, much of the population outside these places does not speak any language other than their own and frequently, written information is in the national language only. Learning the rudiments of Spanish, Portuguese or an indigenous language like Quechua (spoken in Peru and parts of Bolivia) will vastly enhance your travelling experience. The locals will respect your attempt to communicate, you'll be able to get about without the complications caused by a language barrier and you'll feel much more engaged with

Habla Español? Language courses in Latin America

Argentina There are dozens of language schools in Buenos Aires and almost as many in Argentina's second city, Córdoba, as well as Bariloche and – rather bizarrely – Ushuaia, the world's most southern city at the tip of Tierra del Fuego. The ILEE Spanish Schools network (🌐 www.argentinailee.com) is recommended.

Bolivia Bolivia has some of the cheapest deals for courses; centrally located Sucre and Cochabamba are among the most popular places in the country to learn Spanish. The Bolivian Spanish School in Sucre (🌐 www.bolivianspanishschool.com) is highly rated.

Chile The vast majority of language schools in Chile are based in the capital, Santiago, though there are also courses available in Iquique, Pucón, Valparaiso and seaside resort Viña del Mar. Bellavista Language School (🌐 www.escuelabellavista.cl) in Santiago has small class sizes – no bigger than five students – and a good reputation.

Costa Rica The country's capital, San José, is the centre for Costa Rica's language schools: they're mostly US-owned and comparatively expensive, though very well organized. There are also classes in the student town of Heredia and on the beach at Quepos. The Costa Rican Academy of Language (🌐 www.spanishandmore.com) in San José is a small Tico-owned school with a friendly atmosphere and a conversational approach. Outside the city in the Valle Central, the Montaña Linda Language School (🌐 www.montanalinda.com) is located in the pretty village of Orosí with excellent local teachers, a charming informality and the cheapest rates in the country.

Ecuador Ecuador's capital, Quito, is easily the most popular place to study in South America, with over sixty language schools, cheap courses and immersion in the particularly clear local dialect. There are other language schools in Cuenca; both the South American Spanish Institute (🌐 www.southamerican.edu.ec) and Bipo and Toni's (🌐 academia.bipo.net) are rated by ex-students; the latter regularly donates a portion of its profits to environmental projects.

El Salvador While there aren't a great deal of language schools in El Salvador, the well-run El Salvador Spanish Schools organization (🌐 www.salvaspan.com) has schools in San Salvador, Santa Ana and two beach destinations – with optional surfing lessons.

Guatemala One of the most popular places to study Spanish in Latin America is the impressive colonial city of Antigua. Further west, the city of Quetzaltenango is less pretty the culture you're visiting. Additionally, learning a language in its own country means that you'll have instant access to the way it's used by **native speakers** and opportunities to practise and improve what you are learning in a classroom.

While language courses in Latin America will invariably cost less than at home, they're not all good. A multitude of **websites** dedicated to learning a language abroad will help you research schools before you sign up. Amerispan (Ⓦ www.amerispan.com) is a long-standing organization which lists and reviews hundreds of language schools. Also recommended for finding language schools are: Ⓦ www.languageschoolsabroad.co.uk, Ⓦ www.languageschoolsweb.com, Ⓦ www.studyspanish.com. Language courses usually take the form of weekly units of four hours a day for five days and you can choose how many units you'd like. Currently the average price for each week is US$150–200. Most schools will arrange

but boasts some equally good schools in a far less touristy environment. Rapidly growing in popularity for Spanish classes is the backpacker haven of San Pedro La Laguna on the shores of Lago de Atitlán. There are also a number of language schools in the Petén region, within striking distance of Tikal. The website Ⓦ www.guatemala365 .com lists the best and most professional schools as well as providing tips about the relative advantages of different study centres.

Mexico The attractive colonial city of Cuernavaca, 50km south of Mexico City, makes a good base for exploring the capital, the pyramids of Teotihuacán and the silver town of Taxco. The place for learning Spanish in Mexico, particularly popular with young Americans, it has lots of language schools and teaching of a high standard. Other places to learn Spanish in Mexico are the equally attractive colonial cities of Guanajuato and San Miguel de Allende. The longest-standing and most professional school in Guanajuato is the Centro de Idiomas at the University of Guanajuato (Ⓦ www.ugto.mx). In San Miguel de Allende the most prestigious place to study is the Instituto Allende (Ⓦ www.instituto-allende.edu.mx).

Nicaragua Although the colonial cities of Granada and León have several language schools, the pleasant university town of Estelí in the north has the longest established and most professional places, originally set up in the 1980s for the visiting supporters of the Sandinista revolution. Courses here are probably the cheapest in Latin America at around US$150 per week, including full board and lodging with a local family. The most popular school in Estelí is Escuela Horizonte (Ⓦ www.ibw.com.ni/u/horizont) which is particularly known for its excellent teachers. For those who'd prefer to study in Granada or on the coast in San Juan del Sur, Nicaragua Spanish Schools (or NSS; Ⓦ pages .prodigy.net/nss-pmc) has schools in three places and is a cooperative venture run by Nicaraguans.

Peru Backpacker hot spots Cusco and Arequipa both have a handful of language schools, as does the more commercial city of Huancayo in the foothills of the Andes. In Cusco the Amigos Spanish School (Ⓦ www.spanishcusco.com) is a not-for-profit organization which ploughs all its profits into food and education for local poor families. Also recommended is the Academia Latinamericana de Español (Ⓦ www .latinoschools.com).

▲ Studying Spanish in Guatemala

extracurricular activities in your spare time and be able to place you with a local family for the length of your course, so that you can practise what you've learned.

Though by no means the only place in Latin America to learn **Spanish**, Guatemala is by far the most popular and consequently has the widest range of options, with at least sixty well-established schools and very reasonably priced courses. What's more, Guatemalan Spanish is spoken slowly and clearly (partly because the largely Mayan population themselves speak Spanish as a second language). This is also the case in Ecuador, another favourite place to learn Spanish.

Portuguese is only spoken in Brazil; consequently many travellers aren't interested in learning it. However, if you are travelling widely in the country you'll need at least a few words and Brazilians will be delighted that you've made the effort. Additionally Portuguese is almost identical in its grammatical structure to Spanish – if you speak one of the two languages you should be able to attempt the other. There are language schools in Rio de Janeiro, São Paulo and Salvador, geared largely towards businessmen.

Should you be interested, it's also possible to study several **indigenous languages** in Latin America. In Bolivia, which has the largest indigenous population in South America, you can study Aymara and Quechua in Cochabamba at the Escuela Runawasi (Ⓦwww.runawasi.org). The small town of Joyabaj in the Western Highlands of Guatemala has a language centre where you can learn Quiché. In nearby Quetzaltenango, the Centro Maya de Idiomas (🌐www.centromayaxela.org) has classes in five Mayan dialects - K'iche', Q'anjob'al, Kaqchikel, Tzutujil and Mam.

Courses in Latin American culture

If you already speak Spanish and would like to explore the region's culture in a more light-hearted fashion, there is no shortage of options. Again, the internet is the best starting point for finding a suitable course. **Cultural Travels** (🌐www.culturaltraveldirectory .com) lists over 2000 travel agencies and other setups which offer

Courses

Archeological dig Two weeks working on an archeological site in the Peruvian highlands with field trips to Cusco and Machu Picchu. Contact Spanish Abroad (🌐www .spanishabroad.com).

Lens on Latin America: Video and Media Production An opportunity to make a short video under the supervision of award-winning Bolivian documentary producer Ismael Saavedera. Courses are based in Cochabamba and include a visit to the Bolivian film archives in La Paz. Contact the School for International Training (🌐www.sit.edu).

Mayan Culture and Cosmovison Based in Antigua, Guatelmala. Gain a basic understanding of the complexities of Mayan spirituality, with the opportunity to participate in religious ceremonies. Contact the Center for Global Education (🌐www.augsburg.edu).

Mexican cuisine Learn how to cook classic Mexican dishes such as *mole poblano* and *chiles en nogada* in an attractive colonial house in the small town of Tlaxcala in the centre of Mexico. Contact the Mexican Home Cooking School (🌐www.mexicanhomecooking.com).

Permaculture Investigate new ways of creating sustainable human habitats at Ecoversidade, a grassroots ecological institute in tropical Brazil. Contact Living Routes (🌐www.livingroutes.org).

Revolution, Transformation and Civil Society An educational tour with expert local historians and guides of key sites in Nicaragua where Spanish colonial powers, the Sandinista revolution and a brief Contra war have left their legacies. Contact the School for International Training (🌐www.sit.edu).

Tango Learn the most sensuous and complicated of Latin dances in one of Buenos Aires' best dance schools, the Escuela Argentina de Tango. Contact the Grupo de Intercambio Cultural or GICArg (🌐www.gicarg.org).

Teacher Training Practical experience teaching primary schoolchildren in rural Ecuador with opportunities to engage in community politics and on-the-job training. Contact Fundación Brethren y Unida (🌐www.fbu.com.ec).

Sea kayaking Learn how to master a paddleboat in the scenic Northern Patagonian Fjords of Chile. Contact Yak Expediciones (🌐www.yakexpediciones.cl).

Tropical Ecology and Conservation Live and work in a field station in the Monteverde Cloudforest Reserve in Costa Rica. Off-site activities include a trip to Panama to observe marine diversity. Contact CIEE (🌐www.ciee.org).

"**educational holidays**" by theme: these include art, archeology, architecture, cookery, history, marine biology and sport. Your **guidebook** will also detail organizations offering training to visitors. These include national parks, environmental agencies, community centres and the odd eco-lodge or hostel.

Volunteering

A great way to give added purpose to your trip is to work as a **volunteer**. You'll be getting directly involved in **local communities** and experiencing Latin America in ways you can't possibly as a tourist. You'll see first hand how many Latin Americans struggle to survive on a handful of dollars a week and learn about the devastating effects a lack of decent infrastructure and sanitation bring. But you'll also share your working days with local people, learning their particular sense of humour and expressions, what they eat for lunch and what concerns them most in their daily lives. And you'll have

---

Volunteer projects and organizations

Belize The Cornerstone Foundation (ⓦ www.cornerstonefoundationbelize.org), based in San Ignacio, runs volunteer projects such as working with HIV/Aids sufferers and literacy programmes. Based in San Pedro on Ambergris Caye, Green Reef (ⓦ www.greenreef belize.org) volunteers help protect the caye's marine environment and also run bird sanctuaries. The Belize Aubudon Society (ⓦ www.belizeaudubon.org) runs nine of Belize's protected areas and takes on volunteers to help with warden duties and education programmes.

Bolivia The Inti Wara Yassi community in Bolivia runs two animal rehabilitation centres (ⓦ www.intiwarayassi.org) and is always looking for extra help; volunteers can just turn up.

Brazil US-based non-profit organization Globe Aware (ⓦ www.globeaware.org) uses volunteers on short-term placements (1–2 weeks) to help out with its community project in Bahia, where it is building a community centre, teaching children basic computer skills, growing a vegetable garden and working with sufferers of alcoholism.

Chile WWOOF (Worldwide Workers on Organic Farms) has a number of volunteer farming/gardening projects in Chile, including on the pretty Isla de Chiloe and on mainland Patagonia. Contact ⓦ www.wwoofchile.cl for a full list of opportunities.

Colombia Peace Brigades International (ⓦ www.peacebrigades.org/colombia .html), an organization which maintains observer teams in areas of conflict, currently has volunteers in four parts of Colombia – Barrancabermeja, Bogotá, Urabá and Medellín. The Inter-cultural Youth Exchange (ⓦ www.icye.co.uk) organizes several projects in Colombia, including a school for deaf students and rehabilitating sex workers.

Ecuador AmaZOOnico (ⓦ www.selvaviva.ec), an animal refuge and rehabilitation centre on the Río Napo, accepts volunteers to help tend rescued forest animals and show visitors around. The Fundación Jatun Sacha (ⓦ www.jatunsacha.org) accepts volunteers to work in one of its ten biological stations in the Amazon, Andes, coastal lowlands and the Galápagos Islands. Workers get involved in field research, community service, agroforestry and environmental education.

the satisfaction of helping Latin Americans and their environment in ways that go beyond parting with a few bucks. With any luck, you'll establish lifelong connections with communities, projects and people vastly different from those back home.

Volunteering opportunities usually follow one of two themes: working with **nature** (generally conservation or scientific research) or working with **people** (for example, building homes, caring for the homeless, sick or drug-addicted, or teaching). In most cases volunteers have to commit themselves for a certain amount of time (at least one to three months). Once you've enrolled, you'll be expected to work hard – volunteer organizations don't take kindly to their workers choosing their own hours, partying all night and sleeping the day away.

Some projects require volunteers with **specific skills**; others will take on anyone with enthusiasm and energy. The internet has hundreds of volunteering websites; of these, Ⓦwww.volunteerabroad.com has all kinds of useful information and projects while the Lima-based South American Explorers Club (Ⓦwww.saexplorers.org) has a database for

El Salvador Ethical volunteering organization Travel To Teach (Ⓦwww.travel-to -teach-org) has placements on the island of Meanguera, teaching computer skills and English as well as helping with turtle conservation. The AMOR project (Ⓦwww .churchinwales.org.uk), based in Wales is a church organization which runs a day centre for street children in San Salvador as well as outreach programmes.

Guatemala Entremundos (Ⓦwww.entremundos.org), based in Quetzaltenango, has links with a number of projects, including a women's refuge and a scheme to replace smoky open fires with stoves in the rural Western Highlands. Volunteer Petén (Ⓦwww .volunteerpeten.com) is an environmental NGO based in San Andres and has projects for volunteers including park maintenance, reforestation and animal husbandry.

Guyana Canadian organization Youth Challenge International (Ⓦwww.yci.org) sends young volunteers to Guyana to work on a number of projects, including HIV/Aids education and women's groups.

Nicaraga International conservation body Fauna and Flora International (Ⓦwww.fauna -flora.org) needs volunteers to help protect endangered species and habitats on the remote Pacific coast. Most towns in Nicaragua have a local IXCHEN *casa de la mujer* (women's centre) which women volunteers with some Spanish skills are welcome to visit and help out.

Paraguay ECOSARA (Ⓦwww.faunaparaguay.com) welcomes, particularly those interested in biology, to help in the Parque Nacional de San Rafael, Paraguay's most diverse reserve.

Peru Traveller not Tourist (Ⓦwww.travellernottourist.com) is a small local charity based in Arequipa, southern Peru which helps to improve the lives of local children. Volunteers are welcome for a minimum of 2 weeks.

www.roughguides.com

members called Volunteer Resources, which hooks up organizations and potential volunteers, as well as providing up-to-date feedback from people who've taken part in various projects. Language school organization Amerispan (ⓦwww.amerispan.com) also has a section on volunteer opportunities in Latin America as does ⓦwww.planeta.com.

Educational institutes with **Latin American studies centres** are also an ideal starting point for investigating volunteer opportunities – Stanford University's CLAS (Center for Latin American Studies; ⓦwww.stanford.edu/group/las) is a good option, as is the UK-based Latin America Bureau (LAB; ⓦwww.lab.org.uk).

There are essentially two ways of going about getting a volunteer placement. There are now hundreds of international volunteer organizations which have programmes in Latin America (some are listed above; see pp for more details). Many of these are linked to **gap year websites** and offer a wide range of working opportunities which you'll have to apply for months before you arrive in Latin America. The majority of these organizations are highly profitable businesses and, in exchange for finding you a suitable position will charge you a fee (running to several thousand dollars), only a small part of which covers your living expenses while away. Additionally some of these businesses are unscrupulous and fail to monitor each project properly – you may find yourself sweeping floors and washing up rather than saving the planet. Check carefully the **credentials** of your chosen organization and try to get a **personal recommendation** if possible. The advantage of volunteering this way, however, is that you'll be able to organize your schedule in advance and ensure that you have something you're interested in lined up before you set off.

On the other hand you could just turn up while in Latin America and offer your services to a suitable organization, which is much the cheapest way of doing it – locally run schemes won't charge you for the privilege of helping them though you run the risk of not finding anything appropriate, let alone well organized and effective. You'll have to cover your **expenses** unless you have a specific skill – medicine, engineering, teaching – in which case you may be offered a small living allowance. Check your guidebook for lists of locally run organizations in areas you'll be visiting or try asking at the tourist office on arrival.

Working

If you run out of cash and don't want your adventure to end you could always try looking for a **job**. Bear in mind, though, that **unemployment** runs as high as eighty percent in some parts of Latin America and if there aren't jobs for the locals, chances are there won't be jobs for foreigners.

Obviously, if you speak Spanish or Portuguese you'll massively improve your chances of employment. That said, most job opportunities exist in one of two areas: ELT or tourism. ELT (**English Language Teaching**) is the most widespread work available for foreigners in Latin America. *Teaching English Abroad* by Susan Griffith (Vacation Work) is a good starting point if you're planning to take up ELT. More and more locals are keen to learn English and every capital city will have scores of English schools as well as private classes held at large businesses or in individual's homes. Generally the hourly rate of pay is quite reasonable, although your hours (usually before and after the working day) won't be convenient. Although it's not mandatory, having an ELT qualification will greatly improve

Teaching English

While studying Spanish in Antigua, Guatemala, I was recruited by a language academy to work in El Salvador. Most of my fellow teachers were American – perhaps the reason why the students loved my English accent. I fielded innumerable questions about the royal family, Michael Owen, David Beckham and the Spice Girls. In return, I learned a huge amount about postwar society in Central America and the economic and social disparities.

A few adventurous travellers passed through and stayed to teach and share our house – located opposite the presidential palace. I taught government ministers, Latin American diplomats and the captain of the national women's soccer team. After classes, teachers and students would hit the bars and at weekends we'd hit the beach or climb volcanoes.

But the best bit? Undoubtedly teaching English slang to the youngsters. Imagine the thrill of listening to kids running out of class calling each other "geezer" and "bloke".

Gary Bowerman

your chances of employment and increase your status and wages: the best of these is the University of Cambridge **CELTA** (Certificate in English Language Teaching to Adults) which takes a month, full-time, to complete – and is recognized worldwide. Courses are widely available in most parts of the developed world and cost around US$1500 (see Directory for details). Generally acknowledged as the best ELT training centre, **International House** (ⓦwww.ihworld.com) has branches in many countries including several destinations in Latin America. Alternatively you could try just turning up at an English-language school on spec – particularly in places less popular with tourists, there might well be vacancies for English teachers, and all you may be asked for in terms of qualifications is to be a native speaker. There are also occasional admin jobs at English language schools or work as student coordinators. The British Council's website (ⓦwww.britishcouncil.org) and the TEFL website (ⓦwww.tefl.com) both have lists of English-teaching vacancies worldwide.

www.roughguides.com

Additionally, you may find work in **tourist resorts**, especially if you have a special skill or qualification in something like scuba diving, sailing, whitewater rafting or mountain-climbing – ask around at likely spots. Otherwise, you might find a job in a hotel as a chambermaid, waiter or even receptionist. **Backpacker hostels**, especially those run by gringos, often hire broke guests to help serve food and drinks or clean in exchange for board and lodging.

If you have any kind of talent for writing or taking photographs you may also find paid employment working for one of the English-language **newspapers** based in Latin America – most countries have at least one, based in capital cities or major tourist resorts; worth contacting are San José, Costa Rica's *Tico Times* (Ⓦwww.ticotimes.net) which sometimes offers four-month **internships** with a small monthly stipend; *The Buenos Aires Herald* in Argentina (Ⓦwww.buenosairesherald.com) and Mexico's *The News* (Ⓦwww.thenews.com.mx). Alternatively you could work **freelance**, sending in articles and images as you travel – the Lanic website (Ⓦlanic.utexas.edu) has links to dozens of newspapers in Latin America as does World Newspapers (Ⓦwww.world-newspapers.com).

Whatever sort of work you find, however, it's likely to be of an unofficial nature. **Work visas** for Latin America are difficult to obtain: you'll need a contract of employment and endless patience to negotiate the relevant bureaucratic hurdles. Fortunately, many employers will turn a blind eye to your lack of papers.

4

When to go

Obviously, planning when to go to Latin America is largely dependent on your own circumstances, and when you're able to find the time and the money to get away. These constraints aside, it's important to have an idea of what the **weather** will be like in the areas you're planning to visit, and to understand how seasonal variations in climate are likely to affect your travels – with a little planning, it's possible to organize an extended itinerary through the region that makes the best of the weather conditions in each country you're visiting.

However, it's also worth bearing in mind that, in any particular region, the time of year which enjoys the best weather will almost inevitably also be the peak tourist season, particularly if it coincides with the December-to-January, Easter, and June-to-August holiday periods in the US and Europe. Prices for everything from international airline tickets to accommodation are at their highest, and popular destinations can get uncomfortably crowded. If you're prepared to put up with a little rain and visit outside these periods, you'll often be rewarded by lower costs and fewer crowds.

Weather aside, you may also want to arrange your visit around one of Latin America's major **fiestas**. These extravagant festivals encapsulate the heart of Latin American culture and are amongst the most colourful and exciting experiences the region has to offer, so it's well worth making the effort to coincide with one of these, as it's likely to prove one of the highlights of your travels. It's also worth timing your trip precisely if you want to catch other special events – such as music or literary festivals or the arrival of migrating whales on a particular coast line.

www.roughguides.com

THE BIG ADVENTURE

The climate in Latin America

Most of Latin America lies within the **tropics**, so there's no great difference between winter and summer, and seasonal variations in temperature are minimal – Belize City, for example, is 27°C/81°F in January and 31°C/88°F in July. But although temperatures are relatively stable, there are considerable seasonal variations in rainfall and humidity that may affect your plans. Most tropical regions have **wet seasons**, when heavy rain can make travel difficult and uncomfortable.

That said, though most tropical regions receive extremely high annual rainfall, even in the rainy seasons this tends to be concentrated in torrential bursts lasting a few hours or so, after which the skies clear and the sun comes out. In some tropical lowland regions – particularly in the rainforests of the Amazon and the Colombian Pacific coast – it can rain almost every day (it's not called rainforest for nothing), so the occasional soaking just goes with the territory and will only really spoil your trip if roads are washed out, making bus travel impossible.

The best time to visit

What follows is a very broad guide to the best times of year for travelling to each country in Latin America ("best" meaning the driest and mildest conditions). This summary is meant only as a general introduction to help you plan your route; for more detail, check the relevant guidebooks, tourist offices and other sources of information.

Argentina	Dec–May
Belize	Late Dec to March
Bolivia	May–Sept
Brazil	Feb–June
Chile	Nov–March in the south; year-round elsewhere
Colombia	Nov–March
Costa Rica	Nov, April & May
Ecuador	June–Aug in the highlands; Dec–April on the coast
El Salvador	Nov–April
Guatemala	Feb–May
The Guianas	Feb & March, July–Nov
Honduras	March–May
Mexico	Nov–Feb
Nicaragua	Dec–March
Panama	Dec–April
Paraguay	May–Sept (the cooler winter months)
Peru	May–Sept in the highlands and Amazon and Dec–March on the coast
Uruguay	Sept–April
Venezuela	Nov–June

www.roughguides.com

Tropical Latin America is not uniformly hot: **altitude** is a huge factor in determining local climate, particularly in the Andean countries, which sit astride the highest tropical mountain range in the world. Temperatures decrease by about 6–7°C/11°F with every 1000m you ascend, so that in the Ecuadorian capital Quito, for example, which is set at an altitude of 2800m, the year-round daytime temperature never really exceeds a spring-like 20°C/68°F (with much cooler nights), even though the city sits almost directly on the equator. In mountainous countries you can take advantage of local differences in climate caused by altitude: if you can't stand the heat and humidity of the lowlands, you can always escape to the cool of the highlands, while if the bitterly cold nights in one of the cities of the high Andes get too much to bear, you can jump on a bus and head down into the sweltering lowlands for a day or two.

South of Latin America's tropics, the temperate **Southern Cone** region – comprising Argentina, Chile, Uruguay and southern Brazil – experiences far greater annual variations in temperature, with seasons similar (but in reverse) to those of the northern hemisphere. But it's only in the far south of the Southern Cone that the cold weather and short days of the southern hemisphere winter (June–Sept) can limit your options and make travel unpleasant.

Whilst taking seasonal variations into account, you shouldn't let the prospect of very wet or cold weather put you off altogether, as long as you have the right clothing and accept that transport may be less reliable and certain outdoor activities, such as trekking, less enjoyable or even impossible.

Mexico and Central America

Northern Mexico is the only part of Latin America north of the tropics, but the region is so hot and arid that rain and the northern hemisphere winter are no real impediment to travel, though it can get pretty cold at higher altitudes between December and February. **Southern Mexico** lies within the tropics and shares the same seasonal climate patterns as **Central America**, which is generally hot and humid year-round (though, again, cooler in highland regions), but has seasonal variations in rainfall and humidity. The best time to visit southern Mexico and Central America is during the dry season, which runs roughly from November to March. The rainy season runs from around May to October, but even then it doesn't rain all the time, and you'll often get a fine sunny morning followed by a few hours of rain in the afternoon. Along the **Caribbean coastline** of Central America, rain and humidity continue year-round with only slight seasonal variations.

▲ Tulum, Mexico

The tropical Andean countries

Running the length of the western side of South America, the **Andes** are the second largest mountain range in the world, and the highest range in tropical latitudes. In the five tropical countries the Andes pass through – Venezuela, Colombia, Ecuador, Peru and Bolivia – the extreme variations in altitude created by the mountains produce an astonishing number of different climatic zones within a surprisingly small area. The eastern slopes of the Andes, in particular, are so steep that it's possible to experience both subzero conditions and extreme tropical heat in the same afternoon. Colombia is home to so many different microclimates as to make generalization almost impossible, while Peru embraces perhaps the greatest extremes of climate of any country on Earth, ranging from the world's driest desert on its Pacific coast to the glacial peaks of the high Andes and the hot and humid lowlands of the Amazon basin. This enormous variety means that whatever time of the year you happen to be in one of these countries, the weather conditions are likely to be ideal in at least some regions (though it's equally likely to be pouring with rain elsewhere).

That said, there are some broad seasonal differences that you should be aware of when planning your trip. Venezuela and Colombia broadly share the same dry season as Central America, particularly along the Caribbean coast, so November to March is the best time to visit. The rest of the year tends to be much wetter (though rain falls throughout the year in the lowland rainforest regions in both countries and along Colombia's Pacific coast). Further south, the Andean countries of Ecuador, Peru and Bolivia experience more defined seasonal differences. In the highlands, the dry season runs between May and October, with bright, dry, sunny days, and cool nights, particularly at higher altitudes. This is obviously the best time to visit, particularly if you want to do any trekking or mountaineering, though it also coincides with the peak tourist season from June to August. The rainy season runs roughly from November to April, with the wettest weather in January and February. Heavy rains can cause floods and landslides that damage or completely block the generally poor roads, causing frequent travel delays. Rain can also make mountain trekking pretty miserable, while some high-altitude routes become cut off by snow. Those difficulties aside, it rarely rains so much in the highlands as to spoil your day, and the landscape is arguably more beautiful than during the dry season, with crops high in the fields and the mountainsides green with vegetation, rather than parched and brown.

Though the **Amazon Basin** is pretty wet all year round, along its western edge in Peru and Bolivia it is also affected by the Andean rainy season, so between November and April the Amazon regions of both countries see heavy rain and can be impossible to visit, as roads are washed away and large areas are flooded. The **Pacific coast** of Ecuador and Peru is affected by a very different set of seasonal variations. The period from around December to March gener-

Rainy days in Chocó

The region of Chocó in northwest Colombia is among the world's rainiest – unless you go there in its "dry" period (Dec–March) you're likely to get drenched. When I arrived in the region's capital, Quibdó, it wasn't actually raining; the streets were full of colourful fruit stalls and locals sitting idly along the riverfront, shooting the breeze. That evening, though, when I went to bed, the rain began – my modest hotel had a flat tin roof, as did all the other buildings in Quibdó, and the violent drumming noise, like a thousand tap-dancing giants, kept me awake all night. In the morning the streets had been churned into muddy rivers, the rain was still falling heavily and the sky was sporadically lit up with dramatic white flashes of lightning.

The locals, used to the weather, had donned wellies and were splashing happily through the water – I had come unprepared and so stayed in my hotel all day watching the rain from the reception and only periodically rushing out to the nearest café to eat and then race back again. All day it rained and all the next night and then all day again. I couldn't sleep or sightsee or even just stroll through the streets as I would usually have done. The level of noise, both the crashing rain and the cracks of thunder, was incredible – I could barely get myself heard, let alone read in peace. Slowly the water began to seep under the front door into the hotel and the corridors were filled with sodden clothing drying out and a damp cloying mist. After several days the rain stopped – for a while – but by then it was time to move on. When people ask me what Quibdó is like I can only shrug and say "wet".

Polly Rodger Brown

ally sees hot, sunny days along the coast (in comparison to the rains that affect the highlands), but for most of the rest of the year the region is covered by low coastal cloud or mist known as *garúa*, which makes for grey days and cold swimming, even though it rarely ever rains along the entire length of the Peruvian coast.

Brazil

Given its vast size, it's no surprise that Brazil's climate varies considerably between different parts of the country. Brazil lies entirely within the tropics, so it's generally **hot** and **humid** year-round, and in most areas rain can fall at any time of the year, though rarely for long enough to affect your travel plans – in general, most of the country can be visited at any time. The main exception to this is the far south, where the climate is more temperate and seasonal variations are more marked; here, the southern hemisphere winter months from June to August see cooler temperatures and heavy rains which can make travelling miserable, while the peak summer months of January and February are particularly hot and humid and coincide with the main holiday period for Brazilians.

The Southern Cone

South America's Southern Cone, comprising Argentina, Chile and Uruguay, lies almost completely outside the tropics and enjoys a **temperate climate** with more marked seasonal differences in climate between the winter (June–Aug) and summer (Nov–Feb) – the fact that these seasons are the exact opposite of those in the northern hemisphere means that if you time your trip right you can enjoy two summers in one year. Uruguay and the northern parts of Chile and Argentina can be comfortably visited at any time of the year, though the winter months are cooler and drier than the summer, which can be unpleasantly hot: the optimum times are spring (Sept & Oct) and autumn (March & April). The further south you travel in Chile and Argentina, however, the better it is to avoid the winter months, when the days become short and it gets very cold and wet; in addition, heavy snow can prevent access to mountainous national parks and block some passes between Chile and Argentina (though, of course, the same conditions are ideal if you want to go skiing – the season runs from June–October). In the far south, the summer offers the added advantage of long summer evenings, allowing far more time to enjoy the sights.

Fiestas

Latin Americans welcome any excuse for a party, and most countries host a large number of national, regional and local **fiestas**. These are amongst the most vibrant and exciting spectacles Latin America has to offer, and can be worth planning your trip around. For many Latin

www.roughguides.com

Semana Santa

Semana Santa – Holy or Easter Week – is Latin America's biggest festival, even more ubiquitous than Carnival, with celebrations taking place in every city, town and village from Mexico to Argentina. Firstly it's a **public holiday**, when locals head in droves for the beach, national parks and other resorts or else back to their hometowns. Hotels are booked out, buses and domestic flights are crammed full – anyone planning to travel during this period will need to book in advance. More significantly, though, it's a deeply religious occasion with a series of packed masses over the week leading to Easter Sunday and churches lovingly decorated with extravagant flower arrangements. Though ceremonies vary from region to region, they usually include solemn parades of church statues through the town centre and vivid Passion plays with real blood and suffering – the man playing Christ often wears a genuine crown of thorns, staggers under the weight of a solid cross and is sometimes even nailed to it with real nails. The sanctity of the occasion is lightened with street food stalls, traditional live music and noisy firework displays.

The most impressive Semana Santa celebrations in Latin America occur in the colonial city of **Antigua**, Guatemala, and attract tens of thousands of visitors. Locals spend hours carpeting the streets with elaborate patterns of flowers, coloured sawdust and pine needles for the Good Friday parades where life-sized images of Jesus Christ and the saints are carried through the town on massive cedar platforms to an accompaniment of brass band dirges and thick clouds of incense. Elsewhere, some of the best places to witness the festivities include San Miguel de Allende in central Mexico, Popayán in southern Colombia and Ayacucho in the Peruvian Andes.

Americans, fiestas are the most important events of the year and are taken very seriously, often involving lengthy preparation and considerable expense, with the largest featuring thousands of costumed dancers, massed bands, fireworks, copious food and drink, and unrestrained revelry that can continue for a week or more.

The most famous fiesta is without doubt the **Carnaval** in Rio de Janeiro, one of the biggest parties in the world. It's worth remembering that Carnival (originally a religious festival marking the start of Lent) is also celebrated throughout Brazil and the rest of Latin America, albeit on a less spectacular scale, and smaller celebrations often have a more intimate and less commercial feel.

Like Carnival, many of the major fiestas mark important dates in the Roman Catholic religious calendar, so the dates they're held on can vary from year to year – tourist offices should be able to give you precise details of major events. As well as religious occasions like Carnival and **Semana Santa** (Easter), many national and regional public holidays mark significant events in Latin America's post-Conquest history, such as the gaining of independence or the foundation of particular cities; though still treated as an excuse for a party, these tend to be somewhat stuffier affairs, involving interminable civic and military parades.

During major fiestas, transport and accommodation can be very difficult to come by and prices increase dramatically, so it's worth booking well in advance. Even when they don't coincide with an official public

Our favourite fiestas

We've listed some of our favourite fiestas below; any guidebook or local tourist office will suggest many others. It's also worth looking at *Wild Planet! 1001 Extraordinary Events for the Inspired Traveller* by Tom Clynes (Visible Ink Press), which has details of dozens of celebrations throughout Latin America and the rest of the world, or check out the website @www.whatsonwhen.com which lists hundreds of events by country and by month.

Feria de Alasitas La Paz, Bolivia (last week of Jan). This unusual festival sees the streets of central La Paz filled with stalls selling miniature models of items as varied as cars, houses, livestock, wads of dollar bills, and even computers and university degree certificates. Locals buy these to offer to Ekeko, the household god of abundance (portrayed as a diminutive, smiling, moustached man), in the belief that whatever they give him in miniature will be given back to them for real before the year is out.

Carnival (late Feb or early March). Beginning on the Friday before Ash Wednesday, the pre-Lenten *Carnaval* in Rio de Janeiro is without doubt the world's most famous party, a five-day extravaganza that attracts over a quarter of a million foreign visitors each year. The highlights are the processions of the samba schools, each made up of thousands of costumed dancers and myriad decorated floats, who parade along the main avenues and around the purpose-built Sambódromo, competing both to impress the *Carnaval* judges and the huge crowds. The manic celebrations continue through the night at numerous themed *Carnaval* balls, unrestrained parties that start a week before the main event.

Carnival is also celebrated throughout the rest of Brazil and Latin America, albeit on a smaller and less dramatic scale than in Rio, though usually involving the same ingredients of music, dance and licentiousness. If the sheer scale and commercialism of the Rio *Carnaval* puts you off, you may be better off joining a smaller but arguably more authentic celebration somewhere else – many people rate the celebrations in Salvador de Bahia, with its strong Afro-Brazilian traditions, more highly than Rio. Elsewhere, the Carnival in Baranquilla, on the Colombian Caribbean coast, is renowned for its raucousness, while Carnival in the bleak Bolivian mining city of Oruro is amongst the most colourful folkloric fiestas in all Latin America.

Semana Santa (March or April). Semana Santa – the Easter Holy Week – is marked throughout Latin America with colourful religious processions. The celebrations in the city of Ayacucho in Peru and in Antigua in Guatemala are particularly fervent and dramatic. For more on Semana Santa, see the box on p.71.

Qoyllur Riti Peru (May or June). Held at the foot of a glacier in an isolated valley in the Andes south of Cusco in the week before Corpus Christi, this is a celebration of ancient Andean beliefs centred on mountain gods and natural cycles, covered with only the thinnest veneer of Catholicism. Thousands of indigenous peasants make the pilgrimage to a bleak spot at well over 4000m, and costumed dances, accompanied by traditional music and dynamite explosions, continue for three days and nights. This is primarily an

holiday, major fiestas tend to result in pretty much everything shutting down for at least a day or two, so they're not a good time to buy an airline ticket, change money in a bank, or get a visa extension. The same is true of national public holidays, particularly the **Christmas and New Year** period, when buses and trains get very crowded as people travel to visit relations, and international flights are often booked up months ahead by expatriate Latin Americans returning home for the holidays.

indigenous fiesta and though a few Cusco tour agencies take groups, it's only for the adventurous, as you'll have to hike there and camp at high altitude.

Inti Raymi and Corpus Christi Cusco, Peru (June). Inti Raymi (June 24) is a popular and commercial re-enactment of the Inca Festival of the Sun, performed by costumed actors in Sacsayhuaman, the massive Inca fortress that towers above Cusco. The fiesta draws thousands of tourists to the city, and hotels and flights fill up, but it's far from the most authentic of Cusco's many fiestas – that honour belongs to Corpus Christi. Usually held in mid-June, this event involves mass processions of saints' effigies accompanied by costumed dancers, traditional music and street markets selling traditional food.

Yamor Fiesta Otavalo, Ecuador. Held in the first two weeks of September, the Yamor Fiesta is the main annual festival in the Ecuadorian town of Otavalo, best known for its craft market. The indigenous people of the region come into town for several days of bullfights, food, drink, music and dance, in celebration of a pre-Columbian fiesta revived in the 1940s.

Day of the Dead Mexico (Nov 1 & 2). Fervently celebrated throughout Mexico on All Saints' Day, and through the night into the following day (All Souls' Day, the Day of the Dead proper), the Day of the Dead is a time of remembrance that is at once sombre and festive. People converge on cemeteries with food and drink to party with their deceased loved ones and ancestors. In the run-up to the event throughout the country shops and market stalls sell special foods and macabre decorations in the shape of skulls, coffins and the like, which are used to adorn graves, and ceremonial offerings arranged in honour of the dead, who are believed to return to the land of the living and visit their former homes for the day. Precise customs vary from region to region within Mexico – one of the most dramatic places to witness the occasion is on the Lago de Pátzcuaro, about 200km east of Mexico City, where locals converge on an island cemetery in canoes carrying candles and floral offerings. The Day of the Dead is also celebrated in similar fashion in Guatemala, and throughout the Andes, though without the bizarre ritual paraphernalia of Mexico.

Día de la Tradición Argentina (around Nov 10). Also known as the Fiesta del Gaucho, this is a celebration of Argentina's most powerful cultural icon, the gaucho (cowboy) of the pampas grasslands. Centred on the town of Santiago de Areco, the festival involves traditional gaucho folk music and dance, rodeos and horseriding displays, and the consumption of large quantities of the finest beef in the world, roasted on a spit over an open fire.

Día de la Virgen de Guadalupe Mexico (Dec 12). Mexico's patron saint's day is celebrated with extravagant processions and a mass pilgrimage to the Basilica de Guadalupe, outside Mexico City, with many of the thousands of celebrants advancing to the shrine on their knees.

As well as major national and regional celebrations, most towns and villages have their own annual local fiesta, usually held on the day of its patron saint. These celebrations can be much more fun to visit than major fiestas in larger towns, particularly in rural areas of countries with a large indigenous population, where they can last over a week and involve traditional music and colourful costumed folkloric dances. Be prepared to change your itinerary at short notice if you hear of a good local fiesta.

5

How much will it cost?

The **cost** of travelling in Latin America depends hugely on where you're going: from ultra-cheap countries like Guatemala, Nicaragua or Bolivia where you could get by on US$10 a day to places like Argentina, Chile or Costa Rica, where living costs can be similar to those in Europe or North America. Generally, though travelling in Latin America is not as cheap as travelling in other parts of the developing world like Asia, it is much less expensive than travelling in your own country.

Obviously, your **budget** is vital in determining what kind of trip you have, and it's important before you set out to have at least a rough idea of how much you'll need. If you do have a very limited budget, then think about taking a shorter but more satisfying trip. Nothing is more frustrating than not having enough cash to really enjoy your holiday. Imagine getting all the way to Venezuela and not being able to afford the flight to the Angel Falls, or going to the Caribbean islands of Mexico, Belize or Honduras and sitting forlornly on the beach while everyone else goes snorkelling or scuba diving.

However tedious it sounds, it really helps to keep a record of your expenses so that you always know how much money you have to play with. It's all too easy to run out of cash well before the end of your trip, or forgo a special outing because you're saving money when actually you don't need to. Don't be alarmed if you spend a lot of money in your first few days, however – it's well worth the investment just to feel safe and properly acclimatized.

Cost of living

It's difficult to generalize about the **cost of living** in Latin America, which varies wildly even between adjacent countries – travelling in Costa Rica costs two or three times more than in neighbouring Nicaragua, for example, whilst crossing the border from Bolivia into Chile will immediately double your expenses. In general, the richer, more westernized Latin American countries are significantly more expensive to travel in than the poorer, less developed ones.

Parts of Latin America have been – and may again be – subject to periods of economic meltdown and hyper-inflation, as demonstrated by fiscal woes in both Brazil and Argentina, which had a topsy-turvy effect on the cost of living for several years.

Making savings before you go

With a little careful planning, you can start cutting the cost of your trip.

- Begin planning well in advance of your departure date – if you leave everything to the last minute you'll invariably pay over the odds. Shop around for airfares and insurance.
- Wait for the sales to buy your equipment or surf the net for special deals. Alternatively, borrow gear from friends and family – or consider buying secondhand stuff (although you should check important pieces of equipment like backpacks or boots carefully). You could also wait to buy basic clothing until you arrive in Latin America, where it's invariably cheaper than at home.
- Make sure you buy those day-to-day items which cost considerably more abroad before you go – these are usually things that the locals don't use as much, such as computer gear, batteries, suntan lotion, moisturizing cream and tampons.

Making savings on the road

Despite the unavoidable expenses when on the road – mainly lodging, eating and transport – there are plenty of ways to cut costs.

- The slower you travel the cheaper your trip will be. Not only will you cut down on transport costs, which can be considerable, but you should also be able to get a reduced rate on accommodation if you're staying more than a few days
- Travel during the low season, when hotel and tour prices drop (sometimes dramatically) and when the relative lack of tourists gives you more bargaining power.

www.roughguides.com

- Form groups with other travellers for arranging tours, hiring transport and even getting good deals on accommodation. The more there are of you, the cheaper things get.
- Always ask the price of things before you start. Be very wary of menus with no prices and agree fares with taxi drivers.
- Do as the locals do. Take local buses, eat in markets or informal cafés and choose the daily set meal.
- Stay in hostel dormitories. They're often the cheapest accommodation available, and most also have kitchens where you can cook your own meals. You might even want to take a tent – you can often camp in the gardens of hostels or cheap hotels, or in national parks – or buy a hammock, which you can sling up on a willing hotel proprietor's porch for a very small fee.
- Take a water filter or some other method of purifying unclean water. Tap water in Latin America is usually not safe, and bottled water costs as much as other drinks.
- Homestays – staying with a local family – are good for practising your Spanish or Portuguese, a great way to get involved in the community and, above all, cheap.

Tourist prices

You may as well accept right from the start that you'll be paying more for most things than the locals – annoying as you might find this, there's very little you can do about it. In some parts of Latin America, tourists are officially charged more than nationals for things like **entrance fees** to museums and art galleries, national parks and historical sites.

Much more widespread is the **unofficial hike** in prices that happens when a tourist comes to town. Market food, taxi fares and perhaps even hotel rooms and meals will invariably cost more. For more on spending money responsibly, see the section on ethical tourism on pp.124–125.

Bargaining

Latin American countries with a large indigenous population have a long tradition of **flexible pricing** and you may be able to significantly lower the cost of – especially – souvenirs and market handicrafts. Buying more than one item at a time always helps as does an apparent insouciance about what you're trying to buy. But experienced traders, like the Aymara of Bolivia and Guatemalan Mayans, are masters in the art of negotiation and rarely sell goods for the very low prices you might imagine you can bargain them down to. Remember, too that what is small change to you might be more important to the seller. There is nothing uglier than a tourist with a thousand–dollar camera around his neck arguing with a *campesino* over the price of an orange.

▲ Bargaining at a market in Ecuador

Splashing out

In Latin America, quite possibly for the first time in your life, you'll be considered **rich**. And, like it or not, by most Latin American standards, you are – compare the cost of your return airfare with wages in the poorer parts of the continent of as little as US$15 a week (coupled with 75 percent unemployment rates) and you begin to get the picture. Instead of fighting this and irritating the locals by continuing to insist that actually you're an impoverished student struggling to make ends meet, why not make the most of your temporary wealth?

In some parts of Latin America (Asunción in Paraguay for example), US$30 will buy you a night in a plush hotel room with all the frills. On the Atlantic coast of Nicaragua you'll pay less than US$10 for a slap-up meal of freshly caught lobster. You can learn to scuba dive in the Bay Islands of Honduras for as little as a third of what it would cost elsewhere – and the same holds for learning Spanish in Guatemala, whitewater rafting in Peru or mountain-climbing in Bolivia.

Occasionally there may be times on the road when you need to **indulge yourself**. Long bumpy bus rides; lack of sleep caused by poor hotels; bad food; mosquito bites; extremes of heat and cold – all these can take their toll and leave you exhausted. Instead of staggering on until you grind to a halt or fall ill, it's a good idea to take time out by paying more than normal for a decent night's sleep and a proper hot

Sample budgets

The following sample budgets are linked to a few of the itineraries suggested on pp.19–27. They do not include international or domestic flights, insurance or any other pre-trip expenses. Minimum daily living expenses (which cover staying in cheap hotels/hostels, eating *comida corriente* and travelling by local bus) for individual countries are listed on the opening pages of the profiles in "Where to go" (see pp.199–296).

Three weeks on South America's Caribbean coast

Though Colombia is still inexpensive to visit, costs are rising in Venezuela and anywhere on the Caribbean tends to cost more than inland destinations. Still, US$600 will cover your expenses and include a couple of snorkelling or short boat trips (US$30–65). If you want to splash out and spend the odd night in a decent hotel (US$30–50) and eat an occasional posh meal (US$10–20) you could fit that into your budget as well.

One month on the Ruta Maya

Ten days in this part of Mexico and Belize will be relatively expensive – count on US$35 per day to cover fairly basic eating and sleeping arrangements with travel included. The rest of this trip – twenty days in Guatemala, Honduras and El Salvador (where accommodation can cost as little as US$5 a night, as does eating, US$2–3 for a substantial *menu del día* lunch) – will cost much less. Altogether, count on spending US$800 for the month with entrance to the Yucatán's Maya cities (US$8–10) but no frills added. If you want to scuba dive (from US$85 for a one-day "exploratory" course) in Belize, tuck into Mexican "haute cuisine", take an organized day-trip or visit one of the Ruta Maya's amusement parks (such as Xelha) you'll need an extra US$200.

Three months in the Andean highlands

While Chile is one of the priciest countries in South America, the other places on this itinerary – Peru, Ecuador and particularly Bolivia – are among its cheapest. For this trip reckon on a minimum budget of US$2000 which will cover food, accommodation and travel on a fairly tight budget. If you want to ski in Chile (prices start at US$800 for an all-inclusive week-long package), visit upmarket beach resort Viña del Mar or spend any longer than three weeks in the country you'll need to increase your budget. On the other hand both simple accommodation and eating out rarely cost more than a few dollars in the other Andean countries – a month in Bolivia could cost as little as US$350–500.

meal. And when it comes to your **personal safety**, no price is too high to pay. If the only budget hotel in town is down a dark alleyway, don't book in; if the cheapest local guide is clearly a bit of a cowboy, don't hire him; and if the third-class boat you're planning to board looks like it might sink, don't get on it. You'll feel very foolish if something awful happens simply because you were cutting corners.

How to take your money

The best way to keep your money safe is to take it in as many different forms as possible – cash, travellers' cheques, and credit cards. In addition, be sure to check exchange rates on the internet (ⓦwww.oanda.com or ⓦwww.xe.com) so that you know what you should be getting.

US dollars

The **US dollar** rules supreme in Latin America – it's actually the **official currency** of Panama, Ecuador and El Salvador. Every country in the region accepts dollars as payment as well as its own currency, and you should never be without some. Generally speaking, the more expensive the service or goods you're buying, the greater the chance that you'll be able to pay in dollars, while the further away you get from tourist areas, the slimmer your chances of paying in dollars become.

In case you run short, you can also get dollars from some **ATMs** in parts of Latin America – this is easiest in Mexico.

Cash

The easiest and cheapest – though least secure – way to take your money is as **cash**, either in local currency or as US dollars. Don't change too much cash all in one go, though. You'll miss out on local currency fluctuations, which often favour established hard currencies like the dollar, the pound and the euro. More importantly, standard insurance policies only replace small amounts of cash if it's stolen.

Travellers' cheques

With the growing ubiquity of ATMs in Latin America **travellers' cheques** (*cheques de viaje*) are now rarely used by tourists. This means that banks and *casas de cambio* are more reluctant to accept them and you may find them difficult or impossible to change.

However, since if they're lost or stolen they're swiftly replaced, they're still the safest way of carrying funds. Should you want to take some, always buy travellers' cheques issued in **US dollars** and use recognizable brands – American Express or Thomas Cook. You'll be charged a commission when you buy them (1-1.5 percent) and possibly when you cash them as well as getting a low exchange rate.

Credit and debit cards

Credit and debit **cards** are the most convenient, if not necessarily the cheapest, way to carry funds in Latin America. Most banks will give you an advance on your card, and there are increasing numbers of **ATMs** across Latin America where you can withdraw the local currency (and sometimes even dollars) – you can check the location of ATMs in Latin America at ⓦwww.visa.com or ⓦwww.mastercard.com.

It's worth remembering, however, that using a credit or debit card is far from cheap. When it comes to withdrawing money from an ATM, the average cost for using both types of card includes a 2.75 percent handling charge plus a further 1.50 percent commission on foreign exchange – in total, a whopping 4.25 percent (on the plus side, however, ATMs often offer far better exchange rates than local banks or *casas de cambio*). With credit cards, you'll also be paying interest on any money withdrawn from the moment you take it out. Additionally, if you're paying for a room or a meal with plastic you may be stung with an additional charge levied by the hotel or restaurant owner – such additional charges are completely unregulated and can potentially be as high as fifteen percent.

The most popular credit cards in Latin America are **Visa** and **Mastercard** – Visa is the more widely accepted of the two, though it's worth carrying both. If you're travelling for a while, you'll need either to set up a direct debit or ask a friend to pay off your account. It's also possible to get Visa debit cards: these work in most Latin American ATMs (as do other debit cards linked to the Link, Cirrus or Plus networks).

For UK citizens, the current best debit card deal is with **Nationwide** (Ⓦwww.nationwide.co.uk). The one percent charge for taking money out abroad with a FlexAccount debit card is the lowest currently available. Americans can use either a Citibank or Capital One debit card, both of which carry no charges.

If you're using a credit/debit card abroad it's advisable to contact your supplier in **advance** and warn them that you'll be away, where and for how long. It's not uncommon for card companies to put a block on your cards due to what is deemed "unusual activity" – this means that suddenly and without warning you won't be able to withdraw cash from machines or use cards for any payments. You'll have to call your bank or card company and explain what's happening before the block is lifted. In terms of **security**, avoid withdrawing cash from an ATM at night and exercise due caution at all times.

Prepaid cards

An alternative way of carrying funds is with a **prepaid card**. Combining the convenience of a debit card with the security of travellers' cheques these are a safe and easy way to pay your way. Cards are used to withdraw funds from ATMs just like debit cards and are linked to the Mastercard or Visa networks. It's easiest to order them, load them up from your bank account and top them up as you go all online. Lost or stolen cards are usually **replaced** very quickly with funds intact.

Currently the best deals are the Caxton FX Global Traveller (Ⓦwww.caxtonfxcard.com), Ice Travellers cash card (Ⓦwww.iceplc.com) and Visa TravelMoney (Ⓦwww.visa.com). In the UK the **Post Office** (Ⓦwww.postoffice.co.uk) also now has a Travel Money Card (TCM) which has a 2.75 percent transaction charge as well as a minimum £2 fee for each withdrawal – essentially the same costs as most credit/debit cards.

Changing money

The easiest form of money to change is **dollars**: in many parts of Latin America virtually everyone you come across – hoteliers, restaurateurs, shopkeepers, local business people, market traders – will be more than happy to change them for you at the going rate. There are also moneychangers (*coyotes*) on the streets in most Latin American countries who'll change dollars for rates slightly better than banks, and without commission. They normally hang out in commercial areas, like shopping malls or around markets – you'll recognize them by the wads of cash they flick through and wave in your face. Some are licensed, while some are unofficial – be very careful if you decide to deal with the latter, who are adept at all kinds of scams. By contrast, official licensed moneychangers (look for the badge) are often trustworthy, though it's worth checking locally first.

You can also change money at **banks** and **casas de cambio** (exchange bureaux, usually street booths); some will also change travellers' cheques and give advances on credit cards. In some places, banks offer better rates than *casas de cambio*, while in others, the reverse applies. Banks are potentially much more frustrating places than *casas de cambio*, with long queues (although tourists are sometimes ushered to the front) and inflexible set hours for changing money. *Casas de cambio* are generally more user-friendly, with many opening late and over weekends.

Change is in very short supply in many Latin American countries so whenever you're changing money always ask for small-denomination notes and check that they're in fairly good condition – torn or even just grubby notes may be refused by traders (this goes for dollars too). Once you've completed your transaction, be it with a moneychanger, *casa de cambio* or bank, count your money carefully.

Emergency funds

The easiest and fastest way of getting emergency funds is to have someone **wire money** to you. The two main operators are **Western Union** (Ⓦ www.westernunion.com) and **Moneygram** (Ⓦ www.moneygram .com), even quite modest-sized towns in Latin America have an office of one or other (Western Union is more prevalent). Someone at home will have to take the money to the local branch, which is then wired immediately (taking no more than fifteen minutes) to the office you have specified. Remember, though, that wiring money is hugely expensive – costing anything up to fourteen percent of the sum being wired – and should be considered a last resort.

6

Guidebooks and other resources

Whatever the nature of your trip, the chances are that the more you know about Latin America, the more you'll enjoy your time there. Having some idea about the history, politics and culture of the countries you'll be visiting will whet your appetite for travelling and place what you see in a broader **context**.

There are lots of ways of learning about Latin America. The **internet** is an excellent resource; connect to a powerful search engine like Google (Ⓦwww.google.com), type in the subject or place you're interested in and you'll get hundreds of useful links to websites, online articles and photo essays (see p.306 in the Directory and the individual country profiles for some recommended websites). Cities with large Latin American populations in North America, Europe and Australasia all have **specialist resource centres** with libraries and collections of useful videos; they also run courses and lectures, as well as publishing useful leaflets and magazines (see p.306 for details). Their staff are often experts in Latin America. Specialist **travel agencies** (see p.300) and **national tourist boards** should also be able to advise you, particularly on the practical aspects of your trip. Reading novels by some of Latin America's greatest writers, or non-fiction titles exploring the history and politics of the region, will also inspire you before you set off (see pp.86–89).

Guidebooks

A decent **guidebook** is an essential tool in planning your trip. Not only is it a source of all kinds of practical information – from how to buy a plane ticket to how to ask for a sandwich in Portuguese – but it will also give you a reasonable grasp of a country's or region's culture and history. Bear in mind, though, that it's impossible for guidebooks to be one hundred percent accurate – prices change constantly, restaurants open and hotels shut down every week. The other disadvantage of slavishly following a guidebook, especially a popular one, is that you'll constantly bump into other readers following the exact same route as you.

Choosing a guidebook

When it comes to choosing a guidebook, don't leave it till the last minute – good guides are full of useful pre-trip advice. Go to a large bookshop and browse through all the relevant titles; compare the way different guidebooks write up a particular destination, and see what sort of hotels and restaurants they list to work out how relevant they're likely to be to your trip.

Compendium volumes cover several countries in one area – ie Central America, South America, the Amazon, the Andes – and are particularly useful. Budget travellers are also widely catered for: both

▲ A young Rough Guide reader, Peru

www.roughguides.com

Rough Guides (generally mainstream) and Lonely Planet produce guidebooks focusing on **budget travel** and the entire Let's Go series, which is written and produced by Harvard University students, is dedicated to detailing cheap hotels and places to eat. The oldest guide-book to the region, Footprints' *South American Handbook*, is also its longest (almost 2000 pages) and aimed at middle-income tourists as are Bradt publications.

If you've planned your trip round a particularly theme or activity – whether scuba diving, bird-spotting or trekking – you might want to also take a **specialist guidebook**; the best of these are detailed in Chapter 1 under the relevant theme or itinerary.

Maps

Although your guidebook should have **maps** of cities and particular regions, these will inevitably be fairly basic, given the constraints of book format. Although it's not strictly necessary (unless you're travelling under your own steam), it's worth thinking about taking a proper map with you. This will give you a much better overview of where you're going, with enhanced road details and contour markings, so you'll get a much clearer picture of the land through which you're travelling. For a list of good map shops, see pp.305–306.

The best travel maps of Latin America are published by Canadian cartographers **International Travel Maps and Books** (Ⓦwww.itmb .com), who are specialists in the region. Their maps are renowned for their accuracy, for being regularly updated, and for their wealth of detail (including symbols for caves, lighthouses and even oil pipelines). ITMP have the largest-scale maps for most countries in Latin America, including less-visited destinations like French Guiana and Uruguay, as well as maps of particular regions, such as the Amazon Basin, Tierra del Fuego, the Galápagos Islands and Cusco/Machu Picchu. Additionally, **Rough Guides**, in partnership with the **World Mapping Project**, produces its own set of country and regional maps. The maps are highly detailed and printed on waterproof and virtually indestructible paper. There are currently Rough Guide maps to eight countries and regions in Latin America – Argentina, Baja California, Chile, Costa Rica and Panama, Guatemala and Belize, Mexico, Peru and the Yucatán Peninsula. Maps produced by **Borch** (Ⓦwww.borch.com) – which are laminated for extra durability – and **GeoCenter** (Ⓦwww.geocenter.de) are also good.

If you're planning on trekking, most Latin American capital cities have an Instituto Geográfico Nacional or Militar that sells detailed topographical maps of the country.

Background reading

While your guidebook is a good starting point for learning about Latin America, to really flesh out your knowledge of the region's history, geography, politics, society and people, you'll need to consult other sources.

Magazines

A wide range of **travel magazines**, from the very chic (*Condé Nast Traveller*) to the very adventurous (*Outside*) have articles on Latin America on a regular basis. Most feature general information on travelling as well as reviews of the latest equipment and books, plus current travel news. Published in the UK (but available worldwide on subscription), *Wanderlust* (Ⓦwww.wanderlust.co.uk) and *Traveller* (Ⓦwww.wexas.com /travel/traveller) feature off-the-beaten-track destinations with great photographs and well-written articles. Comprehensive sections in both list websites, road-test new equipment and review the latest travelogues and guidebooks. *Geographical* (Ⓦwww.geographical.co.uk), the magazine of the Royal Geographical Society, has special features on exploration and ecological/environmental issues. In North America, the best magazines on adventurous, independent travel are *Outside* (Ⓦoutside.away .com), *Get Lost* (Ⓦwww.getlostmagazine.com) and *National Geographic* (Ⓦwww.nationalgeographic.com) which has several spin-offs – *National Geographic Traveller* and *National Geographic Adventure*. In Australia, *Backpacker Essentials* (Ⓦwww.backpackeressentials.com.au), the magazine of the Australian Youth Hostel Association, is packed with useful travel tips plus features written by backpackers; *TNT* (Ⓦwww .tntmagazine.com.au) runs articles on budget travel and is a good source of practical information on cheap flights and insurance policies.

There are a number of magazines devoted to Latin American society and politics, which are available to read in specialist libraries (see p.306) and on subscription. The best of these are printed in the US: the bimonthly *Americas* (Ⓦwww.oas.org/americas) is published by the Organization of American States and has clearly written features on history, film and food; *Report on the Americas* (Ⓦwww.nacla .org), published by the left-wing North American Congress on Latin America, is more highbrow, though still highly readable. The *Latin American Weekly Report* (available on subscription – and online – from Latin American Newsletters; Ⓦwww.latinnews.com) offers a useful overview of political, economic and financial happenings in the region.

Online magazines and blogs

There are now hundreds of online travel magazines or (**webzines**) – some require a paid subscription but many have travel articles that can be browsed for free. Among the best for independent travellers are *Travel Mag* (Ⓦwww.travelmag.co.uk) and *High on Adventure* (Ⓦwww.highonadventure.com).

There are a couple of good online magazines which focus on travelling in Latin America: *Latin Travel* (Ⓦwww.latintravel.com) which has news stories, expert advice, destination guides and travel features and *Aventura* (Ⓦwww.aventura-mag.com) which specializes in adventure sports travel in Latin America.

For links to hundreds of magazines published in Latin America – on ecology, history, sport, fashion and pretty much everything else – check Ⓦwww.zonalatina.com and Ⓦwww1.lanic.utexas.edu. Both have links to online versions of the magazines which are conveniently listed country by country.

An additional source of useful word-of-mouth information on travel in Latin America are the numerous **travel blogs** posted by people en route – simply typing latin america + blogs into a search engine will bring up thousands of entries on all manner of subjects. Travelblog.org and travelpod.com are two of the biggest blogging websites specializing in travel while National Geographic's blog, "Intelligent Travel" (blogs.nationalgeographic.com/blogs) is award-winning. For further information on the vast cyberworld of blogging, see the *Rough Guide to Blogging*.

Books

There are dozens of good **books** on all aspects of Latin America which will whet your appetite for the countries you're going to visit – if you don't get time to read them before you go you might want to take some of them with you. The *Latin America Review of Books* (Ⓦwww.latamrob.com) is a good source of all the latest Latin America literature with detailed reviews and author interviews. Recommended bookshops with comprehensive travel sections are listed in the Directory (see p.305). Country-specific travel writing, novels and non-fiction books are listed in Where to Go under each relevant country. Detailed below is a comprehensive list of more general books on the whole or parts of the region.

Politics, history and culture

- **Leslie Bethell:** *A Cultural History of Latin America: Literature, Music and the Visual Arts in the 19th and 20th centuries* (Cambridge University Press). Superb and scholarly work of reference with varied types of art forms placed in historical context.
- **John Charles Casteen:** *Born in Blood and Fire: A Concise History of Latin America* (W.W. Norton). Both academic and readable, Casteen uses the lives of prominent historic figures in Latin

America – Simón Bolívar, Lazaro Cardenas, Mayan leader Canek among others – to illustrate how and why Latin America has been shaped into the continent it is today.

- **Michael D. Coe:** *The Maya* (Thames and Hudson). Celebrated general introduction from a renowned Maya expert to one of Latin America's most sophisticated indigenous cultures.

- **Charles Darwin:** *Voyage of the Beagle* (Vintage Classics). The journal of young naturalist Charles Darwin recording his five-year trip around the southern end of South America (1831–36), a journey which inspired his evolutionary theories, with an obvious – though not exclusive – focus on flora and fauna.

- **Wade Davis:** *One River* (Simon and Schuster). Fascinating study of the Amazon's vital environment by US ethno-botanist who specializes in psychoactive plants. Davis weaves his own extensive knowledge with stories of trips made in the 1930s to the Amazon by his great hero, Richard Evans Schultz.

- **Alan Gilbert:** *Latin America* (Monthly Review Press). A highly regarded academic treatise set within a historical context, Gilbert attempts to analyse the development of Latin America since the era of the conquistadors.

- **Eduardo Galeano:** *Open Veins of Latin America: Five Centuries of the Pillage of a Continent* (Serpents Tail). Written some 25 years ago by Uruguayan journalist Galeano, this groundbreaking treatise lays the blame for Latin America's ills squarely on its sixteenth-century European colonizers and, more recently, on the creeping globalization initiated by the US.

- **Duncan Green:** *Faces of Latin America* (Monthly Review Press). Comprehensive and lively introduction to Latin American politics, economics and society, illustrated with deftly chosen accounts drawn from personal experiences.

- **In Focus Guides** (Latin American Bureau). Published by the Latin American Bureau in London, this excellent series of individual country profiles covers more than half of the countries in Latin America, each consisting of a collection of short and clearly written essays organized by theme – history, politics, environment and society.

- **Elisaberth Lambert Ortiz:** *Flavours of Latin America* (Latin American Bureau). Recipes from all over the region as well as poems and prose extracts on a foodie theme.

- **Javier Santioso:** *Latin America's Political Economy of the Possible* (MIT Press). Well-argued and fascinating thesis which charts the rise of pragmatic economic planning in Latin America in the place of past utopian schemes.

87

- **Sue Steward:** *Salsa: Musical Heartbeat of Latin America* (Thames and Hudson). Attractively presented and illustrated history of the ubiquitous history of Latin American dance music style and its offshoots – rumba, mambo, cumbia and merengue.
- **Chris Taylor:** *The Beautiful Game* (Weidenfeld and Nicolson). Fascinating and thoroughly researched history of Latin American football along with an examination of the vital role football plays in the region's culture, politics and society.

Latin American literature

Latin American literature is known principally for its evolution of a literary style which has influenced writers worldwide: **magic realism**. A seamless blend of fact and fantasy, magic realism often takes as its themes the absurdity of murderous dictatorships, brutal regimes and eccentric family life. Latin American writers also have a particularly strong political commitment – both Mario Vargas Llosa (see below) and Chilean poet Pablo Neruda ran for the presidencies of their respective countries. Detailed below are some of the most celebrated Latin American novelists.

- The literature of Nobel Prize-winner **Gabriel García Márquez** (1928–) is one of Colombia's most famous exports. *One Hundred Years of Solitude* is the seminal work of magic realism, telling the story of the pioneering Buendía family and the history of their strange little town, Macondo, in the South American outback. A romantic and humorous love story, *Love in the Time of Cholera* is set on the steamy Caribbean coast. Written much later, *The General in his Labyrinth* is the spare and wonderfully poetic story of the tragic dying days of Simón Bolívar, El Libertador.
- Peru's most famous author and former presidential candidate, **Mario Vargas Llosa** (1936–) is a ubiquitous figure in Peruvian society. *Aunt Julia and the Scriptwriter* is a partly autobiographical and very amusing account of a young radio soap writer's life in which fact and fiction become marvellously confused. Set in the Brazilian backlands in 1897, *The War of the End of the World* is a fictionalized account of the charismatic leader Antonio Conselheiro, his short-lived utopian commune at Canudos, and the brutal suppression of his followers, which left thousands dead.
- Niece of assassinated Chilean president Salvador Allende, **Isabel Allende** (1942–) is the author of several of the most recent popular examples of Latin American magic realism. *House of the Spirits* is a fantastical saga of the wealthy Trueba family which

follows the lives of matriarch Clara and her eccentric, unusual children and grandchildren. Another well-loved book, *Of Love and Shadows* is set against the background of a brutal military dictatorship whose unexplained disappearances mirror those in Chile under Pinochet.

- **Jorge Amado** (1912–2001) was a lavish chronicler of life and culture in the colourful tropical state of Bahia, northeast Brazil. In *Dona Flor and her Two Husbands*, Dona Flor marries a sensible pharmacist after her roguish husband drops dead at Carnaval, only to find her previous husband returning as a ghost. When *Gabriela, Clove and Cinnamon* was made into a TV film in Brazil, the entire country, including the government, downed tools to tune in. Here, Amado chronicles the growing prosperity of the Bahian town of Ilheus in the 1920s due to the creation of vast cocoa plantations, as seen through the eyes of a young mulatto girl, Gabriela.

- **Jorge Luis Borges**'s (1899–1986) *Labyrinths*, a collection of short stories and essays, is a compact introduction to the inventive and philosophical world of Argentina's – and perhaps Latin America's – most esteemed writer. With his original style, comprising an erudite mixture of wild fantasy and intellectual rigour, Borges has often been called the father of magic realism.

- The work of Guatemalan **Miguel Angel Asturias** (1899–1974) interweaves the past, present and future and is often seen as a precursor of magic realism. Asturias's main theme was the deep-rooted and continuing value of indigenous Latin American traditions. In *Men of Maize* he tells the story of a backlash by the Maya against the intended cultivation of maize – a crop woven into their culture and folklore – for profit by outsiders. *The President* chronicles the machinations of a ruthless dictator who plans to rid himself of a political opponent in an unnamed country generally considered to be Guatemala.

Background viewing: Latin America on film

Three countries have long dominated **Latin American cinema**: Argentina, Brazil and Mexico. Brazil's *cinema novo* was one of the world's most vibrant film movements in the 1960s. After quieter years – which coincided, not surprisingly, with military dictatorships in both Argentina and Brazil – all three countries are strongly established once more as making exciting modern films which have attracted critical acclaim and are being shown in mainstream cinemas.

Two annual Latin American **film festivals** are held in London every November – the Latin America Film Festival (@www.latin americanfilmfestival.com) and Discovering Latin America (@www .discoveringlatinamerica.com) while there are numerous festivals in the US, including ones in Washington (@www.oas.org); Austin, Texas (@www.cinelasamericas.org); Chicago (@www.latinoculturalcenter .org) among others. Australia holds its Latin American film festival in Sydney (@www.sydneylatinofilmfestival.org). If you become seriously interested in Latin American films, *Mediating Two Worlds: Cinematic Encounters in the Americas*, *The Cinema of Latin America* (British Film Institute) and *South American Cinema: A Critical Filmography* (Routledge) are all recommended anthologies.

Latin American films

The following films are some of the most memorable movies made in Latin America in either Spanish or Portuguese.

● *Black Orpheus/Orfeu Negro* (1958). Set amidst the Rio Carnaval, this is a vivid reworking of the ancient Greek legend of Orpheus and Eurydice, a fatalistic love story with a tragic ending. The city's dramatic setting is beautifully though rather sentimentally filmed – Rio's *favelas* (slums) look almost pretty – and is accompanied by a bestselling soundtrack by Antonio (Tom) Jobim and Luís Bonfá which ushered in a new style of Brazilian music: bossa nova.

● *City of God* (2002). An extremely stylish – and fictional – portrayal of life in the slums or *favelas* of Rio de Janeiro, *City of God* nevertheless pulls no punches. The film spans two decades, and follows the lives of a gang of children, two in particular, who grow up in the infamous City of God and deal with their hardships in very different ways. Absolutely gripping and horrifying by turns.

● *Maria Full of Grace* (2004). Grimly depressing and stark fictional account of the lives – and deaths – of Colombian drug mules who carry cocaine to the US. Catalina Sandino Moreno deservedly won an Oscar for her spirited performance in this joint American and Colombian venture.

● *The Milk of Sorrow* (2009). An award-winning epic tragedy, set both in the shantytowns of Lima and a wealthy city household, weaves together indigenous Peruvian culture with the legacy of Peru's brutal and bloody past. Magaly Solier gives a heartbreaking performance of a young woman condemned to a life of struggle and sorrow because of her mother's violent rape and staunch Indian fatalism.

- *The Motorcycle Diaries* (2004). Adapted from Che Guevara's diaries which describe a trip he made through South America in 1951, this is a beautifully shot though occasionally sentimental film. Current Mexican heart-throb Gael García Bernal pulls off a fine performance as the fledgling revolutionary though the film's real star is South America itself, which looks dazzling.

- *Nine Queens* (2000). An ingenious con-man comedy set in Buenos Aires over the course of 24 hours, *Nine Queens* also reflects the cynicism and suspicion of Argentines towards their thoroughly corrupt institutions. A remarkably prescient film, made shortly before the country's economic meltdown in 2001.

- *Pixote* (1981). The story of a homeless urchin in São Paulo, *Pixote* is a fictionalized account of the appalling lives of Brazil's numerous street children, and won many awards for its affecting and graphic depiction of a world which, lamentably, still very much exists.

- *Secuestro Express* (2006). Venezuela's highest grossing film is the gritty tale of the kidnap of a wealthy young couple in Caracas. Both funny and stylish, it presses home the enduring social inequality of most Latin American cities.

- *Tony Manero* (2008). Dark comedy set in Santiago during the height of Pinochet's reign of terror. Raul is a serial killer obsessed by John Travolta's character in *Saturday Night Fever* and alternates murderous acts with nights of cheesy disco dancing at the local cantina. Strange, sleazy and gripping.

Films set in Latin America

Predictably many films set in Latin America are made in the US and tend to focus on cowboys, lost-in-the-jungle action movies or civil war. The following include some more critically acclaimed offerings, as well as a couple of documentaries.

- *Aguirre, Wrath of God* (1972). Werner Herzog's crazed masterpiece tells the story of a band of Spanish conquistadors who go up the Amazon in search of El Dorado, the fabled city of gold. Led by the megalomaniac Aguirre, self-styled "Wrath of God", the trip rapidly descends into chaos and death as the group travel from the high Andes into primeval forest.

- *Missing* (1981). Based on true events during the Chilean coup of 1973, *Missing* tells the story of an American journalist who "disappears" and of his family's subsequent search for him, taking a dark look at the human tragedy of murderous dictatorships like Pinochet's, and evocatively portraying a society coming apart at the seams.

www.roughguides.com

- *Salvador* (1986). Arguably Oliver Stone's best film, *Salvador* features James Woods as washed-up American journalist Richard Boyle, who travelled to El Salvador in 1980 in search of a story and instead found himself in the middle of a civil war. Co-written by Boyle himself, the film has brilliant action sequences underpinned by a forceful and sometimes moving polemic.

- *Carla's Song* (1996). Left-wing film-maker Ken Loach's examination of the civil war in Nicaragua centres around the love affair of a Glaswegian bus driver (played by Robert Carlyle) and a Nicaraguan refugee – the film's witty depiction of the Nicaraguan's humour and playful language had the audience at its Managuan premiere in fits of laughter.

- *The Battle of Chile* (1973). Patricio Guzman's three-part documentary on Allende and the Chilean coup d'état is widely feted as among the best documentaries ever made. The three films cover events in chronological order, mixing trenchant political analysis with revealing interviews with some of those who took part in the events described.

- *Señorita Extravida/Missing Young Woman* (2001). Moving and lyrical documentary made by Chicano film-maker Lourdes Portillo about the more than two hundred young women who have been kidnapped, raped and murdered in the border town of Cuidad Juárez, Mexico. Portillo has also made films about the Day of the Dead and the women who march weekly in Buenos Aires for their "disappeared" children.

- *Los Olvidados/The Forgotten* (1952). One of surrealist film-maker Luis Buñuel's best films and his own personal favourite. *Los Olvidados* is a stylish though gritty narrative about the miserable lives of two street urchins living in Mexico City and is in many ways a forerunner to *City of God* (see p.90).

- *Qué viva México!* (1931/1979). Never finished in his lifetime but finally pieced together by the original cameraman, this is Russian director Sergei Eistenstein's poetic meditation on the potency of Mexican culture. The film consists of a series of six non-fictional and fictional episodes which link Maya civilization with the Spanish conquest and the Mexican Revolution.

What to take

The short answer to the all-important question "**what shall I take?**" is as little as possible. Once you realize just how often and how far you're going to have to lug your gear around, you'll understand why it's a very good idea to reduce your packing to the bare minimum. There's nothing like an hour wandering with all your stuff around a hot and unfamiliar town looking for a hotel to make you curse your backpack and everything in it. Remember too that public transport in most Latin American cities and towns consists of a motley collection of beaten-up tin buses, vans and trucks. These are invariably crammed to the gills, and in many cases there literally may not be room for you and your enormous backpack. In addition, the larger your pack, the more likely you are to be marked out as a gringo no matter how well you know the country or how good your Spanish or Portuguese.

Having said that, there is a certain amount of **travel kit** that you will need to take, unless you want the hassle of having to constantly buy stuff as you go along. Travelling light is smart; travelling with too little is not.

Backpacks

Your **backpack** is the single most important piece of kit that you'll take – if you've got any money to spend on equipment, this is the time to splash out. Backpacks vary in price from £50–180/US$75–250, and generally you get what you pay for. Berghaus (⊛www.berghaus .com), Karrimor (⊛www.karrimor.com) and The North Face (⊛www .thenorthface.com) are all recommended makes of backpack. Shop around various specialist travel, camping or adventure-sport shops – the best shops have knowledgeable staff who have travelled widely themselves (see p.307 for listings of recommended retailers).

Backpack sizes are measured in litres (since their actual weight depends on what you put in them). A medium-sized, **50-litre pack** is the most popular size, and you'd be mad to carry anything bigger than 65 litres, even if you're taking camping gear. If you're a really ruthless packer, you might manage with 25–30 litres, the size of a largish daypack. In terms of weight experts recommend that the total contents of your pack don't exceed one-fifth to a quarter of your body weight. In practical terms, this means that most men shouldn't try to carry more than 18–22 kilos, whilst women ought to stick to 13–17 kilos.

The most important element of a backpack is its **harness**. The best harnesses are fully adjustable and have padded shoulder straps, a wide hip belt (essential for transferring weight from your back) and compression straps on the side of the pack which push its contents tightly into your back. If your backpack doesn't come with a built-in harness cover (backpacks usually don't; travel packs usually do – see below), you should consider buying one – this is very useful for airplane holds and other luggage racks because it avoids straps being torn and damaged by baggage handlers, airlines sometimes insist that backpack straps are tidied away with a harness cover or outer sack.

The way the pack is divided into **compartments** is also important. Outer pockets are useful for quick access to essential items, though these are hard to secure properly. Too many outer pockets will make your backpack bulky – the narrower your pack, the easier it will be to manoeuvre while wearing it, and to store it in tight spaces when you're not.

It's essential to try on a backpack before you buy it to check that it fits properly and feels comfortable. First, though, find a knowledgeable shop assistant who will measure your back length (from the top of your hip bone to the seventh vertebra) – this is vital in determining the right size of pack. Backpacks should never be tried on empty – get a shop assistant to fill it with a suitable weight – and you should then walk around the shop to ensure that the pack is stable. A properly fitting pack has a good harness (see above) with shoulder straps and a **hip belt** which fits snugly and doesn't dig. Other features to look for are a ventilated or **mesh back system** which will help reduce sweating, long-lasting and tightly woven fabrics, and **triple-sewn seams** (stress points should have five lines of stitching). Most manufacturers make backpacks specially designed for **women**; these have straps which are closer together to fit narrower shoulders, making them significantly more comfortable.

Toploader and travel packs

There are two basic types of backpack: choosing the right one depends on what kind of trip you're planning. A **toploader** or traditional backpack opens principally at the top, though most brands also have side pockets and a bottom compartment. The long, narrow shape of toploaders gives them an effective **weight distribution** and makes them particularly comfortable to carry – useful if you're planning on doing any serious trekking, mountain-climbing, or even if you just expect to have to lug your pack around a lot.

The newer type of backpacks, known as **travel packs**, are wider than traditional toploaders, with horseshoe-shaped zips, meaning that almost all the pack can be easily accessed (although this does mean that it's less secure), whilst clothes can be packed flat as in a traditional suitcase. Most travel packs also come with a zip-on daypack (see below) and built-in harness covers. If you're not planning to carry your pack around a great deal, a decent travel pack will suffice.

Weatherproofing

Surprisingly, most backpacks aren't entirely rainproof. You can remedy this by waterproofing your backpacks with a can of **waterproofing spray**; these can be bought at most camping and outdoor shops. Use the spray outside, however, and apply it well before you leave – it smells horrible at first and gives off toxic fumes (though these wear off after the first few days). Alternatively, you could buy an elastic backpack **raincover** or a waterproof backpack liner. If you're on a really tight budget you can either line your pack with a binliner or simply pack your stuff in a series of plastic bags before putting it in your pack.

Security

Keeping your backpack and its contents **safe** is a major concern. Essentially, it's impossible to completely secure a pack against a determined thief. That said, most thieves are opportunists, and any attempt to make their job harder and slower will probably encourage them to look elsewhere.

One traditional way of stopping thieves slashing your pack open is to line it with **chickenwire**, which is cheap and fairly tough and can be bought at most hardware shops. It's still a good deterrent – try to get wire with the smallest holes. There are several other ways of making your pack more secure. You can now buy something called **PacSafe**, which works on the chickenwire principle – it's a sheet of very strong metal mesh which fits over the outside of a backpack; it also comes with a padlock so that you can attach your pack to a luggage ruck or other fixed object. Although PacSafe is heavy and not totally foolproof (it can be cut with wirecutters), it does at the very least make getting into your backpack a job for professional rather than amateur thieves.

A further option is a **cable lock**: a long length of thick wire which can be used to lock your pack to fixed objects. Some cable locks come

THE BIG ADVENTURE

with sturdy combination locks and a built-in alarm which goes off if someone touches or tries to move your pack – particularly useful if you're travelling alone and have no one to help keep an eye on your stuff. Finally, you could also take small padlocks to slot through backpack zips and secure openings, but their size and limited strength make it relatively easy to snap them open.

A cheap option for making your backpack slightly more secure and protecting it at the very least from the elements is to carry it in a **large grain sack**, available from local markets in Latin America. This "disguise" may not fool many locals for long but it just might stop your backpack being identified immediately as such and the tough covering will keep it free from dust, rain and mud.

Daypacks and shoulder bags

Once you've arrived at your destination, found a hotel and dumped your backpack, you'll still need a **daypack** to carry essential items – guidebook, water, camera, extra clothing – in. Daypacks are essentially just smaller versions of a backpack (between 15 and 30 litres). Most travel packs now come with matching daypacks zipped onto the front. If you're buying one of these, make sure you unzip the daypack and examine it properly before you buy it – some are sturdier than others. Packs made by Patagonia (ⓦwww.patagonia.com), Osprey (ⓦwww.ospreypacks .com) and Vaude (ⓦwww.vaude.co.uk) are all recommended; the makers of rucksacks mentioned (see above) also make daypacks.

If you're buying a daypack separately it's as important to choose it as carefully as a backpack. You're likely to use your daypack on a daily basis, and it needs to be **tough**, with strong padded straps and sturdy zips.

Money belts

Most travellers nowadays keep their documents and cash in a **slim** and **discreet** money belt with two zipped compartments (one the size of a passport, the other big enough for credit cards), which is tucked away underneath your clothing. The most popular type of money belt goes round your **waist**; other types can be found which hang round your neck; which are strapped under your arm or round your calf; or which hang from your regular belt inside your trousers. Another innovation is an apparently ordinary buckled belt with a narrow, zipped pocket inside where you can hide folded banknotes (though obviously it's no use for larger items like passports).

Obviously, wearing your belt around your waist makes it more **accessible**, though sweat can be a problem (it's a good idea to keep documents, travellers' cheques and notes wrapped in plastic to avoid them getting soggy). Choose a belt made from cotton to keep as cool as possible – it's amazing how much hotter something light round your waist can make you feel. Additionally, a skin-coloured or beige belt is far more discreet. Bear in mind also that thieves in Latin America are all too aware now that foreigners carry their valuables in hidden money belts, although on the positive side they take too long to remove to be regularly stolen.

If you're travelling alone, something else to consider is a **water-safe** or plastic container to keep money and keys in if you want to go for a swim without leaving them lying on the beach. These are worn round the neck and range from fairly bulky containers to slim, wallet-shaped affairs with watertight zip locks. Most specialist travel equipment outlets sell some form of water-safe.

Documents

It's a good idea to take **photocopies** of important documents, such as the personal pages of your passport, with you. Keep these copies separate from the originals; having a copy of the information-bearing pages in your passport hugely speeds up the process of getting it replaced if it's stolen. Alternatively, as a further precaution you could email a **scan** of them to your email address to download in case of emergency. Other useful documents to take with you include your **driving licence** and an **international student card**, which entitles you to various discounts. **Passport photos** are handy for visa extensions or any permits or passes that you might need.

Clothes

Before **packing**, lay out all the clothes you think you'll need, and then halve the amount – remember that you can buy much of what you'll need (and generally more cheaply) once in Latin America. Trainers/sneakers, t-shirts and trousers are sold everywhere, while in Andean countries like Ecuador, Peru and Bolivia you can buy very cheap and wonderfully warm alpaca sweaters, gloves and socks. It's also worth leaving your favourite clothes at home: if they're not lost or stolen, they'll likely be reduced to shreds by the **wear and tear** of constant travelling. Instead, pick up bargain bits and pieces at cheap chain stores, **charity shops** or jumble sales, which can be dumped when they've worn out or you no longer need them.

Remember when you're packing to allow for Latin America's **extremes of temperature**, from the high Andes to sizzling Caribbean beaches. Unless you're only going to one region in one country you'll probably need clothes for both hot and cold weather, and it's always worth erring on the side of caution – even in the warmest climates, you might find yourself on overnight buses with freezing air conditioning. If you're heading into the Andean highlands or Patagonia in winter you'll need to have adequate clothing to deal with temperatures that can fall well below freezing. Don't assume that because these places suffer freezing temperatures they have indoor heating systems – most parts of Bolivia, for example, don't. Conversely, in a city like Manaus in Amazonian Brazil, where it's too hot to move by 10.30 in the morning, even cotton can seem too warm and clothes need to be light and loose.

For more on Latin American dress codes, see p.115. Useful and essential items of clothing for your trip are listed below:

- **Dress** A cool, loose sundress is an excellent piece of all-round clothing: they're generally light, easy to pack and can function for more formal occasions as well as fun nights out.

- **Fleece** Fleece jackets are an absolute godsend: they weigh nothing and are very cosy, so you won't need to take another jacket or jumper. Although the best are expensive (£50–110/US$75–160), they're worth every penny. High-street stores sell fleeces in all shapes and sizes, though they're not as effective as those made by adventure sports manufacturers (see Directory).

- **Hat** A small, foldable hat is a great idea, both for keeping the sun off your head when it's hot and helping retain body heat when it's cold (when a fleece or woolly hat is invaluable).

- **Shirts and trousers** Avoid taking jeans: they're bulky, heavy, difficult to wash and take forever to dry. Much better to take something like cargo pants, which are lightweight, tough and comfortable, although be careful with combat trousers – the soldier-boy look doesn't always go down well in countries which have suffered brutal military dictatorships or, like Colombia, are still in the throes of civil wars. Specialist manufacturers make practical travelling trousers which are made from breathable fabric, dry out very quickly and zip apart to make a pair of shorts. A pair of loose drawstring trousers, cool in the heat and doubling up as pyjamas (recommended if you're sleeping outside in a hammock) is also a good idea. Shirts should also be loose and lightweight – a loose shirt can be much cooler than a t-shirt. Take one with long sleeves for protection against mosquitoes, in case you get sunburnt or need to cover up.

- **Socks** Take several different thicknesses – lightweight for deterring mosquitoes in the tropics and a thermal pair for the mountains and long, chilly bus rides.

- **Tights** If it gets cold, a pair of tights worn under trousers can add a valuable extra layer of insulation.
- **T-shirts** A long-sleeved t-shirt is a good idea for chilly nights, while a short-sleeved t-shirt will be useful during most days. Bear in mind, if you're a woman, that wearing very tight or low-cut t-shirts will attract ogling men.
- **Waterproof jacket** Unless you can afford an expensive breathable Gore-tex jacket, raincoats are too sweaty to be comfortable in Latin America. If you're planning on doing some serious trekking in the rainy season, however, you will need a decent waterproof jacket.

Footwear

Shoes and **boots** are obviously a vital part of your kit, but don't take more than two pairs because that's all you'll need and they take up lots of room. A pair of sturdy **walking boots** is essential if you're planning on doing some serious trekking, and recommended even if you're not. Modern brands are incredibly lightweight and last forever, and a good pair is a great investment. The best come with special gripping soles, supported sides (to protect your ankles) and waterproof lining so that your feet don't get wet. Specialist shops (see Directory) sell a wide range of walking boots, but you won't find them on sale in many places in Latin America, so buy them before you leave. Many travellers take a pair of trainers or sneakers instead – these are cheaper, do pretty well on the road and are easily replaced.

Your other pair of shoes should be **sandals** – make sure they're hard-wearing and waterproof. Again, they're most easily found in adventure sport shops. Leather sandals are sold everywhere in Latin America – in fact shoes of every kind are a Latin American fetish – and are cheap and well made. Flip-flops in every shape and colour are also available absolutely everywhere (though not if you have big feet –

Packing with style

For my travels around Peru in 1999 I had scrunched a very shiny top and completely impractical mini-skirt into a bag at the bottom of my backpack. For five months, through jungle and desert, Ecuador and Colombia, the clothes hitched a ride, apparently pointlessly. But then came December 31st: I was in Cartagena, and I had tickets to a glamorous salsa party in the city square to ring in the millennium. The shiny outfit may have been a little creased, but, well, it just wouldn't have been the same in grubby green trousers that had been over the Andes and back.

In the streets of Latin America, let alone the bars, you don't see many people clumping around in hiking boots and reversible fleeces. Even fairly poor people tend to dress snappily, and when you wind up in a bar or late-night café and are mixing with the locals – as you will, for this is one of the joys of Latin America – you might start to feel a tad silly in that breathable shirt that style forgot.

Rosalba O'Brien

www.roughguides.com

Latin Americans are normally short with small feet and footwear caters accordingly).

Essentials

Below is an alphabetical list of items (apart from documents and clothes) that you're likely to need.

- **Alarm clock** Take the smallest one you can find and make sure it has a light. Alternatively take a watch (not expensive) with an alarm on it.
- **Batteries** Standard batteries are available everywhere (though they're often expensive), but you may have difficulty finding more obscure camera or watch batteries – take spares with you.
- **Cable lock** More useful than a padlock: with a good cable lock you can attach your backpack to fixed objects; fancier models come sealed into a natty hardwearing case with combination lock and with a 100-decibel alarm. You can hang them from hotel doors and windows – particularly useful if you're a lone woman traveller – so that you'll know if someone is trying to get into your room while you're sleeping.
- **Cigarette lighter** Surprisingly useful even if you don't smoke, and much better than matches (which are sometimes so flimsy that they're virtually useless) for lighting mosquito coils, camp fires and candles during power outages.
- **Contact-lens solution and glasses** Contact-lens solution can be difficult to find outside big cities; take supplies with you. If you wear glasses, take a spare pair and your prescription.
- **Contraceptives** Condoms are available pretty much everywhere, but may not reach the same rigorous standards as those at home. If you're on the Pill, take a supply with you – you may not be able to find your prescription in Latin America.
- **First-aid kit** See p.159 for details.
- **Flashlight (torch)** An important piece of kit, since there are still parts of Latin America without any electricity, while power cuts are also common.
- **Guidebook** See pp.82–84.
- **Liquid soap** Special, all-purpose liquid soap (available in specialist adventure shops) can be used to wash yourself, your hair, your clothes and even fruit and vegetables.
- **Penknife** Take a good penknife with a sharp blade, bottle opener and corkscrew (and remember not to fly with it in your hand luggage).

- **Sarong** A sarong is extremely versatile and can be used as an emergency towel, a bedcover, a scarf, a skirt and so on. They're widely available in beach resorts, though you might prefer to bring one with you.

- **Sheet sleeping bag** Useful in hostels where they don't provide sheets and in cheap hotels (if you first spray it with a solution of Permethrin) to ward off fleas, lice and bed bugs. You can easily make one yourself from a folded sheet sewn across the bottom and down the side.

- **Sunglasses** Vital for protecting your eyes from the sun (and also from snow-glare in the mountains). Make sure you get proper UV-resistant lenses – a pair of cheap sunglasses is useless.

- **Sunscreen** Sunscreen is available in big cities and tourist resorts, but the locals don't use it, so it's expensive and sometimes not of the best quality. You'll need at least factor 15 to start with.

- **Toiletries** Keep your washbag supplies to a minimum and transfer things like shampoo and moisturizing cream into smaller travel bottles which you can buy at chemists or in camping shops. Avoid bottles with pop-tops which tend to open in depressurized environments (such as aircraft holds) and will then leak everywhere. The heat and fierce sun mean that one thing you will need loads of is moisturizing lotion; in some parts of Latin America this will cost more than your lunch.

Non-essentials

If you have any space left in your luggage, consider taking several or more of the items listed below. Though not essential they will enhance your trip and/or make travelling more comfortable.

- **Binoculars** Great for bird- and wildlife-spotting. The latest models are tiny and very light; you ought to be able to get a decent pair for £21/US$30.

- **Books** Although there are innumerable book exchanges at backpacker's hostels and cafés across the continent, the quality of books on offer is often pretty dire, so you'll probably want to bring plenty of reading matter of your own.

- **Camera** A good digital camera costs £75–300/US$110–450. These days you should be able to upload your pictures onto a computer in any sizeable town in Latin America and email them home to your friends and family as you travel. You can also save the images in disk format and either mail these home or travel with them. Rewritable discs and USB memory sticks are also widely available in most places. You'll need to carry both the USB cable that links your camera to a computer and your battery charger with you – infuriatingly very few of these are interchangeable with other models.

● For non-digital camera users, standard camera film is still available (though only in specialist camera shops in big cities), but you should take a supply of slide and/or black-and-white film if you use these, since they're not always easy to get hold of in Latin America. It's also worth taking plenty of high-speed film (400 ASA), which is best for naturally dark environments like the rainforest.

● **Camping gear** Obviously, taking camping gear opens up lots of extra possibilities in terms of trekking and saving on hotel costs, although it also means you'll have to say goodbye to travelling light and carry a much larger pack.

● **Compass** Important if you're planning on trekking, and useful anywhere to get your bearings. A more advanced option is a portable GPS (global positioning system) which works with satellites and gives clear instructions on which route to take to reach your required destination.

● **Earplugs** Latin Americans love noise and scarcely seem to notice it, but you might not: a decent pair of earplugs is a godsend if you find yourself in a hotel next to an all-night bar or sitting beside the sound-system on a bus.

● **Games** A pack of cards or a travel chess or backgammon set can help while away the hours waiting for buses, on buses or sitting indoors during rainy-season days.

● **iPod** Great for lazy days in a hammock and long boring bus journeys.

● **Map** A decent map can add hugely to your appreciation of the country you're travelling through, both as a guide during long journeys and as an aid in planning itineraries.

● **Mosquito net** Even if your hotel does have mosquito nets, they may well have holes in them, which makes them pretty useless. Take your own. Some come impregnated with repellent; if not, you can treat it yourself with Permethrin.

● **Neck cushion** An inflatable neck cushion is great for long bus and plane journeys.

● **Needle and thread** Useful for mending clothes and sewing buttons back on.

● **Notebook** Most people keep some kind of diary of their trip – very valuable years after the event when you've forgotten the small details of life on the road that once seemed so crucial.

- **Padlock** Handy for hostel lockers and for locking the door of your room in cheap hotels.
- **Photos and postcards** Photos of your family and home town are a great way of breaking the ice with curious locals. Postcards from your home country make good presents – children, in particular, love them.
- **Plug** A universal plug is useful, since most sinks and baths in cheaper hotels have lost their plugs.
- **Plug adaptor** Sockets in Latin America are the same as those in North America or Europe (ie they take two flat or round prongs); if you're from anywhere else you'll need an adaptor, available from camping shops or at the airport.
- **Radio** Lets you tune into local radio stations and sounds; with a short wave radio you can get the BBC World Service/Voice of America and keep up with news back home.
- **String** Often useful for running repairs, and can also serve as an emergency washing line.
- **Toilet paper** Although toilet paper is sold everywhere in Latin America, it's often not supplied in toilets, so carry your own roll.
- **Towel** If you'd like something more absorbent than a sarong to dry yourself, don't take an ordinary bath towel – they rot easily, smell horrible and take up far too much room. Instead take a special travel towel which looks more like a duster, folds away to almost nothing, is made from incredibly absorbent fabric and can be packed when damp.
- **Water bottle** Take a sturdy water bottle (with a carrying strap) if you're planning on camping, trekking or exploring the wilderness.
- **Water sterilizing kit** A valuable money-saving device – see p.168 for details.

Your first night

E ven for seasoned travellers, arriving in Latin America after a long flight is a daunting prospect. The noisy and chaotic scene that is likely to greet you is hardly an ideal situation when you're feeling exhausted and vulnerable, and it's often difficult to retain a positive attitude and a sense of humour. With just a small amount of **organization**, however, you can make sure your introduction to Latin America is as painless as possible.

Booking hotels in advance

Chances are that you'll be flying into one of Latin America's capital cities, some of which – such as Mexico City and São Paulo – are vast. It will take you days to orient yourself, and half an hour after flying in is not the time to start. Booking a **hotel** in advance is quite possibly the best five minutes you'll spend on planning your trip, and will stop you fretting all the way through the flight (it might even make your mother fret less, too). Your guidebook should list the phone number and email details of a wide range of hotels, as should the relevant tourist board and a host of internet sites (see Directory for details). When choosing a hotel, consider the following:

- **Choose your location carefully**. Decide on the part of the city you want to stay in, as well as a particular hotel. Most cities have two distinct hotel areas – expensive and budget. While expensive hotels are often located in leafy suburbs adjacent to the city centre, budget hotels and hostels are frequently right in the heart of the city or, alternatively, near bus stations and/or markets. It's also best to pick a reasonably central hotel close to several others so that you can swap easily should you want to.

▲ Searching for accommodation

- **Time to splash out.** This is the time to spend more than your allotted daily budget. After a lengthy flight you'll be in need of a comfortable bed and a hot shower, two facilities missing from the very cheapest hostels. Also, a hotel that serves breakfast and has a bar and restaurant will save you wandering the streets of a strange city unnecessarily.

- **Stay a second night.** Consider booking not just your first but also your second night's accommodation. Otherwise, if you arrive late in the day, you'll have to get up early (checkout time is usually noon) and spend your first morning looking for another hotel – sounds fine now, but you might not want to do it with jet lag or altitude sickness.

To make life easy, choose a hotel with a **website** so that you get some idea of what's on offer and are able to book online. Alternatively, some travel agents (see p.299) have a hotel-booking service and can book hotels for you – if you're booking your flights through them, they might do this for free, although the hotels on their lists will probably be three-star or better and cost at least £40/$65 a night. You can also book a bed through various international youth hostelling associations (see Directory).

www.roughguides.com

Arrival

8

Once you've landed and emerged, blinking, from the plane follow the signs – and everyone else – through immigration, baggage reclaim, customs and the arrivals hall and then out onto Latin American soil. This is where **culture shock** kicks in: you'll probably be jet-lagged, and as a tourist you'll be prey to every hustler in the building. Don't let anyone bully you into something you don't want to do or distract you – instead, try to keep focused on getting out of the airport, and at least look as though you know what you're doing.

Immigration

You shouldn't have any problems at immigration, assuming you've filled in all the **forms** correctly (these will usually have been given to you on the plane) and have all the relevant documents to hand, including your passport, return ticket and proof of funds. Your **entry stamp** (see p.47 for further details) will have a number of days written on it by the official dealing with you – make sure you get the days you need for your stay; if you don't, point this out very politely and ask for the right amount. Most immigration officials speak a little English, but will always appreciate the effort if you speak even just a few words of Spanish or Portuguese. Remember there's no absolute guarantee that you'll be allowed into your chosen country, even if you have a visa. The decision to let you enter rests with whichever immigration official deals with you upon your arrival. Although it's pretty much unheard of for anyone to be refused entry without a very good reason, it doesn't hurt to be on your best behaviour.

Baggage reclaim

Baggage reclaim is usually where the chaos begins – this may be the moment to start getting used to Latin American spontaneity and disorder. Keep your eyes peeled for your backpack, and once it arrives don't ever leave it **unattended** until you reach the safety of your hotel room. Beware of any distractions, particularly strangers rushing up to you and shouting in your face – this is a well-known ruse to distract you while a thief makes off with your stuff.

Customs

Unless you're travelling with specialized equipment, you won't need to **declare** anything at customs – obviously, it's not recommended that you bring in weapons, large amounts of alcohol and recreational drugs (unless you relish the prospect of being locked up in squalor for a very long time). In all likelihood you'll be allowed to walk straight through customs past a couple of bored officials; if you've been given a customs declaration to fill in on the plane, this is where you hand it in, having presumably ticked no to every question – are you bringing in contaminated liquids? Explosives? Infected meat? No, no and no.

Arrivals hall

This is where your journey finally begins. Once you've emerged into the arrivals hall – usually not as grand as it sounds – you're now officially on Latin American soil and what you do next is entirely up to you. You might have first to wade through an excited throng waiting for long-lost relatives to emerge, followed by an unholy scrum of airport hustlers pressing in on all sides. Ignore them, and head for a relatively quiet space to orientate yourself and work out where what you need is situated. This is likely to be the ATM and the taxi rank. Don't spend more time in the arrivals hall than you need to, however – like any transport hub anywhere in the world, airports are a favourite hangout for all kinds of unsavoury characters who prey on the vulnerability of new arrivals.

Airports always have somewhere to change money – these days this is likely to be an ATM. In the unlikelihood that there isn't one (or it's not working - much more likely) you may be able to **change money** at a *casa de cambio*. Bear in mind, though, that the exchange rate offered at airports is usually terrible and these places are a last resort. If there's no way of getting local currency at all, all is not lost - there can't be an airport taxi driver in Latin America who doesn't accept dollars, and all you really need to pay for at this stage is a ride to your hotel. There's also likely to be some kind of **tourist information booth** at the airport. Though these are often fairly useless, staff do usually speak some English and can tell you how much you should pay for a taxi ride into the city. They should also be able to recommend a hotel (though these will be mid- or top-range places) if you haven't already got a reservation, and book a room for you. Some might even have a basic city map.

Some travellers arriving in the middle of the night prefer to wait in the airport until daybreak. Note, though, that some airports close after the last arrival; at others, security guards might ask you to move on. It really is much easier to fork out for a taxi to take you to a hotel where you can dump your bags and get a much-needed first night's sleep, but if you do spend the night in the airport, pick a well-lit, secure spot and tie your luggage onto something solid.

Getting into town

Your next challenge is to find a way of getting from the airport to your hotel, whether in a taxi, *colectivo* (a shared taxi) or bus.

www.roughguides.com

The taxista assault course

Just what you need after eighteen hours flying from London – to run an assault course of *taxistas* at San José international airport. It used to be that the taxi drivers would rush the entrance of the terminal, wrest your bag from your hand, and absolutely insist on taking you to the city, whether you had a ride lined up or not. Usually they would charge you the right fare – give or take a couple of dollars. Now the *taxistas* are crowded outside, prevented by airport officials from entering the terminal, so that your first view of Costa Rica might well be a phalanx of slightly hysterical-looking men, all yelling "taxi" of course. It's just like those wildly stereotypical American films where the fresh-faced Yankee hero goes to Latin America and steps from the airport into a cesspit of chaos and corruption. That said, airport taxis are regulated, and pirate cabs can no longer operate freely. So take a deep breath and choose your *taxista*.

By taxi or colectivo

Most Latin American **airport taxi ranks** are at least properly regulated. You'll first have to pay your fare at a ticket booth in the airport (you'll be given a receipt or coupon to hand to your taxi driver) and then have to wait in line at the taxi rank. You can pay in dollars, though prices are fixed and not open to negotiation. Many taxi drivers speak a little English, and are generally friendly and honest, but there are a few things to watch out for. The most common is that your driver, after asking you where you're staying, will tell you that the hotel or area you're going to is dangerous and that he knows somewhere much safer. Always stick to your guns – this is a well-rehearsed ploy to take you to his aunty/mother-in-law/good friend Miguel's hotel, or indeed anywhere where he'll get a slice of your money. Secondly, if you haven't bought a coupon at the airport, always agree the price of your journey first even if the taxi is metered (meters are often doctored) and absolutely refuse to pay any more if your driver tries it on. Thirdly, don't get in any cab if there's someone else riding up front, and never get out of the taxi until you arrive at your destination for whatever reason (in Bogotá, taxi drivers claim that the engine has stopped and that they need your help pushing the car, which then miraculously springs back into life leaving you standing in the middle of the road without your luggage). Be careful, too, that taxi drivers don't drive off with your luggage at the end of your trip when you get out of the vehicle.

As well as private taxis, you may well find **shared taxis** or *colectivos*. These are usually minibuses that, once full, drive round town dropping everyone off at their various destinations. *Colectivos* are much cheaper than private taxis, stringently regulated and more secure – in sum, a much better option. Again you'll purchase a coupon from an official booth in the airport.

Another alternative (but only if you arrive in daylight) is to walk out of the airport to the nearest main thoroughfare and hail a regular taxi;

these will charge you much less than the airport taxi service. A decent guidebook will tell you where to head for, but don't wander aimlessly, and try to make sure you get into a licensed cab (identified by a certain make of car in a certain colour, such as the green Volkswagen Beetles used in Mexico City). A riskier alternative is to go with one of the touts in the airport to his vehicle, which will be parked outside the jurisdiction of the official airport taxi union. These unlicensed taxi drivers are often perfectly decent citizens trying to make a living – but who's to say if they're not? You could be mugged, dumped somewhere dangerous or worse – if you do take a ride with a tout you have only your instincts to decide whether he's honest or not.

By bus

If you arrive in daylight, you might find a **bus** that goes into town from the airport or close by, but you'll need to have a good idea of where you're going and some small change to pay your fare. Local buses are frequently rife with pickpockets, and if you have a huge backpack they may refuse to take you or simply not have enough room. In general airports that don't run a *colectivo* service will instead run airport shuttle buses. These take you on a set route, usually to the city centre or to hotel districts. **Shuttle services** are more expensive than ordinary local buses but are also safer, and frequently come equipped with air conditioning and comfortable seats.

Jet lag

To those who have never suffered it, jet lag might appear to be nothing more than a rich kid's whinge, but unfortunately it's all too real, as you're likely to discover for yourself after your arrival in Latin America, unless you've flown from North America. The condition affects the vast majority of all long-distance travellers, and unless you're one of the lucky few who are immune, it's an inevitable hazard of flying long distances. Jet lag results from the disruption of the human body clock which is caused by rapidly crossing world time zones. If you cross more than three time zones (ie if the time in your departure city is more than three hours different from that at your destination), chances are you will experience jet lag. You're likely to suffer less from jet lag when travelling west rather than east, so Europeans have it easier on the way out to Latin America, while Australasians will have less jet lag going home. The good news for North Americans is that if you're flying directly south from the US or Canada to Latin America you may not even cross a single time zone, thus avoiding jet lag altogether.

Symptoms of jet lag include extreme fatigue, disorientation, lack of concentration, disrupted sleep and dehydration. In the days following your arrival you're likely to feel light-headed and unable to go to sleep and wake up at the appropriate times. Sitting bolt upright in bed at 4am and falling asleep in your breakfast may sound amusing, but disrupted sleep patterns can cause your health and wellbeing to suffer temporarily. According to NASA, for each time zone crossed, you'll need a day before your body clock is properly adjusted – this means that if you're flying from London to Santiago, for example, it'll take six days. And jet lag doesn't really kick in until the second day of your arrival, so don't congratulate yourself on avoiding it prematurely.

There are all kinds of bizarre jet lag treatments available on the market. Some, like **melatonin**, a synthetic version of the hormone which is secreted into the bloodstream when it's time to sleep, have large followings (though its effectiveness is doubted by as many others, and there's no standard dose) – it's available in health-food stores in the US but not Europe. A herbal remedy from New Zealand called **No-Jet-Lag** (Ⓦwww.nojetlag.com) is said to work as is **intensive light therapy** (Ⓦwww.bodyclock.com). In general, though, the best way to minimize the effects of jet lag is to follow the points below:

- Try to avoid 24-hour partying the night before you leave and last-minute panicking – stress and hangovers will only exacerbate jet lag. It's also possible to "save up" sleep by having several decent nights of it before you fly.
- Once on board, set your watch immediately to your destination time zone and start to adjust to the new time.
- Drink loads of water, avoid alcohol and caffeine, and eat light meals. Don't take conventional sleeping pills, which are dehydrating.
- Once you've arrived, continue to follow the local time even if your body is desperate for sleep. Go to bed when the locals do, eat meals at the right time and avoid sleeping during the day.
- Get out into the fresh air and spend as much time in bright natural light as possible – daylight alleviates jet lag by helping to reset your body clock.
- Take some gentle exercise as soon as possible – swimming or walking will combat the stiffness which results from sitting in one place for a long time and may also alleviate symptoms of jet lag such as disrupted sleeping patterns.
- Take it easy for your first few days – put off any non-urgent decisions, since your mental processes will be impaired by jet lag. Now is the perfect time to go to the beach, where the sunshine will aid your recovery.

Culture shock

Don't worry if you find you don't much enjoy your first few days in Latin America. You may well find the change in climate and food and the sheer strangeness of the place overwhelms you, leaving you feeling anxious, disoriented, paranoid, self-conscious or simply exhausted. You may even find yourself wishing you'd never come, shocked by the poverty, appalled by the pollution, confused by the language and disconcerted by the apparent chaos all around you. These are all common symptoms of **culture shock**, a perfectly normal reaction that almost every traveller suffers to some degree. Even experienced travellers sometimes undergo the same feelings of anxiety and alienation when they return to the region after some time away; in many ways, these feelings are part of the exhilaration of travel: if it didn't feel slightly dangerous, alien and exotic, it wouldn't be an adventure.

Culture shock often goes hand in hand with **homesickness**, and some people find it comes and goes in waves during long trips, so that the very same things which one week you find exciting about the country you're travelling through – be it the food, the local culture, the pace of life – can the next week seem deeply frustrating and annoying, making you wish you were back home surrounded by the safe and familiar. Fortunately, culture shock usually fades very quickly after arrival, generally giving way to excitement as you settle in and begin to enjoy all that Latin America has to offer. The following tips should help you overcome any initial culture shock and get through the confusion and strangeness of the first few days.

- If you're going on a long trip taking in several different countries, consider starting in a country that's relatively easy to travel in, such as Chile, Argentina or Costa Rica, before taking on somewhere more challenging, such as Peru or Colombia.

www.roughguides.com

- Take it easy for the first few days after arrival: you may well be jet-lagged after a long flight, exhausted and struggling to cope with a very different climate.

- Start exploring gradually rather than diving into your travels headfirst. Take time to get your bearings and visit a few easy and accessible places before heading off to more remote and adventurous destinations.

- Try and speak a few words of the local language, even if you only know enough to order a beer: this will make you feel less of an alien and make the locals much more approachable.

- Call or write home about your initial experiences – often just telling someone about what you're adjusting to can make it feel much more manageable.

- Chat to other travellers, as they've invariably been through the same thing and can offer useful support and advice, and help you see the funny side of things you might otherwise find exasperating.

- Don't feel obliged to have a completely "authentic" experience right from the start, no matter what other travellers tell you. If you want to stay close to your hotel and eat only familiar food for the first few days, then go ahead – there will be plenty of time to explore further afield and eat more adventurously once you've settled in.

- If after a few days the symptoms of culture shock don't go away, it may simply be that you don't like your first port of call. Try moving to another city or region where the climate or culture makes you feel more comfortable.

Different countries, different customs

Though when you first arrive in a Latin American capital it may seem disappointingly familiar, with its high-rise business district, rushing commuters and international corporate advertising hoardings, it won't be long before you realize that the westernization of the region is a thin veneer. Beneath the sometimes banal globalized veneer, traditional Latin American culture runs deep, and it will quickly become clear that you are in the midst of a society with a very different approach to life and view of the world to what you're used to back home. **Religion** – above all Roman Catholicism – and extended **families** play a far greater role in Latin American culture than you're probably used to, and you may find many of the attitudes you encounter surprising in comparison to those commonly held in Europe or the US. Traditional Latin American values, especially those related to gender roles, inequality and social conformity, may seem stiflingly conservative or even oppressive. Many Latin Americans will find your behaviour equally strange – the very fact of your travelling to far-away countries simply for pleasure may be viewed as an irresponsible eccentricity, while to be unmarried and childless in your mid-twenties will strike some as at best bizarre or at worst indicative of some underlying misfortune.

Though there have been important steps towards more equal rights in recent decades, the culture of **machismo** is alive and well in Latin America. This tradition of gender stereotyping sees men as strong and dominant and women weak and subservient, and many women find it the most challenging aspect of travel in Latin America. Advice on coping with sexual harassment is given on p.190, but you should also be prepared to cope with more general **gender prejudices**. If you're a woman travelling with a man – be it a husband, partner or friend – most conversation will be addressed to him, even if you're the one who speaks the local language; if you're a woman travelling alone, meanwhile, some Latin American men will assume it's because you can't find a man back home, and act accordingly.

Other aspects of Latin American culture that you may well find frustrating include a near-complete disregard for timekeeping, widespread corruption, shocking levels of poverty and inequality and interminable bureaucracy. However infuriating these aspects of Latin American culture can be, there's almost nothing you can do to change them, so railing against them is a waste of time and energy that can really spoil your trip. It's much better to accept such traits as part and parcel of what you came to experience, and adapt accordingly; keeping a sense of humour and perspective will help you to remain calm in testing situations.

Blockbuster movies

When you're travelling, cultural dislocation can make you take a sudden dive for the nearest Burger King, blockbuster movie, or other culturally familiar things you might never consider doing at home. I never see American blockbuster films at home, of course, being a snob. But it's quite entertaining, not to mention instructive, seeing *Speed III* or *Godzilla* in a Central American cinema, surrounded by the increasingly Americanophile teenage sons and daughters of the local scions (cinemas are sometimes too pricey for the average family). The parking lot is full of four-wheel drives, and the foyer stuffed with girls admiring each other's outfits (*Que chivo!, que barbaro!* – roughly, Cool!). You can learn a lot of Spanish by reading the subtitles and comparing them with what comes out of Keanu Reeves' mouth – or perhaps that's not such a good example…

Jean McNeil

www.roughguides.com

113

Gay and lesbian travellers

Traditional macho attitudes to gender roles combined with the influence of the Roman Catholic Church make much of Latin America fairly hostile to homosexuality. In some countries homosexual acts have only recently been decriminalized, and gays and lesbians across the region still face considerable discrimination. For gay and lesbian travellers, it's safest to follow the example of local gay couples and avoid flaunting your sexuality. In rural areas in particular, open displays of affection between two men or two women can still provoke a hostile reaction. You'll find a more tolerant attitude in the cities, particularly in Brazil. Rio de Janeiro, São Paulo and Salvador all have thriving gay nightlife scenes, as do Buenos Aires in Argentina and Santiago in Chile. The website of the International Gay and Lesbian Travel Association (Ⓦ www.igtla.com) has listings of gay-friendly accommodation and travel agents throughout Latin America.

On your best behaviour

However much you may dislike the idea of being an ambassador for your country, this is how many Latin Americans will see you, just as your view of their country will be shaped by how the locals treat you, so it's important to act with **respect** towards the cultural and social norms of the country you're in. No one expects you to transform yourself overnight into a Latin American, but adapting your behaviour to the country you're visiting is polite, makes local people more receptive, and generally makes travel easier and more enjoyable. Mastering the full range of social niceties in any country takes considerable time, but there are a few general behaviour codes you should definitely try to follow.

Even if you're only travelling for a few weeks, it's essential to learn at least a few basic words of **Spanish** or **Portuguese**. As well as being practical, making an effort to speak the local language makes locals react more favourably towards you, even if it's no more than basic greetings. Although few Latin Americans speak good English, many understand enough to know if you're talking about them, and certainly recognize common English obscenities, so be careful what you say.

Though it varies in degree from country to country, Latin Americans generally attach considerable importance to **politeness** and formality. It's normal to shake hands and use a formal greeting such as "good morning" or "good afternoon" before engaging someone in conversation – failure to do so will make you appear rude and can cause offence, or at least make people less helpful. It's also a good idea to use formal titles like *señor/señora* or *don/doña* and, if speaking Spanish, to use the formal *usted* rather than *tú* when addressing older people or those in authority. Politeness is particularly important when dealing with officials such as police officers, for whom the respect accorded their uniform or position is one of the few compensations for low pay and poor conditions. If you're rude or disrespectful, they can make things very difficult for you.

Though you're likely to see a few locals doing it, getting angry and raising your voice will seldom produce results, and is more likely to cause further antagonism, particularly when dealing with people in authority. This doesn't mean you can't be firm and assertive – just do it in as calm and civil a manner as you can manage. Getting involved in any kind of fight is a very bad idea, as the use of fists can easily provoke a reaction with a knife or gun.

You should be wary of discussing **politics** in public and with strangers, as tempers can get very heated, and be cautious about getting directly involved in local politics – a vogue for so-called "guerrilla tourism" in the southern Mexican state of Chiapas has seen many young travellers expelled from the country.

There's a strong **drinking culture** in many parts of Latin America, and if you enjoy a drink, you'll have plenty of locals who are happy to share a few with you. But like everywhere else, public drunkeness – though not unusual – can lead to all sorts of problems.

Dressing the part

Latin Americans attach considerable importance to appearance. Even if they are so poor they only have one set of clothes, they're still likely to be clean

A few pisco sours too many

The conversation around the table has come to an abrupt halt. The old man in the cravat smiles weakly as his leather-faced wife glares at me like an Easter Island statue in Chanel. My new-found drinking companions are turning against me. I try to replay the last few sentences to come out of my mouth but my brain isn't cooperating. Those pisco sours are really moreish.

I'd travelled up from the Central Valley having spent a busy week attending tours entitled "Getting to Know Chilean Wine", even though we'd been acquainted for some time. In search of something stronger I arrived in the idyllic village of Pisco Elqui, home to Chile's oldest pisco distillery. The guided tour I took there was informative but merely foreplay to the tasting session that followed. It started with the weakest, the Seleccion, then gently eased through the Reservado onto the Especial, and finally finished with the strongest of them all, the aptly named Gran Pisco. These were all sampled neat and were really good, but were trumped marvellously by what followed: pisco sours, a delicious cocktail of crushed ice, pisco, lemon juice, sugar, egg white and angostura bitters. And they are lethal. Intent on furthering my education, I headed out to the first bar I could find.

So all of them are just sitting there looking at me, not saying a word. And I honestly can't remember what I have just said to cause offence. Earlier they seemed happy to accept my devastating critique of Pablo Neruda's infantile love songs. Some of them, the two gauchos, were even nodding. Is that a hunting knife hooked onto his belt? I wrack my brain some more and catch a faint echo. I think I just mouthed off about Pinochet. I can't believe I've broken one of the Golden Rules – namely do not be drunk, English, totally uninformed and launch into a rant about a much-loved fascist dictator. I can't have done something that stupid. Stupid pisco sours.

Ross Monaghan

www.roughguides.com

and relatively smart. Although the prejudice against people perceived as hippies is not as strong as it once was, dressing in untidy or dirty clothes is usually viewed unfavourably, whilst having at least one set of reasonably smart attire can get you into places where scruffier back-packers wouldn't be admitted.

It's a good idea to observe **local dress codes** as much as possible. Short shorts, sleeveless shirts and bikinis are fine on the beach, but in towns and cities they are usually frowned upon, and in some isolated rural communities can cause serious offence and even provoke stone throwing. Wearing part or all of the traditional costumes of local indige-nous groups, on the other hand, can provoke ridicule or offence, so save them until you get home. Camouflaged military clothing is also a bad idea, especially in countries with recent experience of armed conflict.

The Roman Catholic **religion** is taken seriously across Latin America, so it's particularly important to dress appropriately and behave respectfully when visiting churches or attending religious ceremonies.

Harsh realities

Unless you've travelled to other developing countries before, the thing you'll find most shocking when you arrive in Latin America is likely to be the **extreme poverty** endured by much of the population. Most major cities are ringed by slums and shantytowns which lack even basic amenities such as water, electricity and sewerage, and whose populations are constantly increasing as a result of migration from rural areas where poverty is even more desperate. Unemployment is high, and wages so low that even those who do have jobs (including professionals such as teachers) often struggle to make ends meet. This poverty is even more shocking in comparison with the extreme wealth enjoyed by small sec-tions of the population: Latin America is home to some of the most unequal societies in the world, and the gap between rich and poor is distressingly pronounced.

The most visible manifestation of poverty you'll come across is undoubtedly the large number of **beggars** on the streets of almost every city. Many Latin Americans of all social classes give generously to beggars, particularly to the old and sick, and their donations act as an informal welfare system in countries without universal health provision or welfare system. Many tourists are unsure how to deal with beggars in Latin America, and you wouldn't be the first to mask your discomfort by averting your gaze while marching by. Obviously, giving is a personal decision, and you may prefer to give to a charity instead, or even to get actively involved in a local charity for a while, see pp.60–62. If you do decide to give money, you may want to follow the example of most locals by targeting the old, disabled and sick rather than those beggars who could otherwise be working for a living. There are also other ways of giving to the poor: paying for small services like **shoe-shining** is an informal way of giving money to the poor whilst encouraging hard work and self-reliance in street children who might otherwise turn to begging or crime.

Mañana, mañana

One of the most striking cultural differences between Latin America and countries in the developed world is in their attitude to **time**. Whereas back home turning up fifteen minutes late is considered at best thoughtless and at worst rude and unprofessional, in most of Latin America arriving hours or even days late for a meeting barely warrants an explanation, never mind an apology. This relaxed attitude to time, whereby almost anything can be put off until tomorrow (*mañana*) and punctuality is considered of little or no importance, is one of the aspects of Latin America that most travellers find most frustrating. Latin Americans are usually aware of this trait (though that doesn't stop them setting very exact agendas which they've no hope of meeting) and often rather bemused by gringos' bizarre obsession with punctuality. Indeed, when they really, truly mean an exact time, they'll emphasize it by using the expression *hora inglés* ("English time").

That they're aware of it, however, doesn't mean they're going to change just for you, and the bottom line is that there's nothing you can do about it. Getting angry because a bus leaves a few hours after the official departure time isn't going to make things happen any faster, so to avoid frustration it's best to allow extra time for every journey and leave enough space and flexibility in your travel plans to accommodate the inevitable delays. It also helps if you can adopt the same laid-back approach to time as the locals, and enjoy the relaxed unpredictability it adds to life: after all, if you want to travel in a country where the trains run on time, you'd be better off going to Switzerland. Finally, it's worth bearing in mind that, according to Latin American travellers' lore, the only time a bus or train does leave on time is when you arrive at the terminal five minutes late.

Being a gringo (what they think of you)

Wherever you go in Latin America, it won't be long before you hear locals refer to you as **gringo** or (if you're female) **gringa**. Strictly speaking, the term originally only applied to people from the US, and this meaning is still retained in most of Mexico, but elsewhere in Latin America "gringo" is used to describe anyone from rich, developed and largely white countries in Europe, North America and Australasia. It can have negative connotations – in Colombia, for example, the expression *hacerse el gringo* ("to act like a gringo") is used to mean "play the fool" – but generally speaking it's not an insult, just a description of which ethnic or cultural group you belong to in Latin American eyes, so it's not worth getting upset about. Latin Americans are equally blunt in describing people of Chinese, African and indigenous descent as *Chino*, *Negro* and *Indio*, and while there is a degree of racism in this system of categorization, with the exception of *Indio* these terms are not generally considered racist in themselves – it depends on the tone and context.

Latin Americans are prone to making assumptions about foreign travellers, just as Latin Americans are often stereotyped in the media back home as superstitious, shiftless, corrupt and prone to thieving and drug-trafficking. Gringos in Latin America are in turn often stereotyped as being ignorant, clumsy, arrogant, rude, naive, sexually promiscuous, obsessively uptight about time and, above all, as inordinately wealthy. However, like all stereotypes, these are easily broken by engaging in a little direct human contact. Often, just making an effort to speak the local language, eating the local food, sharing a drink or a joke, revealing a little about your real life and showing a modicum of interest in local culture or respect for local social norms is enough to shatter these clichés.

Making that contact is also pretty easy, as generally speaking Latin Americans are just as fascinated by you as you are by them, and wherever you go you're likely be engaged in conversation and bombarded with questions. "Where are you from?", "Where are you going?", "What do you think of my country?", "How much did it cost to fly here?" – the same enquiries will come again and again, but though the constant repetition and the assumptions that underlie these questions can be irritating, they're usually just conversation openers. Particularly in areas that see little tourism, a foreign traveller passing through can be an exciting event for the locals, an opportunity to practise their English and satisfy some of their curiosity about the outside world, something few Latin Americans are able to do by travelling themselves. Some travellers like to carry photos of their friends and family to show curious locals what their life back home is really like.

And being a Yanqui...

Latin American attitudes to people from the US – often referred to as **Yanquis** (Yankees) no matter what part of the States they're from – are a complex mixture of love and hate. On one hand, Latin Americans generally admire the wealth, dynamism and material success of the US. Millions have friends and relatives who live, work and study in the US, and millions more would like to join them and live the "American dream" in what's seen as a land of milk and honey. But this admiration is tempered by widespread political resentment of the US government's long record of interference in Latin America, and its deeply hypocritical approach to the "war on drugs". The US is also widely blamed for the poor economic situation in many Latin American countries, especially where the Washington-based International Monetary Fund and World Bank have insisted on swingeing government spending cuts that have crippled social services. There are few political crises that are not blamed in some quarters on supposed CIA conspiracies and US "imperialism". Some US citizens go so far as telling casual acquaintances they are Canadian when travelling in Latin America, but in fact these resentments are rarely directed towards individual travellers and are unlikely to affect you as long as you stay out of heated political discussions, especially in countries and regions where tension is high.

Where are you from?

Searching for the immigration office in downtown Medellín, I soon realized the map in my guidebook was hopelessly out of date. Aware that walking a few blocks in the wrong direction could land me in a very dangerous neighbourhood, I stopped to ask directions from a respectable-looking man. "Where are you from?" he asked in return, and when I told him I was British, he said, "Well in that case, head two blocks down this street, and turn left at the traffic lights." I thanked him politely for his help, but before I continued on my way I couldn't resist asking him why he'd first enquired about my nationality. "Well," he said, "if you'd said you were from the United States, I'd have told you it was in the opposite direction."

James Read

Being a wealthy tourist

All over Latin America, the most common assumption you'll confront is that as a gringo you are, by definition, extremely **wealthy**. You'll find people constantly asking you how much your flight cost and what the minimum wage is in your home country, then gasping in amazement as their preconceived view of your inordinate personal wealth is apparently confirmed. What makes this stereotype almost impossible to dispel is the fact that it is, by and large, entirely accurate. However low your economic position may be back home and however tight your budget, compared to the average Latin American, you're rich. Not only do you come from a wealthy country, you can even afford to take time off work and travel long distances for pleasure, something most locals can only dream about. You can counter

www.roughguides.com

this assumption of endless wealth to a certain extent by explaining how long you had to work to raise the money for the trip, or how prices back home are much higher, but in the end you're unlikely to convince anyone that you're not comparatively rich, because all the evidence points in the other direction.

And why bother, when this comparatively wealthy status, however unusual you find it at first, was probably one of the reasons you chose to go to Latin America in the first place. After all, it can be very enjoyable suddenly to be able to take a taxi whenever you want rather than waiting for a bus, to eat in restaurants every day, and to take part in all kinds of activities that would be too expensive to contemplate back home. While enjoying the freedom wealth allows, however, you should be aware that it involves some **responsibilities**, too. As a person with cash to spend you can drive up local prices just by paying over the odds for a taxi fare or a beer (and many locals will encourage you to do this) as traders may then overcharge future customers, driving inflation up. In the worst cases, goods and services in popular tourist destinations can become so expensive that locals can no longer afford them. Ask locals about prices before buying and try to pay a reasonable price, but conversely don't worry too much about being slightly overcharged: getting angry and frustrated over a few cents really isn't worth the energy. In some countries and regions local traders operate an informal two-tier price system whereby foreign tourists are charged more than locals – some buses in Guatemala, for example, or hotels in Nicaragua. This can be quite annoying, but there's usually not much you can do about it, so it's not worth getting upset about – think of it as an unofficial subsidy for the locals who struggle to afford the same service.

▲ Cooking in Buenos Aires, Argentina

For more on tourist prices and bargaining, see p.76.

Food and drink

Getting used to the local food and drink can be one of the trickiest cultural transitions to deal with while travelling, but in comparison to Asia or Africa, Latin American food and drink isn't so very different to what you find at home, and there are only a handful of dishes – such as iguana eggs, guinea pigs or the dried ants popular in eastern Colombia – which you're likely to find totally alien. In cities and towns you'll find that familiar foods like pizza, burgers and fried chicken are widely available, and in areas popular with budget travellers you'll find restaurants and cafés specializing in the kind of food backpackers eat the world over – muesli, banana pancakes and the like. If you're travelling on a tight budget, you're better off sticking to local food, particularly the very good-value **set menus** for lunch and dinner available in most countries, though you may find you eventually tire of regional staples like rice and beans, maize tortillas, or starchy soups. However, you'll be really missing out on one of the great pleasures of travel in Latin America if you don't sample the local specialities in the countries you visit: from Peruvian *ceviche* (cool, spicy raw fish) and Mexican *chile* to Argentine steaks (the best in the world) and Brazilian *feijoada* (a meaty black-bean stew), the region is a cornucopia of culinary delights.

The one thing to be wary of is the fondness of people in some countries (above all Mexico and Peru) for particularly **spicy food** – Latin America is, after all, the original

What kind of meat?

On the inland roads of the Yucatán, hitchhikers are common, trying to get from the middle of nowhere to the edge of nowhere. I pick up nice-looking women and children to break up the monotony of the greenery and practise my Spanish.

One day, into my car climbed a little bundle of Maya cheer, clad in a traditional flowery dress and toting three huge mesh bags. After the conversational preamble – her Spanish was about as fluent as mine – she asked me, "So, what kind of meats do you eat in your village?" It was such an odd question that I made her repeat it – and I'd already told her I was from New York ("Díos mio!" she gasped), so her saying "pueblito" was also confusing. Baffled, I began to list all the meat words I could think of: pato, pavo, pollo… But she quickly interrupted – this was a question she wanted to answer. In her village, they eat special animals that you only find in the forest, such as…and she rattled off several of them.

To illustrate one, she reached in a bag and pulled out the back half of a forest critter's carcass, splayed out flat and all black from roasting. The little feet were still on, with delicate toes and nails. This was an uhum, she said – it had (once upon a time) a long tail and pointy nose. According to her, it was a great little animal, but they'd been hunted for so long there were hardly any left.

And then she encouraged me to sample some of these endangered hindquarters. A difficult task while driving, but I got a few shreds, and it was quite tasty, though I think that had more to do with the pit-cooking than its innate uhum-ness.

Zora O'Neill

www.roughguides.com

Favourite Latin flavours

These are just a few examples of Latin America's many culinary delights. You don't have to spend much to eat very well, and the best food can turn up in the most unlikely places.

Argentine beef Good steak features regularly on menus throughout Latin America, but nowhere does it match the quality of Argentina's, where preparing the world's best beef has become an art form unto itself. Ordered from a complex diagram of bovine anatomy, Argentine steaks come in many different cuts and have many different names, but they're invariably large and almost always delicious.

Ceviche Peru's unmissable national dish, a cool and spicy combination of fresh fish and seafood marinated in chilli, onions and lime juice, best washed down with an ice-cold beer. Anything served under the same name elsewhere in Latin America seldom lives up to the exquisite Peruvian version.

Chilli sauce The chilli pepper originates in Latin America, and as well as being one of the regions greatest gifts to world cuisine, it's an indispensable everyday condiment in almost every Latin American country. Whether mass-produced in a bottle or handmade to a family recipe, chilli sauce is always on the table and can liven up even the blandest food. In Mexico in particular, the variety of chillies available is amazing. The hottest varieties can bring tears to your eyes, but once your taste buds are accustomed you may find you can't eat without it.

Colombian coffee Coffee may come from Africa originally, but Latin America now has a strong claim to producing the world's finest beans, as well as being home to some of the world's most enthusiastic coffee drinkers. The best is arguably found in Colombia, where sweetened black coffee known as *tinto* is always available, served from thermoses by wandering vendors.

Cuy Bred as livestock for thousands of years, the guinea pig remains the favourite party dish for indigenous people in much of the Peruvian Andes. If you can get past the fact

home of the red-hot chilli pepper. Fortunately for those without the fire-eating habit, chilli is usually served in a side dish, either chopped raw or blended into sauces with all kinds of other ingredients. Be cautious in applying this to your food, as it could well be hotter than anything you've tasted back home; the best remedy if your mouth is on fire is bread or something sweet rather than cold water. In addition, always wash your hands after handling chillies, as otherwise touching your eyes or other more sensitive parts of your body can give you a culture shock of a particularly agonizing kind.

The only reason you're likely to have difficulty with food is if you are a **vegetarian**. Latin America is very much a meat-eating society, and most Latin Americans who can afford to do so eat meat with pretty much every meal. All kinds of fruit and vegetables are of course available, but outside tourist areas they rarely make it onto menus as main dishes. Telling a waiter you're a vegetarian is quite likely to produce a blank stare, while insisting you don't eat meat will probably be interpreted as meaning you don't eat beef, but pork or chicken is okay. If you're a strict vegetarian, be warned that ostensibly vegetarian dishes such as beans are often cooked in pork fat they look like rats once roasted and are better known as children's pets elsewhere in the world, cuys are a tasty treat and certainly something to write home about.

Empanadas A classic snack available throughout Latin America in a variety of guises, empanadas are small pies or pasties, filled with meat, chicken, fish, cheese and/or vegetables and either baked or fried.

Feijoada No visit to Brazil is complete without tasting this classic dish. *Feijoada* is a rich black-bean stew laden with chunks of meat and sausage that's served throughout the country, either as a side dish or, accompanied by rice, as a meal in itself.

Fruit juice Latin America's astonishing variety of sumptuous tropical fruit is best enjoyed juiced and blended with ice. Known by various names including *zumo, suco, vitaminha, batido* and *licuado*, fresh fruit juices are available almost everywhere, providing a delicious, refreshing and inexpensive way to stay healthy on the road.

Mole poblano Only in Mexico, where chocolate originated, could they get away with using it to make a spicy sauce for turkey. But strange as it may sound, the subtle blend of bitter chocolate with several varieties of chilli that is *mole poblano* is excellent. The food of the gods – as the Aztecs considered it – is also used more conventionally in contemporary Mexico, grated from natural blocks to make delicious hot chocolate drinks.

Tortillas You can love them or loathe them, but you certainly can't escape tortillas if you travel in Mexico or Central America. These flat pancakes of maize or wheat flour are the traditional equivalent of bread, served with almost every meal. At their worst they're soggy, dull and repetitive. But at their best – made from hand-ground corn and baked on a stone by a wood fire – they're the very essence of Central America. And as a key ingredient in a host of dishes – tacos, burritos, enchilladas – they're an essential part of Mexico's varied and distinctive cuisine.

for extra flavour. With a little persistence and determination, however, it is possible to be a vegetarian in Latin America. Most large towns and cities have at least one vegetarian or health-food restaurant (often run by Hare Krishnas), and tourist restaurants usually have several vegetarian options. If you stick to local places, however, you may well find yourself consuming a lot of eggs. Shopping for fruit and vegetables in the local market – where a huge range of both is almost always available – and cooking or preparing it yourself is one way to supplement the rather meagre fare available to vegetarians on the road.

Taking photos

For many people, taking **photographs** or video footage is one of the great joys of travel and one of the best ways of preserving memories. The sheer visual magnificence of so much of Latin America makes it an excellent place for photographers, whether you're fully kitted out with professional equipment or snapping away with a basic camera. But not all Latin Americans are happy to have their photo taken by tourists, and

www.roughguides.com

123

there are certain situations where you should be cautious about who or what you photograph. The following guidelines should help you get the picture you want without causing offence or getting into trouble.

- Always ask permission before taking pictures of people, as failure to do so is at best rude and at worst deeply offensive. Remember that you're not in a theme park, and think how you would feel if strange foreigners began taking your picture without so much as a by-your-leave. Be particularly cautious in isolated indigenous communities, where taking people's picture is sometimes considered akin to theft.

- Sometimes you may find people ask you to pay them a small fee in return for allowing you to take their photo. Some travellers view such demands with outrage, but in fact they represent a perfectly reasonable exchange – you get the picture, the usually poor subject earns a little money which may make him or her more receptive to tourists in the future, and locals are encouraged to maintain the colourful and unique costumes and traditions which are probably the main reason you wanted to photograph them anyway.

- Locals will often ask you for copies of the pictures you take of them or their families, as many can't afford cameras or development costs themselves. Though the quality of prints is usually not as good as back home, getting pictures printed locally and giving away a few copies to the people you've photographed makes the whole process a much more equal exchange, and the delight a few pictures can bring to people who have perhaps never seen a photo of themselves can be very satisfying.

- Always ask before taking pictures in churches and during religious processions and fiestas, as it may be considered disrespectful. Flash photography is often banned in churches as it can damage ageing oil paintings and other decorations.

- Don't take pictures of border posts or any kind of military installation, as this can result in you having your film or camera confiscated or even in your being arrested by paranoid military personnel. Always ask permission before taking photographs of police or soldiers.

Responsible tourism

Culture shock works both ways, and with the number of tourists visiting Latin America increasing all the time, it's important not to underestimate the impact the **tourism industry** has on local cultures, particularly in popular destinations. One of the most alarming aspects of reverse culture shock is the tendency for big businesses to take over local enterprises in resort areas, preventing the economic dividends of tourism from reaching local communities. As a first-time traveller you'll probably be on a fairly tight budget and so unlikely to be patronizing international hotel chains, but you may well be tempted to stop off at familiar multinational takeaway food outlets. Where possible, it's much better (as well as cheaper and more enjoyable) to support local shops, restaurants and hotels instead. That way, the money you spend stays within the community and local residents retain control over their own neighbourhood, ensuring that the place keeps its character – which is, after all, what you travelled so far to experience. Though they spend less money than wealthier tourists on short, all-inclusive tours, budget travellers can have a beneficial effect on the countries they visit, as most of the money they do spend tends to go to small **local businesses**, and so can have a more positive impact on local economies.

Local initiatives

It's also important to support **local initiatives** when it comes to visiting traditional indigenous communities, so that the people you go to see – be it Quechua-speaking llama-herders in the Andes or semi-nomadic tribes in the Amazon – gain some economic benefit from your curiosity. All too many tour companies sell trips to visit isolated indigenous groups without giving travellers any chance to communicate with them, turning communities into little more than human zoos and exotic photo opportunities where traditional culture is parodied rather than respected. Where possible, try to organize a tour with a tour guide or agency from within the community you wish to visit, or at least endeavour to actually meet and interact with the people you've travelled so far to see. Tourism can have a dramatic negative impact on remote communities, in some cases plunging them suddenly into an unfamiliar market economy and materialist society. However, if conducted in a sensitive manner, tourism can have a positive effect, reviving local economies and keeping local traditions alive. A growing number of **community-based guides** and tour operators are springing up all over Latin America, offering a far more authentic and positive experience of traditional socie- ties than you'll get with many more mainstream tour agencies. The website ⓦ www.leaplocal.org can put you in touch with local guides and community tourism initiatives in much of Latin America. You could also check out the *Good Alternative Tourism Guide*, published by Earthscan for the campaigning organization Tourism Concern, which lists a selection of successful local tourism initiatives in Latin America

and the rest of the world. Tourism Concern also have a website at
ⓦ www.tourismconcern.org.uk.

The environment

As a responsible tourist, you should also try to reduce your impact on
the **environment**, particularly in national parks and other protected
wilderness areas, where you otherwise risk damaging the pristine
natural beauty you've travelled so far to see. In practice, this can mean
everything from being careful about rubbish disposal to following
strict national park rules. Even if the locals appear unconcerned about
litter, it doesn't mean you should be. In particular, don't dump non-
biodegradable stuff like plastic, cigarette ends and dead batteries in rural
areas: if you can manage to carry it in with you, you can certainly take
it out again. Don't buy souvenirs made from **endangered species** such
as black coral, and avoid eating endangered species such as turtle, which
often make it onto tourist menus.

Ecotourism

In recent years Latin America has seen an explosion in **ecotourism**,
which in theory involves tourists visiting fragile natural environments
such as rainforests and coral reefs whilst minimizing the negative impact
their visit has on them and their inhabitants. In the best cases, ecotourism can even have a positive impact, encouraging environmental
protection by allowing local communities to make a living through
conserving rather than exploiting natural resources. In many instances,
however, tour agencies claim to practise ecotourism to attract clients
but in fact do little or nothing to reduce the negative impact of their
tours, a process known as "greenwashing".

Advice on getting involved in nature conservation work in Latin
America is given in Chapter 2, and you'll find a list of relevant
organizations in the Directory on p.305. You'll also find plenty of
information and advice on ecotourism on the websites ⓦ www
.planeta.com and ⓦ www.ecotour.org.

10

Getting around

As often as it is exciting and exhilarating, travel in Latin America can be unpredictable, frustrating and exhausting. The extremes of terrain, poor infrastructure and the enormous distances involved mean that simply getting people from one place to the other is an enormous challenge, but it's one that Latin American transport operators overcome every day, moving millions of passengers around using planes, trains, passenger ships, river boats, motorized dugout canoes, tourist buses, local buses, open-top lorries, pick-up trucks and shared taxis.

Road transport is the main way of getting around throughout the region, though the quality of this varies enormously. In relatively developed countries such as Argentina and Venezuela, most main roads are well paved and buses are often modern and reliable. In poorer countries, however – and particularly in sparsely populated regions with swampy or mountainous terrain – most roads are unpaved dirt highways in very poor condition which are only kept open by constant labour against floods and landslides, and by the determination and skill of bus and lorry drivers.

Throughout the vast, rainforest-covered basins of the Amazon and Orinoco, meanwhile, roads are few and far between and the mighty river systems form the main highways, served by a variety of **boats** ranging from large ships to canoes hewn from single tree trunks. In many coastal regions, too, ferries and fast launches are the main means of hopping along the shore or reaching nearby islands. Throughout Latin America **local flights**, whether in airliners shuttling between major cities or light aircraft skimming over the treetops, offer a quick and easy way of getting around, saving many hours or even days of hard overland travel at a relatively reasonable price.

www.roughguides.com

THE BIG ADVENTURE

Public transport in Colombia

As the crow flies, it was a distance of 100km from where I was staying to the Caribbean coast of Colombia – a leisurely morning's journey, you might assume. There was no direct route, though – so it took a lot longer than I'd imagined. From inland Mompos I took a crammed jeep – "When does it go?" I asked the driver, who was ordering breakfast from a street stall. "It goes when it's full" was his reply, grunted between mouthfuls of empanada – to the river, then a speedboat to Magangue, a dusty town from where I took a minibus and arrived in Sincelejo in time to find a room for the night. A dawn start the next day began with another minibus ride, which got me at last to the coast – but not the village I was heading for. In Tolu the roads petered out and I climbed into the back of a truck – the only form of public transport other than the local "taxis", bicycles with rickety seats custom-built over the front and back wheels – with the aid of a handy wooden stool that was whipped out by the driver's assistant at every stop so that passengers could climb on. These included local farmers wearing straw stetsons and carrying chickens, businessmen with mobile phones, schoolgirls, and smart women adorned in flowery frocks and gilt jewellery. Another truck ride and then the luxury of a proper bus and I finally arrived in San Bernardo del Viento – seven bus/truck rides, one boat trip and two days later.
Polly Rodger Brown

All this exciting variety must be set against discomfort, poor safety conditions and driving standards, delays and unreliability – enduring characteristics of travel in Latin America. While back home a five-hour bus ride in a comfortable seat may seem interminable, and a fifteen-minute delay a serious inconvenience, if you want to travel in Latin America for any length of time you'll find yourself making a lot of twelve-hour bus journeys in cramped seats and confronting delays of many hours, often for no apparent reason. If you look on the travel itself as part of the **adventure**, you'll have a better chance of keeping things in perspective. The twelve-hour bus journey that turns into a three-day marathon may be a gruelling experience at the time, but when you get home you'll probably look back on it as one of the most memorable adventures of your trip. On most journeys, too, the spectacular scenery you'll pass through and the colourful antics of your fellow passengers are usually compensation for the arduousness of the trip.

Planes

Almost all countries in Latin America have an air network of some sort, and **internal flights** are by far the fastest way to get around. It's also by far the most expensive, and only a very small proportion of Latin Americans can afford to travel this way, although a new generation of budget airlines are starting to change that; among the pioneers of low-cost, no-frills air travel in the region are GOL in Brazil and Volaris in Mexico. Flying is an excellent way of avoiding exhausting overland journeys and saving time if you're trying to fit a lot into a relatively short trip – a one-hour flight between Lima and Cusco in Peru, for example, can cost as little as US$100, not much when you consider that the alternative is an exhausting bus journey lasting at least twenty-four hours. And although you'll miss out on many of the scenic views at ground level, many flights – especially those passing over the high peaks of the Andes or across the endless green carpet of the Amazon rainforest – offer breathtaking views.

You can often book internal flights from home when you book your outward flight (see pp.48–51): though this will cost more than booking in Latin America itself, it's worth doing if you're short on time and want to travel on popular routes, which may be booked up well in advance. Several airlines offer **internal airpasses** at good rates to tourists, which can be worthwhile if you're intending to cover a lot of ground in as short a time as possible (for more on airpasses, see p.51).

In some remote regions like the Amazon you can also travel in small **light aircraft** that carry only five to twelve passengers. Though expensive, this is an exciting way to travel and can save days of arduous overland travel; in some cases it's also the only way to reach the most remote (and therefore most pristine) national parks and wilderness regions.

When using Latin American airlines, the following tips should make your trip easier:

- Some of the airlines flying internal routes are small operators with minimal backup both on and off the ground, so don't expect them to be as efficient or punctual as airlines back home.
- Not all Latin American airlines have the same safety standards as what you're accustomed to at home, and some have poor records: if in doubt, check with your embassy before you book, or visit Ⓦwww.airsafe.com, which lists the safety records of many Latin American airlines.
- It's often easier to book air tickets through a reliable local travel agent for a small fee.
- Having booked a seat, you often need to reconfirm with the airline before travel. Check before you book, and make a careful note of the number you'll need to ring to reconfirm.
- Flights can be cancelled or delayed at short notice due to weather conditions or due to technical problems or lack of aircraft. Build as much flexibility into your itinerary as you can, and, if possible, avoid relying on an internal flight to get you back to the capital on the day your international flight home departs.
- Overbooking – where more tickets are sold than there are seats on the plane – is also often a problem, so make sure you reconfirm,

www.roughguides.com

Squaring up to Bluefields

Tourism is still very much in its infancy throughout Nicaragua, so getting around can require a lot of patience and a good sense of humour, as my friend and I discovered when we flew from Managua to the ramshackle Caribbean town of Bluefields, named after seventeenth-century pirate Abraham Blauwveld.

The *Bluefields Express* was the name of a passenger ferry that used to make its way from the town of Rama to Bluefields (96km away) until it was found in a forest after Hurricane Joan in 1988. You can still travel this journey by boat, or you can fly on one of the most un-aerodynamic aeroplanes you are ever likely to see, also called the *Bluefields Express*.

My friend's aversion to small planes became apparent as soon as we saw the "flying box". He tried to pluck up some Dutch courage with the aid of Nicaragua's lifeblood Flor de Cana rum. Meanwhile, the rum seller had donned his DJ hat and was playing an old Sandinista favourite, aptly titled "Come Take a Ride on The Bluefields Express". The locals literally danced onto the aircraft. I sensed my friend was not in a dancing mood, so I handed him a copy of the local paper to help keep his mind off the flight ahead. It might have worked, had the leading article not been about a man who had taken this same flight one week previously and covered himself in gasoline. Threatening to set himself alight, he demanded to be taken to Costa Rica and then proclaimed to be a "saviour, sent by the Lord". Luckily all passengers survived and the man was arrested, but it did take a while for my friend to see the humour behind the irony.

Rafe Stone

and check in as early as possible as boarding passes are usually issued on a first-come-first-served basis.

● In some countries you have to pay a domestic airport tax before flying. This is often payable only in cash, so make sure you have enough with you before heading to the airport.

Long-distance buses

Most Latin Americans rely on long-distance **buses** when it comes to making extended journeys, and travelling this way is one of the most enjoyable (and also sometimes the most exasperating and exhausting) experiences the region has to offer – all of human life is jammed together, often with a few chickens or pigs thrown in for good measure, travelling at a pace slow enough to really appreciate that landscape you're passing through. The buses are often a sight in themselves, painted with bright slogans and designs and with lavish handmade consoles around the driver, complete with statues of the Virgin Mary that light up when the brakes are applied. Bus travel is also extremely good value – for example, travelling from one end of Peru to the other, a distance of about two thousand kilometres, will cost you less than US$40.

The quality of buses varies enormously both within and between countries. The best ones – variously described as *Pullman*, *primera clase* or *de lujo* – are modern vehicles with air conditioning or heating, comfortable reclining seats, plenty of legroom, chemical toilets, television and video, and even waitresses serving drinks to passengers. These are more common on major inter-city routes and in more developed countries. They tend to be fairly punctual and make fewer stops, meaning that they're faster, but they also tend to cost more than less luxurious buses. At the other extreme are ageing buses with dodgy engines, cracked windscreens, ripped seats and balding tyres; many are old school buses from the US, or even flat-bed lorries fitted with seats.

When there are a number of different bus companies operating the same route, it's worth trying to get a look at the bus before buying a ticket and choosing the one that looks in best condition. These buses tend to stop frequently en route to pick up passengers, who are crammed into every available space. One popular joke asks: "How many passengers fit in a Peruvian [or Bolivian, etc] bus?", with the inevitable answer, *unito mas* – "just one more!"

Seats at the back are always the bumpiest, while those at the front afford the best view of the driver's technique and an earful of his favourite music. Latin American buses are generally designed for smaller physiques – many are made in Japan but refitted with smaller seats to allow for extra passengers – so don't underestimate the stamina required for long journeys, particularly if you're relatively large.

Any journey over four hours or so is likely to involve a meal stop at a roadside restaurant. You'll rarely be told how long this will last, so keep an eye on the bus lest it leaves without you. These meal stops are usually the only opportunity you'll get to relieve yourself, so think carefully before drinking that extra beer or cup of coffee. Anywhere the bus stops it's likely to be boarded by people selling drinks, snacks, sweets, complete meals and whatever is the local speciality or produce of the region you're passing through. It's worth carrying some **food and drink** with you on long journeys, however, as you may not like or trust what's on offer at the roadside, and you never know when a breakdown or other delay might leave you stranded and hungry. It's also worth keeping some warm clothing or even a sleeping bag or blanket with you on the bus, even if it's extremely hot when you set off – nightfall or a climb in altitude can send temperatures plunging, and powerful air conditioning can leave you shivering even as the temperature soars outside.

Generally speaking, journeys are measured in time rather than geographical distance. On well-paved roads between major cities and in more developed countries, buses make good time, but elsewhere roads are often simply rough tracks through tortuous terrain, and what looks like a short distance on your map actually takes far longer to cover than a much greater distance on a good road through flat country.

"Fe en conductor"

Antigua's bus station is located at the market, and it's a hectic place. There are no first-class buses here, only crazily painted old school buses, known fondly as "chicken buses", that make their way around locally or (by some miracle) to far-flung places. Suffice it to say, the adage "Old buses don't die – they go to Guatemala" rings true. It is a common belief that Guatemala's bus drivers have death wishes. With names like Fe en Dios (Faith in God) and Mi Esperanza (My Hope) painted on the windshields, it's easy to wonder if you'll make it to your destination in one piece.

When the bus to Guatemala City pulled away from the curve, there were eight of us in my row – three on my side, and a family of five on the other. The other rows were just as packed, and there were a dozen people standing. It wasn't until there were about seventy people on the bus – including the very uncomfortable 6' 7" gringo with whom I was travelling – as well as a baby chick (honest), that the driver felt he had enough passengers.

A good part of the road from Antigua to Guatemala City is curvy, with some incredibly steep grades. As we sped along I grabbed the only free spot on the seat in front of me and held on for dear life; I felt many things – disbelief, discomfort, amusement, fear, nausea. After a while, I put my faith in the driver (Fe en conductor), as one has no choice but to do, and within an hour, we were nearing my stop. When the moment of truth came, I shoved my way past several tightly packed people and practically fell out the back door onto the street, so very happy to be alive, as the bus pulled away.

Julie Feiner

Punctuality varies greatly between different countries – Chilean buses almost always leave on time, for example, whereas buses in rural Peru frequently leave long after the man who sells you the ticket tells you they will. Often buses will leave only after hours of futile driving around town hooting loudly to conjure up nonexistent passengers, but if they're full, they may even leave early.

Once underway, further delays can be caused by poor road conditions, landslides, police or customs searches, or simply by the driver's desire to spend an hour with his girlfriend in a town en route. All this can be very frustrating, of course, but if you can it's best to take delays with the calm, fatalistic approach adopted by many Latin Americans – if you always expect journeys to take longer than expected, it's a pleasant surprise when you arrive as scheduled.

On long inter-city routes you'll often have the option of **travelling overnight**. Some travellers favour this as a way of saving money on accommodation and making extra time for sightseeing at their next destination. But it means you miss out on the scenery, and unless you're in a luxury bus with fully reclining seats, it can be difficult to sleep in cramped conditions and on bumpy roads, leaving you tired and washed-out when you arrive. You're also more vulnerable to theft, whether by bandits stopping the bus or sneak thieves filching your bag while you sleep, and drivers are far more prone to potentially fatal accidents when travelling by night.

Most larger towns and cities have one or more **bus terminals** for long-distance buses (*Terminal de Buses* or *Terminal Terrestre* in Spanish, *Rodoviária* in Brazil), though in some places buses depart from various offices scattered around town. Usually there's an information desk of some kind, as well as left-luggage offices, restaurants, and cheap (though often insalubrious) accommodation close by. You'll often have to pay a small terminal tax on departure.

Generally speaking it's a good idea to book a seat in advance if you can, though on busy routes served by frequent buses this isn't always necessary – just turn up and buy a ticket for the next departure. If you're travelling from a small town between major destinations or in a remote region where traffic is scarce, your best bet is often to flag down anything passing in the right direction, even though this may involve standing up for some time until a seat becomes available. During public holidays and fiestas people travel in great numbers, and bus tickets can be hard to come by even though prices are often higher.

On more luxurious inter-city buses, your **luggage** will usually be put in a locked compartment under the bus, and you'll be given a ticket with which to claim it at the end of the journey; the compensation this ticket entitles you to if your bag goes missing is paltry, but the system is usually pretty safe. On more basic buses, your bag will often be slung on the roof, it's worth keeping an eye out of the windows when the bus stops to make sure no one takes it accidentally or on purpose. It's not a bad idea to cover your backpack with a sack (available in any market) to protect it from dust, rain, oil and prying fingers. If you're travelling light, you can keep your luggage with you on your seat, and it's worth keeping valuable or fragile items with you in your hand luggage anyway, to prevent theft. For more on backpack security, see 95.

In countries and regions where the tourist infrastructure is more developed, private companies operate special **tourist bus services** exclusively for foreign visitors. These offer a direct, hassle-free and usually faster service between main tourist destinations. The downside is they're more expensive and they deprive you of the colourful (if sometimes infuriating) experience of sharing your journey with ordinary Latin Americans.

Lorries and trucks

In remote areas, and particularly in poorer countries, passengers often travel in heavy goods **lorries** or **trucks** rather than buses. These usually start and stop in designated areas, and pick up passengers from the roadside along the way. There are no timetables, so asking local advice is the key to travelling this way. Sometimes the lorries are specially converted for passengers and fitted with basic seats, but usually you'll simply be standing in the back or sitting on top of the cargo or on a wooden plank placed across the top. On a good day, travelling in the back of an open-top truck with the wind in your face and 360-degree views is a fantastic experience – for the first hour at least. After that the dust, hard wooden seats (when there are any seats at all), exposure to the elements and extremely bumpy ride start to take their toll. Lorries are also slower and generally more dangerous than buses, and stop more frequently. Still, travelling by lorry is a quintessential Latin American experience that's worth trying at least once. For shorter journeys in remote areas, smaller pick-up trucks, known as *camionetas* in Spanish, also carry passengers; these share the same drawbacks and pleasures as lorries, but are slightly faster and less bumpy.

Is it safe?

There is no escaping the fact that road travel in Latin America is often a hair-raising experience, though safety records are generally better in richer countries and regions with more developed infrastructure such as Argentina, Chile and Brazil. Buses and other vehicles often travel far too fast for the conditions – overtaking on blind corners is a regular occurrence – and drivers are frequently poorly trained and work long hours without sufficient sleep. Road conditions can be appalling and vehicles poorly maintained, so not surprisingly, **accidents** do happen – you only need to look out for the white crosses beside the road that mark where the victims of previous accidents have died to realize that bus travel involves a greater degree of danger in Latin America than it does at home. Statistically, however, the risk remains small, and you should remember that even after buying a ticket you can still choose not to climb on board the bus – if it looks too dangerous or the driver appears drunk, it's best to follow your instinct and stay put or travel in a different vehicle.

Trains

Travelling by **train** is often the safest and most memorable way of getting around Latin America, and usually considerably more comfortable than going by bus. Unfortunately, railway travel is very much in decline across Latin America, and many networks have been abandoned, partly as a result of privatization and the withdrawal of government subsidies, but mostly because bus travel along the ever-increasing road network is

Top train rides

Copper Canyon Railway Starting on the Mexican Pacific coast at Los Mochis, this line clings to the wall of the dramatic 2000-metre-deep canyon of the Río Urique, known as the Copper Canyon, as it climbs up to cross the continental divide amongst the peaks of the Sierra Madre before reaching the city of Chihuahua.

Cusco to Machu Picchu This train is the only way to reach the fabled Lost City of the Incas without walking the Inca Trail and is a spectacular journey in its own right, climbing up switchbacks from the city of Cusco and passing high Andean peaks that flank the Sacred Valley before plunging down the deep, narrow ravine of the rushing Río Urubamba to the foot of the ruins at Aguas Calientes.

The Old Patagonia Express A narrow-gauge steam train made famous by Paul Theroux's (rather disparaging) book of the same name, the Old Patagonia Express is a classic South American train journey, lurching across the arid steppe of northern Patagonia for a 1650-kilometre stretch between Esquel and El Maitén.

Panama Railroad The Panama or Trans-Isthmian railroad was the first railway to cross the American continent between the Atlantic and Pacific oceans when it was completed in 1855 at great financial and human cost. It now runs through pristine rainforests alongside the Panama Canal and has recently reopened as a tourist attraction, making it one of the best ways to experience that most impressive of waterways.

Uyuni to Calama Running from the railway junction of Uyuni in Bolivia, this route runs across the dramatic, bleak lunar landscape of the high Altiplano, passing the southern edge of the Salar de Uyuni, the world's largest salt lake and between snowcapped volcanic peaks before crossing the border and descending to the Chilean town of Calama.

generally cheaper and faster. Fortunately governments are waking up to the fact that many foreign visitors prefer to travel by train, and in many countries the most spectacular stretches of line have been preserved as tourist attractions even though most local cargo and passenger traffic now goes by road.

Though they vary between countries and lines, ticketing systems usually involve two or more **classes**: the most luxurious and expensive are tourist-only carriages featuring comfortable seats, heating or air conditioning, restaurant cars, waiter service and additional security; at the other extreme are second-class carriages with hard seats and few facilities which are usually packed to the seams with local passengers sitting, standing and hanging off the sides or on the roof. Buying tickets for the former is usually easy and can also be done through tour agencies as well, while getting tickets for the latter can involve arriving at the station before the ticket office opens and lengthy queuing to get a seat, especially at small intermediary stations. Security issues on trains are fairly similar to those on long-distance buses, except that you'll usually have your luggage in the compartment with you, in which case it's worth locking your backpack to the luggage rack and keeping small bags away from windows at stations.

Boats

Travelling by **boat** can be one of the most exciting ways to get around Latin America. In some regions – particularly among the many offshore archipelagos along the Pacific and Atlantic coasts and throughout the Amazon Basin – it's often the only way of getting around without flying and is usually cheaper than taking a plane – many services are scheduled and depart from official docks, but you can also hire a boat or pay for a ride on anything heading your way. There's a huge range of memorable boat journeys you can make in vessels ranging from the modest motorized dugout canoes which ply the Amazon backwaters to luxury tourist yachts and ships which cruise around the Galápagos Islands and the glaciers of Patagonia. Whatever kind of boat trip you take, however, bear the following points in mind:

- Take a sun hat, sunscreen and sunglasses, as reflected light off the water increases the effect of the sun while cool breezes can disguise its intensity.
- It gets cold at sea, so keep warm clothing close at hand. Waterproof clothing is also a good idea on sea, lake and river trips, as even if it's not raining, you can easily get soaked by spray.
- It's a good idea to take seasickness pills with you for sea voyages, even if you've never suffered before.
- Even if you're a strong swimmer, it is best to make sure life jackets are available before you depart.

Best boat trips

Amazon canoe trips For a closer look at Amazonian wildlife, you can't beat a trip in a motorized dugout canoe along one of the minor tributaries in the Upper Amazon – you can do this either by travelling in a canoe used for local transport, as part of an organized rainforest tour, or by hiring a boat yourself. One of the most spectacular of these journeys is the trip down the Alto Madre de Dios and up the Río Manu into the pristine Manu National Park in southern Peru.

Galápagos cruise A week-long cruise exploring the unique and astonishing wildlife of the Galápagos Islands, 900km off the coast of Ecuador, is one of the world's finest boat trips, though the cost may stretch your budget to the breaking point.

Panama Canal A one-day cruise along the Panama Canal is the best way of appreciating the magnitude and surprisingly rugged beauty of one of the greatest engineering feats of all time. With a little luck you might even get taken on as a line handler on a yacht and be paid for the privilege of sailing down the canal.

San Rafael Glacier The 200-kilometre trip from the port of Chacabuco through the spectacular fjords and islands of southern Chile and along the seemingly unnavigable Río Tempranos into the iceberg-choked Laguna San Rafael, at the foot of the giant glacier of the same name, is one of South America's most magical boat journeys.

- Put cameras and other valuables in plastic bags or other waterproof containers to protect them.
- On longer trips, take your own food and water, as the quality of what's available on board can be poor. Boats sometimes break down or get delayed by bad weather or other factors, so your journey may take longer than expected.
- On long river trips in the Amazon, you should take along your own hammock for sleeping in, ideally fitted with a mosquito net – both are available in most river ports. Most boat captains will let you sleep on board for a day or two while waiting for departure – a good way to save money on hotels.
- For Amazon river trips you may have to wait around a day or two (or longer in remote towns) for a departure. The naval port authority office can usually tell you which boat is likely to leave first.

City transport

Getting around the teeming cities of Latin America can be an intimidating experience. Most have grown incredibly quickly in recent decades, and underfunded and overloaded **public transport** systems struggle to cope with the near-impossible task of moving millions of people around every day. The capitals of more developed countries like Buenos Aires or Mexico City boast modern **subway systems**, but in most Latin American cities urban transport is dominated by a seemingly chaotic array of **buses** and **minibuses**.

However, despite any initial bewilderment, after a few days you'll most likely be able to work out which routes will take you where you need to go. Indeed the process of finding your way around by public transport can be a great way of exploring a new city, even if it means getting on the wrong bus a few times. If all this seems too daunting, or you're short on time or concerned about security, you'll be better off relying on taxis. These are generally plentiful and inexpensive, particularly if you are sharing the fare with one or more other travellers.

Local buses

Most Latin American cities are served by a mixture of large and small buses – often former US school buses or ageing colossuses which lumber around belching diesel fumes as they ferry people in and out of town from outlying suburbs. These are supplemented by an ever-increasing number of **minibuses** and vans known as *combis*, *micros* or *colectivos*, which race around shorter fixed routes, picking up passengers at every street corner.

Fares on all these vehicles are extremely low, but finding out which one will take you where you want to go can be very difficult – official bus stops are rare, and even then they're unlikely to display details of which buses stop there; bus timetables or maps of local services are even harder to come by, if they exist at all. Details of transport to popular tourist destinations, however, should be fairly easy to come by – ask at the local tourist office or in your hotel, or check your guidebook. Many buses have their main destinations written on the windscreen, while their conductors or fare collectors (often children) hang out of the open door at every stop shouting their destinations at the top of their voices. Drivers, conductors and other passengers are generally helpful, though rush-hour commuters around the world aren't known for their patience and Latin America is no exception. The following tips should help you survive the chaos:

● Carry plenty of small-denomination coins or notes, as getting change can be a nightmare.
● Give yourself as much time as you can and keep calm – you'll soon be nipping around town like a local.
● Be wary of pickpockets. Keep your valuables hidden away.
● Most buses and minibuses don't have room for any luggage: if you occupy space that could be filled by another passenger you'll be expected to pay double. If you're travelling with large bags you're better off taking a taxi.

Taxis

Taxis are plentiful and relatively **inexpensive** throughout Latin America – prices vary between cities and countries, but generally speaking a taxi ride in a city centre never costs more than a few dollars, offering a fast, convenient and relatively safe way of getting around, particularly if you're sharing the cost with other passengers. In wealthier countries and larger cities taxis are licensed and marked as such, and have radio controllers, but in many places anyone with a car can become a taxi driver simply by putting a sign in the windscreen of their private car – often the two types of cab operate alongside each other. Informal taxis tend to be cheaper but less reliable. Many Latin Americans from all walks of life moonlight as taxi drivers in their private cars to supplement their meagre incomes, which can make for far more interesting conversation than you usually get from taxi drivers at home.

If you're travelling with heavy luggage, particularly when you've first arrived – and above all at night – it's a good idea to take a taxi straight to your hotel and dump your bags rather than risking public transport – think of the fare as an insurance policy. It's not unknown for taxis to be used by criminals as a means of robbing unwary passengers, but you can reduce the risk of this by telephoning for a cab from a reputable company. In some cities taxis are equipped with meters, but otherwise fares are based on distance or a zone system, though they're generally negotiable. There's a strong tendency to overcharge foreign tourists, so it's best to agree the fare before you set off. You can get an idea of how much it should cost by asking other travellers or at your hotel. **Fares** tend to increase late at night and during public holidays, and taxis to or from international airports (see pp.107–108) usually charge fixed and relatively high fares. In some cities, special tourist taxis congregate outside upmarket hotels and major tourist attractions; these tend to charge far more than ordinary taxis.

If you want to see a lot of sights in a short time, it can be a good idea to hire a taxi for a few hours or a day (or even longer; see below) to take you around town – you can usually negotiate a reasonable rate, especially where business is slow, and with luck you may even find that your driver acts as a good impromptu tour guide.

In some countries taxis are treated almost as a form of public transport: fares are charged per person, and you may be asked to share your cab with a stranger, though you can always refuse this if it makes you uncomfortable. In some places you'll also find **collective taxis** (*colectivos*), which run along fixed routes picking up and dropping off passengers rather like a bus.

Motorbike taxis

In some cities and towns – especially in towns in the Amazon with poor or no road connections to the outside world – motorbikes operate as taxis, offering an exciting but risky way of getting around. These are always cheaper than cars and often faster, and are a good option if you're travelling alone. Obviously they can't carry much luggage, though that rarely stops them trying – if you have a backpack you may have to carry it on your back while riding pillion, which is uncomfortable and precarious. Negotiate the fare before you get on, as with conventional taxis, and always use a helmet if one is available.

Vehicle rental

Renting a **car** is relatively expensive in Latin America but does offer the freedom to visit areas that are otherwise difficult or impossible to reach by public transport. **Costs** vary between countries and regions, but generally speaking you'll be looking at around US$50 per day for a small car; much more for a large vehicle or four-wheel drive (4WD). Most capitals have branches of international rental companies such as

Hertz, Budget and Avis, which means you can book your vehicle in advance from home, but these places are usually more expensive than local companies. As with pretty much everything in Latin America, prices are flexible, so shop around for a good deal and be prepared to negotiate. Obviously sharing the cost and the driving with one or more other travellers makes renting a car cheaper and more attractive. To rent a car you'll need to be over 25 and to have an **international driving licence**. You'll also need a credit card or large quantity of cash as a deposit. Many companies require you to take out additional **vehicle insurance** as well as third party, so make sure you read the small print and know exactly what is covered and what you may be liable for in case of an accident. Renting a car on a casual basis and driving without proper insurance is a bad idea. Most of the time and in most places, if you do want to travel by car you're better off hiring a car with a driver to take you around. This doesn't usually cost much more than renting a car, even though you'll have to pay for the driver's meals and accommodation costs on longer trips, and it means you can sit back and enjoy the scenery. A local driver will probably know the way (or be better at asking if he or she doesn't), and will often have good suggestions about side trips. Obviously you should still check that the car is roadworthy and the driver sober and competent.

Buying a car is only really a worthwhile option if you're staying in one country for a long time, ideally as a resident rather than on a tourist visa, and even then it involves considerable hassle, especially when you come to sell it at the end of your stay. It's possible to drive from the US into Mexico (beyond the immediate border area; see p.43) and on into Central America, but this involves considerable expense and bureaucratic hassle; shipping a car to Latin America entails even more trouble and expense, and really isn't worth it unless you absolutely must have your own vehicle.

If you do decide to drive yourself, the following tips should help:

- Make sure you know the legal speed limits and other requirements, and be aware that many local drivers regularly ignore road signs and traffic regulations, and may not even have driving licences, never mind insurance.
- Find out the local rules of the road. Your guidebook should have some information about these, although be aware that Latin American drivers often show scant regard for official rules – watch how people drive before attempting it yourself.
- Inspect the rental vehicle carefully before you accept it and make a note, signed by the owner, of any scratches or dents, so you don't get charged for these when you return it.

▲ Riding to school, Banos, Ecuador

- Check things you would take for granted on a rental vehicle at home: the lights, horn, windscreen wipers, door locks, petrol cap, seatbelts, and so on.

- Make sure you know how to open the bonnet (hood) and check the spare tyre, jack and toolkit.

- Read the small print on the contract carefully, checking what the insurance covers and what the excess is – the amount you'll have to pay in case of an accident.

- Carry your passport, licence and all documents related to the vehicle with you at all times, as you'll often have to show them to police at roadblocks and impromptu checks. Failure to do so can lead to a bureaucratic nightmare, or at least having to pay a bribe.

- Make sure the rental agency gives you a 24-hour emergency telephone number.

- Secure parking is often a problem, so stay in hotels with garages or car parks. Don't leave a parked vehicle unattended for long, and never leave anything valuable in it. In many cities street children offer to watch over cars in return for a small tip, a service that's well worth taking up.

- Pay close attention when you buy gas, and make particularly sure that the pump gauge has returned to zero before you're served.

www.roughguides.com

Motorbikes

Motorbikes are rarely available for rent in Latin America, and when they are it's usually on an informal basis, often from the same people who act as motorbike taxi drivers. All the tips for driving a car in Latin America also apply to motorbikes, with the added proviso that driver and passenger should always wear helmets and cover up, even if not required to by law. Pillion passengers also need to be careful to avoid leg burns from the exhaust pipe. Be aware that unpaved roads are difficult to ride on and can be very unpredictable, turning from dust to mud depending on weather conditions. Riding a motorbike in Latin America is not for beginners.

Bicycles

Bicycles are available to rent in a growing number of tourist centres in Latin America, with the emphasis particularly on **downhill mountain biking**, which involves taking a bus or truck ride up to a high pass on a mountain road and riding down the other side. This is easiest to do on a guided excursion with a tour agency, but you can easily do it yourself by renting the bike and using public transport. Unsurprisingly the Andean countries – Ecuador, Peru, Bolivia, Chile and Argentina – are the best and most popular places to do this, as they feature innumerable downhill rides, including some of the longest, most exciting and most scenic descents in the world.

For longer trips you're better off bringing your own bike from home, as buying a good-quality bike or renting one for long periods is likely to end up costing you more. Most airlines are happy to carry a bike, often for no extra fee, if you ask them in advance and pack the bike in a bike box. You should bring the best machine you can afford, plus extras like panniers, lights and a strong lock; make sure you also bring plenty of spare parts, and ensure that you're capable of carrying out minor repairs yourself. Though dust, wind, rain, heat, high altitude and unpaved roads mean bicycle touring is often hard work, it is nonetheless one of the most enjoyable ways of travelling around at a slow pace, giving plenty of contact with local people and allowing you to go pretty much at your own pace. If the going gets too hard, you can always stick your bike on top of a bus and relax for a while. For more information, see *Latin America by Bike, A Complete Touring Guide*, by Walter Sienko (Mountaineers Books, US, 1993).

Though common in smaller towns, suburbs and rural areas, bicycles are rarely used as a means of getting around in larger towns or cities, as almost no provision is made for cyclists and the snarling traffic makes riding very dangerous. If you do decide to ride a bike, whether for a day's easy riding, for a hardcore downhill run or for some long-distance touring, bear the following in mind:

- If you rent a bike, try it out before parting with your money, carefully checking the wheels, brakes and gears, and making sure the seat is set at the right height.
- Protect yourself from the sun and carry plenty of water – cycling is thirsty work.
- Carry a pump and a puncture-repair kit or spare inner tubes.
- Local mechanics are usually masters of improvisation when it comes to fixing bikes, but spare parts are difficult to come by, so if you're bringing a bike from home, bring plenty of spares.

Hitchhiking

The cost of transport in Latin America is so low that **hitching** isn't really necessary for tourists, though in out-of-the-way places when the last bus has gone, no taxis are available and there's still a long way to go, it can become the only option. In such circumstances, local drivers who pick you up will anyway expect you to pay something close to what the bus fare would have been – the distinction between public and private transport is a hazy one in Latin America, and in remote regions private vehicles often carry paying passengers. Hitchhiking on roads where public transport is also available is unlikely to get you far for free and involves a greater degree of risk than doing the same thing at home. If you must hitch, never do so alone and, if you're a woman, never do so unaccompanied by a man. If you are suspicious of a person offering you a lift, don't get into the vehicle.

Walking

With all these different means of transport available, don't forget the simplest and cheapest way of all – whether it's a short stroll around a city centre or a long hike in the mountains, **walking** is one of the best ways to enjoy Latin America. If you are planning to do much walking it's a good idea to bring **hiking boots** or at least robust walking shoes with you. When walking around in towns and cities, be very cautious when crossing roads, as Latin American drivers show scant regard for pedestrians and often ignore road signals. For longer walks in rural areas – even for just a few hours – it's important to be properly equipped with warm clothing, rain gear and/or sun protection, as well as food and plenty of water. A huge range of tour companies – both at home and in Latin America – offer organized treks, which take all the hassle out of arranging things like tents, guides and mules, and are often the best way of getting into the most remote and beautiful places.

www.roughguides.com

Organized tours

Throughout Latin America there are an ever-increasing number of national and local **tour companies** and **travel agents** offering all manner of organized trips, from brief city tours to hardcore wilderness adventures. You may leave home swearing to do everything independently, but once you're in Latin America you'll often find it's easy, convenient and relatively inexpensive to go on an organized trip. They're a particularly good way of visiting remote attractions that are otherwise difficult to reach – indeed, many of Latin America's finest attractions can only realistically be reached on a guided tour. Going with a local guide who knows the area and speaks the language can also make it far easier to visit regions where foreigners might otherwise be treated with suspicion or worse, and by acting as a mediator a good guide can give an insight into the lives of local people.

Many tour companies also offer a range of excellent **activities** that are very difficult to do on your own or which require specialist equipment that you're unlikely to be carrying in your backpack, such as climbing, trekking, mountain biking, kayaking and whitewater rafting. If you're contemplating taking an organized tour, bear the following in mind:

- A day or half-day city tour can be a very good way of orienting yourself in a place before setting out to explore on your own, and allows you to see far more than you'd manage in the same time travelling by public transport.
- Unless you have abundant cash, experience and equipment, an organized tour is often the only way to reach many of Latin America's best national parks and wilderness areas.
- Not all tours are luxurious (and therefore expensive) – indeed many are budget trips aimed squarely at backpackers.
- Going on an organized tour means you get to share the expense of things like local guides and boat or jeep hire.
- With longer trips, be sure to find out the full details of the itinerary and exactly what's included before you sign up – make sure, for instance, that a "four-day trip" doesn't leave after lunch on the first day and return early in the morning on the fourth.
- In popular tourist centres, tour agencies tend to be very competitive, so shopping around can get you a good deal. The best way to find out which agencies are reliable and have good guides is by asking other travellers.
- Organized tours are definitely not for everyone: you may find they restrict your independence and freedom of movement.

Accommodation

ome of your best and worst memories will be of **hotels** or **hostels** – these aren't just places to sleep, but also where you'll make contact with other travellers, where you'll hang out whilst recovering from long journeys or bouts of illness, or where you'll retreat to if it's pouring with rain or if you simply can't face the outside world. Finding somewhere good to stay is a real bonus and might even shape your itinerary: it can be difficult to leave a place if you've made friends, if the hotel café has food you've been craving or you have an affordable room with a great view. Conversely, if you've heard that a place has nowhere decent to stay, you might be tempted to drop it from your plans.

Accommodation in Latin America ranges in **price** from a few dollars a night in a basic Guatemalan or Bolivian hostel up to several hundred in one of Mexico's chic *haciendas* or a flash hotel in Rio or Buenos Aires. However, it doesn't always follow that the cheapest countries to travel in have the best-value hotels: in general, the lack of demand and competition means that rooms in less-visited places will often be less keenly priced and often of a lower standard than places in popular tourist centres, which are usually packed with affordable and attractive hostels and hotels.

The cost of accommodation will be a major part of your expenditure if you're on a tight budget. Even so, in Latin America you'll have the chance to stay in some amazing places for a fraction of the price you'd pay back home, and it would be a shame to miss out. There's nothing more guaranteed to restore the spirits after a few days of rough travelling than a decent hotel room with comfortable beds and an en-suite bathroom – so try and factor the occasional posh hotel into your budget before you set out. If you're on a moderate budget you'll have a lot more choice, obviously – the difference between a US$10 room and a US$20

www.roughguides.com

can be surprisingly large, although the downside of staying in mid-range hotels is that you might find yourself rather cut off from other travellers. At over US$30 per day in the Andean countries or much of Central America, you can expect something very comfortable indeed, with all the modern amenities, including air conditioning, television and phone. If you're in Chile, Argentina, Uruguay or French Guiana you'll have to shell out at least US$70 to get something similarly comfortable.

Finding somewhere to stay

The last thing you'll feel like doing when you stumble off a plane or bus at the end of a long journey is finding somewhere to stay. Booking a hotel in advance will ease the pain enormously – this is when a good **guidebook** comes into play. Study the town map in your guidebook first and choose an area which has several appealing hotels close together so that if your first choice isn't right you can easily check out others – hotel accommodation is often clustered conveniently either around the major bus station or in the town centre.

It's important to remember, though, that guidebooks aren't infallible, since they rarely have enough space to list every hotel in town and inevitably go out of date between new editions. Once you get on the road, the **travellers' network** is the most up-to-date source of information about good accommodation. In particular, notice boards and visitors' books in gringo hangouts like hostels and internet cafés usually have personal recommendations of places to stay.

At popular tourist destinations, you might be met by **touts** at the bus station. These will often be boys, and in most cases they're genuine and helpful, either taking you to a relative's hotel or to a hotel where the patron will give them a small fee for each guest checked in. Don't be instantly suspicious – many of the places you'll be shown will be fine, and if you don't like the place, you shouldn't feel under any pressure to stay. If you're lucky they might take you to an excellent local guesthouse not listed in any guidebook. In addition, touts can also save you the bother of reading a map and finding your way around an unfamiliar town (although of course you should always try to keep your wits about you and retain some sense of where you are). The usual common sense applies when deciding whether or not to go with a tout: if it's the middle of the night, if you're on your own or if you just don't like the look of the tout, then politely refuse their services. You should be more wary of **airport cab drivers** in large cities, however, who are notorious for telling tourists that the place they're going to doesn't exist or is dangerous, and then suggesting other hotels, many of which are overpriced or miles out of the way (but which pay commission to the driver).

However you intend to find a hotel, it's best to arrive as early as possible at your destination – this will give you plenty of time to orientate yourself and find somewhere you like. Arriving early will also enhance your chances of getting into the better places – popular backpackers' hostels, particularly those in areas with little competition, often fill up as soon as the previous night's occupants have checked out, often around noon. It's worth phoning these places in advance to see if there's room before you go to the trouble of turning up in person. Looking for a hotel in the dark isn't much fun either – if your bus arrives in the early hours of the morning it might be safer to wait until daylight in the bus station (many stay open all night) before you begin your search. It's also worth waiting since if you check in before dawn (usually 5–6am) you may have to pay for a whole night.

There are also times in certain towns during big **festivals** or **public holidays** (see pp.70–73) when every room gets booked out months in advance. If you're planning on visiting during these times, try to sort out accommodation as far in advance as you can. If you haven't done this, however, don't despair: enterprising locals often respond to tourist influxes by offering visitors rooms in their homes or turning their gardens into campsites.

Types of accommodation

Accommodation in Latin America covers a wide spectrum, from five-star hotels to backpacker dormitories; these are detailed below, in roughly descending order of expense.

Five-star hotels and boutique hotels

Latin America's **five-star hotels** tend to be part of **international chains** and are usually located in the hotel zones of capital cities and expensive tourist resorts such as Cancún in Mexico or Brazil's Rio de Janeiro. Often looking like large tower blocks with hundreds of rooms, they have no shortage of creature comforts but little in the way of identifiable Latin American personality – you could be anywhere in the world.

Boutique hotels are a more attractive option, though rarely within the budget traveller's price range (many cost US$150 or over a night). These are always small, beautifully decorated – some by famous interior designers – and elegantly luxurious. Most boutique hotels are located in well-known areas of outstanding natural beauty, classy seaside resorts and quiet colonial towns. Some of the loveliest are restored *haciendas* in Mexico's Yucatán Peninsula while, citywise, Rio de Janeiro and Buenos Aires have a huge range of attractive small hotels.

www.roughguides.com

147

Eco-lodges and estancias

Each year, more and more **eco-lodges** open for business in Latin America. These have become the region's quintessential accommodation choice, especially feted for their well-chosen **locations** and convenient holiday packages which offer full board plus guided walks and other outdoor activities. Many are situated in places of great natural beauty or private wilderness reserves and the best really are worth splashing out for. Their remoteness means that you'll be expected to book in advance, partly so that you can be given a lift to the lodge. In theory, eco-lodges are **environmentally friendly**, though this is not always the case in practice – look out for those personally run by

Our favourite places to stay

- *Casa Na Bolom* (ⓦ www.nabolom.org) is a fascinating cultural centre in San Cristobal de las Casas, dedicated to the Lacandon Mayans of Chiapas. The complex has 16 atmospheric rooms, all decorated with old furniture, books and working fireplaces.

- The river pools of Semuc Champey are one of Guatemala's natural highlights and in the nearby village of Lanquin, *El Retiro hostel* (ⓣ 00 502 7983 0009) has its own pretty setting in meadows by the river. Dorms are basic but the communal space is very attractive with great gringo breakfasts and happy hour drinking sessions that run long into the night.

- In the highland Honduran village of Copán Ruinas (named after the ruined Mayan city close by), *Hacienda San Lucas* (ⓦ www.haciendasanlucas.com) is a wonderful converted farmhouse with cosy rooms, delicious food and an engaging hostess.

- At one end of Little Corn Island, off the Caribbean coast of Nicaragua, the individual cabins of the *Hotel Casa Iguana* (ⓦ www.casaiguana.net) perch on the cliffs – most rooms are spacious and have porches with hammocks. Evening meals, held family-style in the hotel's reception lodge, are a great way to meet other travellers and swap stories

- *Reserva Selva Bananito*, (ⓦ www.selvabananito.com) on the Caribbean coast of Costa Rica between Puerto Limón and Cahuita, is a private rainforest reserve run by a family determined to protect their piece of the forest from loggers. With nothing but trees and dense vegetation as far as the eye can see, there's not much to do but swim, ride, climb trees, hike, or simply kick back and enjoy the green peace.

- Bizarrely situated in the metallic tower of a former US radar station, *Canopy Tower* (ⓦ www.canopytower.com) in central Panama sits high above the forest with bright comfortable rooms and superb birdwatching. The tower is especially popular in March and October, the migrating seasons of hawks and vultures, who pass over in their thousands.

- Some travellers end up staying for several weeks rather than days at the *Platypus hostel* (ⓦ www.platypusbogota.com) in Bogotá, Colombia. The dormitory rooms are basic but the hostel's owner, German Escobar, is a mine of valuable information about the whole country, which makes this place an essential port of call if you're travelling around Colombia.

- One of Venezuela's loveliest stretches of beach, Playa Cepe on the northwest Caribbean coast, is the location for *Posada Puerto Escondido* conservationists and ecologists. Eco-lodges tend to be on the **expensive** side, although some have a range of accommodation with much cheaper options, often in dormitories.

Another way of getting off the beaten track – and a distinctively Latin American one at that – is to stay at an **estancia** in Uruguay, Argentina and Chile. These are working cattle **ranches** where you can join in the daily life of the farm, riding round on horses and seeing the local gauchos (cowboys) at work. Although generally expensive, estancias are usually fairly posh (often similar in style to a big farmhouse), and all meals are included in the price – you may also get treated to an *asado* (barbecue), with delicious beef roasted on a spit over an open fire.

(Ⓦ www.puertoescondido.com.ve). Reached only by boat, the colonial house is set in a cacao plantation and you can arrange to snorkel or dive with the owner who is also a dive master.

- *Karanambu*, (Ⓦ www.karanambu.com) the largest ranch in the Rupununi area of Guyana is also the first to offer nature-based tourism. Its owner, Diane McTurk, is known for her work rehabilitating the local giant river otters – boat trips to watch them play makes the long trip to the isolated ranch worthwhile.
- *Black Sheep Inn* (Ⓦ www.blacksheepinn.com) is an eco-friendly guesthouse whose owners have a strong commitment to the environment. Lodging is in adobe huts, water and waste are all recycled and the food is organically grown in the inn's garden. The inn also has a stunning setting in the dramatic scenery of Ecuador's Central Sierra of Ecuador and is close to crater lakes, sleepy Andean villages and perfectly shaped Cotopaxi volcano.
- *Albergue Ecologico Chalalán* (Ⓦ www.chalalan.com), Parque Nacional Madidi, Bolivia, was established as part of a sustainable living project for local people and is owned and managed by the Quechua-Tacana community of the Tuichi River. Rooms are in traditional Tacana style, with thatched wooden cabins and solar-powered energy, and the lodge overlooks a lake teeming with birdlife.
- *Hacienda Los Lingues* (Ⓦ www.loslingues.cl) is possibly the grandest hotel in Chile. Still inhabited by the aristocratic family that owns it, staying here is more like being a visitor in a large country house than a hotel guest. Rooms are furnished with antiques and family portraits and there are wine cellars, a chapel and library on site. The *hacienda* also breeds some of the finest horses in South America so there are plenty of horseriding opportunities as well as trout fishing, visits to local wine estates and use of the swimming pool and tennis courts. Rates are high but weekend special offers are sometimes available.
- There are numerous eco-lodges in Brazil's Pantanal but *Réfugio Ecológico Caiman* (Ⓦ www.caiman.com.br) is the most luxurious. Vast grounds with amazing views host its own airstrip and several swimming pools. Numerous activities for guests include nocturnal safaris, boat trips and cattle-drives.
- The scenery surrounding Ushuaia, Tierra del Fuego's capital city, is spectacular but the weather is not. Shelter from the frequent howling storms and downpours in the stylish comfort of *Alto Andino* (Ⓦ www.altoandinohotel.com), which has picture windows with wonderful views, a chic bar and all mod cons.

Pensiones, residenciales and hospedajes

Latin America's mid-range and cheap hotels go under a bewildering variety of names: *pensión, posada, albergue, residenciale, hostal* and *hospedaje*. These names are often fairly meaningless, however, covering fairly basic establishments as well as some rather fancy examples. If you're using a guidebook to select a hotel, room rates are a much more useful indication of the type of service you should expect. The most commonly used name for **mid-range** accommodation is **pensión** (in Brazil, *pensão*) – these are usually small, reasonably priced guesthouses run by local families; they invariably have a lot more character than bigger hotels. Rooms vary enormously in quality, though you should get your own bathroom, towels and soap and have your room cleaned daily. Rates sometimes include breakfast.

Residenciales and *hospedajes* are generally **cheap hotels** with a range of accommodation in dormitories and double and single rooms. Many have shared bathrooms only, fairly basic facilities and desultory cleaning. Guests are usually a mixture of budget travellers and young locals on holiday.

Backpacker hostels

It's likely that you'll end up staying at least some of the time in a backpacker **hostel** – a place geared to the needs of foreign travellers on a budget. As well as having some of the most competitively priced accommodation in town (usually a mixture of singles, doubles and dormitories), they're also a major source of information, with English-speaking staff, travellers' notice boards and internet access.

In general, backpacker hostels offer a good way to ease your way into Latin America – or to retreat to if the going gets tough. Almost all offer **good value** for money and have staff who are used to dealing with budget travellers. Many also have lively on-site **cafés** with all the things you've been missing from home on the menu – bacon sandwiches, proper vegetarian food, pasta (even if you're staying elsewhere you'll usually be welcome to come in and check the notice board or visit the café). Don't assume, however, that these places are automatically cleaner or more comfortable than other hotels, and in terms of **security** you should look after your possessions as you would in any other hotel, and with particular care if you're sharing a dormitory. Additionally and increasingly, you'll need to **book** the most popular hostels in remote places in advance

Youth hostels

Youth hostels (*albergues juveniles* or *albergues de la juventud*) exist in Mexico, Costa Rica, Argentina, Uruguay and Chile, which all have

▲ Playa Norte, Isla Mujeres, Mexico

youth hostels affiliated to the Hostelling International organization (ⓦwww.hihostels.com); if you have an **HI card** (which you can either buy in advance or purchase on arrival at your chosen hostel) you'll be entitled to a discount. Standards vary, but most youth hostels are similar to those worldwide, with bunk beds in dormitories, shared cooking facilities and decent rates (US$12–15 a night). Many travellers eschew youth hostels in favour of backpacker hostels (see above), though the former are often just as good value and a better place to meet young Latin Americans.

Dormitorios

Virtually every town in Latin America has one cheap hotel or **dormitorió** – these are often semi-permanent homes to migrant (male) workers who share rooms, string their washing through the corridors and stomp noisily off to work at four in the morning. Although you'll be welcome and rates will be very low – around £3/US$5, you might feel intimidated if you're female and you shouldn't expect high standards of **hygiene** – particularly in the shared bathroom. Occasionally, the town *dormitorió* is not just unsalubrious but also dangerous – in all cases, inspect the premises, management and clientele if

151

Home sweet home

I arrived in El Castillo, a village on the Río San Juan in Nicaragua, intending to stay in a hotel. Over breakfast at a small café, the owner helpfully ran me through the various options. "And finally," he said, "if you want somewhere really clean for a good price you should stay with Doña Luisa, my wife's aunt."

Doña Luisa had the prettiest house in the place, green-and blue-painted clapboard with potted plants in every corner. Though not a hotelier, she was happy to earn a little extra by putting up the occasional tourist – she gave me her absent youngest daughter's bedroom, which had a poster of the Backstreet Boys on the wall, a shelf of white teddy bears and a pile of well-thumbed teen mags. It also had a priceless view right over the river and all for US$5 a night. Thinking I might be bored in the sleepy village, Luisa introduced me to her brother-in-law, who took me on a horse ride over the hills, and to one of her neighbours, who tried to teach me to fish. In the evening she cooked a delicious meal of freshwater lobster and home-made tortillas, while her husband Luis, home from his farm, talked of the old days, of shooting *tigres* (jaguars) in the woods and paddling a canoe downriver for two days to reach the nearest settlement – now a mere two-and-a-half-hour ride in a motorboat. When I left I knew I'd seen a slice of Nicaraguan life I couldn't have experienced in any hotel – and that I'd contributed directly to the local economy.

Polly Rodger Brown

possible before you check in, and if you don't feel safe, don't stay.

Rooms in private houses

Homestays – staying with a local family in their own home (*casas privadas* or *familiares*) – are popular in some parts of Latin America, particularly the poorest countries of Central America and most remote regions. This is a relatively cheap option (approximately US$10–15 for full board and lodging, or less than US$8 for room only), which contributes directly to local communities and – depending on the family setup, of course, and how long you stay for – gives an insight into daily family life that you might not otherwise get.

Homestays are often arranged in combination with a **language course**, so that you can practise what you've learnt outside the classroom, though it's also possible to arrange a homestay for a night or two without studying – either contact a language school in the area you're interested in, ask at the local tourist office for a list of local homestays, or look out for signs on private homes which say *hay cuartos, cuartos para alquilar, se alquila cuartos* (rooms to rent). Some homestays are formal arrangements where you'll get a room and have little or no contact with the family involved while in others, particularly those used by language schools, you'll eat three meals a day with your family, have your clothes washed and even go on outings with family members. In most cases, rooms in private homes are simple but scrupulously clean.

In various parts of Latin America without accommodation for tourists (such as the Solentiname Archipelego in Nicaragua) there might be an informal network of homestays. In this case you'll be met on arrival by family members, often children, who'll take you to their home – and if not, you could try asking around. You shouldn't assume, however, that families will always be willing to take in tourists if you offer to pay – where this is not the norm don't insist or you'll risk causing offence.

Short-stay hotels

Short-stay hotels, which charge by the hour and are euphemistically called "**love hotels**" or motels, exist all over Latin America. They're usually found on the outskirts of towns and advertise themselves with gaudy neon signs and lurid names. If you get stuck with nowhere to stay, don't rule out motels – the staff won't turn you away, and while they won't have the cheapest rates in town, rooms are often good value for money, with en-suite bathrooms and (not surprisingly) comfortable double beds.

Other hotels in Latin America used for short stays include cheap hotels, particularly those situated around bus stations or the local market, which double up as informal **brothels** – this should be fairly obvious when you walk in though, again, you're unlikely to be turned away if you want to stay for the whole night. While some of these places are deeply insalubrious, others are clean and safe, if rather noisy.

Camping and sleeping in a hammock

Camping is obviously one of the cheapest forms of accommodation, although the inevitable hassle of having to carry a tent, sleeping bags, mats and cooking equipment might outweigh the savings you make. Remember too that **organized campsites** only exist in significant numbers in Costa Rica and the countries of southern South America (Brazil, Uruguay, Argentina and Chile). In these countries, where accommodation is relatively expensive and camping is popular with young locals as well as tourists, it's well worth considering – although also bear in mind that the south of Argentina and Chile are freezing cold in the winter (June–Sept). If, on the other hand, you're only going to the region's cheaper Andean countries like Bolivia or Peru, then it's only really worth taking a tent if you're planning on doing a lot of trekking, given the cheapness of accommodation, the lack of proper campsites, and the challenging mountain temperatures. Likely locations for campsites are seaside resorts, national parks and popular scenic areas. Backpacker or youth hostels (see p.150) with gardens often keep some space free for tents.

Camping in the **wild** isn't recommended, since you risk upsetting local landowners (unless you specifically ask permission) and you put yourself at risk of robbery or attack. Never camp on a beach unless

www.roughguides.com

Amazon accommodation

By mid-afternoon, on the first full day of my boat journey from Iquitos to Yurimaguas, the air was still and the deck had become uncomfortably hot. I tried to sleep because I couldn't bear to do anything else, but the children in the hammock "next door" had become restless. The baby was cranky, and in trying to cheer her up her older siblings had become rambunctious, banging me every so often, starting the domino effect; I banged my travelling companion, and he banged the next person, and so on. With so many hammocks crammed into such a small deck area, there was a lot of banging going on. Once in a while a little foot would pop over into my hammock, then an arm. Then I felt tiny little hands below me – the baby was underfoot, with her hair in a ponytail straight up on her head. Suddenly she was swept up and put in the hammock and covered up as if in a cocoon, where she squealed with delight, content with her game of hide-and-seek. Meanwhile her father slept beneath me on his plastic tarp, his head resting on my backpack. It was a lesson in patience, typical of Amazon journeys. Everyone pokes and prods and everyone gets poked and prodded, and people are amazingly tolerant. At bedtime, I realized my neighbours had shifted in such a way that their hammock (holding four of them) was practically on top of me. They were fast asleep, and I could feel the weight of their bodies no matter which way I turned. There was nowhere to go but up, so I raised my hammock and happily drifted off to sleep, no matter that I was completely lopsided.

Julie Feiner

it's standard practice to do so. The exception is if you're on a guided trek, since you'll have safety in numbers and your guide should be able to find a good secure base for the night.

Even cheaper than camping is using a **hammock**. These are ubiquitous in many parts of Latin America, particularly port or riverside towns – and if you're planning any long **river trips** you'll need to take your own. Hostels and other cheap hotels sometimes have a dedicated space for travellers to hang their hammocks or will be happy to let you hang it in a corridor, yard or garden for a few dollars a night. Laid-back **beach resorts** like Tulum in Mexico will have sets of bamboo huts or *cabañas* on the beach furnished with nothing but a pair of hammock hooks. Remember that you'll need to sleep diagonally across a hammock rather than along it if you want to avoid backache, so you'll need one that's a decent size – ask for a *matrimonial* (or couple-sized) hammock.

Inspecting the facilities

Never take a room without inspecting it first. Obviously, if you don't like a room you're shown you're under no obligation to stay, but try to avoid being rude when you leave in case, for any reason, you have to come back.

● Ask if the room you're being shown is the best room they have available. Hotel staff will often show potential guests the worst or most expensive room available first in the hope of getting rid of it. If you don't like the room you're being offered or can't afford the rate, ask to see another one – it's surprising how much rooms in the same hotel can vary in size and price.

- Try to avoid rooms next to shared bathrooms or communal areas unless you fancy spending your entire time listening to the sound of flushing toilets or blaring televisions.

- Check if the bathroom is clean, particularly if it's shared – some are filthy enough to put you off immediately. Also ask if there's hot water and for how long each day, and find out whether towels, soap and toilet paper are provided.

- Sit on the bed to see how comfortable it is – beds in cheap hotels often have thin foam mattresses which sag terribly and give you chronic backache if you stay for several nights.

- Check if there's a fan or air conditioning (fairly essential in a hot climate), turn it on to see that it works without sounding like a traction engine.

- Is the room secure? Make sure the windows close properly, particularly if you're on the ground floor, and that the room can be properly locked.

- Check whether there's a curfew: if you're out on the town, you might not be able to get back in until morning.

Room rates and checking in

Although room rates vary enormously, you ought to be able to find a bed in a hostel dormitory for US$12–15 per night in the most expensive countries in Latin America, while in the cheapest, the same sum will get you a comfortable en-suite room in a small hotel with breakfast included. Don't assume that room rates are standard across a country (sometimes a popular seaside resort will charge twice as much for its rooms as a small mountain village, or vice versa), and don't be surprised if the rates quoted in your guidebook no longer exist – waving your book at a bemused hotel owner won't usually get you anywhere. Having said that, rates are pretty **flexible**. If you're travelling in low season, if the hotel is almost empty or if you're planning to stay for several nights it's always worth **bargaining**; this may save you a dollar or so, although you won't get a huge discount unless you're staying for weeks.

Check-in procedure is fairly standard. If the hotel is full and you arrive early you'll have to wait until guests vacate the rooms before you can check in. Usually you'll be welcome to dump your bags so you can go for lunch while your room is cleaned. Otherwise it's simply a question of filling in a **basic form** with your name, address, nationality and passport number and, in most cases, paying in advance for the room. You shouldn't surrender your passport to hotel reception, and it's unlikely that you'll be asked to do so, unless you choose to put it in the hotel safe for security (for more on hotel security, see pp.180–184).

Showers and toilets

There are a few differences between the showers and toilets you'll be used to at home and those in Latin America. There's no hot water of any kind in many parts of Latin America, partly because of the climate, partly because hot running water is perceived as an unnecessary luxury. If you're staying in a cheap hotel in a warm part of Latin America your shower will invariably only have **cold water**, and although it's a shock to the system at first you'll quickly get used to it. Take showers during the heat of the day if it's too cool in the evenings or upgrade yourself to a more expensive hotel if you really can't bear it. Water pressure is often inadequate too, and hotels almost never have bathtubs.

In colder parts of the continent, cheaper hotels and hostels have come up with a device known to travellers as the "killer" (or "suicide") shower. This involves attaching a small electric unit to the top of the shower that heats the water as it passes through. Most are controlled by water pressure – the slower the flow of water, the hotter it will be. In most cases they're pretty unsatisfactory and provide a thin trickle of lukewarm water at best, and because they consist of a combination of water and electricity they're also highly dangerous and **electric shocks** are not uncommon. Be very careful when using them and if possible wear a pair of flip-flops or rubber-soled shoes – never fiddle with the electric unit while standing in the shower with the water on.

The other thing to know about Latin American **plumbing** is that it's pretty basic and you can't throw anything into the toilet bowl without risking it getting blocked. It's standard practice in virtually every country to put toilet paper, sanitary towels and tampons into a basket beside the toilet (these should be emptied regularly). Don't ignore this custom even if you find it distasteful – the other option, a blocked and overflowing toilet, is far worse.

12

Staying healthy

Despite dramatic extremes of climate, unclean drinking water and often poor standards of hygiene, visitors to Latin America are unlikely to suffer from anything more serious than a bout of **diarrhoea** or a touch of **sunburn**. However, the majority of travellers to Latin America inevitably suffer from the change in environment, usually manifesting itself as diarrhoea and/or nausea and vomiting – both can be very unpleasant, though far from life-threatening (if symptoms persist beyond a few days, though, they could be indicative of something more serious and you should see a doctor). Resign yourself to the fact that you may well lose a few days of your trip to illness, and make sure there's enough flexibility in your itinerary to ensure you don't have to travel when you're feeling awful. And just in case you have the misfortune to suffer a serious health problem, make sure you get a comprehensive **insurance** policy which covers all medical expenses in an emergency, including repatriation – see p.53 for more details.

Although most countries in Latin America don't have free or subsidized health care, **private health clinics** abound in large cities and are often very good. And even the most expensive will be more affordable than their equivalent at home. The prescription system doesn't exist in Latin America, which means you can buy any drug over the counter. Locals frequently don't bother consulting a doctor but instead go straight to the pharmacy, where staff are often very knowledgeable and are used to offering informal diagnoses. It's also worth memorizing the generic names of useful general **antibiotics** (such as metronidazole, trade name Flagyl – useful for clearing up giardia or dysentery), so that you can get the right drug fast.

Latin Americans love discussing medical problems in gory detail. If you do get ill, the staff at your hotel will all have an opinion on what

www.roughguides.com

157

you have, who you should consult and what to take. Most locals, particularly in the countryside, have some idea of natural or **indigenous cures** (usually an infusion made from local plants) – these often work wonderfully well. That said, it's important that you don't self-diagnose if you're feeling very sick – you must consult a professional doctor. Local medical services – public or private – in Latin America will be aware of the diseases listed in this chapter and should be able to treat them adequately.

There are lots of excellent sources of information on travellers' health (see Directory for websites). Books include the *Rough Guide to Travel Health* and *Where There Is No Doctor* (Macmillan Educational), which is particularly good if you're planning to stray far from accessible medical care.

Vaccinations

Unless you're a frequent traveller to the tropics, you'll need several **vaccinations** before you set off. Don't leave them to the last minute – some require more than one dose, others need to be given a few days apart from each other so that they don't cancel each other out or cause reactions, and all vaccinations take several weeks for full immunity to develop; it's best to start getting inoculated around three months before you depart.

You will probably have been inoculated as a child against certain diseases, including diphtheria, polio and tetanus; in these cases you'll require only a **booster jab**, if that. Other diseases that you'll need to be vaccinated against are typhoid and hepatitis. **Combined injections** now exist which lessen the ordeal. Two more vaccinations you might consider having are yellow fever (which is mandatory for visits to some countries; the World Health Organization website, ⓦwww.who.int, has a list of these) and rabies.

If your home country has a public health service, you may be able to get some of your vaccinations (tetanus, for example) **free** or at a greatly reduced cost from your local doctor. Less commonly requested jabs (such as yellow fever) are not always available and will cost as much as going to one of the many **private travel clinics** (see Directory, pp.303–304) which deal exclusively with vaccinations and information about tropical diseases. These clinics have expert staff and generally offer much more rapid and convenient consultations, although prices for ordinary jabs can be much higher than your doctor charges. Additionally, there are several premium-rate phone lines in the UK, North America and Australasia that give specific health advice for travellers, plus various websites where you can pay for an online consultation (see p.304 for details).

First-aid kits

Travel clinics, adventure sports shops and large pharmacies all now sell comprehensive travel health kits with a combination of the following – alternatively, it's easy enough to put together your own:

- Anti-diarrhoeals, for emergencies only, such as unavoidable journeys
- Antihistamines, for itchy bites, rashes and allergic reactions
- Antiseptic cream, very important for the tropics where strong humidity exacerbates the infection of wounds
- Antiseptic liquid soap, the best way to ensure you're really clean
- Insect repellent with DEET
- Painkillers (Ibuprofen, for example)
- Band-aids/plasters in several sizes, a length of bandage, surgical tape and scissors
- Rehydration salts, for coping with the dehydrating effects of diarrhoea and sickness
- Sun block (SPF 15+)
- Sterile needles
- Tweezers, for removing splinters and sea-urchin spines

Antibiotics

Available only on prescription at home, though you may be able to persuade your doctor to give you a course of general antibiotics such as metronidazole or ciprofloxacin (both of which kill diarrhoea-causing bacteria) in advance. Or you could just buy them over the counter in Latin America if and when you need to. It's vital to take the whole course, and make sure you get your illness diagnosed before starting treatment.

Alternative medicine

Increasingly popular, alternative medicine offers, to various degrees of effectiveness, natural treatments – consult your local health food store or homeopath for detailed information. Particularly useful remedies to take include arnica or calendula cream for bruises and bites; echinacea to boost your immune system; citronella, eucalyptus or lavender oils to ward off mosquitoes and other nasty bugs; tea tree oil, which acts as an antiseptic; tiger balm for headaches; and Rescue Remedy, a Bach Flower Remedy which calms the nerves in stressful situations. Additionally, if you're planning on wilderness trekking or going into the jungle for a lengthy period, vitamin supplements, particularly vitamins B and C, will help to keep you healthy.

Diseases you should know about

- **Chagas' disease** (aka American trypanosomiasis) Transmitted by reduviid beetles, also known as "assassin bugs", Chagas' disease is rife in some parts of Latin America (particularly northeastern Brazil) and, though you're unlikely to be affected, can be fatal if left untreated. Try to avoid staying in the adobe or mud huts that the reduviid beetle lives in (if you can't, then be sure to sleep well away from the walls), and if you are bitten, disinfect the bite with antiseptic and don't scratch it. Should a fever develop within ten days, get a blood test as soon as possible – if you have the disease you'll need to be hospitalized. Other symptoms are localized swelling around the bite, swelling of the lymph glands and an itchy rash.

- **Cholera** Cholera is spread by contaminated water or by eating contaminated shellfish and manifests itself as a particularly nasty bout of diarrhoea and/or vomiting. There's currently no effective vaccine – the best way to avoid catching cholera is by being careful about the water you drink. Diagnosis is by stool sample and treatment is with antibiotics such as doxycycline.

- **Dengue fever** A virus spread by the Aedes mosquito, which bites in the early morning or late afternoon. Initial symptoms (similar to those of malaria) typically appear five to eight days after being bitten and include fever, headache, joint pains and backache, as well as short-lived but severe diarrhoea and a fine rash. Diagnosis is made by blood test; you should check for malaria at the same time if you have this particular collection of symptoms. Dengue fever has no specific cure and is usually treated with bed rest. The disease can, however, develop into dengue haemorrhagic fever (though rarely – it most commonly affects children aged 15 and under), which is life-threatening – seek immediate medical attention if you go into shock (characterized by clammy skin, a weak pulse and shallow breathing) or start to bleed from any orifices.

- **Hepatitis** Hepatitis (an inflammation of the liver) exists in several different forms. Hepatitis A is a virus spread by contaminated water or intimate contact; symptoms include nausea, loss of appetite, weight loss, fatigue and abdominal pain and, most distinctively, jaundice, which turns the patient's skin and eyeballs yellow. Hepatitis B is a more severe and longer-lasting form of the disease; it's spread by blood through sexual contact, sharing needles or blood transfusions. Both forms are usually treated with several weeks of bed rest. Effective vaccinations for both hepatitis A and B exist and can be given in one combined shot. Immunization is recommended. Other strains of hepatitis also exist–C, D and E–but have no vaccination.

- **Leishmaniasis** Found in many parts of Central and South America, leishmaniasis is transmitted by sandflies and exists in several forms. Most common in Latin America are the cutaneous and mucocutaneous strains: these cause the sandfly bites to develop into itchy red skin ulcers which can leave severe and permanent scarring. Diagnosis is made by a skin biopsy and treated with a ten-day intravenous course of drugs. There is no vaccine, although sandflies are low-flying, and sleeping above ground level will lessen your chances of being bitten, as will using an insect repellent. Mosquito nets, however, will not protect you, since sandflies are small enough to pass through the mesh.

- **Malaria** See p.162.
- **Rabies** Rabies is spread by the bite of an infected animal (usually a dog) and is a serious paralysing and potentially fatal disease that rapidly becomes incurable. Symptoms initially include fever, nausea and loss of appetite, muscle aches and sore throat; they may also include unpredictable or aggressive behaviour followed by muscle spasms, fear of water and paralysis. A three-dose vaccine exists which will partly protect you against the disease developing, but if you're bitten, even if you've been immunized, you must seek urgent medical attention. Treatment consists of a further course of injections. Thorough cleaning of the wound also helps to reduce the chances of becoming infected.
- **Schistosomiasis** (or Bilharzia) is now the second most prevalent tropical disease worldwide after malaria. Minute larvae that live in fresh water penetrate human skin, grow in the liver, mate and then release their eggs via faeces or urine. An initial itchy rash may be the only specific symptom of schistosomiasis, which can cause kidney failure and damage to the heart, lungs and central nervous system. The disease presents itself 2–12 weeks after exposure to contaminated water. There is no vaccine but the oral drug Praziquantel is an effective cure. Travellers who wade, swim or bathe in fresh water (lakes and rivers) in Latin America are at risk – if any of the above symptoms persist you'll need to undergo screening tests (blood and stools) to detect the disease before treatment.
- **Tetanus** Tetanus spores live in soil, dust and manure and infect humans through open wounds. Symptoms develop following

Footworms in Brazil

When you've finally reached that perfect beach – powdery white sand and palm trees – one of the first things you want to do is kick off your shoes and walk barefoot along the shore. So when I found my beach on an island in Brazil, that's exactly what I did. Two days later I had an itchy big toe and, on examination, a small swelling right by my toenail – it wasn't an insect bite, though. José, the man who ran my hotel, knew what it was as soon as he saw me scratching furiously – "Ah," he said phlegmatically – "you have a *bicho de pé*", which he went on to explain was a footworm, a small maggotty insect fond of crawling into the cracks between human toes and toenails and then moving into the bloodstream. Once I'd recovered from the shock, José explained that I'd have to remove it as soon as possible. "Oh God," I said, "and how do I do that?" Footworms, it appeared, have to be dug out with a thorn from a lemon tree – the native way – or with a sewing needle – the gringo method. However I did it, it wasn't the first and last footworm I dug out of my toe – every evening as sun set, examining my feet for the telltale signs became a nightly ritual. The locals were definitely wearing shoes on the beach for a reason.

Polly Rodger Brown

www.roughguides.com

an incubation period of between five and twenty days and include headache, fever, irritability and jaw-muscle spasms which spread to the neck, limbs and torso and may result in breathing difficulties. Tetanus is potentially fatal, with various complications including blood clots, pneumonia and heart problems; treatment requires hospitalization. Most people in the developed world are vaccinated as children, though you'll need a booster if it's been over ten years since your last immunization.

- **Typhoid** Typhoid is carried in contaminated water or food and, like cholera, is fairly widespread in unsanitary areas. Symptoms are similar to cholera and include fever, headache, lethargy and stomach pains. In some cases, coughing, temporary deafness and pink spots on the torso also occur, and what begin as mild symptoms may deteriorate over two weeks into serious illness. Diagnosis is through a blood or stool test, and the disease can usually be treated with antibiotics such as ciprofloxacin. An effective typhoid vaccine exists, and immunization is recommended.

- **Yellow fever** The yellow fever virus is spread by mosquito bites and is found throughout the Amazon region. Mild though sudden symptoms of fever, abdominal pain and vomiting often disappear rapidly, only to recur in fifteen percent of cases along with jaundice, kidney failure, bleeding and shock. This secondary yellow fever is potentially fatal and there's no specific treatment. There is a vaccine, however, and in various parts of Latin America (specifically Brazil, and in Amazonian areas in general – check with a travel clinic) you may be asked to produce an International Certificate of Vaccination proving that you've been immunized. If you can't, you run the risk of being immunized on the spot in potentially less than sanitary conditions. Immunization lasts for ten years and is recommended.

Mosquitoes and malaria

Malaria, a potentially fatal disease spread by the bite of the female Anopheles mosquito, is one of the world's most **widespread** diseases, with an estimated 300 to 500 million cases every year and between one and three million deaths. Although outbreak patterns change from year to year, parts of Latin America, particularly the **Amazon region**, are generally considered high-risk. There's no vaccine yet and anyone going to tropical or subtropical Latin America should take a course of **preventative drugs** and try to avoid being bitten.

The initial symptoms of malaria are worryingly similar to flu or more general fever. Typically, sufferers start feeling very cold and shiver, then develop a very high temperature and finally begin to sweat – these three stages continue in one- to three-day cycles. There are four different strains of the malaria parasite; the most dangerous, *p.falciparum*, can become potentially fatal in a matter of hours.

Your local doctor and specialized travel clinics, phone lines and websites (see p.304) will have up-to-date advice on **malarial areas** and **anti-malarial drugs**. There is some controversy about anti-malarial drugs because of their side effects and efficacy (none is one hundred percent effective), but all offer at least some (and usually much more) protection against contracting the disease.

Treatments

There are several **anti-malarial drugs** on the market; which one you take will depend on your medical history, where exactly you're going and for how long. The longest established anti-malarial, chloroquine, is also the most widely available, the cheapest and has no significant side effects (it can be taken continuously over a five-year period). However, its heavy use over the years has led to *p.falciparum* (see above) mutating to become chloroquine-resistant and thus rendering chloroquine **ineffective** in many areas. In Latin America, *p.falciparum* exists throughout the Amazon basin (which covers every country in South America apart from Paraguay, Uruguay, Argentina and Chile), and if you're travelling in this region you'll need another anti-malarial.

Of the other drugs currently available, mefloquine (Lariam) is the most effective, can be taken for up to a year and works well against most strains of malaria – although strains are starting to become resistant to it. However, there have been reports of disturbing **side effects**, including hallucinations and psychosis, as a result of taking Lariam – be aware of the risks if you decide to take it. It's also the most expensive anti-malarial. Doxycycline is effective against *p.falciparum* only and can be taken for three months, though its side effects include increased risk of sunburn, nausea and vaginal yeast infections. It's not easily available in the US. Malarone is the most recent anti-malarial on the market, is effective against all strains of malaria and has few side effects – though it shouldn't be taken for more than 28 days.

All anti-malarial courses must be started before you reach the malarial zone, from two days for doxycycline to one to three weeks for mefloquine, and continued for up to a month after you've left. You'll have to pay full price for anti-malarial drugs (and most aren't cheap), but buying them before you set off is recommended since their availability and quality in Latin America can't be guaranteed.

In terms of alternative medicine, a **Chinese remedy**, *qinghaosu* (sweet wormwood) or *artemisinin*, has attracted much interest from the tropical medicine community and is now marketed in various forms – you can buy it online at ⓦwww.OrganicPharmacy.org. or from ⓦwww.Amazon.com. Note however that the World Health Organization recommends taking the drug in combination with other anti-malarials. Demal2000™ is a homeopathic anti-malarial which enables the immune system to develop antibodies to fight the infection. Developed in Indonesia and widely used in the region since 1989, the drug reportedly has very high success rates and is also available for sale online (ⓦwww.blueturtlegroup.com).

How to avoid getting malaria

The best way to avoid getting malaria is to avoid being bitten (and bear in mind that as well as transmitting malaria, mosquitoes may also carry dengue and yellow fever). The following **precautions** will help when in malarial areas:

- Mosquitoes are mainly nocturnal – and malaria-carrying ones particularly love dusk, which is when you're most likely to be bitten. Cover up as much as possible, wearing long-sleeved shirts and trousers tucked into socks. Mosquitoes are drawn to strong dark colours – white is your best bet for keeping them at a distance.
- Buy an effective insect repellent and use it diligently. The best repellents contain varying levels of DEET (from 15 to 100 percent), and although it smells nasty, can sting sensitive skin, and actually melts plastic, it does work (but try not to apply it in a closed environment or near other people, unless you want to asphyxiate them). If you want to use natural repellents, citronella, eucalyptus and lavender essential oils (mixed into a base of oil or water) are effective for several hours. Bizarrely, Avon's Skin-So-Soft moisturizing lotion, available from drugstores in North America (and parts of Latin America), is one of the best repellents of both mosquitoes and sandflies. It's also claimed that mosquitoes love perfume, pregnant women and sweat, but hate the smell of garlic and vitamin B.
- Sleep under a mosquito net – it's best to take your own (those in hotels invariably have holes); good ones roll up into a small and virtually weightless pouch. In addition, soak your net in permethrin – widely available in travel stores – before you set off or choose one that's already been treated. You can also impregnate your travelling clothes with permethrin, which will act as a further line of defence.
- Burn mosquito coils in your room – they're the most popular local form of repellent and so are usually cheap and readily available.

- If you're not on a tight budget, choose a hotel room with **mesh screens** over the windows. Both air conditioning and powerful ceiling fans prevent mosquitoes from getting near you because they find it hard to fly in circulating air currents.
- Even if you're not in a malarial area, mosquito bites can be distressing. If you are bitten, try not to **scratch** the bite – this only spreads any infection further. Calamine lotion, tea tree oil or an antiseptic cream may help to soothe the irritation; if the itching becomes unbearable, **antihistamine** tablets or cream will calm it considerably.
- The website ⓦwww.malaria.org is a good source of information on the disease – otherwise check the general travellers' health websites.

Heat and cold

While all of Mexico and Central America – bar a few mountainous areas – enjoys tropical or semi-tropical weather, South America has extreme differences in temperature, from very hot and dry (in the Atacama Desert of Chile, for example, during the day) to humid (in the Amazon) through to freezing cold in the Andes and Patagonia. Whichever itinerary you plan to take, it's best to consider, and plan for, the intense heat and cold you could potentially encounter once in Latin America.

Sun exposure

Apart from stomach upsets, you're most likely to fall ill during your trip as a result of exposure to the sun. Remember that the sun is at its hottest between 11am and 3pm, and you should try to avoid being outside in direct sunlight for too long during these hours. Bear in mind also that the effect of sun is stronger at high altitudes and anywhere where light is reflected, such as snowscapes, or in and on the water; if you're on a boat, cooling breezes may mask the strength of the sun. Be extra careful in both these environments and **cover up** in a lightweight shirt and long trousers.

When you do venture out into the sun, always use a **sunscreen**, with at least **SPF 15** and choose one that protects against both UVA and UVB rays and is waterproof; this will help protect you against skin cancer and premature ageing – however much you want to return from your trip with a healthy-looking tan, you could be seriously damaging your long-term health if you're not properly protected from the sun's ultraviolet rays. Apply it twenty minutes before you go out and reapply it diligently every couple of hours. Take a large bottle of sunscreen with you from home – it's often very expensive in Latin America – and once on the road, stock up in big cities since smaller places often don't have anything suitable. Also take a sunscreen stick for your lips.

The other important item to take is a decent pair of **sunglasses** with UV-resistant lenses. You may also want to take a **hat** to stop your head getting burnt. If you do get burnt, there's little you can do about it except slather yourself in a soothing after-sun lotion (anything with aloe vera in it is wonderfully cooling), increase your fluid intake (but avoid alcohol) and stay in the shade until the redness and soreness have gone.

Heat and humidity

As well as direct exposure to the sun, you'll also probably have to deal with the overall heat and humidity. Acclimatizing to these takes a while – weeks rather than days – so don't rush around or undertake strenuous exercise immediately after you've arrived. You should also increase your **fluid intake**, and if you do start to feel you're over-heating, bathe frequently in tepid or cool water. **Prickly heat** or heat rash results from inflamed sweat glands, caused by over-exposure or over-exertion in high temperatures, and manifests itself as small itchy pink/red spots on the head, neck, shoulders and other sweaty parts of the body. As well as taking cool showers, treat heat rash by wearing loose lightweight clothing, using talc to keep dry and sooth-ing after-sun creams to stop the itching. **Heat stroke**, by contrast, is a potentially life-threatening condition. If your body temperature rises significantly (above 40°C/106°F) and you experience nausea, sensitivity to light, rapid breathing and, most significantly, stop sweat-ing, you need urgent medical attention.

Hypothermia

At the other end of the scale, in the Andes the temperature can fall well below **freezing**. It may be hot during the daytime in the mountains, but as soon as the sun sets the temperature drops alarmingly fast – if you're out hiking, take layers of **warm clothes** with you. At worst, severe cold can lead to hypothermia (when the human body tem-perature drops beneath 35°C/95°F). Symptoms include slurred speech, stumbling and shallow breathing; if untreated, hypothermia can lead to coma and then death. If you do get very cold, you can warm yourself up by consuming **high-energy foods** like chocolate and hot, sugary drinks (alcohol should be avoided because it dilates blood vessels near the surface of the skin, meaning you actually lose heat). Sharing your companion's body heat (and/or sleeping bag) is another highly effective way of increasing your own body temperature.

Altitude

Altitude sickness, known as *soroche* in Spanish, is caused by insufficient **acclimatization** to high altitudes (over 2500m) and the body's inability to cope with reduced levels of **oxygen**. You should be particularly wary of altitude sickness if you fly into La Paz in Bolivia (3636m), Cusco (3500m), Quito (2800m), Bogotá (2650m) or Mexico City (2400m) – plan on taking things easy for the first few days after your arrival if you're arriving at any of these cities from a low altitude. Symptoms of altitude sickness include persistent headache, vomiting, dizziness and breathlessness. Drinking lots of **water** will help enormously; in Bolivia, the local coca tea (*mate de coca*) is an effective remedy as is chewing coca leaves, widely available in mountain markets, though these are illegal in many other countries. There is also a homeopathic remedy, *coca*, which like other homeopathic remedies is not readily available in most parts of Latin America and should be purchased before you set off.

At very high altitudes (3000m or more, for example when climbing in the Andes) altitude sickness can worsen to become **acute mountain sickness** (AMS), which is much more serious and potentially fatal. Symptoms of AMS, caused by increased fluid and swelling on the brain and lungs, include lethargy and confusion, coughing and a bluish tinge to lips, nails and skin. If you're planning to climb in high altitudes you should be in good physical shape. Spend several days acclimatizing before you set off, limit your ascent to no more than **300m** each day and keep hydrated by drinking at least **three litres** of non-alcoholic fluids a day. The only effective cure for AMS is to descend immediately – even several hundred metres will instantly make you feel better – although the drugs dexamethasone, frusemide and nifedipine (which should only be used under medical supervision) might buy you some time while you descend.

Water

Probably the biggest single health hazard travellers to Latin America face is **contaminated water**, the cause not only of travellers' diarrhoea and dysentery, but also of much more serious diseases like cholera, hepatitis and typhoid. Avoiding contaminated water, however, isn't that easy. Though the water situation has improved considerably in recent years, **tap water** in Latin America isn't always safe to drink. Obviously, you should only drink and clean your teeth with **bottled** or purified water, as well as avoiding **swimming** in fresh water and (although it sounds stupid) taking a shower with your mouth open. In addition, avoid salads, which in most restaurants are washed in tap water, and check that ice and fruit juices (*jugos, licuados* or *batidas*) are made with purified water – this is increasingly the case in places popular with Western tourists.

Bottled water is widely available and inexpensive; alternatively, if you're on a very tight budget, in a remote area or camping, you can purify local water yourself with either chlorine or iodine drops that can be purchased back home in camping shops. Iodine can only be used for up to six weeks continuously although it has the advantage of killing the giardia parasite (see opposite), which chlorine doesn't. Both make water taste unpleasant, although you can add neutralizing crystals that mask most – but not all – of the taste (iodine tablets are available with neutralizers already added). Your other options are portable **water filters** or, better, purifying kits that both filter and sterilize water – although water filters won't get rid of every nasty organism, water purifiers clean water to a high level. They range vastly in price (US$25–100) and come in several sizes; consider weight, efficacy and ease and speed of use before you buy one. If you're carrying a camping stove it's easier to just **boil water** (for at least five minutes; longer at higher altitudes) to rid it of any harmful bacteria.

Food

Food that isn't properly cooked or is unhygienically prepared is another source of diarrhoea and sickness. When choosing where and what to eat, bear the following points in mind:

- Look at hygiene standards: if the floor is swept, tables wiped and ashtrays emptied regularly, chances are the same approach to cleanliness extends to the kitchen.

- You don't have to completely avoid eating street food – some stalls are scrupulously maintained, with ingredients covered and food freshly cooked. Look around for the busiest places – often the best way to tell if somewhere is worth going to.

- Conversely, don't assume that gringo cafés will be more hygienic than local places – they may not be.

- Choose places where food is cooked to order – food that's been left sitting around attracts flies and harmful bacteria.

- Undercooked meat and reheated rice could give you serious food poisoning and salad is often washed in unclean tap water – you should avoid all three. Be particularly careful with shellfish, which is prone to contamination because of the large amounts of polluted seawater they filter while feeding. Additionally a handful of people die every year in Chile from eating shellfish contaminated by the *marea roja* ("red tide"), a very poisonous algae – although the government does issue warnings when it's present. Also avoid fruit that you haven't peeled yourself, and unpasteurized milk and cheese.

Diarrhoea, vomiting, dysentery and giardia

However careful you are, chances are that at some stage in your travels you'll come down with some kind of **stomach bug** or bout of diarrhoea/vomiting – often shortly after arriving. This may be as much to do with a dramatic change in environment as anything, and the good news is that most cases of even severe diarrhoea and sickness clear up within days and can be easily treated without a visit to the doctor.

Diarrhoea and vomiting

If you do come down with something, try to **rest** for a few days until you feel better – you'll also make the experience less unpleasant for yourself (and other guests) if you check into a hotel with a private bathroom. You probably won't feel like eating if you're sick, and cutting back on food intake will give your guts a much-needed break, although the latest thinking is that it's best to eat at least something. Avoid anything spicy or strongly flavoured – stick to plain, freshly boiled rice, bananas and dry biscuits. Unless you have to travel, don't take anti-diarrhoea medication, which works by blocking you up, thus preventing your body from expelling the bacteria which caused your illness in the first place.

The most important thing, if you're suffering from diarrhoea and vomiting, is to ensure that you don't become **dehydrated**, since your body will be losing vital fluids. If you have a dry mouth and tongue, a loss of skin elasticity, dark urine, headaches and backache, then you've already become seriously dehydrated and need to start rehydrating immediately – try to avoid reaching this stage by increasing your fluid intake as soon as diarrhoea and vomiting start. Adults need to take in 2–3 litres of liquid a day (not including alcohol, coffee or tea, which further dehydrate your system) – more in particularly hot or humid climates. Although in the worst stages of a particularly bad bout you may not be able to keep down anything at all, it's important to keep trying. Take sips of bottled water at frequent intervals; even better, add **oral rehydration salts** to boiled or bottled water to replace lost salt and sugar. If you don't have any in your medical kit you can prepare your own by adding half a level teaspoon of salt and eight level teaspoons of sugar to a litre of clean water. Alternatively, if you're feeling up to it, try drinking flat Coca-Cola (thought to soothe stomach upsets) and eating salty crackers. If more than three or four days pass without you being able to keep down liquids, or if you stop urinating altogether and start to feel drowsy, you may need an intravenous drip and should go to a **hospital** for treatment.

There are several **homeopathic remedies** for diarrhoea – *arsenicum album*, *china officinalis* and *veratrum album*. Ginger helps to alleviate feelings of nausea, while live yoghurt (not easily found in Latin America) or acidophilus tablets will repopulate your intestines with good bacteria after a serious bout of sickness. Locals may also have some ideas – this may well involve a herbal tea of some kind, usually foul tasting but often effective.

Dysentery and giardia

While most cases of diarrhoea and vomiting clear up within a few days, there are several more serious gastrointestinal illnesses which have similar causes and symptoms. The most notable of these are **amoebiasis** (amoebic dysentery) and **giardia**. Both are caused by **parasites** which enter the gut via contaminated water or food and are characterized by abdominal cramps, fever, nausea and weight loss. If you have amoebic dysentery, you may also be passing blood and in severe cases, where the parasite has reached the liver and caused an abscess, suffer intermittent pain on the upper right-hand side of the abdomen; giardia is very distinctive, with sulphurous or eggy burping and farts and a bloated stomach. Both can cause long-term intestinal damage if left untreated; treatment is with **antibiotics** (metronidazole).

Other serious illnesses with similar symptoms to travellers' diarrhoea are hepatitis, cholera and yellow fever, amongst others (see pp.159–162) – if you continue to feel ill after five days, have a high fever (above 39°C/102°F) or severe abdominal pain, seek medical advice.

Wildlife and parasites

You'll probably have the jitters about **creepy-crawlies** if you've never been to Latin America, and particularly if you're planning to visit the rainforest, but in truth you're extremely unlikely to be bitten by any poisonous creatures. That said, there are many species of poisonous snakes and other unpleasant insects and parasites in the region, particularly in the Amazon, and it's worth following the points below to minimize the risk of being bitten.

- Tread carefully in jungle terrain and make as much noise as possible – which gives snakes, rarely aggressive, the chance to slither away. If you are bitten by a snake, get to a doctor as soon as possible and try to stay calm since panicking will pump the venom faster around your body. If you're able to kill the snake and take it to be identified, you may hasten the process of diagnosis and treatment. Attempting to suck out venom is not recommended.

- Avoid swimming in rivers, lakes and lagoons, particularly in tropical South America, where cayman (alligators), electric eels and piranha fish make their home. Although cayman aren't generally aggressive, they have been known to attack if protecting young or just plain hungry. The *candiru* fish is native to the Amazon and swims up the urethra and lodges there or in the bladder, which results in severe blood loss and infection and may be fatal; removal is by surgery. Other nasty parasites also live in tropical fresh water, such as those that cause schistosomiasis (also known as bilharzia; see p.61).

- Shake out your shoes every morning – they're a favourite habitat of scorpions and spiders. If you are stung by either (which is highly unlikely, and rarely fatal), apply ice or cold compresses to the bite and take antihistamines and pain

A close encounter

Sitting around the campfire in the midst of the pristine Amazonian rainforest of Peru's Manu National Park, our tour guide, Barry, had warned us to watch out for the bushmaster. He said the most venomous snake in the Americas was also extremely aggressive, and had been known to pursue those who disturbed it, using infrared vision to track them down before delivering a lethal bite with its fangs. According to the locals, Barry said, the person walking third in line on a jungle trail was most at risk from the bushmaster: the first person passing by would disturb it, the second annoy it, and the third would pay the ultimate price. And so I was slightly concerned when, as we set out on a night walk through the forest an hour or so later, I found myself walking up a narrow trail with only Barry and one other ecotourist ahead of me. Within minutes, Barry suddenly stopped and took a step back, shining his torch at what looked like a stick lying across the path. "Bushmaster," he whispered, and I watched as one end of the stick rose vertically into the air, revealing it as a two-metre-long snake, angry and ready to strike. Even Barry seemed pretty unsettled at the sight, lighting a cigarette and puffing nervously as we peered over his shoulder. When asked what the striking range of the snake was, however, he was still cool enough to reply "Oh, he could get me from there." We waited at a safe distance until the bushmaster slithered into the forest and we could continue along the trail. I didn't realize quite how fortunate we'd been until a year later, when I ran into Barry in a Cusco bar. A few weeks after our trip, he told me, another tour group had run into a bushmaster in the same region. The snake had pursued one ecotourist and bitten him on the ankle. "What happened to him?" I asked, and Barry said he'd been lucky: after being airlifted to a Lima hospital, he'd lived to tell the tale, though only after having his leg amputated.

James Read

⑫

relievers. Seek urgent medical advice if you show an allergic reaction to the bite.

● Avoid walking barefoot, especially on beaches or any other area where dogs roam freely (ie most of rural Latin America), no matter how tempting. Jiggers are small fleas that penetrate the skin, normally around the toenails, and lay their eggs. The only way of getting rid of them is to pick them out with a sterilized needle. If you see and feel a dark itchy bump on one of your toes you must remove the flea or risk gangrene and septicaemia. Bathing your feet in hot water after walking in an infested area may help dislodge the fleas before they've become firmly attached, while the liberal use of insect repellent is sometimes effective.

● If a tick – which looks like an eight-legged woodlouse and can carry nasty diseases – attaches itself to you, remove it carefully using tweezers so that you don't leave part of it embedded in your flesh.

● Leeches are not dangerous and will drop off once they've satiated themselves on your blood, though if you'd rather not wait, applying a lit cigarette usually persuades them to leave sharpish. As with ticks (see above), don't pull them off.

● Try not to sleep in mud or adobe buildings. These harbour the assassin bugs that cause potentially fatal Chagas' disease (see p.159).

HIV, AIDS and contraception

HIV/AIDS (*sida*) is just as common in Latin America as in Europe, the US and Australasia – indeed Brazil has one of the world's highest number of infected people. All the usual precautions apply: never have unprotected sex or share needles. If you're planning on being sexually active, take a supply of **condoms** (*preservativos*) with you – the quality of those in Latin America may not be as good as brands you find at home.

If you're on the Pill, take supplies with you, since your particular brand may be hard to find. Bear in mind that prolonged periods of diarrhoea and vomiting will affect the efficacy of the Pill, so take extra precautions following any gastrointestinal upset. Also be aware that taking the **Pill** does increase your risk of **thrombosis**, as does travelling at high altitudes – if you're planning on trekking above 4000m you should seriously consider coming off the Pill during this period (consult your doctor for advice). Alternatively, if you're planning some kind of adventure holiday and would rather not have to deal with periods, it's possible to prevent bleeding for up to three months with no problems by taking the Pill continuously and ignoring the monthly Pill-free week. If you're at all concerned, discuss your trip with your doctor.

13

Keeping in touch

Keeping in touch with home during your travels in Latin America is now inexpensive and uncomplicated, thanks to the **internet**, which has revolutionized communications in Latin America just as it has done everywhere else. Postal and phone networks too, though much less used by tourists nowadays, have been largely privatized and are now fairly reliable. There are obviously regional variations in communication networks – for specific details on keeping in touch check your guidebook, which should have a section covering the relevant issues in the country you're visiting.

Email and the internet

Internet access is widely available in Latin America. Every city and decent-sized town in even the poorest or least touristed of countries now has at least one internet café. In addition, post offices, telephone centres, universities and libraries also often offer cheap internet access – it's always worth asking at these places.

Costs for internet access in Latin America average US$1–2 per hour; there's usually a minimum charge of ten or fifteen minutes. You may have to be patient, though – particularly in poorer countries and rural areas, connection times can be very slow, and occasionally you may not be able to get through at all. If you get stuck, many staff in places with internet access speak some English. It's also worth knowing that the @ **symbol** (*arrobá* in Spanish) is not on every Latin American keyboard – you have to hold down the "Alt" key and then type 64. On those keyboards where it appears you may have to use the Alt Gr key to activate it.

www.roughguides.com

In general the best areas to find internet cafés are around **universities** and in heavily touristed towns; in addition, many backpacker hostels now have internet access and even **wi-fi facilities**.

VOIP, instant messaging and social networks

VOIP (Voice Over Internet Protocol) is a way of using the internet as a phone. Though there are several different systems – those run by Vonage, Tesco Internet are fairly new – by far the most popular is **Skype** (ⓦwww.skype.com) which has millions of users worldwide.

Skype can be downloaded onto any computer for free and if you are "calling" family or friends who have also downloaded Skype and are online then the calls between you cost nothing. You'll need to ensure that the internet café you're using also has all the necessary software – increasingly this is fairly common though many internet cafés charge a little more than their standard rate for using the service. Additionally you can call landlines and mobile phones using Skype. Although very cheap (several pence/cents a minute) it's not free and you'll need to set up a Skype account to be able to do this.

If you're not bothered by needing to hear your loved ones' voices (talking into a computer is not for the self-conscious) then you could use **instant messaging**. Like Skype it's free and instead of talking you type out a conversation in real time. Windows Live Messenger and Yahoo Messenger are two of the most popular forms of instant messaging, though this is also possible with Skype (using their Chat facility).

Social networks **Facebook** (ⓦwww.facebook.com) and **Twitter** (ⓦwww.twitter.com) are also hugely popular ways of letting your family and friends know what you're up to. You can post photos, videos and pictures, use an instant messaging service (see above) and write to each other, all for free.

Phoning home

With the ubiquity of the internet, **phoning home** from Latin America is a rare occurrence these days. However, it's usually a fairly straightforward procedure, although you have several choices in how to make your call. Bear in mind that, although **public phones** do still exist on Latin American streets, using these is a highly inconvenient process – you'll have to buy a phonecard (increasingly hard to find with the ubiquity of mobile phones) and you'll have trouble making yourself heard. It is possible to call from many hotels but this is usually (very) expensive.

Mobile phones

Once a highly complicated and extortionate process, it's much easier to use **mobile phones** abroad these days. Latin Americans almost all have at least one handset – even in the most remote of places - cities are full of phone shops and there are increasingly good call rates. It's easiest to take your own phone – though roaming charges can be high and you may still have to pay to receive as well as make phone calls. Bear in mind also that not all phones and/or networks work in Latin America – though the **GSM** (Global System for Mobile communications) now has widespread coverage in most Latin American countries you'll need a tri-band model in the majority of places rather than the dual band phones used throughout Europe. Check Ⓦwww.gsmworld.com for updates on which country has which **band width**. Alternatively you could get your phone **unlocked** from your network before you travel and then you can buy a local SIM card which may well be cheaper to use than your fixed contract. If you're going to lots of different countries **Global Sim Card** sells a SIM card which can be used in 175 countries (Ⓦwww.gosim.com). Failing all these options, you could buy a phone in Latin America – these cost as little as US$20–and use it while travelling.

Telephone centres

All cities and towns in Latin America (and, nowadays, even some villages) have a **telephone centre** (*centro de llamadas* or *caseta de teléfono*; *locutorio* in Peru and Argentina; *posto telefônico* in Brazil) – generally a branch of the national telecom company. These usually have a series of numbered **booths** which make them, at least, much more private than

▲ Phoning home, Cancún

using the internet. You'll be charged by the minute, although there may be a minimum charge. Telephone centres vary enormously when it comes to rates – some charge little more than the cost of a call made in a public phone, while others hike up the prices substantially. Generally it costs about US$0.75–$2 per minute to make an international call. Telephone centres may not always have the cheapest rates available (see below), but are often the simplest (and most private) way of making a phone call. In addition, telephone centres in larger towns and cities often offer a **fax service** and provide **internet** access.

Calling cards

Calling cards have lots of advantages when phoning from abroad: they're often cheaper to use than calling from a public phone or telephone centre, and can also be used when calling from private phones – including those in hotels – at no extra charge. While some calling card services are **prepaid**, the majority are now charged to a **credit card account** or home phone number, and you can top up the service as you go. The procedure is fairly straightforward – you dial a specified operator, quote your PIN number and then the number you wish to call.

Thousands of **telecom companies** now offer calling cards: the best-established include AT&T, MCI and Sprint in the US and Canada; BT and Mercury in the UK; Telstra in Australia; Telecom in New Zealand and Telkom in South Africa. Additionally, American Express offer a prepaid card, and it's also possible to use a Visa credit card (@www.visa .com). E-kit (@www.ekit.com) offer an advanced **calling card service** which offers a seventy percent discount on international calls, can be recharged online and has voicemail so that your friends and family can leave messages which you later pick up. With so many services to choose from, you should compare rates – US-based calling cards are often the best value and are increasingly available in Europe and Australasia – or use a service like **Planet Phonecard** (@www.planetphonecards.com) which sells dozens of different types of card.

Mail

Postal services in Latin America are fairly **reliable** (though this varies from country to country: Chile and Belize have excellent postal services while Guatemala's is dire and hugely expensive) but slow (up to three weeks to Europe and longer to Australasia, although post to the US usually arrives within a week): always send letters **airmail.**

There aren't many **mailboxes** in Latin America; it's easiest to send mail from post offices. It's also best not to post mail from remote areas, where it may be collected only sporadically; wait instead until you reach a big town or city where post is sorted every day – your post home might arrive weeks earlier as a result. Stamps (*estampillas* in Spanish or *sellos* in Brazil) are available in general stores as well as post offices and are relatively expensive.

If you're having letters sent to you via **poste restante**, you can collect them at any post office: mail should bear your name followed by the words "Lista de Correos" (*Posta Restante* in Brazil; *General Delivery* in Belize), Correo Centrale, and then the town and country name. Every main post office will have a *Lista de Correos* section where they keep mail for at least a month. Letters are often filed erratically, however: ask the clerk to check

> **Dear Mom,**
>
> Glad you're enjoying my stories. Not much to report at the moment. Spent Christmas Eve on top of a Coca-Cola truck driving around Iquitos with Santa Claus, and Christmas Day morning with a monkey on my head. The night before Christmas Eve, I went to an Evangelical church dinner with a Brazilian boat captain who once worked with Jacques Cousteau. During the meal I talked with a (female) judge who fights drug trafficking in the Amazon.
>
> That's about it.
>
> Hope you had a great Christmas.
>
> Love,
> Julie
>
> Julie Feiner

under both your first name and surname. You'll have to present some form of ID (preferably your passport) when collecting post, and in some countries you'll also have to pay a small fee.

While letters usually get through safely, **packages** are likely to be tampered with or go missing – it's best to avoid having these sent to you at all via national postal networks. If you really need something sent to you, use a worldwide courier service (see below). To send a parcel, you'll need to find a large central post office, preferably in a capital city, where there'll be a special section. Take the contents of your parcel unwrapped – they'll have to be inspected by a customs official and you may then have to wrap them a certain way. Fortunately, all the materials necessary will be conveniently on sale, either in the post office or on the streets outside.

Alternatively, you can send anything home via an **international courier company** – both Fedex and DHL have offices all over Latin America and offer an expensive but efficient service. In some very touristy places, such as Antigua in Guatemala or San Miguel de Allende in Mexico, private shipping companies exist who will send home your souvenirs safely – for a price.

The media

As well as speaking or writing to your friends and family you might want to know what is happening in the **news** back home. If you're

www.roughguides.com

from North America, keeping in touch with the news is relatively easy, particularly in Mexico and Central America. Europeans and Australasians, however, may have a hard time finding newspapers and TV stations carrying news from home.

Newspapers

The most commonly found **foreign newspapers** in Latin America are all from the US and include the *Miami Herald*, the *International Herald Tribune* and the *New York Times*, which can be bought at newsstands in capital cities throughout Latin America. The news magazines *Time*, *Newsweek* and *The Economist* are also widely available, though expensive. If you're really desperate to know the news you're better off logging onto the website of your favourite newspaper back home.

Most countries also have an **English-language weekly** of some kind, usually found in capital cities and places with large expat communities who provide a ready market for English-language news, as well as contributing articles and columns. These papers tend to concentrate on local community issues and have little foreign news. The *Buenos Aires Herald* is the longest established English-language paper in Latin America and is broad-ranging – so are the *Tico Times* of Costa Rica and Chile's *Santiago Times*; all have news gathered from the whole of Latin America as well as the rest of the world.

If your Spanish or Portuguese is up to it, you could try reading **national newspapers**. The *Folha de São Paulo*, *El Mercurio* from Chile and Mexico's *La Jornada* and the relatively new *Reforma* are some of the best-regarded Latin American papers.

Television

Television is something of an obsession in Latin America, and increasingly numbers of Latin Americans are now subscribing to North American **cable and satellite services**, meaning that if you have a TV in your hotel room you'll probably have access to CNN, at the very least. In backpacker centres and big resorts you'll also find bars with **sports channels**, MTV and (if they're run by Europeans) the international BBC news channel, all in English.

Radio

Radio is also a good way of keeping up with news from home via the Voice of America (Ⓦ www.voa.gov) or the BBC World Service (Ⓦ www.bbc.co.uk/worldservice), but you'll need a good **shortwave radio** to pick them up. It's also worth checking out frequencies in advance – you can do this online – since these change with baffling rapidity from region to region and at different times of the day.

14

Crime and safety

From what you learn about Latin America in the news back home, it's easy to get the impression that the entire region is dominated by earthquakes, floods, violent crime, drug-trafficking and civil disorder. In reality, although such problems do exist, they're unlikely to affect you – instead, you're much more likely to experience more mundane hassles like petty theft and con-tricks of one kind or another. The information in this chapter should help you avoid the pitfalls that await the unwary and ensure you join the great majority of those who visit Latin America without experiencing any problems with crime or personal safety.

It's worth reiterating that on no account should you set foot in Latin America without adequate **insurance**; see pp.52–54 for more information on this.

Avoiding trouble

In most of Latin America the threat of **crime** is not that much greater than in North America or Europe. The difference is that, whereas back home you blend in and can spot potential danger signs much more easily, in Latin America you probably stand out like a sore thumb – a very wealthy sore thumb, moreover, at least in the eyes of most Latin Americans. The most important rule is not to suspend the instincts that keep you safe at home. It's better to become slightly paranoid than to wander around oblivious to potential dangers. Once you get used to local cultural norms and pick up some of the local language, you'll find you can judge whether or not to trust people just as effectively as you can at home.

www.roughguides.com

179

It's also important to stay informed. Supplement what's in your guidebook with up-to-date information from newspapers, magazines and websites. Natural disasters, civil wars and the like don't make it into the pages of guidebooks until months or years after the event, but they'll be all over the international news media within hours. Travellers' newsgroups and bulletin boards on the internet are also an excellent resource (see p.306 for a list of some of the most useful), and most governments have a department to advise on safety abroad (see p.304) – contact them or check their website to find out the current situation in countries you're planning to visit. In the event of an emergency while you're travelling, contact your nearest **embassy** or consulate (addresses are given in the country profiles, see p.192 for details on how they can help you). It's important to keep such information in perspective. If you hear about civil unrest or a natural disaster in a country you're about to visit, be sure to check it out, but be aware that the problem may well be limited to a remote region hundreds of kilometres from anywhere you're intending to go.

Once you're travelling, heed advice from locals and other travellers, whether it's about a region affected by bandits, an area of a city affected by crime, a hotel where rooms are frequently robbed or a dodgy tour company. Such advice is often much more reliable and up to date than what's in your guidebook.

Passports

In most Latin American countries you are legally required to carry your **passport** with you at all times; failure to produce **identification** when asked for by a policeman can result in arrest or lay you open to a bribe. A scanned copy of your passport sent to your webmail address makes it easier to replace if lost or stolen, and in some countries you can have a printed copy authorized by a public notary for use as a temporary form of identification if you leave your passport in safe-keeping. If you're staying in the same country for a while, consider registering with your embassy; this can also save lots of time if you have to replace a lost or stolen passport.

Theft

Opportunistic **theft** of one kind or another is the most common crime tourists face. More often than not it's simply the result of carelessness, and by using common sense, staying alert and taking some simple **precautions** you can greatly reduce the chances of becoming a victim.

The following guidelines should help reduce your chances of being robbed, and make it easier to deal with the consequences if you are.

- Carry money, credit cards and vital documents like your passport close to your body and concealed under your clothes at all times. Money belts (see p.96) are good for this, but you can also buy secure wallets that hang under your shirt or from a loop on your belt under your trousers; a hidden pocket sewn inside your trousers or a belt with a secret zip for cash are even more difficult for thieves to find. Some Latin American women hide cash inside their bras.

- Make a careful note of your plane ticket numbers, the phone numbers you'll need if you have to cancel your credit cards, travellers' cheque numbers (always keep the purchase receipt separately) and insurance details, and keep all these separate from your valuables. It's also worth emailing these details to your webmail address together with a scanned copy of your passport.

- Keep your day's cash separate from your main stash, so your hidden money belt isn't revealed every time you buy a cup of coffee.

- Keep a separate stash of emergency cash hidden somewhere about your person for use if your main money belt gets stolen.

- Don't flaunt your wealth. Avoid wearing expensive jewellery, use a cheap watch and carry your camera concealed in your daypack rather than round your neck.

In at the deep end

Matthew arrived in Bogotá shortly after his eighteenth birthday at the start of a nine-month circuit of South America with an overland tour truck company. He wasn't due to meet up with his group until the next morning, so he headed out onto the streets to do some sightseeing, revelling in the excitement of his first day in Latin America. Within minutes of stepping out of his hotel, however, he was held up at knife-point by a gang of youths. They took his passport, camera, traveller's cheques, daypack, even the jacket off his back. Deeply shocked, he returned to his hotel, wishing he'd never even thought of setting foot in what seemed a benighted continent. The next day, however, with the help of his tour guide, he was able to arrange a new passport and new traveller's cheques. He picked up a secondhand camera (probably stolen from some other tourist, he said) in the market, and replaced the jacket and bag with local equivalents during the course of his travels.

When I met up with him months later in Peru, he said that while at the time the robbery had been frightening and deeply disheartening, on reflection he actually felt it had liberated him from much of his anxiety about travel in Latin America. Everything he'd lost that he hadn't been able to replace locally now seemed to him an unnecessary encumbrance he was better off without. And once you've been robbed, he said, you realize it's not the end of the trip, much less the end of the world, so you don't live in fear of it happening again.

James Read

- Mugging and violent robbery usually occur at night, so try to avoid having to walk down empty or poorly lit streets in the early hours, particularly on your own. ATMs are an obvious target for robbers – don't use them at night, if possible. If the robbers are armed, do not resist.

- Better hotels often have a safe or strongbox at reception where you can deposit valuables. This is usually safe, though it's best to leave stuff in a tamper-proof holder (anything with zips which can be padlocked will do). Make sure you get an itemized receipt for whatever you leave, and count cash carefully before and after.

- A small padlock is useful for replacing or supplementing the one on your hotel room door if you're worried about security.

- Don't leave valuables on the beach when you swim. Most travel shops sell waterproof canisters which you can wear in the water; alternatively, just take enough cash for your immediate needs and keep it in a small plastic bag in a pocket in your swimming trunks or tucked into your swimsuit.

- Don't automatically trust other travellers – a small minority fund their travels by ripping off others.

Safety on the move

- You are at your most vulnerable, and have the most to lose, when you're on the move or arriving in a new town and have all of your luggage with you. Bus stations are a favourite hunting ground of thieves the world over: try not to arrive after dark, keep a close eye and hand on your bags at all times, and consider taking a taxi from the bus terminal to your hotel as a security precaution.

▲ Backpacks left in a risky spot...

- Unless you travel very light, when moving around by bus or train you'll often have to put your backpack into a luggage compartment or on the roof. This is usually safe, and some bus companies will give you a baggage reclaim ticket, but it's still worth keeping an eye out when the vehicle stops to make sure no one takes your bag.

- Some travellers like to chain their bags together or onto an immovable object when waiting around transport terminals, and onto the roof of the bus or train luggage rack when travelling. You can also buy lockable lightweight metal meshes to fit over your pack for extra security.

- Transport terminals, markets, city centres, fiestas and other crowded public places are favoured by pickpockets and thieves. If you're carrying a daypack, keep it in front of you where you can see it to avoid having it slashed; when you stop and sit down, loop a strap around your leg to make it more difficult for someone to grab.

- Beware of accepting food, drink or cigarettes from fellow passengers on journeys. Some thieves use these to drug their victims, making off with everything they own while they sleep it off.

- Though usually safer than walking, taxis can also carry an element of risk, as they're usually poorly regulated and drivers can be criminals too. Don't share a cab with strangers, and lock passenger

A trained eye

Travelling through Bolivia in a freezing cold, uncomfortable, third-class train carriage, we slept intermittently, marking time by the stations that came and went, and with them encounters with the local kids – burnt cheeks, snotty noses and matted pigtails. We bought alpaca bobble-hats and traded pens and fruit for photos. Finally, we pulled into Oruro, our final destination, 37 long hours after our journey began. As happened at every other station, our arrival caused widespread excitement and much clambering on and off the train. In retrospect the clambering on should have seemed strange, as this was where the train terminated. But so eager were we to get off the train that the constant watch over our bags faltered for a brief moment and my daysack was whipped away in the fervour. As quickly as it happened – whilst I was hoisting my large rucksack on my back – all three of us leaped off the train and scoured the crowded platform. On the advice of a local man I rushed outside and in my best Spanish yelled at all departing taxis to stop and please open their boots. Needless to say the next few hours were spent in the police station making a report of the theft. I didn't lose my passport, tickets, money or traveller's cheques as they were tucked away in an under-garment money belt, but I did lose letters and photos, which to me were priceless. I did learn from the experience, though – sometimes it's worth paying a bit more to get some sleep and arrive in a new place with your wits about you.

Claire Southern

www.roughguides.com

doors to stop people jumping in beside you. Where possible, it's better to order a cab by phone rather than flagging one down in the street.

Common scams

The common scams practised on tourists in Latin America change, evolve and become ever more elaborate. The best source of information about all the latest cheats and tricks is other travellers, so talk to other people on the road and learn from their mistakes. Here are a few **classic scams** you should watch out for:

- Thieves pose as plainclothes police officers, complete with fake documents, and ask to see your documents or check for fake currency, often calling on a "passer-by" (read accomplice) to verify their identity. Don't show them your valuables or get in a car with them, and insist on going to a genuine police station.
- Criminals pose as tour guides with the intention of robbing and/ or raping you once they get you out in the middle of nowhere. Only go on trips with reputable tour companies and – particularly for trips to remote areas – with other travellers you trust.
- Your bag or clothing is mysteriously sprayed with mustard or the like. A "friendly passer-by" points this out and offers to help you clean it while his accomplice (who sprayed it there in the first place) picks your pockets or grabs your bag. If you are sprayed, walk away quickly and refuse his or her "help" – you can always clean up later.
- Something valuable – cash, a credit card – is dropped at your feet. A passer-by spots it and asks you to check your wallet to see if it's yours, or offers to share it with you. The story ends either with your own money disappearing by sleight of hand or with you being accused of theft. Ignore anything dropped at your feet and walk away as quickly as possible.
- Someone asks you to carry a package or letter to their friend or relative in another town or country – they may be smugglers and the contents could well be drugs. With this in mind, don't carry packages for other people.
- Some street moneychangers are adept at ripping you off by sleight of hand while counting notes, or of passing you forged notes; some even have specially rigged calculators. If you can, change money or travellers' cheques at a bank or *casa de cambio* – rates aren't much different these days anyway.

Kidnap

The threat of kidnap in Latin America used to be limited to the rich. But in recent years the proliferation of credit/debit cards and ATMs has made travellers (as well as middle-class Latin Americans) a target for what's known as **express kidnapping**. This involves armed men, sometimes disguised as police, entering the taxi or minibus the victim is travelling in (usually with the complicity of the driver) and taking them to a secret location where they are forced to reveal their credit card PIN and held for several hours or days while the account is drained. The same precautions for avoiding theft listed above should help ensure this doesn't happen to you: don't share taxis with strangers and be wary of people claiming to be police. If you think you're being abducted, alert passers-by and get out of the vehicle if you can. If the worst happens and you are taken captive by force, it's best to cooperate to ensure you come out of the experience alive. You can reduce your financial exposure by arranging a low maximum daily withdrawal amount on your ATM; by having a low limit on your credit or debit card or drawing from an account with limited funds which you periodically top up from another. Prepaid travel credit cards also limit the amount you can lose.

Hazards of nature

Latin America is home to pretty much the full range of dangerous **natural phenomena**, including lava-spewing volcanoes, catastrophic floods, landslides and earthquakes, not to mention deadly venomous snakes. However scary these might all sound, the chance of you experiencing any of them is remote.

If you're the sort of person who likes to prepare for any eventuality, *The Worst Case Scenario Survival Handbook*, by Joshua Piven and David Borgenicht, has detailed tips on everything from surviving a shark attack to wrestling an alligator.

Earthquakes and volcanoes

The western edge of Central and South America runs along the Pacific rim, at the meeting point of two of the earth's major tectonic plates, which means it experiences an unusually high level of volcanic and seismic activity. El Salvador, Colombia, Mexico and Peru have all experienced major **earthquakes** in recent decades, while the capitals of both Mexico and Ecuador, as well as many smaller cities and towns in the region, live in the shadow of active **volcanoes**. The Pacific coast of Latin America is also vulnerable to tsunamis. Seismologists are notoriously poor at predicting when earthquakes will strike, and while major volcanic eruptions are usually detectable some time in advance – and you should check the state of alert before travelling near active volcanoes – they can also strike with frightening suddenness. Realistically, though, the chances of you being caught up in a major natural disaster are very small.

If you are unlucky enough to be caught in a major earthquake, it's best to stay inside unless you're close to a large open space, as falling debris from buildings is a major cause of fatalities. Stay away from windows to avoid splintering glass, and shelter under a doorway or strong table if the building looks like it might collapse. Try to contact friends or relatives at home as soon as possible to let them know you're safe.

Hurricanes and floods

The **hurricane season** in Mexico and Central America runs from roughly October to November and affects both the Atlantic and (to a lesser extent) Pacific coasts. Hurricanes are usually predicted well in advance (you can check the latest forecasts in the local media or on the US National Hurricane Center website at Ⓦwww.nhc.noaa.gov), but they can change course fairly quickly. If you're in the path of a hurricane, get out of the area if you can. If you can't, stay indoors away from windows, preferably on high ground to avoid the risk of flooding, taking plenty of food and water with you. As well as loss of life, hurricanes can cause massive damage to transport and other infrastructure, and drinking water may become contaminated: if a region you're planning to visit is hit by a major hurricane, think seriously about revising your itinerary.

Snakes and other potentially dangerous creatures

The chances of encountering **venomous snakes** is obviously greater in, say, the Amazonian rainforest than in most places back home (the same goes for other dangerous creatures like spiders and scorpions). But though the thought of a snake in your sleeping bag or a tarantula in your trousers might make you wish you never thought of visiting Latin America, in reality you're highly unlikely to suffer anything worse than a few mosquito bites, especially if you listen to local advice and take sensible precautions.

- Trek with local guides who know the terrain and potential hazards.
- Give snakes a wide berth, and don't ever antagonize them. Most snakes are usually as scared of you as you are of them, and they tend to avoid humans as far as possible, although they will strike

if they feel threatened. Wearing thick boots and long trousers, watching where you step and making plenty of noise all reduce the chances of getting bitten.

- If a snake bites you, chances are it won't have injected enough venom to be dangerous, so try to remain calm. Clean the wound, immobilize the limb and avoid movement. Seek medical help immediately and try to identify the snake if possible.

- Shake your shoes or boots out every morning: spiders and, especially, scorpions sometimes sleep inside. It's also a good idea to look before you place your hand on the ground or a branch in outdoor areas – arachnids won't look to attack you, but if you disturb or threaten them they will bite or sting, and some species are extremely dangerous.

- Though fairly rare, rabies does exist in Latin America and does kill people, so give dogs a wide berth. Even if not rabid, dogs are often aggressive and can be dangerous, though you can usually dissuade them from matching their bark with a bite by waving a stick or throwing a few stones in their general direction (for more on rabies see p.161).

Hazardous activities

Activities like whitewater rafting, kayaking, mountain-climbing, and skiing are not known as **dangerous sports** for nothing, and though the degree of risk is minimal, safety standards in Latin America are not generally as high as they are back home. Some of the companies that offer such activities may not even be licensed or insured, their "expert" guides may not be properly trained, and their equipment may be shoddy or even dangerous. Don't suspend your usual criteria for judging danger just because you're travelling, check your insurance covers you for specific activities before you undertake them, and always go with a recommended and reputable company, even if it means paying more.

Swimming

Swimming in the sea can be hazardous due to sharks, poisonous creatures such as sea snakes and jellyfish, heavy surf that can batter you unconscious, and dangerous currents that can drag you out to sea (rip-tides) or drag you under the water (undertows). Only the most popular resort beaches have lifeguards, so it's best to exercise caution before going for a swim – if you do get into difficulties in the water you can't count on getting rescued. The best guide is to ask locals whether it's safe to swim before getting in the water: if no one else is swimming, you should definitely ask why before doing so yourself. If you get caught

www.roughguides.com

in a riptide and find yourself being dragged out to sea, don't panic or exhaust yourself by trying to fight it and swim back to shore. Instead, try to attract the attention of people on land, and when the current slackens after taking you away from the shore, swim back in at a 45-degree angle so as to avoid being caught in the current again. **Undertows**, which drag you beneath the surface of the water, are more difficult to escape: the best thing is to avoid getting in the water in the first place, so always check if the beach is safe before swimming. The same goes for **dangerous sea creatures** such as sharks and jellyfish: ask local people if it is safe to swim before getting in the water, and get out quickly if you see a shark or other hazard.

Swimming in **fresh water** can also be hazardous. River and lake currents can be deceptive, while buoyancy in fresh water is less than in salt water – a dangerous combination that increases the risk of drowning. Piranha fish, found in tropical South American rivers, are far less dangerous than books and films would have you believe (most eat fruit rather than humans), but they pack a painful bite and do sometimes attack in shoals, especially when concentrated in small pools at the end of the dry season, or if their victim is already bleeding. Other freshwater hazards include electric eels, which pack a powerful shock equivalent to 500 volts, and the infamous candiru, a small, parasitic eel-like fish with a penchant for swimming up the urethra to feed on blood and lodging there using its sharp barbs, an extremely painful – and even fatal – condition which can only be cured by surgery; always wear swimming trunks or a costume and don't urinate in the water while swimming. Always check with locals before swimming in tropical rivers and lakes. Freshwater stingrays also pose a risk, so wear shoes or boots and probe sandy riverbeds with a stick before wading across them. Finally, though many of the volcanic hot springs scattered around Latin America are safe to bathe in, it's always a good idea to check the temperature before plunging in, as this can vary from day to day, and some unfortunate travellers have been badly scalded by springs which were generally considered perfectly safe.

Guerrillas, bandits and civil unrest

Until the early 1990s, many countries in Latin America were riven by bloody civil wars and other armed conflicts, usually between Marxist **guerrillas** and oppressive military regimes. Fortunately, most of these have now been resolved, and democracy is now the rule across the region. A notable exception to all this is Colombia, large areas of which remain off-limits to travellers because of fighting – the risk of being kidnapped or caught in the crossfire between left-wing rebels, right-wing paramilitaries and the security forces is very real. Research the current situation carefully before visiting Colombia, and take local advice on which areas are safe when there. This conflict sometimes spills over into the border areas of neighbouring countries. Some remote parts of Peru are still off-limits because of the presence of remnant bands of the Shining Path (*Sendero Luminoso*) rebel group.

The end of the region's armed conflicts has left many countries awash with arms and with former combatants who have few prospects and little to lose; some of these have turned to **banditry** (itself a long-standing Latin American tradition), holding up cars and buses on isolated roads. However, this is usually confined to very localized areas and the risk of encountering bandits is small: take local advice on which regions or roads are dangerous and avoid travelling by night where possible.

Many Latin American countries – including in recent years Argentina, Peru, Bolivia, Ecuador, Venezuela, Nicaragua and Guatemala – are still subject to periods of serious

A revolutionary encounter

Being pulled over at impromptu police and military roadblocks is not an uncommon experience when travelling by road in Colombia, so it was only after the bus drew to a halt that I realized that the armed figures in camouflaged fatigues that had emerged from the forest on either side of the road were not members of the security forces but battle-hardened guerrillas from the ELN – the National Liberation Army. Fears of kidnap, robbery or worse immediately flashed through my mind. To my surprise we were instead treated to a long speech on Colombian politics, Marxist theory and the justifications for armed struggle, delivered by an earnest young woman carrying an assault rifle. She ended by asking for donations to the revolutionary cause, an invitation that in the circumstances seemed foolish to refuse. Along with the other passengers, I handed over the equivalent of a few dollars. The bus moved on, and for weeks to come I was able to entertain other backpackers with the story of my brush with the guerrillas, turning what was probably a lucky escape into an archetypal Latin American traveller's tale.

James Read

political and economic upheaval. This is unlikely to spoil your travel plans, though strikes, roadblocks or protests can sometimes paralyse cities or entire countries, so it's worth keeping an eye on local and international news sources (check ⓦwww.bbc.co.uk or ⓦwww.cnn .com). It's best to steer clear of **political demonstrations**: these can spiral out of control very quickly and police responses can be extreme. If you get caught up in any major political upheaval it's best to sit tight in your hotel and wait until things blow over – everything's likely to be shut anyway.

Sexual harassment and homophobia

Though it varies in degree between countries and regions **machismo** – the cultural stereotype that characterizes women as weak and submissive, and men as strong and dominant – is alive and well in Latin America, and attitudes to gender equality and the rights of women are a long way behind those you're probably used to at home. Under traditional machismo stereotypes, women are viewed either as virgins or whores – foreign women in particular are widely considered to fall into the latter camp, an attitude reinforced by films and magazines. The perception of **female travellers** is often one of sexual availability and promiscuity, so as a female traveller you're likely to face some degree of verbal or physical harassment, something many Latin American women suffer from as well. Having said that, most female travellers to Latin America don't experience any serious problems, even when travelling alone, and if you rely on the instincts you use to avoid sexual harassment at home, you should be able to prevent it from spoiling your trip. Latin American attitudes to **homosexuality** are also generally conservative. Though some countries (especially Brazil) and cities have thriving gay communities, in much of the region homosexuality is frowned upon and kept under wraps. **Gay travellers** are unlikely to suffer any direct abuse, but it's best to be discreet and avoid public displays of affection.

The following tips may help you avoid or deal with sexual harassment:

● Don't walk alone down dark streets at night; avoid hiking or camping alone or in small groups; avoid taking taxis alone at night and, if you do, try to call a radio taxi rather than flag one down on the street.

● Always carry enough cash on you in case you need to take a taxi back to your hotel.

● Make sure your hotel room is secure, taking care to check door and window locks. You may want to use your own padlock.

● Harassment usually takes the form of whistling or cat-calling: the best way to deal with it is to ignore it.

● Be aware of the different interpretations that may be placed on your behaviour in Latin America: what may pass for simple flirtation or even just friendly conversation back home may be seen as a direct come-on by Latin American men.

● Be assertive: if you find yourself the subject of unwanted male attention don't be afraid to politely but firmly tell them where to go. Men who grope or harass you can be shamed into leaving you alone if you draw public attention to their actions.

- Observe how local women dress. While skimpy bikinis and figure-hugging lycra may be all the rage in some regions, in others they can cause deep offence and may even get you chased out of town.

- Many Latin American bars are pretty much men-only and should be avoided: if you want to go out for a drink, choose more upmarket places or those frequented by other travellers.

- If you're not married, invent a mythical husband: some unmarried women travellers wear a wedding ring to ward off potential pests.

- Don't automatically trust male travellers just because of cultural familiarity or shared language.

Drugs

The production and trafficking of **illegal drugs** – particularly cocaine, but also marijuana and heroin – is a major industry in many countries in Latin America, largely for export but also for local consumption. However, though drugs are widely available (and usually of high quality) in most areas penalties for possession – never mind trafficking – are very severe. Under heavy pressure from the US to stamp out the drug trade, local authorities are particularly happy to throw the book at foreign offenders, and being caught with even small amounts of an illegal substance can get you a long sentence in a Latin American jail.

If this doesn't put you off, be warned that in tourist areas, setups by dealers and the police are commonly used as a way of extorting money from unwary travellers. Areas where drugs are produced – particularly the coca-growing regions of Bolivia, Colombia and Peru – should be given a wide berth, as you may be taken either for a trafficker or a foreign drug-enforcement agent. **Coca leaf** itself – the raw material from which cocaine is produced – is legal in Peru and Bolivia, where it has been used for thousands of years by local indigenous people as a mild stimulant and a key ingredient in traditional rituals and medicine, but it's illegal everywhere else.

Corruption and the police

In general, the **police** rarely trouble tourists, and with any luck, your contact with them will be limited to frontiers and road checkpoints. Even so, it's important to be **polite** in any dealings you have with them, as they can easily make problems for you if you're not. Bear in mind that police officers are invariably armed, and may well shoot if you run away

www.roughguides.com

191

from them. Anyone claiming to be an undercover policeman is probably a thief or confidence trickster (see p.184); don't get in a car with them or show them your documents or valuables, and insist on the presence of a uniformed officer. If you do need to contact the police, it's best to go to the tourist police, where they exist; they'll probably have a better understanding of your problem, and are more likely to speak English.

Latin American police are generally very poorly paid, and in many countries graft has become an accepted part of the job. It's not unusual to be offered an opportunity to **bribe** a policeman even if you've done nothing wrong. Often they're just trying it on, and there's no need to pay if you're innocent of any misdemeanour: refusing politely or acting like you don't understand is usually enough. In some circumstances, however, it can work to the advantage of both parties – if you've committed an offence, paying a small bribe is certainly preferable to going to jail. Beware of initiating a bribe unless you're very sure of your footing and speak the language reasonably well, however, as doing so can sometimes cause offence and make the situation worse; in Chile, for instance, the police have a scrupulous reputation for honesty and won't take kindly to being offered a bribe.

Corruption is by no means limited to the police: throughout much of Latin America it's very much a normal part of everyday life that involves everyone from presidents down to minor officials – there may be times when you're invited to pay a bribe or a "tip" to ensure you get a seat on that plane or get through border formalities without hassle or delays. Once again, there's no need to pay if you don't want to – asking for a **receipt** is a good way of avoiding irregular payments to officials – but there may be occasions when it's easier just to hand over a small sum and be on your way.

If disaster strikes

If disaster strikes and you're robbed or find yourself in trouble with the authorities, your embassy or consulate abroad can:

- Issue emergency passports – having a photocopy of the original will speed this up immediately.
- Contact friends and family and ask them for help with money or tickets.
- Put you in touch with local doctors and lawyers.
- Contact or visit you in prison.
- Inform next-of-kin in case of serious illness.
- Evacuate you from the country in the event of major political upheaval or civil war.

However, your embassy or consulate cannot:

- Give you money (though they may give an emergency loan under very strict criteria).
- Pay to fly you home, other than in very exceptional circumstances.
- Get you out of prison. You won't get much sympathy or help if you're on a drugs charge.

You may also need to:

- Contact the police if you have been the victim of a crime, and to get a written report for insurance purposes if you've been robbed.
- Contact your insurance company. You should carry your policy number and emergency contact details with you and leave a copy at home. Be aware of the procedures you need to follow in the event of robbery or illness, as failure to do so could invalidate your claim. In the case of theft or loss of possessions, you can usually wait until you get home, but in the event of serious medical emergencies you'll need to contact your insurer promptly, especially if you need them to cover hospital or air-evacuation costs.
- Cancel your credit cards if they're stolen – make sure you have an international 24-hour hotline number for doing this. If your travellers' cheques are lost or stolen you'll need to contact the issuer with full details to order replacements.

15

Coming home

E veryone expects to experience **culture shock** when they travel to Latin America, but culture shock works both ways, and after a long period away you may find returning home a surprisingly difficult transition to make. Even though it's initially exciting to be surrounded once again by familiar things and people, normal life back home may soon seem tedious and banal compared to the excitement of travel, and friends and relatives may not be able to relate to experiences of life on the road. You may find that your outlook on life has been transformed by your travels, even while those closest to you hope you've "got it out of your system" and are now ready to settle down. At worst, exchanging the freedom of travel and the joy of experiencing new things every day for the sometimes humdrum realities of work and life back home can be very depressing. Short of immediately setting off on further travels, there's no real antidote for the homecoming blues. However, the following tips should make it easier to cope with:

● Before you go away, try to set aside some money as your coming-home fund – returning home is bad enough, never mind doing so without a penny to your name.

● While you're still on the road make some plans – however basic – for the immediate future after you get home. Returning home with nothing to look forward to is the worst possible scenario; having a job, university place or some other project lined up makes the transition much easier to deal with.

● Make sure you keep in touch with people back home who are important to you, so they're aware of your experiences and thoughts. That way, they won't be too surprised by how you may have changed while you've been away.

- Don't expect everyone at home to be enthralled by your traveller's tales and photographs. Some people may find your experiences boring or difficult to relate to, while others may simply feel envious that you've been off having an adventurous time while they've been stuck in the same old routine.
- Get in touch with other travellers you've met on the road, and with friends and relatives who've been travelling themselves: they will probably understand what you're going through and will be much more interested in hearing about your trip.
- Keep in touch with locals you've met during your travels, and send out those photos you promised them.
- If you live in a large city with a Latin American community, seek out their bars, restaurants and cultural events where you can relive some of your favourite experiences. Taking salsa classes, learning to cook some classic Latin American dishes, reading books and watching films about Latin America are also all good ways of keeping the experience alive.
- If you find your wanderlust is still burning as strong as ever, start planning and saving money for your next trip. If that's not possible, remember Latin America will always be there, so you will be able to go back one day.

Getting involved

However much you enjoy travelling in Latin America, the chances are you will have found some aspects of life there depressing and shocking, such as the extreme poverty faced by most of the population, the corruption and political oppression, the dearth of basic public services and lack of opportunities. You may also have been dismayed by the rate at which many of the beautiful natural environments you've experienced are being destroyed in the name of economic development. If so, getting involved with some of these issues when you return is a good way of maintaining your interest in Latin America; it's also a positive way of using your experiences and of making sense of all that you saw and did while you were there. The following are just some of the **organizations** that campaign about issues in Latin America and make a contribution towards tackling some of the problems you may feel strongly about.

- **Amnesty International** (🌐www.amnesty.org) Leading international human rights organization which publishes reports on political oppression in countries around the world, including many in Latin America. Their website has a huge amount of information (including much which governments would prefer you didn't see) as well as excellent links to other human rights-related sites.

- **Latin America Bureau** (ⓦwww.latinamericabureau.org) London-based independent research and publishing organization working to broaden public understanding of human rights and social and economic justice in Latin America and the Caribbean. Publishes a huge range of non-specialist books and is the main point of reference in the UK for people interested in Latin America, with a website full of information and a list of organizations sending voluntary workers to Latin America.

- **One World** (ⓦwww.oneworld.net) A network of more than a thousand human rights, anti-poverty and environmental organizations, with masses of information on Latin America, as well as lists of job vacancies and volunteering opportunities.

- **Rainforest Action Network** (ⓦwww.ran.org) International campaign network working to prevent rainforest destruction and protect the human rights of forest peoples, with a website full of information on Latin America's dwindling forests and links to other relevant sites.

- **Survival International** (ⓦwww.survival-international.org) Campaigns for the rights of tribal people all over the world and against governments, armies, corporations, banks, missionaries and anyone else who threatens their future.

- **Washington Office on Latin America** (ⓦwww.wola.org) US-based group that campaigns for human rights and democracy in Latin America and produces a huge range of books and reports.

Making your trip work for you

After your travels you may be looking for **work**, either at home or overseas. Your prospects with future employers will be better if you can not only describe your trip as an enjoyable adventure but also show that you developed useful abilities or experiences while travelling. Doing some kind of voluntary work during part of your trip always looks good on a CV or résumé. Speaking Spanish or Portuguese is a valuable skill, so you might want to polish what you picked up while travelling by taking further language tuition.

Working in the travel industry

In the longer term, your experiences in Latin America can help pre-pare you for work in the **travel industry**, either working for a travel agency at home or as a guide back in Latin America. To get work as a tour guide you'll need to speak pretty good Spanish and/or Portuguese and convince the tour operator that you have the necessary background knowledge, social skills and ability to take responsibility before they entrust a group of paying clients to your care. Look out for job adverts in the travel press and don't be afraid to approach tour operators if you think you've got what they need. When you are travelling you may well run into people working in the industry who you can ask about what the work is like, and what potential employers are looking for. Back home, travel fairs are a good place to find out more.

Travel writing and photography

If you've taken good photographs or written about your travels you may be able to make some money out of it when you return, or even turn it into a career. If you want to sell **photos** or **travel stories**, it's worth having a good look at the kind of material different newspapers

▲ Looking at travel images with local children, Brazil

THE BIG ADVENTURE

and magazines favour before you go. Unless you have good contacts or previously published work you're unlikely to elicit much interest before you set off on your trip, and you'll have to submit articles and photos to publications on spec when you get back. Obviously, travel magazines with small circulations or which are distributed free are much more likely to look at your work than national newspapers and major magazine titles. They don't pay much, but the first step is to get something into print, which you can then use to approach other publishers. In several Latin American countries there are small **English-language newspapers**, which can be a good place to get your picture or stories published. Most national newspapers and travel magazines run annual travel-writing competitions for young people, which are an excellent way of getting into the industry – even if you don't win, a good entry can get you noticed and bring future commissions. Photographers are better off approaching picture agencies and libraries rather than magazines – remember, if you're hoping to sell your photos, you'll really need to take slides or high-resolution digital images rather than colour prints. Both travel writing and photography are difficult areas to break into, and even if you succeed you still may well struggle to make a living, but it's a big industry that always has room for new talent. Have a look at Guy Marks' very useful *Travel Writing and Photography, All You Need to Know to Make it Pay* or Louise Purwin Zobel's *The Travel Writer's Handbook, How to Write and Sell Your Own Travel Experiences* for further advice.

First-Time
Latin America

Where to go

Mexico & Central America

●	Mexico	201
●	Belize	207
●	Costa Rica	211
●	El Salvador	216
●	Guatemala	220
●	Honduras	224
●	Nicaragua	228
●	Panama	232

Mexico

Capital Mexico City
Population 110 million
Languages Spanish and various indigenous languages, including 8 distinct Mayan dialects and Nahuatl
Currency Peso ($)
Climate Varies widely, from tropical to desert, with most of the country having two distinct seasons, wet (June–Sept) and dry (Oct–April)
Best time to go October–April (dry season), November 1 for the Day of the Dead
Minimum daily budget US$25–35 (depending on whether you visit major tourist resorts or not)

Mexico is overwhelmingly the most visited country in Latin America. Yet in spite of the modern resorts and sophisticated facilities catering to foreign tourists, much of this large country remains steadfastly traditional, with daily life continuing as it has done over hundreds of years.

Geographically, Mexico is the only Latin American country in North America, and it has strong ties with that region, both historic – Texas and California were both once part of Mexico – and modern, through the North American Free Trade Agreement and the fact that so many Mexicans go to the US to work, often illegally. It's partly this dichotomy – between the desire for US-style consumerism and material prosperity on the one hand, and traditional Latin American values on the other – which lends the country so much of its particular character.

For visitors, however, it's the longevity and diversity of Mexican culture that's likely to make the strongest impression. It is home to two of the greatest of Latin America's pre-Conquest civilizations, the Aztec and Maya, as well as countless others, and the country's indigenous populations – among them Maya, Mixtec, Zapotec – live much as they have done for hundreds of years, speaking their own languages and cultivating their land in the same way as their forebears did. The monuments of these ancient cultures can be seen everywhere – at the great Maya sites of the Yucatán Peninsula; at the Zapotec sites of Monte Albán, Yagul and Mitla in Oaxaca state; and at the majestic Aztec sites of Tenochtitlán and Teotihuacán, in and close to present-day Mexico City. The country also boasts one of Latin America's richest legacies of colonial architecture, including florid churches and perfectly preserved cities, ranging from the Zócalo (main plaza) in Mexico City to the picturesque silver-mining towns to the north. All of which offers the visitor a heady mix of cultures – Mexico City, for instance, boasts Aztec ruins, atmospheric Spanish-colonial architecture and ultramodern architecture within the space of a few miles.

Geographically, too, Mexico offers an embarrassment of riches, from the arid canyons and cactus-strewn badlands of the north to the tropical rainforests of the south – not to mention the thousands of kilometres of Pacific and Caribbean coastline which includes a number of world-class surfing spots and long swathes of idyllic white-sand beaches lined with palm trees.

Mexico's comparatively well-developed economy means that the country has a good infrastructure, with decent roads and public transport. There are many holiday resorts on both coasts, and accommodation is varied and widespread. Costs vary enormously between established tourist resorts where they are relatively high and traditional inland regions where they remain low. Most of Mexico is safe to travel in, with the inevitable exception of Mexico City – take care at night - and at the time of writing, the border area with Texas as well as Tijuana, which is currently riven by violent warfare between drugs gangs.

Main attractions

● **Day of the Dead (Día de los Muertos)** Taking place annually on All Souls' Day and its eve (Nov 1 & 2), this is the occasion for Mexicans to honour their dead family members and friends. Although a deeply religious ceremony, with all-night vigils held in cemeteries and shrines built in every home, it's also an incredibly picturesque event – papier-mâché skeletons, sweets shaped like skulls and banks of chrysanthemums abound. The night vigil on the island of Janítzio in Lago de Pátzcuaro, 200km west of Mexico City, is particularly intense; locals converge on the island by canoe as dusk falls, their boats each lit by a single candle.

● **Guanajuato** To the north of Mexico City, in the fertile hills and valleys of the Bajío, are the country's finest colonial remnants, cities founded by the Spanish on the wealth brought by silver and gold

mining. The most beautiful of these is Guanajuato, for centuries the wealthiest city in Mexico, which was declared a UNESCO World Heritage Site in 1988. A maze of steep lanes and leafy squares surrounded by the grand mansions of the mine-owners, Guanajuato also has a unique network of subterranean streets running under the city. The city's most distinctive draw is the grotesque Museo de las Momías (mummy museum), which displays over a hundred mummified bodies, some, buried alive with "silent screaming" features and others with their burial clothes still intact. On a lighter note, visitors to Guanajuato enjoy the *callejoneadas*, walking tours led by student minstrel groups, and the city's superb café life.

● **Maya sites in the Yucatán** Much of Latin America's spectacular pre-Hispanic ruins can be found in Mexico. The best known of these are the Maya cities situated on the plains of the Yucatán Peninsula in the country's southeast along an easily travelled circuit known as the Ruta Maya. Chichén Itzá is the most impressive site with its vertiginous temple, snail-shaped observatory and distinctive reclining statues or Chaac-Mools. Calakmul, though only partly restored, is the largest ruined city in Mesoamerica with the base of its great pyramid covering five acres and the view from the highest temple extending, on a clear day, as far as Guatemala. The smaller site of Uxmal is celebrated for its decorative geometric style and stone mosaic friezes. Palenque, while not strictly in the Yucatán but rather in neighbouring Chiapas, has the loveliest setting, surrounded by jungle-clad hills.

● **Mexico City** The country's capital and the world's second largest city (with a staggering 19 million inhabitants), Mexico City sits at the spiritual and geographical heart of Mexico and is

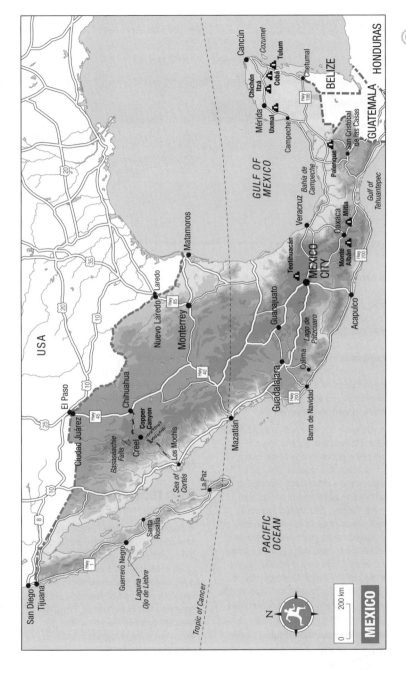

▲ Tulum, the Yucatán

a fascinating blend of pre-Columbian, colonial and modern architecture and culture. Its long list of attractions includes the impressive colonial Zócalo, the world-famous Museo Nacional de Antropología, and Diego Rivera's celebrated murals of historic events such as the enslavement of native Indians by the Spanish and the 1910 Mexican revolution, not to mention fascinating markets and frenetic street life.

● **Oaxaca** 500km southeast of Mexico City, Oaxaca is a colonial town of enduring charm in one of the country's most traditional regions. The city's main square is famously atmospheric, with live music in the evenings and local Zapotec and Mixtec Indians in indigenous costumes selling brightly coloured *faldas* (skirts made of striped woven cloth) and *huipiles* (embroidered blouses). Don't miss the lavish gilded interior of the Santo Domingo church or the Saturday market for locally made shawls, leatherwork, pottery and fried grasshoppers.

● **The Yucatán's Caribbean coast** In the far southeast of the country, the Yucatán Peninsula's Caribbean coast offers long beaches of white sand and azure sea. Although much of the coast south of Cancún is being developed by large resorts, there are still pockets of relative tranquillity, like Puerto Morelos, Xpu-ha and Tulum. The "Riviera Maya", so named by the Mexican Tourist Board, also fronts the world's second largest coral reef, which extends as far as Honduras and makes for breathtaking scuba diving and snorkelling: the nondescript island of Cozumel is its mecca with a world-class series of drop-offs, walls and coral gardens.

Also recommended

● **Bahía de Navidad** Directly west of Mexico City, Bahía de Navidad is one of the most beguiling stretches of Pacific coast in Mexico. Neither deserted nor overdeveloped, the entire length of the large bay is edged by fine sand and has two small communities, Barra de Navidad and San Patricio-Melaque, which are wholly Mexican in feel and great places to chill out.

• **San Cristóbal de las Casas** San Cristóbal, at the centre of Chiapas state, is an attractive and relaxing mountain town. There are a number of small museums and colonial churches to visit, an atmospheric local market and an abundance of attractive restaurants and places to stay in all price ranges. San Cristóbal also makes a perfect base for exploring the indigenous Maya communities which dot the surrounding hills, notably the nearby village of San Juan Chamula, whose famous church offers a rare insight into syncretized religion, with rituals and imagery drawn freely from both Catholicism and pre-Conquest indigenous beliefs.

• **The train ride from Los Mochis to Chihuahua** The thirteen-hour train journey from the Pacific town of Los Mochis to Chihuahua is one of the most scenic in the Americas, crossing the Sierra Madre and offering breathtaking views over the 2000-metre-deep Copper Canyon. The best stopping point for tourists keen to explore the area on foot is Creel, with its nearby canyons, pine forests and the Basaséachic Falls, claimed as North America's highest single cascade at 254m.

• **A tram ride through Campeche** The capital of Campeche state, on the Yucatán Peninsula, is a lovely walled city with immaculately kept narrow streets and pastel-coloured houses. One of the best ways to see the city is on a picturesque tram ride – trams run along the seafront to the city's archeological museum, housed in an old fort, which includes jade death masks from the Calakmul Maya site among its treasures.

• **Whale watching in Baja California** During January and February, California grey whales arrive from Alaska to give birth in the relatively warm waters of the Laguna Ojo de Liebre, off the coast of Baja California. The scruffy town of Guerrero Negro serves as a base for Mexico's most memorable whale-watching excursions, which afford the chance of a close encounter with the newly born calves swimming calmly alongside their parents.

Routes in and out

Mexico is one of the easiest countries in Latin America to reach, with daily flights from the US to a range of cities and resorts, including Mexico City, Cancún, Acapulco, Monterrey and Veracruz. There are also daily flights from Madrid to Mexico City and Cancún, several weekly flights from London to Mexico City, as well as dozens of regular charter flights to Cancún. By land there are dozens of border crossings between the US and Mexico, the most popular being between San Diego in California and Tijuana; El Paso in Texas and Ciudad Juárez; and Brownsville on the Gulf of Mexico and Matamoros. The most popular land frontiers between Mexico and Guatemala are from Tapachula to either Talismán or Tecun Umán on the Pacific coast of Guatemala. Hourly buses leave from Chetumal in southern Quintana Roo state to Corozal in Belize and on to Belize City. There are also several river crossings in northern Chiapas to the Petén region of Guatemala: Frontera Corozal–Bethel (30min by boat) and La Palma–El Naranjo (4hr) are the least complicated.

Books

Sybil Bedford *A visit to Don Octavio* (Eland). Wonderfully idiosyncratic and vivid account of a visit to Mexico in the 1950s.

Graham Greene *The Power and the Glory* (Vintage). Based on Greene's own travels, this first-class novel takes as its theme the anticlerical purges in the southern states of the country in the 1930s and wonderfully evokes the tropical torpor of Mexico's backwaters.

Malcolm Lowry *Under the Volcano* (Penguin). Set in Cuernavaca over the course of a single day in 1948, the novel painstakingly unravels the last hours of alcoholic British Consul Geoffrey Firmin's life through a haze of mescal and the macabre celebrations of the Day of the Dead.

Subcomandante Insurgente Marcos *Our Word is our Weapon* (Serpent's Tail). A collection of writings from the famously erudite and poetic leader of the Zapatistas, the Mexican revolutionary movement who are fighting for land rights for indigenous peoples in southern Mexico.

Mexico online

Mexico Connect Ⓦ **www.mexconnect .com** Monthly e-zine providing information on all aspects of Mexico.

Mexico Travel Guide Ⓦ **www .go2mexico.com** Online travel guide with features and articles on culture, the environment and living in Mexico.

Mexicanwave Ⓦ **www.mexicanwave .com** Excellent English-language

website with book reviews, articles on Mexican culture and life, shopping and links.

Mexican embassies

Australia
Embassy of Mexico, 14 Perth Ave, Yarralumla, ACT 2600 Ⓣ02/6273 3963, Ⓦwww.mexico.org.au/

Canada
Embassy of Mexico, 45 O'Connor, Suite 1000, Ottawa, Ontario K1P 1A4 Ⓣ613/233-8988

New Zealand
Embassy of Mexico, 111 Customhouse Quay (level 8), PO Box 11510, Ⓣ04-4720555, Wellington Ⓦwww .mexico.org.nz

South Africa
Embassy of Mexico, Parkdev Building, Brooklyn Bridge, 570 Fehrsen St, Brooklyn, 0181 Pretoria Ⓣ12-4601004

UK
Embassy of Mexico, 16 St George St, Hanover Square, London W1S 1FD Ⓣ020/7499 8586, Ⓦportal.sre.gob .mx/reinounidoeng/

US
Embassy of Mexico, 1911 Pennsylvania Ave, Washington DC, 20006, Ⓣ(202) 7281600, Ⓦportal.sre.gob.mx/usa/

Belize

Capital Belmopan	**Climate** Tropical with a rainy (May–
Population 301,000	Nov) season and a dry season
Languages English, Spanish, Maya	(Jan–April)
languages, Garífuna	**Best time to go** January–April (dry
Currency Belize dollar (fixed to US$	season)
at a rate of 2 to1; BZ$)	**Minimum daily budget** US$30

Belize is one of the smallest countries in Central America and the least densely populated, with a quarter of a million people occupying an area the size of Wales or Massachusetts. A British colony (known as British Honduras) until 1981, Belize has as much in common with the English-speaking islands of the Caribbean as with the Spanish-speaking Latin American mainland (although the presence of immigrants from other Central American countries is gradually eroding this distinction). This Anglo-Caribbean culture, known as creole, is evident in the country's biggest city, Belize City, with its balconied clapboard houses, reggae dancehalls and vibrant carnival, held in September.

Belize's biggest attraction is its offshore cayes, which sit on the largest coral reef in the Americas, stretching from Mexico to Honduras. The whole area is a protected marine park, teeming with hundreds of species of brightly coloured fish and other marine creatures. Away from the coast, Belize is a sleepy backwater country of dense forests and easy-going rural communities. The interior is home to the highest waterfall in Central America, myriad rivers and caves and a network of national parks and reserves – Belizeans are very conscious of their environment and over forty percent of the national terrain is now protected by law. Ecotourism is seen by many Belizeans as the country's economic future and there are some spectacular eco-lodges to stay in. Also in the interior are Belize's ancient Mayan ruins which, though less impressive than those in Guatemala and Mexico, are well worth visiting – and Tikal in Guatemala is easily accessed from Belize. In the far south of the country, dotted through the foothills of the Maya mountains, traditional Maya live in small communities, similar to those in Guatemala, where you can stay and in some cases participate in village life.

Belize is one of the safest countries in Latin America – crime against tourists is minimal and its capital city, Belmopan, is one of the safest, though dullest, in Central America. You should exercise caution in the former capital, Belize City, which has a much larger population and a slightly seedy atmosphere. Prices are fairly high for the region – if you arrive from Guatemala you could find your costs doubled overnight.

Main attractions

● **Ancient Maya sites at Lamanai, Caracol and Xunantunich** Belize's atmospheric sites are not as historically significant as the Mayan ruins of Mexico, but they are less crowded, with excellent English-language visitor centres and museums on site. Striking Lamanai, in the north of the country, is set in a 950-acre reserve and has wonderful views across the jungle from its temples. In western Belize, Caracol's largest structure, Canaa or the Sky Palace, is still one of the tallest buildings in the country at 42m. Conveniently located en route from Belize to Guatemala (and Tikal), Xunantunich's Maya ruins include a restored stucco frieze carved with abstract designs, human faces and jaguar heads.

● **Caye Caulker** Laid-back Caye Caulker is much smaller – just over 7km long – and less touristy than neighbouring Ambergris Caye and has long been popular with independent travellers. Most visitors come to scuba dive or snorkel, and day-trips go to top diving spots, such as the Lighthouse Reef and the Blue Hole, a complex network of caves and crevices made famous by Jacques Cousteau. On the island itself it's possible to birdwatch – there are many bird species and some, like the black catbird or white-crowned pigeon, are rarely glimpsed elsewhere; rent kayaks or take a boat trip to the reef, which lies just 1.5km offshore.

● **Mountain Pine Ridge Forest Reserve** The range of rolling hills, peaks and gorges that comprise the Mountain Pine Ridge Forest Reserve in western Belize are perfect for hiking and mountain biking. Coursing through the area is the picturesque Río On, which forms a series of natural swimming pools before plunging into a gorge, and the Thousand-Foot Falls – actually 1600ft waterfalls.

● **Rio Bravo Conservation and Management Area** In the northwest of Belize, the Rio Bravo Conservation and Management Area protects 260,000 acres of diverse terrain ranging from forest-covered limestone escarpments through river valleys to palm- and pine-covered plains and swamp. The area has 240 endemic tree species, tapirs, monkeys, river turtles, crocodiles, all five of Belize's big cat species and 400 kinds of bird. If you're feeling flush, the nearby *Chan Chich Lodge* is one of the finest eco-lodges in the world.

Also recommended

● **Belize Zoo** The Belize Zoo, 40km west of Belize City, is widely recognized as the best in Central America and has achieved international acclaim in the fields of conservation education and captive breeding. Its collection of indigenous species includes tapirs, jaguars, toucans and crocodiles, all housed in spacious enclosures that replicate their natural habitat.

● **Placencia** One of the few places in mainland Belize with wide, sandy beaches, Placencia is a laid-back fishing village with a range of inexpensive accommodation and funky reggae and *punta* rock venues; it also makes a good base for day-trips to the nearby coral reef and cayes.

● **Spelunking** Western Belize's (and particularly Cayo District's) limestone hills are home to a spectacular subterranean network, with the Chiquibil cave system in the south of the region ranking as the longest in Central America. Maya ceramics and carvings can be found inside, and some caves have underground rivers which you can float down on inner tubes or in canoes. A good starting point for a caving experience is *The Caves Branch Jungle Lodge*, 19km from Belmopan, which is run by the founders of the Belize Cave and Wilderness Rescue Team.

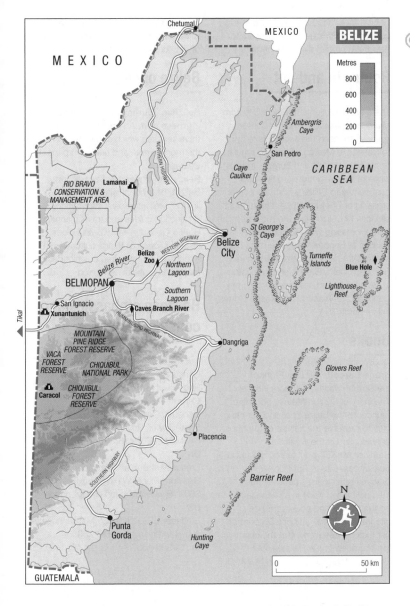

- **Toledo Environmental Association (TEA)** Based in Belize's southernmost town of Punta Gorda, the TEA has an excellent visitors' programme that encourages tourists to stay in the Maya villages of the surrounding area. Visits are tailored to individual interests and may include storytelling, guided walks or boat trips, and traditional harp music concerts. All fees go to the villagers to help them protect their environment.

Routes in and out

There are daily flights to Belize City from Miami and Houston. Another convenient way to reach the country is to fly to Cancún in Mexico, served by regular flights from the US and Europe, from where it's a straightforward five-hour bus journey to Belize – from the border crossing at Chetumal there are frequent services to Belize City. The most popular border crossing with Guatemala (for Tikal) is at Benque Viejo. There are boat services from Punta Gord in southern Belize to Puerto Barrios and Lívingston in Guatemala and, less frequently, from Dangriga and Placencia to Puerto Cortés in Honduras.

Books

Bruce Barcott *The Last Flight of the Scarlet Macaw* (Random House). The story of Sharon Matola, eccentric founder of the Belize Zoo, and her struggles to preserve the habitat of the "most beautiful bird in the world".

Heather McKillop *In search of Mayan Sea Traders* (Texas A&M University Press). Archeologist's detailed study of the ancient sea trade in salt and jade on the islands and coast of Belize, integrated with the author's account of her experiences working in the country.

Ian Vasquez *In the Heat* (Minotaur Books). Acclaimed Caribbean Noir thriller by first-time novelist, born in Belize City, which evokes the sleaze and corruption of dirty dealings in paradise.

Belize online

Belizean Journeys Ⓦwww.belizean journeys.com An online magazine with travel features which concentrate on the more remote and unknown parts of Belize.

Belize Net Ⓦwww.belizenet.com Belize's best portal with hundreds of links as well as general information, destination guides and travel planning.

Belize Online Ⓦwww.belize.com Useful guide to all things cultural, with a focus on tourism, free downloadable maps and a useful news blog.

Belizean embassies and consulates

Australia
Consulate of Belize, 5/1 Oliver Rd, Roseville, NSW 2069 Ⓣ02/9880 7160
Canada
Honorary Consul of Belize, Suite 3800, South Tower, Royal Bank Plaza, Toronto, ON M5J 2JP Ⓣ416/865-7000
UK
Embassy of Belize, Third Floor, 45 Crawford Place, W1H 4LP Ⓣ0207/7223 3603, Ⓦwww.bzhc-lon.co.uk/London
US
Embassy of Belize, 2535 Massachusetts Ave NW, Washington DC 20008 Ⓣ514/288-1687

Costa Rica

Capital San José
Population 4.2 million
Languages Spanish, Creole English on the Caribbean
Currency Colón (¢)
Climate Tropical on the coast, cooler in the mountains, with distinct dry (Dec–April) and rainy (May–Nov) seasons
Best time to go December–April (dry season)
Minimum daily budget US$30

In a region synonymous in many people's minds with civil war and natural disasters, Costa Rica – often described as the "Switzerland of Central America" – stands out as a beacon of prosperity and stability. Today, as Costa Ricans will proudly tell you, the country has no army, more teachers than policemen, free and compulsory primary education, and a literacy rate of ninety percent. For the visitor, Costa Rica's overwhelming draw is its outstanding range of natural attractions and accessible wildlife. Around a quarter of the country is now protected by a widely admired system of national parks and reserves which cover a fascinating diversity of terrains, from mysterious cloud- and rainforests to active volcanic peaks and stunning stretches of palm-fringed coast. And found within these parks is a remarkable array of biodiversity, including some 850 species of bird, more than in the US and Canada combined.

Away from the nation's national parks and reserves, there are outstanding beaches to be found on both coasts, some world-class surfing and whitewater rafting. Man-made and cultural attractions are few, however, although the Jamaican-descended black population which lives around Puerto Limón on the Caribbean coast supplies a welcome splash of cultural diversity (and nightlife) in the country's overwhelmingly mestizo population.

Costa Rica is the most popular tourist destination in Central America and has a well-developed infrastructure, including some of Latin America's most memorable eco-lodges and an efficient public transport network, though some of the country's roads remain pretty appalling. It is, however, perhaps the most expensive country in Central America to travel in, with daily costs almost twice those in neighbouring Nicaragua. On the plus side, it's still amongst the safest countries in the region, though parts of San José should be avoided at night.

Main attractions

● **Osa Peninsula** Much less well known than other parts of Costa Rica, the Osa Peninsula is difficult to reach – getting to both the village of Aguijitas in Bahía Drake and Carate on the edge of the Parque Nacional Corcovado entails lengthy and uncomfortable boat or bus rides – but the few travellers who make it here are rewarded with stunning scenery. Corcovado, with its series of rainforest-fringed beaches populated

www.roughguides.com

by flocks of scarlet macaws, is one of Costa Rica's most beautiful national parks, and there's wonderful marine life and snorkelling at Bahía Drake.

● **Parque Nacional Tortuguero** Most visitors come to Tortuguero to see hawksbill, green and leatherback turtles laying their eggs on the beach (March–May & July–Oct), but the park's network of inland waterways also teems with other forms of wildlife, particularly birds. The most popular way to experience Tortuguero is on an organized package tour with accommodation in comfortable, though pricey, lodges and all meals included. If you want to travel independently, the village has several cheap hotels and is extremely pretty, with pastel-coloured wooden houses.

● **Puerto Viejo de Talamanca** Situated on the southern end of Costa Rica's Caribbean coast, the funky fishing village of Puerto Viejo de Talamanca has easily the liveliest nightlife in the whole country, with several buzzing beach-side clubs. By day, there are miles of clean, sandy beaches to lounge about on, plus excellent surfing and snorkelling.

● **Reserva Santa Elena** In northern Costa Rica, the Reserva Santa Elena comprises a small area of virgin cloud-forest with dense walls of dripping vegetation and brightly coloured birds and flowers. Though it's only a third of the size of the famous Monteverde Cloudforest just down the road, it's also much less visited, more tranquil and profits go to local schools. The surrounding area was colonized by a group of US Quakers (a progressive and pacifist Christian movement) escaping the draft in the early 1950s, and now offers a rural idyll of small dairy farms and mountain scenery.

● **Volcán Arenal** One of the western hemisphere's most active volcanoes, Arenal spews out rivers of molten red lava on an almost nightly basis, although you'll need a clear night to see this amazing pyrotechnic display. The best views are from the north and west sides, however it's forbidden to enter the park at night unless you're on an organized tour. During the daytime hike one of several trails around the volcano and across its solidified lava fields.

Also recommended

● **Liberia** In the northern province of Guanacaste, calm Liberia is Costa Rica's most attractive town, with wide streets of whitewashed houses lined with mango trees. The town's main street, the Calle Real, has been restored to its original nineteenth-century glory and its buildings are the best example of colonial architecture in Costa Rica. Liberia is also a good jumping-off point for several national parks, the Nicaraguan border and the popular beaches of Guanacaste – tranquil Playa Sámara is the least developed of these while gringo-friendly Tamarindo is popular with surfers.

● **Orosí** The peaceful Orosí river valley, 25km southeast of San José, is little visited by tourists but has much to offer, with a dramatic setting in a deep bowl of steep forested hills. There's a series of lovely walks and waterfalls in the area, and the very pretty village of Orosí has two outdoor swimming pools fed by hot springs and one of the oldest churches in Costa Rica, an evocative adobe and red-tiled structure built in 1735.

● **Parque Nacional Rincón de la Vieja** Also in Guanacaste, Rincón de la Vieja is distinguished by its dramatically dry landscape with rock-strewn savannah, bubbling mud pots and sulphurous subterranean springs. The walking trail to the summit of the still-smoking volcano which gives the park its name is one of the most scenic in the

Peñas Blancas

NICARAGUA

COSTA RICA

CARIBBEAN SEA

PARQUE NACIONAL RINCÓN DE LA VIEJA

Liberia

PARQUE NACIONAL VOLCÁN ARENAL

Tortuguero

PARQUE NACIONAL TORTUGUERO

PARQUE NACIONAL PALO VERDE

RESERVA SANTA ELENA

San Carlos

RARA AVIS NATURE RESERVE

RESERVA BIOLÓGICA BOSQUE NUBOSO MONTEVERDE

NICOYA PENINSULA

Puerto Limón

SAN JOSÉ

Turrialba

OROSI VALLEY

Puerto Viejo de Talamanca

Sixaola

PARQUE NACIONAL CHIRRIPÓ

PARQUE INTERNACIONAL LA AMISTAD

PANAMA

Metres
2000
1500
1000
500
0

PACIFIC OCEAN

Bahía Drake

OSA PENINSULA

N

0   50 km

country, passing through fields of purple orchids and deciduous forests. Resident animals include tapirs, peccaries, monkeys and all the country's big cats, while birders may spot oropendolas, trogons and spectacled owls.

● **Rara Avis** A private rainforest reserve and research station 80km northeast of San José, Rara Avis offers one of the best ecotourism experiences in the country. Getting to the forest is half the adventure – its remoteness means that it's only accessible by a tractor-drawn cart from the nearest village along a muddy track, with great views of the surrounding countryside and of toucans in the trees. Once there you can walk one of several excellent trails through the forest, check out the abundant flora

(including rare palm species and orchids) or swim in a waterfall pool.

● **Turrialba** In the Valle Central, Turrialba is a friendly agricultural town with few tourists. The pretty surrounding countryside, spreading over the eastern slopes of the Cordillera Central, is filled with a fresh mountain air that provides a welcome change from the stifling heat of the nearby Caribbean coast. Adrenaline junkies can sign up for a whitewater rafting or kayaking trip on the Reventazón or Pacuaré rivers, while the most important archeological site in Costa Rica – Monumento Nacional Guayabo – is 20km away. Several nearby alfresco restaurants serve delicious local fare – barbecued meat and *pozol*, a corn and pork soup – in attractive rustic settings.

www.roughguides.com

▲ Bungee jumping over the Río Colorado

Routes in and out

There are direct flights daily to San José from Miami, Chicago, Houston, Dallas and several other US cities as well as regularly scheduled flights from Madrid, Frankfurt and Amsterdam. The border between Costa Rica and Nicaragua is at Peñas Blancas, close to the Pacific coast, and has direct bus routes on to Managua; it's also possible to cross the Río San Juan from Los Chiles to San Carlos. There are two main borders with Panama: Paso Canoas on the Pan-American Highway, and Sixaola on the Caribbean, convenient for the popular Panamanian resort of Bocas del Toro.

Books

Jack Ewing *Monkeys are made of Chocolate* (Pixyjack Press). Series of short stories and essays about the flora and fauna of the Costa Rican Atlantic coast written by the venerable owner of one of the country's first eco-lodges.

Mavis Hiltunen Biesanz *The Ticos: Culture and Social Change in Costa Rica* (Lynne Rienner Publishers). Wide-ranging discussion of all angles of Costa Rican society, divided neatly into topics – from economics to religion and food.
Anacristina Rossi *The Madwoman of Gandoca* (Edwin Mellen Press). Autobiographical tale of the dark side of conservation politics which uncovers a secret plot to develop a protected area of the Costa Rican Caribbean coast.

Costa Rica online

Cocori.com Ⓦ www.cocori.com
Excellent series of well-written articles on all aspects of life in Costa Rica, including food, scuba diving and spelunking.
Costa Rica Net Ⓦ www.costaricanet .net Links to thousands of Costa Rican websites and those set up by Costa Rica aficionados in the US.
Info Costa Rica Ⓦ www.infocosta rica.com Well-organized portal with hundreds of good links as well as in-house articles and a message board.

Costa Rican embassies and consulates

Australia
Consulate of Costa Rica, 30 Clarence St, Sydney ☏02/9261 1177

South Africa
Consulate of Costa Rica, 56 Dennis Rd, Blandford Ridge, Sandton,
Johannesburg PO Box 68140, ☏11-7053434

UK
Embassy of Costa Rica, Flat 1, 14 Lancaster Gate, London W2 3LH ☏0207/706 8844, ⓦwww.embcrlon.demon.co.uk

US
Embassy of Costa Rica, 2114 S St NW, Washington DC 20008 ☏(202) 2342945, ⓦwww.costarica-embassy.org.

www.roughguides.com

El Salvador

Capital San Salvador	distinct seasons, rainy (May–Oct)
Population 7.2 million	and dry (Nov–April)
Languages Spanish, Nahua	**Best time to go** November– April
Currency US dollar ($)	(dry season)
Climate Tropical on the coast and	**Minimum daily budget** US$20
temperate in the highlands with two	

El Salvador is the smallest country in Central America, the most densely populated and one of the least visited, largely as a result of the violent civil war which raged from 1980 to 1992, and whose memory still colours outside perceptions of the place. Now, almost two decades after the end of the conflict, El Salvador is making good progress in rebuilding itself, a process which wasn't helped by the series of massive earthquakes which devastated the coastal and central regions in 2001, during which a thousand people died and 145,000 homes were destroyed, leaving the country with a clean-up bill of US$2.8 billion – a sum which El Salvador can ill afford.

Nevertheless, El Salvador is a beautiful place, a land of mountain peaks and rolling green hills studded with no fewer than 25 volcanoes – some of them active – not to mention a long swathe of palm-fringed beaches on the Pacific – one of the loveliest stretches of coastline in the region. Salvadorans, though sometimes initially wary of foreigners (particularly if you're North American), are known throughout Central America for their wry humour, vivacity and industriousness.

El Salvador was, until recently, almost devoid of tourists. However

(though it still remains much less visited than neighbouring Guatemala and Nicaragua) travellers are increasingly attracted by the friendliness and peace of this small nation. It has a growing tourist infrastructure and there are now decent places to stay in all the country's beauty spots. And public transport, in the form of Bluebird buses, is incredibly cheap and well organized. While most of the country is safe to travel in, San Salvador is a hectic place and its city centre should be avoided after dark.

Main attractions

● **Bosque Montecristo** The remote and pristine Bosque Montecristo "El Trifinio" straddles the borders between El Salvador, Honduras and Guatemala. The reserve rises through two climatic zones to its peak at Cerro Montecristo (2418m), surrounded by an expanse of virgin cloudforest home to orchids, huge oak and cypress trees, monkeys, jaguars and quetzals.

● **Islas del Golfo de Fonseca** In the sheltered bay which straddles the coastal El Salvador–Honduras border, these four islands are secluded, peaceful

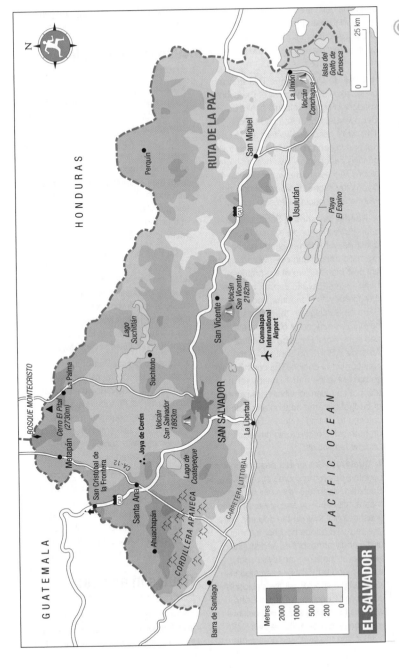

EL SALVADOR

www.roughguides.com

and have calm seas for swimming and uncrowded hiking trails. The largest, Meanguera, has a small hotel, and *comedores* (dining halls) in the local village serve fresh seafood.

● **Lago de Coatepeque** This stunning crater lake lies in the west of the country, shadowed by the volcanic peaks of Cerro Verde, Santa Ana and Izalco. The lake's deep blue waters are fed by hot springs and ringed by walking trails offering panoramic views over lush green slopes. Access to the water is easiest if you stay in one of several simple but wonderfully peaceful lakeside hotels.

● **Pacific beaches** El Salvador has a long sweep of undeveloped Pacific coastline, with palm-fringed beaches, dramatic cliffs, mangrove swamps and unspoilt islands. Two of the prettiest beaches are Playa El Espino, towards the border with Honduras, and Playa Barra de Santiago, in the far west; both have a basic range of places to stay and eat – *Hotel Paradise in Central America* in Barra de Santiago is the only upmarket choice. The coast's main settlement is the rather shabby fishing town of La Libertad, which has plenty of budget accommodation and café life catering to visiting surfers – beaches on both sides of the town have good, uncrowded waves.

● **Suchitoto** Set amidst beautiful rolling countryside on the shores of Lago Suchitlán, Suchitoto (the Nahuatl name means "city of birds and flowers") is the finest colonial town in the country, with low, red-tiled adobe houses, a tranquil and friendly atmosphere, and stunning views over the lake – an idyllic spot to swim and fish. Those interested in local culture should visit the decidedly eccentric Museo de Alejandro Cotto, which is housed in a restored colonial mansion with a beautiful garden overlooking the lake, and an eclectic collection of local paintings, indigenous artefacts and musical instruments.

Also recommended

● **Ahuachapán and the Cordillera Apaneca** Ahuachapán, close to the Guatemalan border, was one of the first Spanish settlements in El Salvador and is now a comfortably bourgeois city with quiet streets, a lively market and several attractive churches. The surrounding area, the Cordillera Apaneca, is covered with mountain peaks laced with pine forest and coffee plantations, which are at their most picturesque when their white flowers blossom in May.

● **La Palma** Known throughout El Salvador for its naif and brightly coloured artesenía (arts and crafts), La Palma is a sleepy mountain town with wooded outskirts and several excellent hiking trails – the most adventurous of these, to the summit of Cerro El Pital, the country's highest peak, takes several days.

● **Ruta de la Paz** Part of a major project to develop tourism in the northeast of El Salvador, the so-called Ruta de la Paz ("Peace Route") encompasses a beautiful mountainous region dotted with small villages and a series of caves containing pre-Columbian wall art.

● **Santa Ana** El Salvador's second city is a relaxing place with some lovely colonial architecture and a magnificent neo-Gothic cathedral. Set in the verdant Cihautehuacán valley, the city is close to three volcanoes, including the highest in the country, Volcán Santa Ana (2365m).

Routes in and out

There are flights daily to San Salvador from various cities in the US, including Los Angeles, Miami, Houston and New

York, as well as daily flights from all the other Central American capitals and Mexico City. There are no direct connections from Europe, Australasia or South Africa. You can cross overland into Guatemala at La Hachadura, near the Pacific (which is used by international buses heading to Mexico and is closest to Guatemala's Western Highlands); Las Chinamas, an hour from Ahuachapán, which has buses to Guatemala City; and, if you're visiting the Montecristo cloudforest, Anguiatú, which has connections to Esquipulas. The main crossings between El Salvador and Honduras are at El Amatillo, on the Panamerican Highway, and at El Poy in the north.

Books

Sandra Benitez *Bitter Grounds* (Picador). Epic and vivid saga which relates the story of three generations of women – poor and rich – in twentieth-century El Salvador.
Joan Didion *Salvador* (Granta). Controversial but deeply felt and lyrical impressions of El Salvador by a renowned US intellectual who spent a short time in the country in 1982.
Jose Ignacio Lopez-Vigil *Rebel Radio* (Latin American Bureau). The engrossing story of Radio Venceremos, the voice of the Salvadoran rebel movement – the FMLF, which broadcast live reports of army assaults alongside music.

Larry Towell *El Salvador* (W.W. Norton). Beautiful and moving photographs taken by a Magnum photographer, which document the country's civil war and its aftermath.

El Salvador online

El Salvador Gringo ⓦwww .theelsalvadorgringo.com
Wide-ranging blog with posts on places of natural beauty, cultural activities and general tips on travelling in the country.
Gateway El Salvador ⓦwww .gatewayelsalvador.com
Comprehensive travel website run by the owner of a large *finca* with an interesting blog on running a working plantation and all kinds of other information for visitors.
The Other El Salvador ⓦwww .theotherelsalvador.com Interesting and in-depth articles and essays written by travellers with photos and a comprehensive series of links.

Salvadoran embassies

UK
Embassy of El Salvador, Third Floor, Mayfair House, 39 Great Portland St, London W1N 7JZ ☎0207/436 8282
US
Embassy of El Salvador, 2308 California St NW, Washington DC 20008 ☎(202) 2659671, ⓦwww.elsalvador.org.

Guatemala

Capital Guatemala City	**Currency** Quetzal/US dollar ($)
Population 13.3 million	**Climate** Hot and humid in the
Languages Spanish, plus twenty	lowlands; cooler in the highlands
indigenous languages including	**Best time to go** February–May (dry
Quiché, Cakchique, Kekchi, Mam,	season)
Garífuna and Xinca	**Minimum daily budget** US$20

After decades of civil war, Guatemala has transformed itself into one of Central America's most popular tourist destinations. Its memorable natural landscapes, outstanding archeological sites and indigenous Maya culture attract many visitors. Almost half the country's population is pure-blooded Maya, speaking their own languages, living in small rural communities which have barely changed in centuries and continuing long-standing traditions. These are most visible in the colourful traditional costumes worn across the highlands and in absorbing markets and riotous fiestas.

Guatemala's outstanding Maya ruins are testament to the strength and longevity of Maya culture; they include not only Tikal, perhaps the most impressive archeological site in Latin America, but also dozens of less well-known sites, many of them atmospherically buried in the pristine rainforests which cover much of the country's eastern lowlands, known as the Petén.

Maya culture apart, Guatemala also boasts some of Central America's most memorable landscapes, from the towering volcanoes which surround magical Lago de Atitlán in the highlands to the vast expanses of the Petén jungle.

In addition, Guatemala is home to Antigua, Central America's loveliest and liveliest colonial city and one of several excellent places in the country in which to study Spanish.

The country is relatively safe to visit, although incidents of armed robbery and rape are still reported, especially around Lago de Atitlán – don't walk alone, especially at night.

Main attractions

● **Antigua** Formerly the capital of Guatemala, and probably the most beautiful colonial city in Central America, Antigua retains its tranquil atmosphere despite a vibrant gringo scene, based around the city's dozens of language schools. Dating back to the Spanish Conquest, the city's Semana Santa (Easter Week) celebrations are the most extravagant in the country.

● **Lago de Atitlán** In the highlands, a hundred kilometres north of Guatemala City, Lago de Atitlán is hemmed in by three soaring volcanoes and surrounded by a string of intriguing lakeside Maya villages, where traditional life continues more or less unchanged, despite the hordes of visiting tourists. It's possible

GUATEMALA

Metres
2100
1200
300
150
0

0   50 km

N

Tikal

Lago de
Petén Itzá

Flores

BELIZE

MEXICO

PETÉN

CARIBBEAN
SEA

CUCHUMATANES
MOUNTAINS

Livingston

Puerto
Barrios

IXIL
TRIANGLE

Lanquín

Río Dulce

La Mesilla

Todos
Santos

Chajul

Nebaj   Cotzal

CA1

Cobán

Semuc
Champey

Lago de
Izabal

CARRETERA AL ATLÁNTICO

Chichicastenango

HONDURAS

Sololá   Panajachel

GUATEMALA CITY

Lago de
Atitlán

Antigua

CA1

Volcán Pacaya

EL SALVADOR

PACIFIC OCEAN

to walk around the lake in four or five days – the less energetic will also find plenty of day-hikes, while boats regularly travel across the lake from village to village. Panajachel is the lake's principal community and the area's main base, with an abundance of cheap hotels and a long-established gringo scene.

● **Semuc Champey** Situated in the heart of Alta Verapaz, one of Guatemala's loveliest regions, Semuc Champey is a series of cool river pools with sparkling turquoise water hidden away in the

forest. The nearby village of Lanquín has several cheap *pensiones*, as well as the *El Retiro* lodge which has a picturesque riverside setting and a very popular bar.

● **Sololá market** Set high up on a hillside overlooking Lago de Atitlán, every Friday the picturesque village of Sololá is home to one of Central America's finest markets, with thousands of Maya traders in colourful woven clothes descending at dawn from the surrounding hills to sell traditional brightly coloured fabrics and ceramics.

221

▲ San Pedro church, Antigua

● **Tikal** Considered by many to be the finest of all Maya sites, the ruined city of Tikal – which at its height in around 500 AD was one of the most powerful and populous cities in the region – lies in the far east of the country. Its ruined temples soar majestically out of undisturbed rainforest which is home to monkeys, toucans and parakeets.

● **Volcán Pacaya** Just south of Guatemala City, Pacaya is one of Central America's most active and spectacular volcanoes, with dramatic night-time eruptions of molten orange lava. Pacaya is easily reached by public transport and has impressive views from its summit, which can be climbed in a day – but check on the volcano's current state of activity first.

Also recommended

● **Ixil triangle** Set in the verdant Cuchumatanes mountains at the northern edge of the Western Highlands, the remote Ixil region is one of the country's most traditional areas, whose Maya inhabitants speak a rare language, Ixil, and live much as their ancestors did centuries ago. The area has some beautiful walking trails, while its three main towns – Nebaj, Chajul and Cotzal – are made of up picturesque white adobe houses and cobbled streets.

● **Santo Tomás, Chichicastenango** The attractive small town of Chichicastenango is home both to a colourful indigenous (though touristy) market and also to one of Guatemala's most intriguing churches, Santo Tomás. Originally built in 1540 on the site of a Maya altar, the church offers a fascinating glimpse into the unique world of Maya religion, with its strange mix of indigenous and Catholic beliefs, incorporating in equal measure Christian saints and native shamans.

● **Travelling along the Río Dulce** Starting in Lívingston on Guatemala's Caribbean coast, the spectacular journey along the Río Dulce passes through a steep, narrow gorge, hemmed in by sheer walls of tropical vegetation, before opening out into tranquil Lago de Izabal, which has some lovely beaches to swim from and boat trips around its shores.

Routes in and out

There are direct daily flights to Guatemala City from cities in the US including Miami, Houston, Chicago and Los Angeles. In Europe there are only direct flights from Madrid and many travellers choose to fly directly to Mexico City or Cancún and make their way overland. Travelling overland, Guatemala has frontiers with four countries – Mexico, Belize, Honduras and El Salvador. The border at Florido is conveniently close to the ruins of Copán in Honduras. A bus from Flores (near Tikal in the Petén) goes to Belize City and straight through Belize to the Mexican border town of Chetumal; there are numerous other border crossings between Guatemala and Mexico as well. The most popular crossing to El Salvador is at Asuncíon Mita on the Pan-American Highway.

Books

Horacio Castellanos Moya *Senselessness* (W.W. Norton). Sarcastic and humorous novel which ridicules Guatemalan society in the aftermath of the civil war, as well as the foreign volunteers, human rights workers and journalists who flooded the country during this time.
Ralph Lee Woodward *A Short History of Guatemala* (Editorial Laura Lee). An academic study, drawing on almost fifty years of research by a US professor and regional expert, which details the country from its ancient Maya heritage to the

modern day with special emphasis on the nineteenth and twentieth centuries.
Rigoberta Menchu *I, Rigoberta Menchu – An Indian Woman in Guatemala* (Verso). Fascinating memoirs of a young Quiché woman which document her complex culture as well as her personal experiences during Guatemala's brutal civil war.

Guatemala online

Guate Living Ⓦwww.guateliving .com A variety of insights on matters big and small, stories and advice in a blog written by an American living in the country.
Guatemala Photos Ⓦwww.atitlan .net Photos, news, essays and links, mostly relating Lago de Atitlán and its surrounds, but also covering other parts of the country.
Guatemala Web Ⓦwww.guatemala web.com Excellent website created by the owner of the *Posada Belén* hotel in Guatemala City, with articles and links on everything from the current government, visa requirements and the locations of cash machines to Guatemalan charities, festivals and cuisine.

Guatemalan embassies and consulates

Australia
Consulate of Guatemala, 41 Blarney Ave, Kilarney Heights, NSW 2987 ☏02/9451 3018
UK
Embassy of Guatemala, 13 Fawcett St, London SW10 9HN ☏0207/351 3042
US
Embassy of Guatemala, 2220 R St NW, Washington DC 20008 ☏(202) 7454952, Ⓦwww.guatemala-embassy.org.

Honduras

Capital Tegucigalpa
Population 7.8 million
Languages Spanish, Creole
English, Garífuna
Currency Lempira (L)
Climate Subtropical in the lowlands
and temperate in the mountains;
the rainy season runs from May to
November, while hurricane season is
in October and November
Best time to go March to May (dry
season)
Minimum daily budget US$20

Honduras is the original "Banana
Republic". From the late 1800s until the
1950s it was largely run by powerful
US fruit companies who controlled
not only the national banana trade but
also its railways, banks and factories.
The US influence lasted well into the
twentieth century – while El Salvador
and Nicaragua suffered years of civil
war, Honduras infamously served as
the training ground for CIA-funded
counter-revolutionaries, and was
consequently kept stable by US
investment and support throughout
the 1980s. Nevertheless, it remains
one of Latin America's poorest,
least developed and least visited
countries.

In October 1998, Hurricane Mitch
ripped through Central America, causing
most of its destruction in Honduras,
where it killed seven thousand people.
The country spent years reeling from
the aftershock, with widespread poverty
and soaring levels of street crime. In
recent years successive governments
have made extravagant pledges to bring
order to the country and to put an end
to the notorious *maras* (violent gangs)
that menace Honduran cities, with little
success.

Geographically, Honduras boasts
similar terrain – a cool, mountainous
interior fringed by a humid Caribbean
coastline – to neighbouring Guatemala
and Nicaragua. Much of the country is
protected by an extensive network of
national parks and reserves, including
the misty cloudforest of Sierra de
Agalta in the east and the spectacular
Río Plátano Biosphere Reserve in the
remote wetlands of Mosquitia, two
of the largest stretches of pristine
forest in Central America. The country
is sparsely populated, while foreign
tourists are also pretty thin on the
ground – you'll have the place pretty
much to yourself, apart from at the
backpacker hot spots of Copán and
the Bay Islands.

The bad news is that Honduras is
one of the most dangerous countries
in Central America – you'll need to be
particularly careful in the Caribbean
towns of Tela, La Ceiba, Trujillo – after
dark, while the country's second city,
San Pedro Sula, is very dangerous,
with rife crack cocaine usage and gang
warfare. You should also avoid walking
on deserted beaches. Honduras is,
however, very cheap, with daily costs
among the lowest in Latin America.

Main attractions

- **Bay Islands** Honduras's biggest draw comprises three small Caribbean islands set on a coral reef. The scuba diving is superb and the Bay Islands' calm turquoise waters have become a mecca for divers, with some of the world's cheapest scuba courses on offer. Utila is the most popular of the islands with backpackers and has a firmly entrenched gringo party scene. The largest island, Roatán, is much quieter, with good hiking trails and more upmarket accommodation.

- **Copán** Copán is one of the most impressive of all Maya sites. Although not large – it's dwarfed in scale by Tikal and Chichén Itzá – the site boasts some of the Maya region's most magnificently carved sculptures, as well as the remarkable Hieroglyphic Stairway and an outstanding on-site Museum of Maya Sculpture. The nearby town, Copán Ruinas, is an attractive and relaxing place to spend a few days.

- **Garífuna villages** Surrounding Tela on the Caribbean coast is a string of sleepy villages with palm-thatched huts which are populated by friendly Garífuna people – the descendants of African slaves brought to the Caribbean to work on banana plantations. Weekends are the best time to visit, when you'll have the chance to hear the seductive drum rhythms of Garífuna music performed by local musicians.

- **Parque Nacional Sierra de Agalta** In the eastern Olancho region of Honduras, the Parque Nacional Sierra de Agalta protects a vast area of pristine and rarely visited cloudforest, which is home to many rare animals including tapirs, jaguars and ocelots, as well as over 400 species of birds, including no fewer than 33 different kinds of hummingbird.

- **Río Plátano Biosphere Reserve, La Mosquíta** Northeast Honduras is covered with remote and marshy wetlands, known as La Mosquíta after the Miskito Indians who still inhabit it. La Mosquíta is rarely visited – you'll have to fly in which is relatively expensive – but it is home to the most significant nature reserve in Honduras, the Río Plátano Biosphere Reserve, which is inhabited by eighty percent of the country's animal species.

Also recommended

- **Lago de Yojoa** Set among the mountains and coffee plantations of Honduras's western highlands, the expansive Lago de Yojoa boasts sparkling blue water and hundreds of bird species. Busy at weekends with wealthy Hondureños, during the week the lake is calm and peaceful.

- **Nightlife in Tela and La Ceiba** These two Caribbean towns are home to the country's wildest nightlife, with vibrant dancehalls, patronized both by locals and foreign tourists, which churn out Garífuna punta rock music, reggae and Latin sounds. The best time to visit is during La Ceiba's carnival in May, during which 200,000 revellers descend on the town and dance until dawn.

- **Parque Nacional Pico Bonito** South of La Ceiba, the Parque Nacional Pico Bonito protects a remote expanse of broadleaf, cloud- and pine forests that's crisscrossed by twenty rivers and dominated by the dramatic peak of Pico Bonito (2435m). There is an abundance of wildlife – including armadillos, monkeys and pumas, while the Río Cangrejal has some of the best Class III and IV rapids for whitewater rafting in Central America.

Routes in and out

There are direct international flights daily from the US (Miami and Houston) to Tegucigalpa, as well as to Honduras's second city, San Pedro Sula, and Roatán. There are no direct flights from Europe, Australasia or South Africa. The most popular and useful overland border crossing into Guatemala is at El Florido (close to Copán), though there are several others; you can also cross overland from Honduras into El Salvador and Nicaragua. A weekly boat goes from the Caribbean town of Puerto Cortés to Belize; you may also be able to find a boat leaving from one of Honduras's Caribbean towns to Puerto Cabezas in Nicaragua. Large groups might be able to charter a boat from Omoa to Lívingston in Guatemala.

Books

Medea Benjamin *Don't be afraid gringo: A Honduran woman speaks from the heart* (Institute for Food and Development Policy). A story of rural peasant life told through the real experiences of Elvia Alvarado, a community leader opposed to the destructive influence of US foreign policy on her people's long-standing way of life.
Lucila Gamero de Mendina *Blanca Olmedo* (Diana). A lushly romantic Romeo and Juliet love story between the classes in the nineteenth century. It caused controversy at the time of its publication because of its brave critical stance against both the Catholic Church and the stifling social mores of Honduran high society.

Adrienne Pine *Working Hard, Drinking Hard: On Violence and Survival in Honduras* (University of California Press). Well-considered sociological study which chronicles the messy lives of factory workers, shanty towns and gang culture in urban Honduras.

Honduras online

Country of Honduras ⓦwww.honduras.com Extensive website with general and travel information and essays on culture and history.
Honduras This Week ⓦwww.hondurasthisweek.com Award-winning website of the English-language newspaper, with national news coverage, tourist information and listings.
In-Honduras.com ⓦwww.in-honduras.com Comprehensive portal with hundreds of links to media, arts and entertainment, political and tourist websites – and also to personal websites featuring the travel journals of people who have visited Honduras.

Honduran embassies and consulates

Australia
Consulate of Honduras, 42 Carpenter St, Brighton Beach, Vic 3186 ☎03/9593 1595
UK
Embassy of Honduras, 115 Gloucester Place, London W1H 3PJ ☎0207/486 4880
US
Embassy of Honduras, 3007 Tilden St NW, Washington DC 20008 ☎(202) 9667702, ⓦwww.hondurasemb.org.

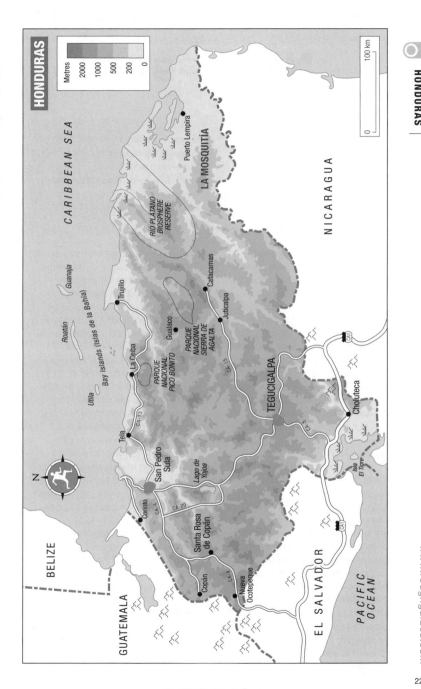

HONDURAS

Metres
2000
1000
500
200
0

N

BELIZE

GUATEMALA

CARIBBEAN SEA

Guanaja

Roatán

Bay Islands (Islas de la Bahía)

Utila

La Ceiba

PARQUE NACIONAL PICO BONITO

Trujillo

Gualaco

PARQUE NACIONAL SIERRA DE AGALTA

RÍO PLATANO BIOSPHERE RESERVE

Puerto Lempira

LA MOSQUITIA

Catacamas

Juticalpa

CA-15

Tela

CA-13

San Pedro Sula

Lago de Yojoa

Corinto

CA-4

CA-20

Santa Rosa de Copán

Copán

CA-1

Nueva Ocotepeque

TEGUCIGALPA

CA-5

Choluteca

CA-1

Isla El Tigre

NICARAGUA

EL SALVADOR

PACIFIC OCEAN

100 km

WHERE TO GO

Nicaragua

Capital Managua
Population 5.9 million
Languages Spanish, Creole
English on the Caribbean coast,
plus indigenous languages including
Sumo, Rama and Miskito
Currency Cordoba (¢)

Climate Tropical in the lowlands,
cooler in the highlands; rainy season
June–October
Best time to go December–March
(dry season)
Minimum daily budget US$20

Despite over a decade of peace, Nicaragua is still associated in many people's minds with the long civil war between the left-wing Sandinistas and the US-backed Contras which devastated the country from 1979 to 1990 and in which some 30,000 Nicaraguans died. Indeed, whatever has changed in the last ten years, Nicaragua is still paying the price for that war – as well as for the 45 years of brutal dictatorship which preceded it – and currently has one of the lowest per capita incomes in Latin America, along with eighty percent unemployment.

Yet, the country has started to realize its potential as a tourist destination – one of the last countries in Latin America to do so – and is rapidly changing. Though many roads are still in a terrible state, more and more decent (and decently priced) accommodation is now available as well as other tourist services. A foreign presence is most notable in the beautiful colonial city of Granada, which sits on the shores of Lago de Nicaragua – cheap property prices and labour costs have encouraged a wave of expat Americans to invest in second homes and even

to start planning large seafront resorts. The unspoilt Nicaragua of old seems like a fast disappearing memory.

For the moment at least, other compelling attractions in the country include two long coastlines, picturesque highland scenery and a landscape dotted with lakes and volcanoes, including the vast Lago de Nicaragua (the largest in Central America).

Nicaraguans are famously friendly and have yet to become blasé or cynical about tourists in the way that the inhabitants of more visited countries can be. With so much unemployment, some families (particularly in touristy areas) are happy to take in visitors as paying guests for as little as US$15 a day, with all meals included. This is a great way to gain an insight into daily life, to contribute directly to the local economy and to practise your Spanish.

Nicaragua doesn't have the most temperate of climates – it's very hot and very dry some of the year and very hot and wet the rest – nor does it offer luxurious or even comfortable travel. It is, however, among the cheapest countries in Latin America to visit, as well as being one of the safest.

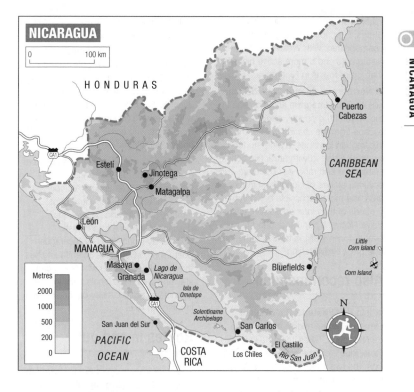

NICARAGUA

| 0 | 100 km |

HONDURAS

Puerto
Cabezas

*CARIBBEAN
SEA*

Estelí
Jinotega
Matagalpa

León

MANAGUA

Metres	
2000	
1000	
500	
200	
0	

Masaya
Granada
*Lago de
Nicaragua*

*Isla de
Ometepe*

Bluefields

*Little
Corn Island*

Corn Island

*Solentiname
Archipelago*

San Juan del Sur

San Carlos

*PACIFIC
OCEAN*

El Castillo

COSTA
RICA

Los Chiles

Río San Juan

N

Main attractions

● **The Corn Islands** Two tiny islands in the Caribbean, Corn Island and Little Corn are a world apart from the rest of Nicaragua, with a largely black population of Jamaican descent. The islands make a perfect place to kick back for a few days, with sandy, unspoilt beaches, a laid-back pace and locally caught (and fantastically cheap) lobster on every menu; there's also superlative snorkelling around Little Corn.

● **El Castillo** Situated on the Río San Juan roughly halfway between Lago de Nicaragua and the Atlantic, the village of El Castillo sits like a mirage in the midst of the remote and scarcely inhabited

wetlands that line the river. It's a pretty little place, with wooden houses on stilts over the water and a ruined Spanish fort on a grassy knoll. There's little to do except sit and watch boats sail down the river, though you could try persuading a local fisherman to take you out on a trip or rent a horse to trek into the forest.

● **Granada** A long-standing tourist favourite, Granada is one of the oldest and most attractive colonial cities in Latin America. Founded in 1524, the city's position on the shores of Lago de Nicaragua led to it being an important commercial centre, though it now exists in a peaceful somnolence, with wide streets of imposing mansions and a leafy Parque Central. The city is changing fast, though – due to an influx of second-homers from the States, Granada is rapidly becoming cosmopolitan, with Western-style restaurants and a more active nightlife than other towns in Nicaragua.

● **Northern highlands** The cool green hills around Matagalpa and Jinotega in the north of the country offer the perfect escape from the searing heat of the Nicaraguan lowlands, a pine-studded landscape dotted with attractive coffee plantations and ranches. There are also several patches of cloudforest in the area, the most accessible being in the grounds of the *Hotel de la Montaña Selva Negra*, a popular eco-lodge with over a dozen walking trails into the forest and great birdwatching.

Also recommended

● **Isla de Ometepe** The island of Ometepe, in the middle of vast Lago de Nicaragua, takes its name (originally Ome Tepetl, or "the place of two hills") from the two striking volcanoes, Volcán Concepción and Volcán Maderas, which tower over it. Most visitors come to climb the volcanoes – it takes eight strenuous hours to ascend and descend Maderas, the smaller of the two, but the view from the top is stunning.

● **Masaya** The market town of Masaya is home to several beautiful churches and an enduring tradition of skilled craftsmanship; the locally produced hammocks are particularly impressive – you can watch them being woven and even have one custom-made. The best time to visit is during October and November when the town stages a two-month festival to celebrate its patron saint, San Jerónimo. This kicks off with two colourful processions (Sept 30 & Oct 7), when the saint's image is borne on a gaily decorated plinth round the town. Every Sunday throughout the festival is marked by fireworks, dancing and live marimba music.

● **San Juan del Sur** Set on a bay surrounded by towering cliffs, with a string of smaller, undeveloped beaches stretching down the coast nearby, San Juan del Sur is a laid-back seaside town with a growing gringo scene, thanks to the surfers who come here in search of uncrowded Pacific waves.

● **Solentiname** Situated in the southern corner of Lago de Nicaragua, the tiny islands of the Solentiname Archipelago represent one of the country's most remote, peaceful and picturesque destinations. Home to an artistic community established by Nicaraguan poet Ernesto Cardenal, Solentiname has three inhabited islands where you can stay and watch the locals paint in their distinctive primitive style, or simply swim in the calm lake.

Routes in and out

There are several direct flights daily from Miami to Nicaragua's capital, Managua, as well as a once-daily service from Houston. If you're travelling from Europe, there's a well-priced Martinair flight several times a week from Amsterdam to San José in Costa Rica, from where you can make your way overland (around 9hr by bus). There's one land crossing between Nicaragua and Costa Rica at Peóas Blancas; you can also cross by river from San Carlos to Los Chiles. There are several land borders between Nicaragua and Honduras – the most popular is El Guasaule in the north of Chinandega province.

Books

Gioconda Belli *The Country Under my Skin* (Bloomsbury). Autobiography of former Sandinista journalist, poet and critic who describes her adventures during the revolution.

Edward Marriott *Savage Shores* (Owl Books). Nicaragua's bull sharks are the most bloodthirsty in the world and in tracking down the men who hunt them, Marriott evokes the rackety atmosphere of the country's Atlantic coast.

Salman Rushdie *The Jaguar Smile: A Nicaraguan Journey* (Vintage). Invited to Nicaragua by the Sandinistas, Rushdie spent 3 weeks in the country in 1983 and wrote this thought-provoking account of his stay when he returned.

Nicaragua online

Manfut Ⓦ**www.manfut.org** Very comprehensive website (Spanish only), mostly featuring photos and videos of every corner of the country.

Nicanet Ⓦ**www.nicanet.org** Website of a US organization committed to social and economic justice for the people of Nicaragua, with information on current campaigns and issues.

Nicaragua.com Ⓦ**www.nicaragua .com** Extensive portal with dozens of links to Nicaraguan general information, news, sport, travel and culture.

Nicaraguan embassies and consulates

UK
Embassy of Nicaragua, Suite 12, Vicarage House, 58–60 Kensington Church St, London W8 4DB ☎0207/938 2373

US
Embassy of Nicaragua, 1627 New Hampshire Ave NW, Washington DC 20009 ☎(202) 9396570.

Panama

Capital Panama City	**Climate** Tropical
Population 3 million	**Best time to go** December–April
Languages Spanish, English and	(dry season)
minority indigenous languages	**Minimum daily budget** US$30
Currency US dollar ($), also referred	
to as Balboa (B)	

Occupying the narrow isthmus that links the two American continents, Panama is often overlooked by travellers to Latin America, partly because the forests of the Darién Gap (see p.42) still block overland travel between Central and South America. Yet Panama packs an extraordinary range of attractions into compact geography, and has emerged from a long history as a virtual US colony as a confident and outward-looking society. Long before the construction of the famous canal linking the Atlantic and Pacific oceans, this was one of the great crossroads of the world, and Panama City is one of the most cosmopolitan and dynamic cities in Latin America. In dramatic contrast to the high-rise modernity of the capital, rural Panama is home to some of the most fascinating and unassimilated indigenous cultures in Central America, such as the Kuna, who govern themselves on a remote and idyllic archipelago.

Though Panamanians have not yet become jaded with foreign visitors, the fact that it's now often described as "like Costa Rica twenty years ago" suggests Panama is finally catching on with travellers to Central America keen to escape the crowds. With 1600km of Pacific and 1280km of Caribbean coast, the country boasts innumerable unspoiled beaches and coral reefs, making it a great place for snorkelling, diving, surfing or just lying out in the sun. And although it is Costa Rica that has achieved world renown as an ecotourism destination, in terms of pristine wilderness and ecological diversity, Panama has little reason to envy its neighbour. Over half the country is covered by dense tropical forest, and large areas are protected by a system of nature reserves and national parks. With little tourist development, the infrastructure for visiting these protected areas is rather limited, but those who make the effort are richly rewarded: whether watching turtles laying their eggs by night on pristine stretches of sand or searching for resplendent quetzals in the high cloudforest, visitors to Panama's national parks are unlikely to share the experience with more than a handful of other people

Main attractions

● **Bocas del Toro** Long one of the best-kept travellers' secrets in Central America, the remote and beautiful Bocas del Toro archipelago on Panama's north-western Caribbean coast is now the

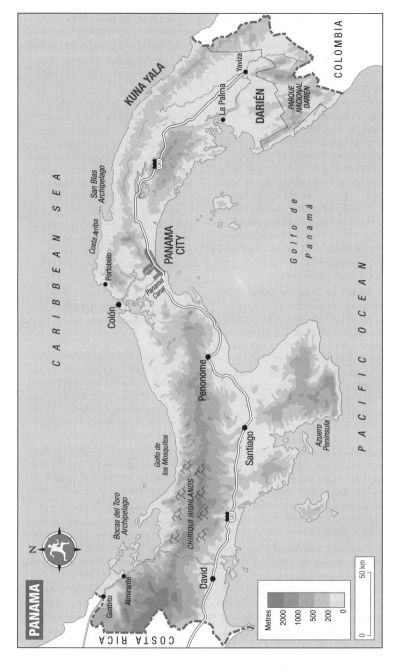

PANAMA

COLOMBIA

KUNA YALA

Yaviza

La Palma

DARIÉN

PARQUE
NACIONAL
DARIÉN

CARIBBEAN SEA

San Blas
Archipelago

Costa Arriba

Portobelo

PANAMA
CITY

Golfo de
Panamá

Colón

Panama
Canal

PACIFIC OCEAN

Penonome

Golfo de
los Mosquitos

Santiago

Azuero
Peninsula

Bocas del Toro
Archipelago

CHIRIQUÍ HIGHLANDS

N

Almirante

David

Guabito

COSTA RICA

PANAMA

Metres	
2000	
1000	
500	
200	
0	

0   50 km

scene of rapid tourist development. So far though, the archipelago's richly varied ecosystems – tropical forests, deserted beaches, coral reefs and crystalline waters – are still largely unspoilt.

● **Chiriqui Highlands** In the far west of Panama on the Costa Rican border, the Chiriqui Highlands are a beautiful region of cloudforest-covered peaks, fertile valleys dotted with orange groves and coffee plantations, and peaceful mountain villages. From the town of Boquete you can walk or drive up to the peak of the 3475-metre Volcán Barú, from where (on a clear day) you can see both the Pacific and Atlantic oceans, while the pristine cloudforests of nearby Parque Nacional La Amistad are perhaps the best place in all Central America to see the rare resplendent quetzal.

● **Kuna Yala** Stretching almost 400km along the northeastern Caribbean coast, Kuna Yala – also known as the San Blas Archipelago – is the self-governing homeland of the indigenous Kuna, who live in splendid isolation on a series of tiny palm-fringed coral atolls strung out along the densely forested mainland. Best known for the distinctive costumes worn by the women, the Kuna enjoy almost total autonomy, a status that has helped them maintain their unique and compelling traditional culture and way of life. This wildly beautiful region can easily be reached by light aircraft from Panama City, and basic accommodation and other services – run by the Kuna themselves – are available on several islands.

● **Panama Canal** Almost a century after its construction, Panama's most famous landmark is still an astounding feat of engineering, impressive both for its sheer magnitude and its unexpectedly rugged beauty. Linking the Pacific and Atlantic oceans, the canal cleaves a narrow path through pristine rainforest

and can easily be visited on a day-trip from Panama City, either by taking a cruise through the canal, riding the train that runs alongside it, or visiting the locks where massive ships are raised and lowered.

● **Panama City** With a spectacular setting on the Pacific coast, Panama City is one of Latin America's most cosmopolitan capitals, combining the intrigue and energy of its modern high-rise banking district with the laid-back street life and Spanish-colonial architecture of its historic city centre. Its food and nightlife are both excellent, and beautiful beaches and rainforests are within easy reach. Panama City is also the best base from which to explore the rest of Panama, including the canal.

Also recommended

● **Azuero Peninsula** Jutting out into the Pacific southwest of Panama City, the dry and scrubby Azuero Peninsula is considered the cradle of Panamanian rural traditions and folklore and is home to many vibrant religious fiestas. It's also fringed with huge, deserted white-sand beaches and boasts two offshore nature reserves: Isla Iguana, which is excellent for diving and snorkelling, and the rarely visited Isla Cañas, where sea turtles nest in large numbers.

● **Parque Nacional Darién** Though guerrillas, drug traffickers and bandits make the adventurous journey overland across the Darién Gap to Colombia (see p.42) strictly off-limits, the splendid wildlife-rich rainforests of Parque Nacional Darién – one of the most biodiverse regions on earth – remain largely safe to visit, either independently or on an organized tour from Panama City.

● **Portobelo and the Costa Arriba**
Though the infamously poor and dangerous Caribbean port of Colón should be avoided, the nearby Costa Arriba, which stretches northeast of the city, covers an isolated and enticing region of palm-fringed beaches, coral reefs and laid-back fishing villages, while the historic town of Portobelo preserves its formidable colonial fortifications, built to protect Spanish treasure fleets from pirate attack.

Routes in and out

Panama City is a major transportation hub and is well connected by plane to other Latin American capitals, the US and Europe. Travelling overland, there are road crossings between Panama and Costa Rica on both the Pacific and Caribbean coasts – as a consequence, western Panama sees more backpackers than the rest of the country combined. Overland travel between Panama and Colombia is virtually impossible, however. Drug trafficking and guerrilla and bandit activity have made the famous crossing of the Darién Gap (see p.42) extremely dangerous – several travellers have been kidnapped and killed in recent years. The ferry service between Colón and Cartagena in Colombia no longer operates, but private yachts often carry travellers on this route, passing through the beautiful San Blas archipelago, for about the same price as a flight – ask around at the yacht clubs in Balboa (Panama City) or Cristóbal (Colón), or at the *Voyager International Hostel* in Panama City.

Panama books

Dougles Galbraith *The Rising Sun* (Picador). *Tour de force* of historical fiction set during the doomed Scottish attempt to colonize Darién during the late seventeenth century.

Graham Greene *Getting to Know the General* (Vintage). Fascinating personal reminiscences of the celebrated author's unlikely friendship with General Omar Torrijos, who ruled Panama between 1968 and 1981.

John Le Carré *The Tailor of Panama* (Sceptre). Highly entertaining satire by the master spy novelist, which paints Panama City as a labyrinth of drugs, dirty money and corruption.

David McCullough *The Path Between the Seas*. (Simon and Schuster). Compelling and authoritative account of the epic struggle to build the Panama Canal. Detailed and well researched, it nonetheless reads with the pace of a thriller.

Panama online

ANCON Ⓦ **www.ancon.org** Website of the National Conservation Association, Panama's biggest and most influential environmental group, with general information on Panama's national parks, ecology and endangered species and voluntary work opportunities.

ANCON Expeditions Ⓦ **www .anconexpeditions.com** Website of Panama's foremost ecotourism operator, with information and booking details for their exclusive lodges in Darién and guided tours throughout the country.

Panama Canal Authority Ⓦ **www .pancanal.com** Official site with plenty of information and news, a history of the canal in English and Spanish, pictures of the canal and a live webcam.

Panama Tours Ⓦ **www.panamatours .com** One-stop resource for travel to Panama, with plenty of general information on the country's highlights and links to a range of related sites.

Panamanian embassies and consulates

Canada
Embassy of Panama, 130 Albert St, Suite 300, KIP 5G4, Ottawa, Ontario ☎613/236-7177

South Africa
Embassy of Panama, 229 Olivier St, Brooklyn, Pretoria ☎012-4606677, ⓔpanamaembassy@bodamail.co.za

UK
Embassy of Panama, Panama House, 40 Hertford St, London W1J 7SH ☎0207/409 2255

US
Embassy of Panama, 2862 McGill Terrace, NW Washington, DC 20008 ☎(202) 4831407 ⓦwww.embassy ofpanama.org/cms/index3.php.

First-Time
Latin America

Where to go

South America

● Argentina	239
● Bolivia	245
● Brazil	250
● Chile	257
● Colombia	263
● Ecuador	268
● The Guianas	273
● Paraguay	278
● Peru	282
● Uruguay	288
● Venezuela	292

Argentina

Capital Buenos Aires
Population 41 million
Languages Spanish
Currency Argentine peso ($)
Climate Most of the country is temperate, though it varies from tropical in the northeast to sub-Arctic in southern Patagonia

Best time to go March–May; the Argentine autumn, with fair temperatures for hiking and pretty foliage in Patagonia, lower prices and bearable heat
Minimum daily budget US$35 (US$50 in Patagonia)

Argentina is an enormous country – the eighth largest in the world – attractions within its ample borders range from the elegant, European-style boulevards and cafés of Buenos Aires to the sub-Arctic glaciers and Andean mountains of Patagonia in the south. Despite its size, however, Argentina is culturally one of the most homogenous of all Latin American countries – the result of mass immigration from Europe during the late nineteenth century, as well as the almost complete extermination of the native populations. Most Argentines have Italian (or to a lesser extent, Spanish) ancestors – and in the cities, at least, the spirit of Europe is never far away.

Outside the major urban centres, however, a distinctively Argentine culture has developed. Known as *argentinidad* it

▲ Thelonious jazz club, Buenos Aires

is exemplified by the legendary gaucho, or Argentine cowboy, a legacy of the days in the early twentieth century when cattle ranching in the vast pampas of the interior made the country one of the wealthiest in the world. Even now, gaucho culture lives on in the Argentine obsession with meat-eating, while the famous gaucho drink, maté – an invigorating herbal infusion drunk through a metal straw from a colourful gourd – remains the national drink.

For the visitor, Argentina's biggest draws, apart from its atmospheric capital, Buenos Aires, are largely outdoors. The southern third of the country, Patagonia, is the principal destination. Here, an extensive series of national parks protects some of the most extraordinary – and extreme – scenery the continent has to offer.

Argentina's natural attractions extend far beyond Patagonia, however. One of the world's great natural wonders, the Iguazú Falls, dominates the northeast of the country, whose flat swamplands are home to hundreds of bird species. The northwest is a beguiling mix of jungle-clad cloudforests, high Andean plateaus (known in Argentina as *puna*) and deserts roamed by flocks of llamas. Further south lie the rolling green hills of Argentina's wine region while most of central Argentina is pampa or cowboy country.

Long considered among the safest and best organized countries to visit in Latin America, Argentina is also one of the region's most expensive places for tourists, particularly Patagonia – pricey by anyone's standards.

Main attractions

● **Buenos Aires** Argentina's capital city is one of the most atmospheric in Latin America. Though its wide tree-lined avenues and architecture were inspired by Paris, Buenos Aires is very much its own place, with distinctive barrios – football-crazy La Boca with its colourfully painted streets, bohemian San Telmo, home to the best tango shows in town, and exclusive Recoleta, site of the magnificently grand cemetery where Eva Perón is buried.

● **Iguazú Falls** One of the world's most dramatic series of waterfalls, the majestic Iguazú Falls straddle the border between Argentina, Brazil and Paraguay. A staggering 275 falls plunge over a precipice 80m high and 3km wide – you'll hear the deafening noise long before you can see anything. Although the best overall view of Iguazú is from Brazil, the falls' most extensive portion lies in the subtropical Argentine Parque Nacional Iguazú, with a well-organized system of walkways which run right to the edge of the roaring water, boat trips and plenty of wildlife. The most spectacular spot is the Garganta del Diablo (Devil's Throat), where fourteen separate falls merge to form the world's most powerful single waterfall in terms of the volume of water flow per second.

● **The Lake District** Often billed as the "Switzerland of Argentina", the Lake District is characterized by vast lakes and densely wooded forests in a mountainous setting. Hugely popular among Argentines as a holiday destination, the area is known for its network of accessible national parks which are strung out along the western cordillera. Bariloche is the region's main holiday hub, with 700,000 visitors annually, many of whom come in winter to hit the slopes at the nearby ski resort, Cerro Catedral. The city is also a starting point for the Ruta de los Siete Lagos, one of Latin America's most scenic drives, offering superb fishing en route.

ARGENTINA

Metres
5000
3000
1500
1000
400
200
0

N

BOLIVIA
La Quiaca
La Quebrada de Humahuaca
Salta
PUNA CATAMARQUEÑA
Antofagasta de la Sierra
Tucumán

BRAZIL
PARAGUAY
Puerto Iguazú
Iguazú Falls
Corrientes
Posadas
RESERVA NATURAL DEL IBERÁ
BRAZIL

CHILE
CORDILLERA DE LOS ANDES

Córdoba
Mendoza
Laguna Mar Chiquita
Santa Fe
Rosario
San Antonio de Areco
Río Paraná
Río Uruguay
URUGUAY
BUENOS AIRES

PACIFIC OCEAN

Santa Rosa
Bahía Blanca

LAKE DISTRICT
Bariloche
Río Chubut
PATAGONIA
Puerto Madryn
Península Valdés
Trelew
Río Negro

ATLANTIC OCEAN

Perito Moreno
La Cueva de las Manos Pintadas
▲ Fitz Roy Massif
PARQUE NACIONAL LOS GLACIARES
Glacier Perito Moreno
Río Gallegos
Punta Arenas
TIERRA DEL FUEGO
Ushuaia
Cape Horn
Straits of Magellan

Argentine Antarctic Territory

FALKLAND ISLANDS (Islas Malvinas)

0   200 km

• **Parque Nacional Los Glaciares**
Parque Nacional Los Glaciares in Patagonia is home to possibly the most impressive scenery in South America. Glaciar Perito Moreno in the south of the park is one of the few advancing glaciers in the world and offers an enthralling spectacle as it fragments into massive chunks of ice, some weighing hundreds of tons, which split off in spectacularly noisy fashion. The Fitz Roy Massif, a collection of mountain peaks centring on Monte Fitz Roy (3445m) on the park's northern boundary, is notably dramatic, its sheer needles of rock set in circles and rising up several kilometres into the Patagonian sky. If you're not an experienced mountaineer, the area, laced with lakes, hiking trails and spectacular *miradors* (lookout points), still has plenty to offer.

• **Península Valdés** A treeless headland in northern Patagonia, Península Valdés is one of the world's most important marine reserves. As well as colonies of penguins, sea lions, elephant seals, dolphins and killer whales, the area's sheltered waters play host to over a thousand southern right whales between May and December – the giant mammal's breeding season, when visitors are virtually guaranteed to get within a few metres of one of these gentle creatures.

• **Quebrada de Humahuaca** A dramatic gorge sliced through the high plains and mountains of northwest Argentina, the Quebrada is framed by striped rocks and laced with rivers and atmospheric mountains towns with a distinctly Bolivian atmosphere.

Also recommended

• **Cueva de las Manos Pintadas (Cave of the Painted Hands)**
Decorated with over 800 black, white and red handprints made by Paleolithic hunter-gatherers and dating as far back as 7300 BC, the cueva is really a series of overhangs in a cliff face. Containing probably the finest examples of rock painting in South America, the cave, in southern Patagonia, is best approached via a beautiful two-hour trek up the Cañon de Río Pintadas.

• **Puna Catamarqueña** The altiplano of Catamarca province is an eerie and remote place, flanked to the west by the Andes and Chile and dotted with flocks of grazing vicuñas and flamingos on frozen lakes. The region's only settlement, Antofagasta de la Sierra, has a 2000-year-old mummified baby in its museum and a tranquil population of highland farmers and herdsmen. Bring some warm clothes, as temperatures drop at night to – 30ºC/22°F.

• **Reserva Natural del Iberá** A watery network of lakes, marshes and floating islands, the Reserva Natural del Iberá is a vast (13,000 square kilometres) protected area in the northeast of Argentina offering wonderful wildlife-spotting opportunities. Locals in the village of Colonia Carlos Pellegrini take visitors out in small motorboats to see birds, monkeys and caymans at close range.

• **Salta** Colonial capital of the beautiful northwest region, Salta is lively and youthful with well-preserved architectural gems (such as the Iglesia y Convento San Francisco) and a surprisingly vibrant nightlife. The town also makes an ideal base for visiting the nearby Quebrada del Toro, a dramatic gorge sliced into multicoloured rock.

• **San Antonio de Areco** Just over 100km west of Buenos Aires, the charming town of San Antonio de Areco, with its cobbled streets and colonial facades, is Argentina's centre of pampa culture. Every November the town hosts a popular gaucho festival, the Día de la Tradición (see p.73), when gauchos parade in their traditional outfits and display their cowboy skills, including *jineteadas* (bronco riding) and horse-breaking. A traditional *asado con cuero* when beef is cooked over an open fire rounds up the festivities.

● **Tierra del Fuego** A collection of windswept islands at the southernmost tip of South America, Tierra del Fuego has long held a fascination for travellers. Its largest island, Isla Grande, is home to the region's capital, Ushuaia, which is beautifully situated between mountains and the sea. The city is also the starting point for boat trips along the Beagle Channel to the historic Estancia Harberton, a farmstead which became a refuge for Yámana, Selk'nam and Mannekenk Amerindian tribes, and today is home to the outstanding marine mammal museum, Museo Acatushún.

Routes in and out

Buenos Aires is easily reached by daily direct flights from Europe (London, Madrid, Paris and Rome), the US (New York, Miami and Chicago) , Australasia (Sydney and Auckland) and South Africa (Cape Town and Johannesburg). There are principal border crossings to Brazil and Paraguay at Puerto Iguazú; from La Quiaca to Bolivia; and by ferry across the Río Plata to Uruguay. There are many border crossings with Chile – the scenic Paso Mamuil Malal in Patagonia connects with the popular Chilean backpackers' resort of Pucón, while the equally picturesque Cruce Internacional de los Lagos crossing links with Puerto Montt.

Books

Roberto Arlt *The Seven Madmen* (Serpent's Tail). The best-known work

of one of the greatest Argentine writers, noted for his distinctive and influential prose style. The antihero goes looking for his soul – literally – in a hostile and ragged Buenos Aires.

Bruce Chatwin *In Patagonia* (Vintage). Inspired by tales of his grandmother's cousin, a sailor who settled in Punta Arenas after his ship sank in the Straits of Magellan, adventurer Chatwin set off to explore the strange and wild plains and peaks of southernmost Latin America.

Jose Hernandez *El Gaucho Martin Fierro* (State University of New York Press). Epic nineteenth-century poem which details the life and times of an impoverished gaucho and his battles with both authority and Native peoples.

Maximiliano Ruiz *Graffiti Argentina* (Thames and Hudson). Enlightening aesthetic and political study of Argentineo street art – which is now ranked as some of the best in the world.

Harry Thompson *This Thing of Darkness* (Headline Review). A fascinating homage to Vice-Admiral Robert Fitzroy who captained HMS *Beagle* – the boat known for taking Charles Darwin on the voyage that informed *The Origin of Species*. The landscape of Tierra del Fuego is evocatively described as is the striking culture of the Patagonian Indians on board.

Argentina online

Argen1tina Ⓦ**www.argentina.ar** Huge portal with hundreds of articles and news items on an extensive range of subjects – tourism, politics, sport.
Bloggers in Argentina Ⓦ**bloggersinargentina.blogspot .com** Hundreds of blogs from all over the country linked together, written by expats, travellers and Argentines.

El Sur del Sur Ⓦ www.surdelsur
.com Excellent online archive of
essays on Argentina's history,
geography and culture, with links to
regional websites.

Argentine embassies

Australia
Embassy of Argentina, PO Box 4835,
Kingston, ACT 2604 Ⓣ02/6273 9111,
Ⓦwww.argentina.org.au

Canada
Embassy of Argentina, 90 Sparks
St, Suite 910, Ottawa, ON K1P 5B4
Ⓣ613/236-2351, Ⓔconargen
@ram.net.au

New Zealand
Embassy of Argentina, Sovereign
Assurance Building, Level 14, 142
Lambton Quay, PO Box 5430, Wellington
Ⓣ04/472 8330, Ⓦwww.arg.org.nz

South Africa
Embassy of Argentina, 200 Standard
Bank Plaza, 440 Hilda St, Hatfield,
Pretoria, PO Box 11125 0083 Ⓣ27/12-
430-3524

UK
Embassy of Argentina, 27 Three Kings
Yard, London W1Y 1FL Ⓣ020/7318
1340, Ⓦwww.argentine-embassy-uk.org

US
Embassy of Argentina, 1600 New
Hampshire NW, Washington DC 20009
Ⓣ(202) 2386400.

Bolivia

Capital Sucre (official); La Paz (seat of government)
Population 10 million
Languages Spanish, Quechua, Aymara, Guaraní, plus thirty other minor indigenous languages
Currency Peso boliviano (B/)
Climate Ranging from hot and humid in the tropical lowlands to extremely cold and dry in the highlands
Best time to go May–September (dry season); between November and March rain make many roads impassable, particularly in the Amazon lowlands
Minimum daily budget US$20

Landlocked and isolated in the centre of the continent, Bolivia is the forgotten heart of South America, home to some of its most dramatic landscapes and deepest cultural traditions. From the glacial peaks of the Andes to the vast rainforests and savannahs of the Amazon, Bolivia's geography is not just extremely varied, it's invariably extreme. This natural diversity is matched by the ethnic and cultural diversity of the population: the majority of Bolivians are of indigenous descent, and the vitality of native cultures here is perhaps greater than anywhere else in Latin America.

Indeed, to think of Bolivia as part of Latin America at all is something of a misconception. Though three centuries of Spanish colonial rule have left their mark on the nation's language, religion and architecture, this European influence is just a thin veneer. Most Bolivians speak indigenous languages and are conscious inheritors of cultural traditions that stretch back long before the Conquest, and which are rooted in an intimate relationship with the land itself. With their traditional costumes, beliefs and ways of life, these distinctive native cultures – alongside the breathtaking landscapes they inhabit – constitute Bolivia's most powerful attraction.

Bolivia is divided into two main regions: the Andean highlands in the west and the tropical lowlands to the east and north. The highlands boast dramatic high mountain ranges where you can trek along Inca trails between traditional Quechua and Aymara villages, fine colonial cities, and the astonishing scenery of the Altiplano, a vast high-altitude plateau which in parts (such as Salar de Uyuni salt lake) possesses an otherworldly beauty. The vast tropical lowland regions of tropical rainforest and savannah include some of the wildest and most pristine protected areas in the Amazon basin (such as Parque Nacional Madidi) where you can see an extraordinary range of wildlife including jaguars, howler monkeys, toucans and pink river dolphins.

Bolivia is about the poorest and least developed country in Latin America, and this combined with the harsh geography makes getting around a bit of a challenge: roads are poor, conditions tough and journey times

www.roughguides.com

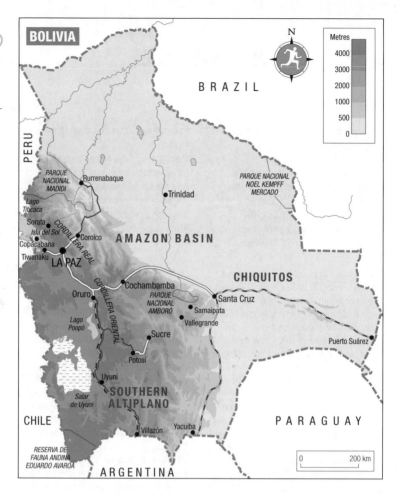

unpredictable. It also suffers frequent bouts of political turmoil, something the election of Evo Morales as the first indigenous president has done little to change. But most travellers who do make it here find it well worth the effort, and are rewarded by arguably the most raw and authentic experiences of South America. In addition, Bolivia is one of the least expensive countries in the region for travellers – if you're on a tight budget, you'll find costs here a

welcome relief after countries like Brazil, Argentina and Chile.

Main attractions

● **The Bolivian Amazon** The Bolivian Amazon is relatively undeveloped and boasts some of the most pristine and biodiverse protected areas in the region. The laid-back jungle town of Rurrenabaque is one of the cheapest and easiest places to organize trips by motorized canoe deep into the Amazonian wilderness. From here you can explore the rainforests of Parque Nacional Madidi (where you can also stay at the excellent *Chalalán eco-lodge*, operated by the local indigenous Tacana community) or head along the Río Yacuma, which flows through savannah-like pampas and supports an astonishing density of wildlife including cayman, capybaras and pink river dolphins.

● **Inca trails** North of La Paz lies the Cordillera Real, a jagged ridge of soaring, glacial peaks that forms a barrier between the high Altiplano and the Amazon lowlands. The range offers some of the finest walking in the Andes, including several treks following pre-Columbian stone-paved roads – the so-called "Inca trails" – that plunge down into the humid subtropical valleys of the Yungas. The charming colonial town of Sorata, nestled in a deep valley at the northwestern end of the range, also makes an excellent base for trekking along the trails.

● **Isla del Sol** Reached by boat from the pilgrimage centre of Copacabana on the Bolivian shores of Lago Titicaca, the idyllic Isla del Sol is the spiritual centre of the Andean world, revered as the place where the Sun and Moon were created and the Inca dynasty was born. Scattered with Inca ruins, and populated by traditional Aymara communities, it's the best place to enjoy the scenic beauty of the vast, high-altitude lake that straddles the border with Peru.

● **La Paz** Spectacularly set in a deep canyon at an altitude of over 3500m, Bolivia's de facto capital is the highest in the world. With a largely indigenous Aymara population, it's also amongst the most fascinating: a cultural crucible where banks and government offices coexist with vibrant street markets

selling all manner of ritual paraphernalia for appeasing spirits and mountain gods.

● **Potosí** Set at an altitude of over 4000m, the legendary silver-mining centre of Potosí is the highest city in the world, and at once one of the most interesting and tragic cities in Latin America. The city's magnificent colonial architecture reflects the fabulous wealth it once generated, but a visit to see the almost medieval working conditions endured by indigenous miners in the labyrinthine mineshafts that honeycomb the mountain overlooking Potosí reveals the horrific price in human lives paid for that wealth.

● **The Salar de Uyuni and Reserva Eduardo Avaroa** The desolate landscapes of the far southern Altiplano are amongst the most extraordinary in all Latin America. From the forlorn railway town of Uyuni jeep tours head across the Salar de Uyuni, the world's biggest salt lake, a vast, perfectly flat expanse of dazzling white surrounded by high mountain peaks. Further south lies the Reserva de Fauna Andina Eduardo Avaroa, a remote region of high-altitude deserts, surreal wind-blasted rock formations, icebound volcanic peaks and half-frozen mineral-stained lakes which is home to a surprising array of wildlife, including great flocks of pink flamingos and herds of vicuña.

● **The World's Most Dangerous Road** Linking La Paz with the subtropical Yungas, the infamous Coroico road descends 3500m over a distance of just 64km, plunging down from the high peaks of the Andes through dense cloudforest. The road clings to steep mountainsides above hair-raising precipices, with views so spectacular that many travellers choose to go by mountain bike rather than by bus, an arduous and exhilarating downhill ride.

Bike trips are easy to organize with tour companies in La Paz.

Also recommended

● **The Che Guevara trail** Admirers of the Argentine revolutionary hero can follow the last steps of his doomed guerrilla campaign in Bolivia in the scrub-covered mountains to the west of Santa Cruz. The town of Vallegrande is the best base from which to visit the places where Che fought and the hamlet of La Higuera where he was killed.

● **The Jesuit missions of Chiquitos** Spread across a vast, sparsely populated region in the tropical lowlands of eastern Bolivia, the Jesuit mission churches of Chiquitos offer a splash of incongruous splendour in the midst of the wilderness, a reminder of the time in the eighteenth century when a handful of European missionaries organized the indigenous Chiquitanos into utopian agricultural communities where music, art and sculpture flourished.

● **Oruro Carnaval** Of all Bolivia's innumerable religious fiestas, the Carnaval celebrations (late Feb or early March) in the otherwise dour Altiplano mining city of Oruro are the country's most colourful and dramatic. Combining Catholic and indigenous religious beliefs, the festivities are marked by thousands of dancers in extravagant costumes parading through the streets accompanied by massed brass bands, while revellers indulge in heavy drinking and indiscriminate water fighting.

● **Parque Nacional Noel Kempff Mercado** Occupying the far north-eastern corner of Bolivia on the border with Brazil, this is Bolivia's finest national park, with abundant wildlife, exuberant Amazonian rainforest and magnificent waterfalls tumbling down from the plateau that supposedly inspired Sir Arthur Conan Doyle's *The Lost World*.

● **Sucre** Known as the White City, Bolivia's official capital is a jewel of colonial architecture and a lively university city that combines serene dignity with an easy provincial charm. The beautiful highland region surrounding the city is populated by traditional Quechua-speaking communities famous for their exquisite weavings, which are best seen (and bought) at the Sunday market in the nearby town of Tarabuco.

Routes in and out

La Paz and Santa Cruz are both served by direct flights from Miami in the US and major South American capitals though flights to Bolivia are considerably more expensive than to neighbouring countries like Peru. There are no direct flights from the UK or the rest of Europe apart from Madrid – so you'll have to change planes there or in Miami or São Paulo. Bolivia can be reached overland from Peru via Puno on the shores of Lago Titicaca, and is connected to northern Argentina and Chile by road and rail. The railway journey between Uyuni in southern Bolivia and Calama in Chile passes through spectacular high Andean scenery, and you can also travel between Uyuni and San Pedro de Atacama in Chile via the remote border crossing at Laguna Verde as part of an organized jeep tour of the Reserva de Fauna Andina Eduardo Avaroa. The main border crossing with Brazil is in the far east of Bolivia at Quijarro, opposite the city of Corumbá in the Brazilian Pantanal, from where there's a direct train link to Santa Cruz: this is the best route to take if you're travelling overland between Brazil and the Andean countries on the western side of South

America. There are also several remote road border crossings between Bolivia and Brazil along the northern frontier in the Amazon. In the May to September dry season you can travel between Santa Cruz and Asunción in Paraguay by bus or lorry along a rough road that runs through the heart of the great thornbrush wilderness of the Chaco.

Bolivia books

Percy Harrison Faucett *Exploration Fawcett* (Phoenix). Rip-roaring account of the adventures of an eccentric nineteenth-century British explorer who mapped Bolivia's borders before disappearing while searching for a mythical lost city.
Ernesto "Che" Guevara *Bolivian Diary* (Pathfinder Press). The iconic Argentine guerrilla's account of his doomed attempt to launch a continent-wide revolution from the backwoods of Bolivia.
Michael Jacobs *Ghost Train through the Andes: On My Grandfather's Trail in Chile and Bolivia* (John Murray). The best recent travel book on Bolivia, retracing the author's grandfather's life as a railway engineer in Bolivia and uncovering an extraordinary love story.
Rusty Young *Marching Powder* (Pan). Hilarious and terrifying account of a small-time British cocaine smuggler's experiences locked up in La Paz's notorious San Pedro prison.

Bolivia online

Bolivia community tourism Ⓦ**www .tusoco.com/** Excellent site with details of community tourism initiatives throughout Bolivia, so you can arrange to stay with locals in some of the country's wildest and most beautiful regions.
Boliviaweb Ⓦ**www.boliviaweb.com** Good general Bolivian site with links to many other Bolivia-related webpages and general background information on subjects such as Bolivian art, history and food.
Coca Museum Ⓦ**www.cocamuseum .com** Brilliant little English-language Bolivian website dedicated to the history of the controversial coca leaf, full of fascinating detail and astonishing photos of its many different uses and meanings.

Bolivian embassies and consulates

Australia
Bolivian Embassy, 7 Culgoa Circuit, O'Malley, ACT 2606, Woden ☏61-2-6290-2968
Canada
Bolivian Embassy, 130 Albert St, Suite No. 416 Ottawa Ontario, K1P 5G4 ☏1-613-236-5730
New Zealand
Bolivian Embassy, 95 Victoria Ave, Remuera, Auckland 5 ☏64-9/5205071
South Africa
Bolivian Consulate, No. 2 Meadowbrook Close French Lane, Morningside, 2057 Johannesburg ☏11-8833416
UK
Bolivian Embassy,106 Eaton Square, London SW1W 9AD ☏0207/235 4248, Ⓦwww.embassyofbolivia.co.uk
US
Bolivian Embassy, 3014 Massachusetts Ave, NW, 20008, Washington ☏(202) 4834410, Ⓦwww.bolivia-usa.org.

Brazil

www.roughguides.com

Capital Brasília	and north Nov–March; northeast
Population 199 million	April–Aug) and a temperate zone
Languages Portuguese, Spanish	in the south with winter chills and
in border areas, plus around 180	occasional snow
indigenous languages	**Best time to go** February (for
Currency Real (R$)	Carnaval) or December–March
Climate Mostly tropical with distinct	(summer in southern Brazil)
rainy seasons (south, southeast	**Minimum daily budget** US$35

The fifth largest country in the world, Brazil occupies half the entire landmass of South America and encompasses all its diverse terrains – bar any mountains that match the height of the Andes. Its enormous interior (which takes four days and nights to cross) consists of sparsely populated scrub, swampland and Amazon rainforest, with two-thirds of Brazilians living on or close to its 8000-kilometre coast and over half living in cities.

It isn't just its size which sets Brazil apart from the rest of South America. The country was formerly part of the Portuguese empire, and consequently Portuguese is the dominant language rather than Spanish (although Spanish is widely understood). The Portuguese built attractive colonial towns much like those of the Spanish colonies – some of the prettiest, such as Ouro Preto and Tiradentes are in the state of Minas Gerais. Virtually nothing is known of Brazil's indigenous culture before the Portuguese arrived in 1500 – there were no cities built in stone like those of the Inca, Aztecs and Maya, no metal or flint artefacts – although it is thought that 5 million pure-blooded Amerindians were

scattered across the country in various tribes. Of these some 300,000 remain, most living deep within the Amazon where it's believed that some tribes remain undiscovered by the outside world.

The Amazon rainforest, the world's largest at six million square kilometres, covers over half of Brazil's landmass and extends into neighbouring Venezuela, Colombia, Peru and Bolivia. With 6000 known species of plant (and thousands more yet to be identified), one in five of all the earth's birds and one-fifth of the planet's fresh water, the Amazon is a vital part of the earth's biosphere. Increasingly, though, deforestation threatens the Amazon and large tracts of the rainforest have been felled by loggers and cattle ranchers. The rainforest remains a highlight of many tourists' visit to Brazil and there are a growing number of eco-lodges close to the region's capital, Manaus.

Brazil's other natural attractions are impressive, too – the Pantanal swamp-land, which borders Bolivia to the west, is one of the best places to see wildlife in Latin America, with jaguars, rare blue macaws, armadillos and anacondas all

▲ The cable car to Sugar Loaf mountain

commonly sighted. The Foz do Iguaçu waterfalls in the south of Brazil are another of Latin America's most visited attractions, a truly spectacular series of cascades surrounded by subtropical forest. Brazil's long Atlantic coastline has some lovely beaches, too, which remain mostly unspoilt with surprisingly little mass-market tourism.

Thanks to rapid postwar growth, Brazil is one of the most industrialized countries in Latin America, although most of the wealth is concentrated in the southeastern region around Rio de Janeiro and São Paulo, the biggest city in Brazil – and South America – with over 11 million inner-city inhabitants. Though it lacks the spectacular setting of Rio de Janeiro, São Paulo has long surpassed it as the cultural powerhouse of the country and its international contemporary art exhibition or biennale, held every two years, is rivalled only by Venice's in prestige. The capital of Brazil is neither of these cities but Brasília, a planned city in the interior built in the 1950s, and interesting only on an architectural level – the Brazilian politicians and bureaucrats who work there arrive on Monday morning and leave on Thursday for the weekend.

Brazil is celebrated for its vibrant music and dance forms, the most diverse in South America – bossa nova and samba are two of the best known. Brazilians are famously hedonistic too, with tolerant attitudes to sexuality and a gregarious openness unsurpassed elsewhere in Latin America. The annual *carnaval* brings all these things together in five days of relentless partying.

Unfortunately, Brazil is not always safe to travel in. Opportunistic theft is rife in larger towns and cities – particularly São Paulo, Rio de Janeiro and Salvador. You should only go out at night with enough money for the evening, never leave your bags unattended or wear an expensive watch or jewellery. Public transport is reliable with a network of comfortable modern coaches, though distances are huge (24-hour journeys are not uncommon); if you have limited time, consider buying an airpass.

251

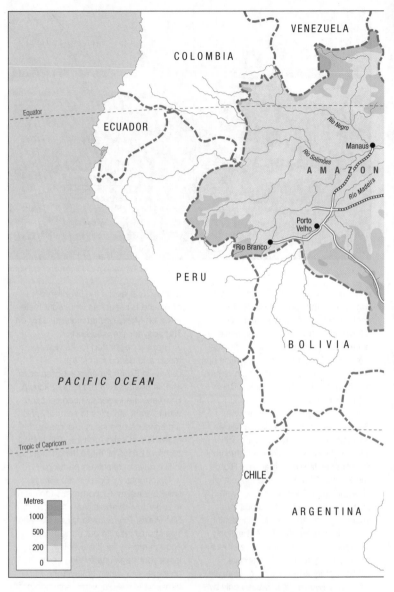

Main attractions

● **Amazon** Both the world's largest tropical rainforest and longest river,

the Amazon has 15,000 animal species, countless different plants and unique indigenous cultures. A boat ride along the vast river is a

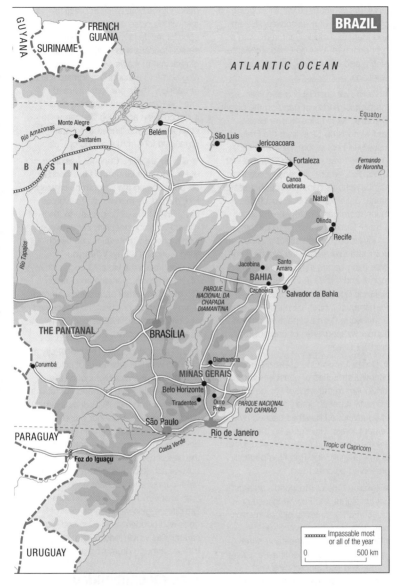

BRAZIL

ATLANTIC OCEAN

Equator

GUYANA

SURINAME

FRENCH GUIANA

Rio Amazonas   Monte Alegre

Santarém

Belém

São Luis

Jericoacoara

Fortaleza

Fernando de Noronha

Canoa Quebrada

Natal

Olinda

Recife

B A S I N

Rio Tapajós

Jacobina

Santo Amaro

BAHIA

PARQUE NACIONAL DA CHAPADA DIAMANTINA

Cachoeira

Salvador da Bahia

THE PANTANAL

BRASÍLIA

Corumbá

Diamantina

MINAS GERAIS

Belo Horizonte

Tiradentes

Ouro Preto

PARQUE NACIONAL DO CAPARÃO

São Paulo

Rio de Janeiro

Tropic of Capricorn

PARAGUAY

Costa Verde

Foz do Iguaçu

URUGUAY

Impassable most or all of the year

0   500 km

www.roughguides.com

hypnotic and memorable adventure, although you'll have to venture down one of its tributaries – the rios Negro, Madeira, Solimões and Tapajós – to see Amazonian wildlife at close hand. Manaus, the region's capital, is the starting point for jungle expeditions; you shouldn't head into the rainforest without a guide. Communities worth stopping off on the stretch of river between Belém and Manaus include Santarém, with a river beach at Alter do Chão, or Monte Alegre and its 10,000-year-old rock paintings.

● **Carnaval** Justifiably recognized as the biggest and best party on the planet, Carnaval takes place all over Brazil, for five nonstop days from the Friday (usually in Feb) before Ash Wednesday. There are three renowned Carnaval hot spots: Rio, where gorgeously costumed samba schools parade through a seated arena; Salvador in Bahia, which has a much more participatory celebration – many Brazilians claim it to be the country's best – with street parades dominated by electrifying *blocos*, large drumming bands that practise all year round; and Olinda (a UNESCO World Heritage Site adjacent to Recife in Pernambuco), host to an intimate and picturesque Carnaval packed into the narrow winding lanes of one of Brazil's prettiest towns.

● **Costa Verde** One of Brazil's most beautiful stretches of coast which runs for 300km to the west of Rio de Janeiro, the aptly named "green coast" is a string of undeveloped beaches backed by verdant forest. Highlights on the route are the island and former penal colony of Ilha Grande, and Paraty, a perfectly preserved colonial town.

● **Iguaçu** One of the world's greatest natural sights, the Foz do Iguaçu or Iguaçu Falls is a series of 275 interlinking waterfalls stretching over three kilometres. Iguaçu is located on the far western Brazil–Argentina–Paraguay border and surrounded by a vast subtropical nature reserve woven with hiking trails.

● **The Pantanal** A vast swamp the size of France in the far west of the country, the Pantanal's flat open terrain

makes it the best place in Brazil to see wildlife close up. Over 250 bird species reside here, including jabiru storks, toucans and magnificent flocks of hyacinth macaws, while the area is also home to anacondas, anteaters and armadillos. There are very few roads into the Pantanal and its size makes it inaccessible and even dangerous to enter alone – you'll need to take an organized tour from Corumb or Cuiab.

● **Rio de Janeiro** Cariocas (residents of Rio) say that God made the world in six days and on the seventh he created Rio, the *cidade marvilhosa* (marvellous city). One of the world's most exciting cities, Rio is spectacularly set between jungle-covered mountains and beach-lined Guanabara Bay. While you shouldn't miss the vibrant beach culture of Copacabana, Ipanema and Leblon, Rio has many other attractions – among them the statue of Christ the Redeemer at Corcovado and a cable-car ride to Sugar Loaf mountain.

● **Salvador da Bahia** The oldest city in Brazil with fine examples of colonial architecture, Salvador was once the country's main slave port and still retains a strong African feel. As well as a largely black population, Salvador pulses with the best music scene in Brazil, a uniquely spicy cuisine characterized by the use of palm oil and coconut, and cultural activities dating from the slave era – *capoeira* (an elegant non-contact martial art) and *candomblé*, an Afro-Brazilian religion with a large cast of gods and goddesses (*orixas*) and ritual ceremonies which induce wild, reeling trances through drumming and dancing.

Also recommended

● **Bahia State** It isn't just Bahia's regional capital Salvador which makes the state worth visiting. The lush green plains of the surrounding Recúncavo countryside have two pretty colonial towns, Santo Amaro and Cachoeira. Inland, the arid plains of the *sertão* have an outback cowboy culture best seen during Monday's leather market in Feira de Santana and in the friendly mining town of Jacobina. Further inland are the waterfalls, strange rock formations and rivers of Parque Nacional Chapada Diamantina. Popular Bahian beach destinations include Porto Seguro, famous for its dancehalls, and Morro de São Paulo, actually a string of white sandy beaches with a laid-back hippy atmosphere and low-key development, located on the island of Tinharé and reached by boat.

● **Cidades historicas** Brazil's so-called "historic cities" are a string of colonial towns in Minas Gerais, the state directly north of Rio. Once bustling mining communities, created on the discovery of a plenitude of gold and diamonds in the area at the end of the seventeenth century, the towns are now tranquil and carefully preserved architectural gems. Ouro Preto, Diamantina and Tiradentes are three of the finest examples.

● **Fernando de Noronha** A pristine archipelago 350km off the coast of Pernambuco, Fernando de Noronha is a marine national park and prime ecotourism destination with a wide variety of birds and sea creatures to spot, including turtles, sharks and whales.

● **Football** Football is Brazil's passion and you shouldn't miss the opportunity to see a stadium match with all its attendant hysteria, live samba and fireworks. Rio's Maracaña Stadium is the world's largest, holding 200,000 people, and during November and December matches are held here three times a week. Otherwise fishermen and other locals play together, usually at dusk, on almost every beach in the country. Gringos are very welcome to join in, though the standard is always high and the game is played barefoot. In 2014 the world cup is being hosted in Brazil, a tournament which will be fantastically exciting.

● **Parque Nacional do Caparão** In the east of Minais Gerais state, the Parque Nacional do Caparão has some of Brazil's most spectacular scenery, divided into two ecological zones: thickly forested valleys, hills and streams in its lower section which give way to craggy mountains and treeless alpine landscapes. Brazil's highest peak, Pico da Bandeira (2890m), is not difficult to climb and on a clear day those who reach the top will be rewarded with a panoramic view over the states of Espírito Santo and Minas Gerais.

Routes in and out

Direct international flights usually land in Rio or São Paulo. These depart from New York, Los Angeles and Miami in the US; London, Paris, Amsterdam and Madrid in Europe; and Sydney via Auckland in Australasia. From Miami you can also fly straight to Brasília, Recife, Manaus and Belém. Brazil borders every country in South America apart from Chile and Ecuador, so there are myriad spots to arrive and leave the country. Overland border crossings are fairly straightforward, though the only direct access to Suriname is via plane from Belém (very expensive) or through its neighbours, Guyana or French Guiana. Another option is to take a boat into and out of Brazil via the Amazon River. Standard routes link to Iquitos in Peru or, less popularly, Leticia in Colombia.

Books

Peter Fleming *Brazilian Adventure* (Northwestern University Press). Classic traveller's tale recording Fleming's disastrous expedition into the Amazon in search of lost explorer Colonel Fawcett.

Joao Guimaraes Rosa *The Devil to pay in the Backlands* (Alianza Editorial). Written in archaic language and distinctive grammar and structures without paragraphs or chapters, this story of banditry in the dusty inland plains of Brazil is recognized as one of the most influential South American novels ever written.

Claude Lévi-Strauss *Tristes Tropiques* (Penguin). Seminal work by the legendary French anthropologist describing a working trip to Brazil in the 1930s to study the Nambikwara and Tupi-Kawahib Indians, this witty and insightful account documents the ups and downs of travelling in a strange culture.

Joseph Page *The Brazilians* (Da Capo Press). Acclaimed and weighty tome which attempts to unravel Brazil's culture through the history of its complex population.

Peter Robb *A Death in Brazil* (Bloosmbury). Genre-defying book which examines history, food, politics and culture to create an absorbing portrait of Brazil, past and present. Robb has lived in the country for many years and his research and observations are deftly woven with his own vivid experiences of life there.

Brazil online

BrazilMax ⓦwww.brazilmax.com Billed as "The hip gringo's guide to Brazilian culture and society", this internet magazine is written by American journalist Bill Hinchberger and has an excellent selection of articles – particularly on cultural activities – with an eclectic reading list, archived travel writings and further links.

Cities in Brazil ⓦwww.cities-in -brazil.com Series of articles on all things Brazilian as well as insight into Brazil's most important cities – Rio de Janeiro, São Paulo and Brasilía and a useful Brazil blog on day-to-day living experiences.

Info Brazil ⓦwww.infobrazil.com Weighty independent analysis of Brazilian current affairs with good links.

Brazilian embassies

Australia
Brazilian Embassy, 19 Forster Crescent, Yarralumla, Canberra, ACT 2600 ☏02/6273 2372

Canada
Brazilian Embassy, 450 Wilbrod St, Ottawa, ON K1N 6M8 ☏613/237-1090

Ireland
Brazilian Embassy, Europa House, Block 9, Harcourt Centre, 41–45 Harcourt House, Dublin 2 ☏01/475 6000

New Zealand
Brazilian Embassy, 10 Brandon St, Level 9, PO Box 5432, Wellington ☏04/473 3516, ⓦwww.Brazil.org.nz

UK
Brazilian Embassy, 32 Green St, Mayfair, London W1Y 4AT ☏0207/499 0877, ⓦwww.brazil.org.uk

US
Brazilian Embassy, 3006 Massachusetts Ave NW, Washington DC 20008 ☏(202) 2382700 ⓦwww.brasilemb.org.

Chile

Capital Santiago
Population 16.5 million
Languages Spanish, plus minority
indigenous languages
Currency Peso Chileno (CH$)
Climate Temperate, with warm
days and cool nights in the north
and centre, colder in the south,
particularly during the winter months
from June–September

Best time to go November–March
is the best time to visit Chile because
of the summer weather, though the
north can be visited at any time.
Avoid June–September, when winter
brings cold weather to the centre
and south
Minimum daily budget US$30

An implausibly narrow strip of land
running down the west coast of South
America, Chile measures over 4000km
in length – the same distance as that
from Britain to West Africa – though its
width rarely exceeds 180km. Absurd as
it may seem, however, this bizarre shape
makes perfect sense geographically:
hemmed in by the South Pacific to the
west, separated from Argentina to the
east by the Andes, and divided from
Peru to the north by the arid expanse
of the Atacama Desert, Chile is a
geographically self-contained unit.

These natural barriers helped create
a nation very distinct from the rest
of Latin America. Of all the countries
in the region, Chile is the one where
European cultural influence is strongest,
a result of the Spanish colonial period,
subsequent waves of immigration from
elsewhere in Europe, and major British
and US commercial involvement in the
nineteenth and twentieth centuries. Now
free of the shadow of the notorious
dictator Augusto Pinochet, who ruled in
the 1970s and 80s, Chile has resumed
its long tradition of political stability,

civilian government and the rule of law.
Compared to the rest of the continent,
Chile is a modern and relatively affluent
society, and is without doubt one of the
safest and easiest places to travel in
South America. The police are generally
helpful and efficient, the infrastructure is
well developed and – most amazingly for
Latin America – the buses run on time.

Though it lacks the diverse and
deep-rooted indigenous traditions
of other Andean countries like Peru
and Bolivia, Chile more than makes
up for it with its astonishing variety
of dramatic landscapes, which range
from the Atacama Desert, the driest
in the world, to the glaciers and ice
fields of Patagonia. Between these
extremes are beautiful beaches; fertile
valleys where vineyards and orchards
flourish; huge temperate forests and
dazzling emerald lakes; stunning fjords
and bleak Patagonian steppes; and,
towering above it all and running the
length of the country, the jagged spine
of the Andes, with its glacial peaks and
smouldering volcanoes. Moreover, with
a population of less than seventeen

million, largely confined to a few cities in a country three times the size of Britain, much of Chile's vast expanse is virtually uninhabited wilderness. Coupled with a well-organized tourism industry, this makes Chile an excellent country for the outdoor enthusiast, whether your preference is for skiing, birdwatching, sea kayaking, whitewater rafting, trekking, mountaineering, horseriding or fly fishing. As if all this wasn't enough, Chile also incudes in its territory far-flung Easter Island, almost 4000km out from the mainland in the Pacific Ocean, which was home to the Rapa Nui, one of the world's most mysterious and remarkable prehistoric cultures, best known for the enormous stone idols that still dot the island's shores.

Chile's climate is much closer to that of Europe or the US than to most other Latin American countries, ranging from an almost Mediterranean climate in the centre of the country, to much colder conditions in the far south. Seasonal variations become more pronounced as you travel south, so while the southern hemisphere winter between June and September brings extremely cold weather in the far south, with heavy snow blocking access to many of the best national parks, the summer months from November to March enjoy good weather and long sunny evenings. This means you can fit much more into a day, and makes southern Chile the perfect place to escape from the winter back home.

Main attractions

● **The Carretera Austral** Stretching over a thousand kilometres south from Puerto Montt to the remote settlement of Yungay, the Carretera Austral – the Southern Highway – is one of the most dramatic roads in Latin America. It carves its way through great tracts of untouched wilderness between soaring, snowcapped mountains, ancient glaciers, narrow fjords, emerald rivers and swathes of temperate rainforest.

● **Chiloé** Just south of the Lake District and reached by boat from Puerto Montt, Chiloé is a peaceful and isolated archipelago famous for its traditional rural culture and rich folklore and mythology. The windswept west coast of the main island, Isla Grande de Chiloé, is covered with dense forest, much of it protected by the Parque Nacional Chiloé, while the more sheltered east coast is dotted with quiet fishing and farming communities, distinguished by colourful wooden churches and traditional wooden houses built on stilts.

● **Lake District** Stretching some 340km between the towns of Temuco and Puerto Montt in the south of the country, the Chilean Lake District is a beautiful region of lush farmland, dense forest and deep, clear lakes which sit at the foot of a series of spectacular snow-capped volcanoes. Much of the stunning wilderness scenery of the region is protected by national parks such as Puyehue, which offer excellent hiking opportunities, with the added bonus of numerous volcanic hot springs where you can relax and soothe tired legs after a hard day's walking.

● **Parque Nacional Laguna San Rafael** Reached from the port of Chacabuco by a spectacular 200km boat journey through labyrinthine fjords, the iceberg-choked Laguna San Rafael, at the foot of the glacier of the same name, is one of the most awe-inspiring sights in Chile. A great place for observing penguins, sea lions, albatrosses and other marine wildlife, it is the centre of a vast national park that encompasses huge ice fields, high mountain peaks, primeval forests and hundreds of glacial lakes.

www.roughguides.com

259

▲ Volcán Parinacota, Northern Chile

● **Parque Nacional Torres del Paine** Situated in the far south of Chilean Patagonia, this remote park encompasses Chile's single most famous attraction, the stunning Torres del Paine, a small mountain range of magnificent near-vertical granite pinnacles that soar more than 2000m above the surrounding plains, amidst a pristine wilderness of glaciers, lakes and primeval forests – a paradise for walkers and mountaineers.

● **Valparaíso and the Litoral Central** The coastal city of Valparaíso, about 120km northwest of Santiago, is Chile's biggest port and a wonderfully atmospheric place, with labyrinthine cobbled streets lined with ramshackle, brightly painted houses that cover the steep hillside down to the seashore. Known as the Chilean Riviera, the stretch of coast either side of Valparaíso boasts bay after bay lined with beautiful white-sand beaches and

twenty or so resort towns, the largest and most famous of which is the upmarket Viña del Mar.

Also recommended

● **Atacama Desert** Stretching over 1200km south from the Peruvian border, the Atacama is the driest desert in the world, a desolate plain of rock and gravel that contains areas where no rain has ever been recorded. The region also boasts a spectacular coastline, geysers, ancient petroglyphs and abandoned nitrate-mining ghost towns. The best way to explore the Atacama is on a jeep tour from the oasis village of San Pedro de Atacama, which is close to the otherworldly landscape of the Valle de la Luna.

● **The Central Valley** Many travellers speed through Chile's Central Valley – the rich agricultural heartland stretching from Santiago 400km or so south to the Río Bío Bío – without stopping as they head to more spectacular attractions further south. They are missing a lush, pastoral landscape dotted with orchards and vineyards, splendid colonial haciendas and tranquil villages, and a traditional rural culture; this region rewards those who stop off and explore away from the main road.

● **Easter Island (Rapa Nui)** Isolated in the vastness of the Pacific Ocean almost four thousand kilometres west of the Chilean mainland, tiny Easter Island – known to its indigenous Polynesian inhabitants as Rapa Nui – is one of the most remote places on earth, and home to the extraordinary monuments left by one of the world's most enigmatic prehistoric cultures. The coast of the island – which measures just over 20km across at its widest point – is dotted with huge, ancient monolithic stone statues of squat human torsos and heads, the origin and meaning of which remain a mystery.

● **Skiing** Chile boasts arguably the best skiing in South America: some skiers say that the very dry powder snow (known as "champagne snow") found on the country's high-altitude slopes is of a quality found nowhere else. The season runs from June to September and the best slopes and resorts – El Colorado, La Parva and Valle Nevado – are conveniently close to Santiago.

Routes in and out

The Chilean capital Santiago is served by regular flights from London and Madrid, and from cities in the US, as well as from Australia via New Zealand, Papeete and Easter Island in the Pacific; it also has regular flights to all the main South American capitals. By land, it's easy to enter and leave Chile across the northern border with Peru and at many points along the long eastern frontier with Argentina – if you visit Patagonia you may well find yourself crossing the border between Chile and Argentina several times. There's a good road link between Arica in northern Chile and La Paz in western Bolivia, but you can also cross into Bolivia by train from Calama to Uyuni – a route that passes through spectacular high Andean scenery – or by jeep as part of an organized tour from San Pedro de Atacama, passing through the stunning Reserva de Fauna Andina Eduardo Avaroa in the far southwest of Bolivia.

Chile books

Isabel Allende *Of Love and Shadows* (Dial Press). A love story set in a country of arbitrary arrests, disappearances and executions, this is a fine example of the magical-realist style of Chile's most famous modern novelist.

Roberto Bolaño *By night in Chile* (W.W. Norton). A short haunting tale by Latin America's most fashionable contemporary novelist, in which a priest confronts his last night on earth, exposing the brutal normality of military rule in Chile and the routine oppression of the dispossessed worldwide.

Marc Cooper *Pinochet and Me: A Chilean Anti-Memoir* (Verso). First-hand account of the coup that brought the notorious dictator General Pinochet to power and the regime he imposed, written by an American journalist who was a translator for the man he overthrew: president Salvador Allende.

Pablo Neruda *Selected Poems* (Penguin Classics). A good selection of the exceptional work of Chile's Nobel laureate, ranging from erotic love poems to revolutionary epics and odes to Chile's extraordinary landscape.

261

Chile online

Chilean Patagonia ⓦ**www.chile austral.com** A detailed and practical tourist information site on Patagonia, with useful links and inspiring picture galleries.
Chip Travel ⓦ**www.chiptravel.cl** Government-sponsored English-language site offering a clear introduction to Chile's attractions, lots of useful practical information as well as online hotel booking and car rental.
Easter Island ⓦ**www.netaxs .com/~trance/rapanui.html** A good introduction to the history and culture of Easter Island, with plenty of good pictures, practical information and useful links.
Sernatur ⓦ**www.sernatur.cl** High-quality National Tourist Board site with useful general information on the main attractions, plenty of pictures and maps, and links to online hotel bookings and other government websites.
Visit Chile ⓦ**www.visit-chile.org** Extensive general tourist information site with information on all the main attractions and activities from skiing to wine tours, as well as links to airlines, hotels and car rental companies.

Chilean embassies

Australia
Chilean Embassy, 10 Culgoa Circuit, Red Hill, ⓣ20-62862430, ⓦwww .embachile-australia.com
Canada
Chilean Embassy, 50 O'Connor St, Suite.1413, Ottawa, Ontario K1P 6L2, ⓣ613/235-4402, ⓦwww.chile.ca/en/
New Zealand
Chilean Embassy, 19 Bolton St, Wellington, ⓣ04-4716270 ⓦwww .embchile.co.nz/
South Africa
Chilean Embassy, Brooklyn Gardens Building, Corner of Veale and Middel sts Block B-1th, New Muckleneuk, Pretoria, ⓣ12-4608090, ⓦwww .embchile.co.za
UK
Chilean Embassy, 12 Devonshire St, London W1G 7DS ⓣ0207/5806392
US
Chilean Embassy, 1732 Massachusetts Ave, Washington DC ⓣ(202) 7851746, ⓦwww.chile-usa.org/

Colombia

Capital Bogotá
Population 46 million
Languages Spanish, plus over a dozen indigenous languages and English Creole
Currency Colombian peso (Col$)
Climate Large variations in temperature: tropical along coast and eastern plains with wet (April–May & Sept–Nov) and dry (Nov–March) seasons; cooler in the Andean highlands
Best time to go November–March (dry season)
Minimum daily budget US$25

To most people, Colombia means only three things: coffee, cocaine and civil war. The country has been blighted by over fifty years of fighting between left-wing guerrillas and right-wing paramilitaries, with hundreds of thousands of Colombians losing their lives and many more being made homeless. Colombia also reels under the influence of the billion-dollar cocaine trade – it is both the world's largest grower of coca (the raw material of cocaine) and the world's leading processor of the drug – the economic and social consequences of this permeate all levels of society – from peasant farmers coerced into growing coca to corrupt politicians in the pay of drugs cartels. Not for nothing is Colombia nicknamed Locombia, or "Mad Country".

In recent years, hardline President Alvaro Uribe's government has achieved huge success in quelling the rebel forces – two leaders of main left-wing guerilla group FARC were killed by the armed forces in 2008 and the level of kidnapping has declined by 80 percent (from its height of 3500 kidnappings in 2000). However, Uribe's tough tactics haven't won favour with everyone. The huge cost of waging war on drugs has meant cuts in the social infrastructure of the country, there are more displaced people than ever and right-wing paramilitary organizations retain a lot of unchecked power.

Still Colombia is safer to visit now than it has been for many years and the country – a longtime travellers' "secret" – is on the verge of a nascent tourist boom. Certainly, Colombia has a lot to offer, including one of the most geographically diverse landscapes of any Latin American country, with the Andes stretching right through its western side, unspoilt Caribbean and Pacific coastlines, and a large area of remote Amazon basin. Uniquely in South America, it's possible to see the ocean from the snowcapped Sierra Nevada de Santa Marta (rising to 5800m), while the lower Andes are dotted with a series of pretty colonial towns and traditional highland villages, along with several unique pre-Columbian sites.

But the country's greatest attraction is perhaps the Colombians themselves, a more homogenous people than that of most other South American countries, with over 75 percent of the population mixed (both mestizo and mulatto) race. Renowned for their exuberance and

www.roughguides.com

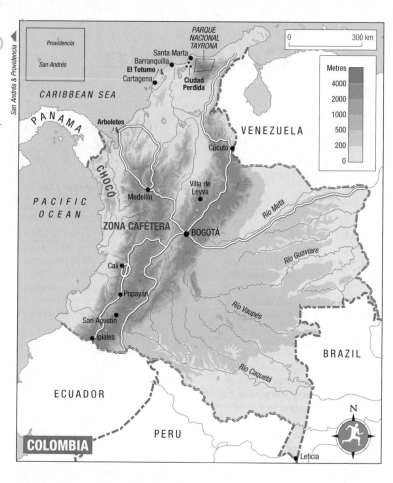

friendliness, they celebrate life with noisy parties whenever possible, and welcome the few tourists they see wholeheartedly. In spite of its continuing violence and criminality, Colombia remains a spontaneous, vibrant and remarkably open society.

Main attractions

● **Cartagena** Founded in 1533, the great walled city of Cartagena de Indias,

on the Caribbean coast, was the main Spanish port in northern South America for several hundred years. Cartagena's thick walls and ring of outer forts, built to protect the city from pirate attacks, are part of the unique character that makes it Colombia's main draw and one of the finest colonial cities in the Americas. You could easily spend days wandering through its maze of narrow streets, arcaded squares, grand buildings and ruined forts. Adjacent to the old city is a vibrant modern beach resort, and at night Cartagena comes alive with a mixture of live music, salsa and beachfront clubs.

● **Chocó region** This remote and unspoilt region encompasses the northern half of Colombia's Pacific coast, with virgin rainforest running down to miles of empty beach, a tropical backwater atmosphere and traditional communities of Chocó and Ember Indians. The region's capital is the ramshackle riverside city of Quibdó – it's better to head straight for the remote and unspoilt coastal resorts of Nuquí, El Valle and Parque Nacional Ensenada de Utría. Highlights of the area include tiny Isla de Salomòn, which has the prettiest white-sand beach around, and the small village of Tribug, both stop-offs on the boat ride from Nuquí to El Valle.

● **Parque Nacional Tayrona** The most popular national park in Colombia, Tayrona protects a 35-kilometre stretch of Caribbean coast, with glorious sandy beaches set in palm-fringed bays and backed by lush rainforest. A well-known hippy hangout, it's the perfect place to take a break from travelling, though if you feel energetic you could make the five-day trek from the park to the Ciudad Perdida ("Lost City") or Teyuna – its indigenous name – of the Tayrona Indians, dating back to 500 AD, which occupies a spectacular location at 1100m on the northern slopes of the Sierra Nevada de Santa Marta. A group of trekkers were kidnapped at the Ciudad Perdida in 2003, though they were all released unharmed.

● **Salsa in Cali** Salsa is one of Colombia's most celebrated forms of music and dance and nowhere in the country is it more popular than in the *salsatecas* (salsa clubs) of Cali, an inland city with tropical temperatures and an atmosphere to match. Cali's citizens, *caleños*, are among Colombia's

friendliest locals – try and persuade them to take you to the authentic *salsatecas* in the barrio of Juanchito, which can be dangerous if you go alone. If not, there are salsa clubs dotted along Avenida Sexta, the city's main street for nightlife.

● **San Agustín** Principally known for a number of mysterious carved statues in a series of nearby sites, San Agustín is a pretty market town in the rolling green foothills of the Andes, with a traditional cowboy culture and a thriving backpacker scene. The surrounding countryside is strikingly beautiful, and there are several impressive waterfalls close to the town.

Also recommended

● **Bogotá** Colombia's noisy, gridlocked and exciting capital is well worth a visit, despite its (largely undeserved) reputation for danger. The city's lovely colonial quarter, La Candelaria, makes an atmospheric retreat from the city bustle, while other highlights include the world-famous Museo de Oro, noted for its extensive collection of fine indigenous crafts made from gold, and the monastery of Montserrate, perched high above the city and boasting wonderful views – not to mention one of the best club scenes in Latin America.

● **Coffee fincas** The *tierra paisa* or countryside around Medellin is known as the *zona cafetera*, where Colombia's coffee is grown. As well as enjoying the local stimulant it's possible to stay in one of 300 picturesque coffee farms. Hosts will organize horseback riding and guided walks amidst the pretty and peaceful surroundings.

● **Leticia** A small town in the south-eastern tip of Colombia, Leticia is the tourist centre of the country's remote

265

Amazon region. The town itself is fairly ordinary but the surrounding area is dense rainforest dotted with Ticuna and Yagua settlements. Popular trips go to Parque Nacional Amacayucu, 75km upstream, where there are walking trails through the forest, and the Lago de Tarapoto, a beautiful lake featuring the famous *Victoria Amazonica* water lily and occasional sightings of pink dolphins. From Leticia (which you'll have to fly to from within Colombia) it's possible to get a boat down the Amazon River to Brazil and Peru.

● **Mud volcanoes** Arboletes and El Totumo are the two most impressive of the series of natural mud lakes that stretch along the Caribbean coast of Colombia. Both have craters filled with the warm, thick mud, in which you can bathe: it has beneficial healing properties and leaves your skin baby smooth – a weird and unforgettable sensation.

● **Popayán** Situated in the southwest of the country, Popayán is one of Colombia's most perfectly preserved colonial towns, boasting several noteworthy Spanish-built churches and hosting spectacular Semana Santa (Easter) parades. It's a small, tranquil place with a mild climate, and there's little to do here other than wander through the pretty squares and cobbled streets, though it makes a good base from which to visit the Tuesday market at Silvia, where the local Guambiano Indians can be seen weaving textiles in their colourful blue and fuchsia costumes.

● **San Andrés y Providencia** A small archipelago in the Caribbean (it's actually closer to Nicaragua than Colombia), San Andrés y Providencia has a unique fusion of Jamaican and Colombian culture, marked by *soca* music and Creole-speaking inhabitants, while the islands' clear blue waters and coral reefs make them a great destination for snorkelling and scuba diving.

Routes in and out

There are direct daily flights to Bogotá from several cities in the US (principally Miami and New York), plus direct flights from Miami to Cartagena and Medellín. From Europe there are frequent direct flights from Madrid, Paris and Frankfurt to the capital. Overland border crossings from Venezuela to Colombia are at Cúcuta and the less popular Maicao, on the northern Guajira Peninsula. The border between Colombia and Ecuador is at Ipiales. Boats go irregularly from Colón in Panama to Puerto Obaldía (2–4 days), from where you can take an *expreso* or speedboat to the Colombian resorts of Capurganá and Acandi. The famous overland crossing of the Darién Gap (see p.42) is extremely dangerous and should on no account be attempted at present.

Colombia online

Colombia Journal ⓦ**www.colombi ajourna.org** Campaigning American website with left-wing perspective which examines civil unrest and the drugs trade in Colombia in depth.
Colombia Support Network ⓦ**www .colombiasupport.net/** Website of the largest grassroots organization in the US working to improve human rights in Colombia, with articles and background information on the current political crisis.
Colombian Blog ⓦ**colombianblog .com/** Huge discussion forum for Colombiaphiles with links to an eclectic range of other websites.

Books

Mark Bowden *Killing Pablo: The Hunt for the World's Greatest Outlaw* (Atlantic Books). Thrilling journalistic account of the rise and demise of the notorious drug lord Pablo Escobar and the environment which created him.

Forrest Hylton *Evil Hour in Colombia* (Verso). Detailed history of 150 years of political conflict in Colombia with detailed analysis of the causes of the country's troubles.

Gabriel García Márquez *News of a Kidnapping* (Penguin). Using interviews and diary entries, Márquez skilfully recreates the stories of several brutal kidnappings (Colombia is the kidnap centre of the world, with over a thousand annually) by infamous drug lord Pablo Escobar – by turns gripping and grimly illuminating.

Charles Nicholl *The Fruit Palace* (Vintage). A humorous and thrilling investigation into the 1970s cocaine trade, exposing the ubiquitous corruption and craziness that continue to underscore Colombian life and business.

Colombian embassies

Australia
Colombian Embassy, Level 2 , Colombia House, 101 Northbourne Ave, Turner, Canberra, ACT 2612 ☎02/6257 2027

Canada
Colombian Embassy, 360 Albert St, Suite 1002, Ottawa, ON K1R 7X7 ☎613/230-3760, ⓦwww .embajadacolombia.ca

New Zealand
Colombian Embassy, PO Box 17072, Karori, Wellington 5 ☎04/476 9857

UK
Colombian Embassy, 3rd Floor, 15–19 Great Titchfield St, London W1N 7FB ☎0207/589 9177

US
Colombian Embassy, 2118 Leroy Place NW, Washington DC 20008 ☎(202) 3878338, ⓦwww.colombiaemb.org.

Ecuador

Capital Quito
Population 14.5 million
Languages Spanish, Quechua, plus minority indigenous languages
Currency US dollar ($)
Climate Hot and humid in the tropical lowlands of the coast and the Oriente, cooler in the highlands
Best time to go June–August in the highlands, December–April on the coast, and any time outside the June–August rainy season in the Amazon lowlands
Minimum daily budget US$20

Sitting on the equator between Peru and Colombia, Ecuador is the smallest of the Andean countries, covering an area only slightly larger than the United Kingdom. But despite its diminutive size, the country is packed with dramatic scenic contrasts, encompassing snow-capped volcanic peaks, palm-fringed beaches lapped by the warm Pacific, and the steaming tropical rainforests of the Amazon basin. Ecuador is also home to a diverse population, including a wide range of indigenous groups, while many of its towns and cities contain magnificent examples of colonial architecture. As if this wasn't enough, Ecuador's attractions are crowned by the Galápagos Islands, the famous archipelago whose unique and extraordinary wildlife played a key role in shaping Charles Darwin's theories on evolution.

Ecuador is a kind of pocket-sized South America, making it the ideal destination for travellers who want to experience a wide range of the continent's manifold attractions but only have limited time available. Unlike larger South American countries, where moving between different regions involves travelling vast distances, Ecuador's compact size means that getting around is straightforward and relatively quick, with few destinations more than a day's journey from the capital, Quito. It also has a relatively well-developed tourist infrastructure, making it easy to arrange guided tours and treks, rainforest expeditions, or climbing, riding and mountain-biking trips.

Like the other Andean countries, Ecuador suffers from chronic political instability, with frequent changes of government, though it has become calmer since the election of the left-wing president, Rafael Correa. The periodic bouts of upheaval are rarely violent, but they can cause severe disruption, so it's important to check on the current political situation before you arrive.

Main attractions

● **Avenue of the Volcanoes** South of Quito, the two parallel chains of the Andes that run the length of Ecuador rise to their most dramatic and spectacular, forming a double row of soaring, snowcapped peaks. The fertile basin between the two chains is the indigenous heartland of Ecuador, dotted

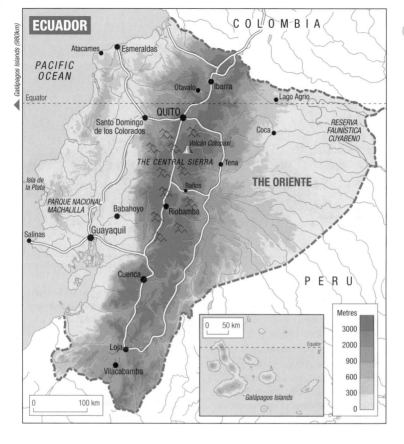

ECUADOR

COLOMBIA

PACIFIC OCEAN

Galápagos Islands (980km)

Atacames Esmeraldas

Equator

Otavalo Ibarra

Lago Agrio

QUITO

Santo Domingo de los Colorados

Coca

RESERVA FAUNÍSTICA CUYABENO

Volcán Cotopaxi

THE CENTRAL SIERRA Tena

Isla de la Plata

Baños

THE ORIENTE

PARQUE NACIONAL MACHALILLA Babahoyo

Riobamba

Salinas Guayaquil

Cuenca

PERU

Metres
3000
2000
900
600
300
0

0   50 km

Equator 0°

Loja

Vilacabamba

Galápagos Islands

0   100 km

with traditional farming villages and peaceful market towns, many of which can be visited in a 200-kilometre loop known as the Quilotoa Loop.

● **Cuenca** Set amid the gentler mountain scenery of the southern Sierra, Cuenca is Ecuador's most captivating city, graced with elegant colonial architecture including glorious churches and monasteries. It's also within easy striking distance of the ruins of Ingapirca, Ecuador's only major Inca site, as well as the starkly beautiful wilderness of Parque Nacional El Cajas, which offers excellent hiking and trout fishing.

● **Galápagos Islands** Lying almost 1000km east of the Ecuadorian mainland, the extraordinary Galápagos Islands – which inspired Charles Darwin's theory of evolution – are Ecuador's best-known attraction, home to a unique, abundant and virtually fearless range of wildlife including marine iguanas, giant tortoises, whales, dolphins, sea lions, penguins and boobies. Visiting the islands is relatively expensive – flights from the mainland, the national park entrance fee and the cost of a seven-night cruise around the archipelago will set you back well over $1000 – but

▲ Marine iguanas sunbathing in the Galápagos Islands

few travellers who come here regret splashing out to experience one of the most astonishing nature-tourism destinations in the world.

● **Parque Nacional Machalilla** Away from the unappealing industrial port cities of Guayaquil and Esmeraldas, Ecuador's varied Pacific coastline is lined with glorious beaches, dense mangrove swamps peaceful Afro-Ecuadorian fishing villages, and several lively resort towns. One of the coastal highlights is Parque Nacional Machalilla, northeast of Guayaquil, which combines stunning unspoiled beaches, pristine tropical forests and, on the offshore Isla de la Plata, an inexpensive alternative to the Galápagos for viewing boobies, frigate-birds and albatrosses.

● **Quito** Set at an altitude of 2800m in a valley at the foot of the soaring Pichincha volcano, the Ecuadorian capital has a beautiful old colonial quarter of narrow streets lined with exquisite churches, monasteries and mansions. The modern new town is packed with hotels,

restaurants, tour companies and other useful facilities, and makes a convenient place to recuperate between trips around the country.

● **Reserva Faunística Cuyabeno** Though the ravages of oil development mean it's generally not as pristine as similar regions in Peru or Bolivia, Ecuador's Amazon lowland region – known as the Oriente – is fairly easily accessible from the highlands, making it an easy place to experience the Amazon rainforest. The best place to head for is the wildlife-rich Reserva Faunística Cuyabeno, in the northern Oriente, which you can visit on an organized tour from the oil town of Lago Agrio or by staying with one of several indigenous Amazonian communities that accept visitors.

Also recommended

● **Baños** With a warm, subtropical climate and a spectacular setting amid lush green hills streaked with waterfalls, the tranquil spa town of Baños is deservedly popular with Ecuadorian and foreign tourists alike. It's a good base for hiking, horseriding, mountain biking and whitewater rafting in the surrounding mountains, after which you can relax in the natural thermal baths that gave the town its name. Check the latest information before travelling here, however, as Volcán Tungurahua, which towers above the town, has been particularly active in recent years.

● **El Nariz del Diablo train ride** From the pleasant city of Riobamba in the Central Sierra, a dramatic train line runs down to the village of Sibambe, zigzagging down a near-vertical wall of rock known as El Nariz del Diablo – "The Devil's Nose".

● **Otavalo's market** Every Saturday the Andean town of Otavalo, to the north of Quito, hosts one of South America's most famous and colourful indigenous markets, where locals from the surrounding mountains come to sell their beautiful textiles. With their proud indigenous heritage and highly distinctive costumes – the men in black ponchos and ponytails, the women in elaborately embroidered white blouses – the Otavalo Indians themselves are a major attraction. But it's their excellent marketing sense and skilled handiwork that make the market a real draw. Quite touristy, but still a great place to pick up a poncho, jumper or handmade musical instrument.

● **Parque Nacional Cotopaxi** Surrounding the perfectly symmetrical cone of Volcán Cotopaxi – at 5897m the highest active volcano in the world – the beautiful Parque Nacional Cotopaxi is Ecuador's most popular mainland park, with numerous hiking trails, campsites and mountain refuges that make it easy to explore the pristine ecology and stark landscape of the high Andean grassland or Paramó. Even if you've little or no technical mountain-climbing experience, as long as you're fit and acclimatized you can reach the summit with a guide.

● **Vilcabamba** Set in an idyllic valley surrounded by crumpled mountains, the village of Vilcabamba first came to international attention in the 1950s, when it was hailed as the "Valley of Eternal Youth" after researchers claimed its inhabitants enjoyed unusually long life spans, with many living well over a hundred years. These days, it's an archetypal gringo hangout popular for its beautiful scenery and laid-back atmosphere. It's also a good base for exploring the cloudforests of the nearby Parque Nacional Podocarpus.

Routes in and out

Quito and the coastal city of Guayaquil are served by regular flights from most major South American capitals, several cities in the US, and Amsterdam and Madrid in Europe. The main land crossing with Colombia is at Tulcán on the Pan-American Highway north of Quito. For Peru, the main border crossing is at Huaquillas on the southern coast; if you're heading to or from the highlands, it's much more convenient to cross the border at Macará in the Southern Sierra – you can travel on this route on direct buses between the southern Ecuadorian city of Loja and Piura in Peru. Following the resolution in 1998 of a long-standing border dispute with Peru it is – in theory at least – possible to cross the border at Nuevo Rocafuerte in the Oriente, travelling by irregular riverboat along the Río Napo – check with the immigration authorities and the Peruvian Embassy in Quito, however, before attempting this rarely travelled route.

Ecuador books

Joe Kane *Savages* (Pan). Moving account of the Huoarani Indians' fight to protect their lands in the Ecuadorian Amazon from oil companies, written by an activist involved in the struggle.

Paul D Stewart, Richard Dawkins *Galápagos: the Islands that Changed the World* (BBC). Fascinating and beautifully illustrated description of the unique natural history of the Galápagos Islands, and their role in the development of evolutionary theory.

Carlos de la Torre, Steve Striffler (eds) *The Ecuador Reader: History, Culture, Politics* (Latin America Bureau/Duke University Press). Excellent introduction to the history and culture of Ecuador in all its diversity, with contributions from a formidable range of Ecuadorian writers.

Ecuador online

Ecuador Explorer ⓦ**www.ecuador explorer.com** Excellent tourist information site with plenty of background on Ecuador's main attractions, practical advice for travellers, and details of an extensive range of tour operators and hotels.

Ecuaworld ⓦ**www.ecuaworld.com** Another general tourism site offering a fine introduction to the country and plenty of useful information including latest travel news and weather.

Galápagos Islands ⓦ**www.darw infoundation.org** Website of the Charles Darwin Research Station on Isla Santa Cruz, with masses of information on the ecology and biology of the Galápagos, the latest conservation and research news, details on volunteering opportunities, and good links to related sites.

Volcanoes ⓦ**www.vulcan.wr.usgs .gov/Volcanoes/Ecuador/framework .html** Comprehensive links to sites with information and photos of Ecuador's major volcanoes.

Ecuadorian embassies

Australia
Ecuadorian Embassy, 6 Pindari Crescent, O'Malley, Canberra, ACT 2606 ☏00612/6286 4021

Canada
Ecuadorian Embassy, 2055 Peel, Oficina No. 501, Montreal, Quebec H3A 1V4 ☏001514/874-4071, ⓦwww .consecuador-quebec.org/

UK
Ecuadorian Embassy, Flat 3b, 3 Hans Crescent, London SW1X OLS ☏0207/5841367

US
Ecuadorian Embassy, 2535 15th St, Washington DC, NW 20009 ☏(202) 2347200, ⓦwww.ecuador.org/

The Guianas

Guyana
Capital Georgetown
Population 773,000
Languages Creole English, Hindi, Urdu
Currency Guyanese dollar (G$)
Climate Tropical – hot all year round, with two rainy seasons (Dec–Jan and April–July)
Best time to go February and March and August–November (dry season)
Minimum daily budget US$30

Suriname
Capital Paramaribo
Population 480,000
Languages Dutch, Hindi, Javanese, Chinese
Currency Surinamese Guilder (Sf)
Climate As Guyana, above
Best time to go As Guyana, above
Minimum daily budget US$30

French Guiana
Capital Cayenne
Population 177,500
Languages French, Hindi, Chinese, some indigenous languages
Currency Euro (E)
Climate As Guyana, above
Best time to go As Guyana, above
Minimum daily budget US$50

Perched on the northern coast of South America, the three small countries known collectively as the Guianas (Guyana, Suriname and French Guiana) are the least visited in Latin America, with a complex blend of races and cultures unique to the region. Additionally, all three countries comprise a largely unsettled wilderness, with vast tracts of unspoilt rainforest – more than in the whole of Central America. Not surprisingly, ecotourism is beginning to take off in the Guianas and there are wonderful opportunities for wildlife spotting, trekking off the beaten track and bush camping – either in a spartan tent or at one of many swanky eco-lodges.

The three countries share an early history, all originally inhabited by Arawak and Carib peoples. In the sixteenth century, they were settled by the Dutch, English and French, rather than by the Spanish and Portuguese. Slaves were brought in from West Africa until slavery was abolished, after which indentured labourers were imported from other colonies, especially India and Indonesia. Today, Guyana and Suriname reflect this racial history with Creole, Hindi and Javanese spoken alongside official languages, and temples and mosques almost as common as churches. French Guiana, on the other hand, is still a department of France – and the only remaining colony in mainland South America – with European living standards and prices to match.

Infrastructure in the Guianas is still very basic and exploring these countries is not for the faint-hearted. Travelling might mean taking a

www.roughguides.com

horrendously bumpy truck journey on one of the few roads in existence or, more likely, an uncomfortable boat ride down one of many rivers. For the most part, the Guianas are relatively crime-free, with the exception of Georgetown, which is a major drug-smuggling centre as well as Guyana's capital – even during the day, some areas of the city are best avoided.

Main attractions

● **Central Suriname Nature Reserve (Suriname)** This 1.6 million hectare rainforest park was formed in 1998 and is one of the most remote parts of the Amazon rainforest accessible – just about – to tourists. The area includes the Coppename River and the Voltzberg peak, which is usually climbed at sunrise for spectacular views. It's best to take an organized tour – these usually include a visit to indigenous villages and rapids

in the area – since the park is hard to reach otherwise.

● **Îles du Salut (French Guiana)** These tiny islands were the location of the notorious penal colonies which Henri Charrière made famous in *Papillon*. Popular with visitors because of their atmospheric ruins, they also have abundant wildlife and wild, palm-fringed beaches.

● **Iwokrama Rainforest Programme (Guyana)** This 3880-square-kilometre conservation project is home to an exceptionally wide range of wildlife and is one of the best places in Latin America for spotting jaguars. You can also take guided treks through the forest to Mount Iwokrama and boat trips along the Burro-burro and Essequibo rivers.

● **Kaieteur Falls (Guyana)** The Kaieteur waterfalls, situated on the upper Potaro River and surrounded by unspoilt forest, are among the world's most spectacular, plunging down a sheer drop of 228m. Most people fly in on a day-trip from Georgetown – January, June and July are the best months to see the falls at their fullest.

● **Paramaribo (Suriname)** Suriname's lively capital is a melting pot of the country's diverse cultures – a wooden cathedral rubs shoulders with one of the biggest mosques in the Caribbean, and several Hindu temples are also situated nearby. There's some fine Dutch colonial architecture to boot, while on Sundays you can witness the unusual spectacle of the locals taking their pet birds to Independence Square for the weekly birdsong competition.

● **Plage les Hattes (French Guiana)** A few kilometres from the Suriname border, at the mouth of the Maroni River, Plage les Hattes is arguably the best of the Guianas' turtle-nesting spots. The beach is home to an abundance of the most impressive species of turtle, the leatherback. Affordable accommodation is plentiful, and reaching the beach – four kilometres from the nearest town – is relatively easy.

Also recommended

● **Bartica (Guyana)** The oldest and most enjoyable of Guyana's towns, Bartica is situated on the confluence of the Essequibo, Mazuruni and Cuyuni rivers. Its rowdy atmosphere – with many bars and nightclubs – is in no small part due to the miners and lumberjacks who populate the town, but they are an extremely friendly and engaging bunch.

● **Carnival (French Guiana)** Carnival in French Guiana is Afro-Caribbean in style, with four days of unique and colourful parades, including Lundi Gras, which mocks the institution of marriage with men dressed as brides and women as grooms, and Mardi Gras, the next day,

which sees locals dressed as devils in red outfits with horns and pitchforks.

● **Centre Spatial Guyanais (French Guiana)** Kourou is the location for a large space station that houses the European Space Agency's Ariane programme. With advance reservations, it's possible to tour the site which is as impressive as NASA's site in Florida; the rocket launch towers and state-of-the-art technology rising out of the dense jungle create a surreal sight. If you write for an invitation it's also possible to watch one of the bimonthly rocket launches which are best seen from one of Kourou's official observation points.

● **Lethem (Guyana)** In the far southwest of Guyana, Lethem is the gateway to a number of wildlife adventures and several of the country's best eco-lodges. Here, the Rupununi savannah, a large area of flat grassland, has great bird-spotting; there are waterfalls at Moco-Moco; and the Amerindian villages of Annai and Surama have set up ecotourism projects that take visitors on night trekking, boating and Land Rover trips. The town itself is friendly and hosts a rodeo at Easter which attracts cowboys from all over the savannah.

Routes in and out

There are daily flights to Guyana from both New York and Miami; from Europe you'll have to go via Antigua, Port of Spain or Barbados in the Caribbean. To Suriname, there are direct flights from Amsterdam several times a week, as well as from Miami, Port of Spain and Curaçao in the Dutch Antilles. There are daily flights to French Guiana from Paris, Guadeloupe and Martinique, plus several times weekly from Miami.

It's not possible to travel by land between Guyana and Venezuela. Border

www.roughguides.com

crossings between the Guianas are complicated and because smuggling is rife, you may be checked several times – many tourists prefer to fly from one capital to another. Between Guyana and Brazil there's just one remote border crossing by ferry near Lethem in the Rupununi savannah (not always accessible in the rainy season). Between Guyana and Suriname, a ferry runs from Corriverton to Niew Nickerie, both coastal towns. Suriname and French Guiana are connected by frequent ferries from Albina to St Laurent-du-Maroni and a good connecting road to Cayenne. To reach Brazil from French Guiana, you'll need to hire a motorized canoe to take you across the Oiapoque River (15min) from St-Georges de L' Oiapoque (which is only accessible by plane from Cayenne) to Oiapoque and onto Macapá – it's much easier to fly all the way.

Books

Leon-Gontan Damas *Pigments* (o/p). French Guianan poet Damas founded the Negritude movement of French-speaking black intellectuals and this volume of calypso-inspired rhythmic poetry is its manifesto.

Roy Heath *The Georgetown Trilogy* (Persea Books). A tragic and complex family saga written by Guyana's best-known novelist, which details middle-class and mixed-race issues in Georgetown.

Sally Price *Co-wives and Calabashes* (The University of Michigan Press). Anthropological investigation into the art forms and way of life of the Saramakas, tribal people of the Suriname rainforest.

Andrew Westoll *The Riverbones: Stumbling after Eden in the Jungles of Suriname* (McClelland and Stewart). Travelogue which explores the remote

and mysterious rainforest cultures of Suriname, written by an enthralled Canadian biologist.

The Guianas online

Guyane Guide ⓦwww.guyane-guide.com Website in French only, with essays and information on the geography, history, gastronomy and tourism of French Guiana.

Guyana Outpost ⓦwww.guyanaoutpost.com Lovingly maintained website of Guyanan Wayne Moses, with a comprehensive list of features, news items, recipes, folkloric stories, a bookshop and useful information for tourists.

Suriname Tourism Foundation ⓦwww.suriname-tourism.org Website of private tourism organization with useful travel tips, news and comprehensive features.

Embassies

French Guiana

Australia
Embassy of French Guiana, Level 26, St Martin's Tower, 31 Market St, Sydney, NSW 2000 ☎02/9261 5779, ⓦwww.consulfrance-sydney.org

Canada
Embassy of French Guiana, 42 Sussex Drive, Ottawa, ON K1M 2C9, ⓦwww.ambafrance-ca.org

Ireland
Embassy of French Guiana, 36 Ailesbury Rd, Dublin 4 ☎01/260 1666

New Zealand
Embassy of French Guiana, 34–42 Manners St, PO Box 11-343, Wellington ☎04/384-2555, ⓦwww.ambafrance.net.nx

UK
Embassy of French Guiana, 58 Knightbridge, London SW1X 7JT

ⓣ0207/073 1000, ⓦwww.ambafrance
.uk.org
US
Embassy of French Guiana, 4101
Resevoir Rd, NW, Washington DC
20007 ⓣ(202) 9446211, ⓦwww.france
-consulat.org

Guyana

Canada
Embassy of Guyana, 505 Consumers
Rd, Suite 206, Willowdale, Toronto, ON
M2J 4V8 ⓣ416/494-6040
UK
Embassy of Guyana, 3 Place Court,
Bayswater Rd, London W2 4LP
ⓣ0207/229 7684

US
Embassy of Guyana, 2490 Tracy Place,
NW, Washington DC 20008 ⓣ(202)
4836960

Suriname

US
Embassy of Suriname, 4301 Connecticut
Ave, NW, suite 460, Washington DC
20008 ⓣ(202) 2447488, ⓦwww
.surinameembassy.org.

www.roughguides.com

Paraguay

Capital Asunción	hot and humid in the east, hotter
Population 7 million	and semi-arid in the west
Languages Spanish and Guaraní	**Best time to go** May–September
Currency Guaraní (G/)	(dry season)
Climate Subtropical to temperate;	**Minimum daily budget** US$20

A remote backwater hemmed in by giant neighbours, Paraguay is one of the least visited countries in South America. Very few travellers come to Paraguay, and those that do tend to pass through only briefly as part of a multi-country trip. The reason for this is simple: in terms of conventional tourist attractions, Paraguay has little to offer, especially when compared to neighbouring countries like Brazil and Argentina. There are no soaring mountain ranges, beautiful beaches or lost cities here, and the lack of infrastructure and limited tourist development make the more interesting wilderness areas difficult to reach. That said, Paraguay is not without appeal, and just coming here takes you firmly off the beaten track, offering a far more authentic (if less dramatic) experience of Latin America than many more popular destinations.

Paraguay's geographical isolation has combined with a history of traumatic wars and long-running military dictatorships to create an inward-looking society with a strong sense of national identity. Although few Paraguayans would describe themselves as indigenous, almost all speak the indigenous language Guaraní as well as Spanish, making Paraguay the most bilingual country in the region. Both are official

languages, but outside the cities Guaraní is far more widely used, and even in the capital, Asunción, you'll hear its musical lilt every time you pass Paraguayans gathered to share a chat and sip the ubiquitous yerba mate – a stimulating herbal tea drunk from gourds through metal straws

Paraguay is one of the poorest countries in South America, its economy based largely on agriculture and smuggling goods to neighbouring Brazil and Argentina – the black economy is still thought to account for up to half Paraguay's gross domestic product.

Geographically, Paraguay is divided into two distinct regions by the river that gives it its name. East of the Río Paraguay is the country's traditional rural heartland, a rich agricultural region of rolling hills covered by well-watered grasslands and patches of subtropical forest. North and west of the river stretches the Gran Chaco, a harsh wilderness region of low plains covered by swamp and impenetrable thorn scrub stretching north to the Bolivian border, an area rich in wildlife and home only to scattered indigenous groups and remote settlements of German-speaking Mennonite farmers. In neither region is the scenery particularly spectacular,

but travelling across the Chaco is still one of the great wilderness journeys in South America, particularly if you're heading to or from Bolivia, while the more populous agricultural region east of the Río Paraguay, with its deep-rooted cultural traditions and sleepy towns and villages, has an understated but timeless rural charm.

Main attractions

● **Asunción** Though it's the political and commercial heart of Paraguay, Paraguay's riverside capital retains the sedate atmosphere of a provincial backwater, with elegant nineteenth-century public buildings and some interesting – though rather militaristic – monuments and museums, largely dedicated to former dictators and war heroes. The pretty countryside and traditional farming towns of the surrounding rural heartland – including the lace-making centre of Itauguá – can be visited on day-trips from the city.

● **Gran Chaco** Covering more than half of Paraguay, the Gran Chaco is one of the last great wilderness regions of South America, a vast stretch of thorn scrub, savannah and swamp inhabited only by indigenous tribes and hardy colonies of Mennonites, a German-speaking religious sect. Comparable to the Amazon in plant and animal biodiversity and largely pristine, the Chaco is extremely rich in wildlife, and a paradise for birdwatchers. The inexpensive way to visit is by making the arduous journey by bus or truck through the heart of the region and on into Bolivia. However, to get a closer look at the wildlife you're better off taking a tour from Asunción – a number of companies there offer jeep trips into the remote Parque Nacional Defensores del Chaco.

● **Jesuit missions** In Trinidad and Jesús, close to the southern city of Encarnación on the Argentine border, stand the ruined churches and other buildings of the utopian Jesuit mission settlements established here in the eighteenth century, their well-preserved stone structures a vivid testimony to the artistic heights reached by the indigenous Guaraní under the tutelage of a handful of European priests.

● **Parque Nacional Ybicuy** One of the last remaining areas of Paraguay's original rainforest, this reserve is noted for its forested hills and rushing waterfalls. It has plenty of good hiking trails, and is easily accessed from Asunción, 120km away.

Also recommended

● **A boat ride down the Río Paraguay** Travelling on one of the irregular passenger boats that ply the mighty Río Paraguay between Asunción and Concepción is one of the best ways of seeing the tranquil rural heartland of Paraguay.

● **Itaipú Dam** Close to the unattractive smuggler's paradise of Ciudad del Este on the Brazilian border lies the massive Itaipú Dam, one of the world's biggest hydroelectric projects. Completed in 1984, it's a monumental sight – though

apparently nowhere near as spectacular as the dramatic waterfalls drowned by the reservoir after it was built.

● **Working on an estancia** A number of farms and estancias or ranches accept paying guests, rather like "dude ranches" in the US, allowing you first-hand experience of the traditional way of life in rural Paraguay.

Routes in and out

The international airport at Asunción has frequent direct flights to most other South American capitals, a number of other cities in Brazil, and to Miami in the US. By land, you can cross the border from Brazil between Foz de Iguaçu and Ciudad del Este in the east and between Ponta Porã and Pedro Juan Caballero in the northeast. From Argentina there are road crossings between Asunción and Clorinda and between Encarnación and Posadas in the south, and you can also enter Paraguay from Puerto Iguazú via Foz de Iguaçu in Brazil. The overland route to and from Bolivia is along the Trans-Chaco Highway, an adventurous journey through the heart of the great Chaco wilderness. Alternatively, you can also enter and leave Paraguay on one of the irregular riverboats that travel the Río Paraguay between Asunción and Corumbá in Brazil.

Paraguay books

John Gimlette *At the Tomb of the Inflatable Pig: Travels through Paraguay* (Arrow). Witty and informative travelogue that delves deep into Paraguay's extraordinary history and idiosyncratic society.
Sian Rees *The Shadows of Elisa Lynch: How a 19th Century Irish Courtesan Became the Most Powerful Woman in*

Paraguay (Headline Review). Well-written account of the extraordinary life of Elisa Lynch, Irish mistress to President Francisco López, who led Paraguay to disaster in a war against Brazil, Argentina and Uruguay.

Augusto Roa Bastos *I, the Supreme* (Dalkey Archive Press). Epic meditation on the nature of power by one of the giants of South American literature, based on the life of Paraguay's founding president, the enlightened dictator and perpetual tyrant, Dr Franco.

Paraguay online

Senatur Ⓦwww.senatur.gov.py Official Paraguayan tourist office site with good general information on the country's attractions and links to relevant sites.

Yagua.com Ⓦwww.yagua.com Comprehensive Paraguayan internet directory with links to all manner of Paraguay-related sites, including tourist information and the media.

Paraguayan embassies and consulates

Canada
Embassy of Paraguay, 151 Slater St, Suite 501, Ottawa, Ontario K1P 5H3 ☎613/567-1283, Ⓦwww.embassy ofparaguay.ca/

South Africa
Embassy of Paraguay, 189 Strelitzia Rd, Waterkloof Heights 0181, PO Box 95774, Waterkloof 0145, Pretoria, ☎12-347-1047/8, Ⓔembapar @iafrica.com

UK
Embassy of Paraguay, 3rd Floor, 344 Kensington High St, London, W14 8NS ☎020/7610 4180, Ⓦwww .paraguayembassy.co.uk

US
Embassy of Paraguay, 2400 Massachusetts Ave NW, Washington, DC 20008, ☎(202) 4836960, Ⓦwww .embaparusa.gov.py/

Peru

Capital Lima	much cooler with altitude in the Andes
Population 29.5 million	
Languages Spanish, Quechua, plus more than thirty other indigenous languages	**Best time to go** May–September (dry season for the highlands and Amazon), December–March for summer weather on the coast. The best of the Andean fiestas are in May, June and July
Currency Nuevo Sol (S/)	
Climate Tropically hot and humid in the Amazon lowlands, drier along the desert coast and	
	Minimum daily budget US$25

Peru is arguably the most varied and fascinating country in Latin America, a place to which even seasoned travellers return again and again, drawn by a landscape of magnificent extremes and a culture of extraordinary depth and irresistible vitality. It's best known as home of the Incas, the rulers of the largest and most powerful of Latin America's pre-Columbian empires, and as the location of Machu Picchu, the original lost city in the jungle. But though Machu Picchu and the Inca heartland around the unforgettable city of Cusco are rightly the main draws for visitors, their fame sometimes obscures the extraordinary attractions of the rest of the country. The Incas were just the last and best known of many civilizations that rose and fell in Peru before the Spanish conquest, and the whole country is dotted with magnificent archeological sites, with major new finds – from lost cities in the Andes to golden tombs in desert pyramids – being regularly discovered.

This astonishing archeological heritage is set amidst fabulously varied scenery, ranging from the deserts of the Pacific coastal strip through the high peaks of the Andes to the seemingly endless expanse of the Peruvian Amazon rainforest. Peru is one of the most biodiverse countries on earth, home to an incredible range of different ecosystems that support an extraordinary variety of plant and animal life. It's also an ideal setting for all kinds of adventure sports, including trekking, mountaineering, whitewater rafting and mountain biking.

The huge range of landscapes is more than matched by the diversity of the population, an intriguing blend of indigenous, Spanish, African and Asian peoples. The most distinctive cultures are found in the Andes and the Amazon, where most people are of indigenous descent, maintaining their own languages and deep-seated cultural traditions and beliefs. These are manifested most vibrantly in their music and dance and in the many colourful fiestas that punctuate the year.

Since emerging from a long period of political violence and upheaval in the 1980s and 1990s, Peru has been

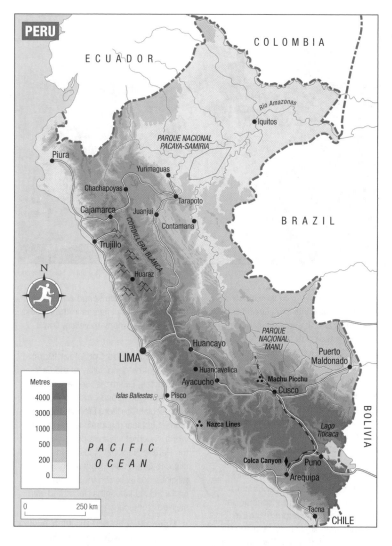

enjoying steady economic growth and relative stability, though some remote areas should still be avoided. It still has an unfortunate reputation for theft and other scams, but you shouldn't let this put you off. Most Peruvians are extremely open and welcoming to foreigners.

Main attractions

● **Arequipa** Set at the foot of the snowcapped El Misti volcano, the city of Arequipa boasts a lovely climate and some of the finest colonial architecture in Peru, including the beautiful Monastery

▲ Llama, Machu Picchu

of Santa Catalina. From the city it's easy to organize trips into the surrounding mountains and the spectacular Colca Canyon, the world's deepest, which is an excellent place for trekking, whitewater rafting and condor-spotting.

● **Cusco** The ancient heart of the Inca Empire, Cusco is Peru's most famous attraction and one of the most compelling destinations in Latin America. A beautiful colonial city built amidst the magnificent ruined temples and palaces of the Incas (and still largely inhabited by their Quechua-speaking descendants), Cusco is surrounded by spectacular mountain scenery and remarkable Inca archeological sites, including the monumental fortress of Sacsayhuaman, which towers above the city, and the numerous temples and palaces of the nearby Sacred Valley of the Incas. Cusco is also a great base for trekking, climbing, mountain biking and whitewater rafting trips, and for expeditions into the rainforests of the southern Peruvian Amazon. Combined

with a lively nightlife scene and some of the most colourful fiestas in the Andes, it's no wonder many travellers find it hard to leave.

● **Huaraz and the Cordillera Blanca** Nestled in the deep valley of the Callejon de Huayllas, Huaraz is the perfect base for trekking and climbing in the spectacular Cordillera Blanca, the highest tropical mountain range in the world, much of which is protected by the Parque Nacional Huascaran. It's also close to Chavín de Huantar, an ancient religious complex of ruined temples and underground labyrinths decorated with stylized stone carvings.

● **Machu Picchu and the Inca Trail** Of all Peru's archeological attractions, the most famous and dramatic is the lost city of Machu Picchu, set amid the dense forests north of the Inca capital, Cusco. You can reach the ruins by taking a stunning train journey from Cusco or by hiking the Inca Trail, a well-preserved though usually overcrowded stone-paved Inca road that passes through spectacular high mountain scenery and numerous Inca sites before plunging down through the cloudforest to Machu Picchu. If the crowds sound too much for you, consider hiking one of the many other Inca trails that criss-cross the Andes around Cusco, many of them linking archeological sites. One of the best of these is the newly opened route to the Inca citadel of Choqueqirao.

- **Nazca Lines** Set in the arid coastal strip south of Lima, the Nazca Lines are one of the most mysterious and dramatic ancient sites in South America, a series of massive geometric shapes and animal figures drawn into the ground over some five hundred square kilometres of stony desert – their origins and meaning remain unknown, despite endless speculation. The Lines are best viewed from the air, and it's easy to arrange an overflight in a light aircraft from the town of Nazca. For those on a tight budget, there is also a viewing tower where you can get a good look of some of the best sections.

- **Peruvian Amazon** Covering over half the country, the rainforests of the Peruvian Amazon are amongst the best preserved and least explored in South America. They're also amongst the least accessible, so you may want to save time by flying to one of the Amazon towns from where you can organize a rainforest expedition rather than make the arduous journey by land down the eastern slopes of the Andes. The best place to visit in the region is undoubtedly the stunning Parque Nacional Manu in the southern Peruvian Amazon (accessible on organized tours from Cusco), arguably the most pristine, biodiverse and wildlife-rich national park in all South America. A cheaper alternative in the south is the more accessible Tambopata-Candamo Reserve, reached by boat from Puerto

Maldonado, while in the northern Amazon the city of Iquitos, on the banks of the mighty Amazon itself, is the best-organized and established tourism centre, with plenty of companies offering everything from luxury cruises and eco-lodges to rugged survival expeditions and trips into the vast and virtually untouched Parque Nacional Pacaya-Samiria.

Also recommended

- **Ayacucho** Once the centre of Sendero Luminoso guerrilla activity in the 1980s and 1990s and long off-limits to travellers, the highland city of Ayacucho is now safe to visit. And, with its fine colonial architecture and strong indigenous cultural traditions, you really should make the effort to see it, particularly if you're making the tough overland journey between Cusco and Lima, and especially during Easter, when it stages fabulous Semana Santa celebrations.

- **Cajamarca** A friendly market town in the northern Andes, Cajamarca is second only to Cusco in the grace of its architecture, the drama of its mountain setting and the resonance of its Inca past. It has so far escaped mass tourism, and is a perfect spot to relax for a day or two as you journey through northern Peru.

- **Chachapoyas** Set in the often overlooked northern highlands, the remote town of Chachapoyas is the centre of a beautiful region of cloud-forest-covered mountains dotted with scarcely explored pre-Inca ruins, including the spectacular walled city of Kuelap.

- **Lago Titicaca** The lakeside city of Puno is the perfect base for exploring the magical scenery of the altiplano, the high Andean plateau, and above all

www.roughguides.com

for making boat trips out across Lago Titicaca to the idyllic islands of Taquile and Amantani, where you can get a real taste of traditional rural Andean culture by staying with an indigenous family.

● **Lima** With its sprawling shantytowns, chaotic traffic and dismal, fogbound climate, Lima can seem a pretty daunting and unattractive place. But beyond these first impressions the capital has much to offer, including an elegant colonial city centre that's gradually being restored and excellent museums such as the Museo de Oro, with its huge collection of pre-Columbian gold artefacts. Lima also boasts some of the finest restaurants in Latin America and a vibrant nightlife scene.

● **Trujillo and the North Coast** The handsome colonial city of Trujillo on the north coast is surrounded by beautiful deserted Pacific beaches, peaceful fishing villages, and an amazing collection of ancient archeological sites, including the massive earthen pyramids of the Huaca del Sol and Huaca de la Luna, and the monumental ruined adobe city of Chan-Chan. It also boasts Peru's finest regional cuisine, based above all on the excellent local seafood. Favourites include Chupe de Camarones – an exquisite shrimp soup; Picante de Mariscos – a spicy shellfish stew; and of course ceviche in all its many forms.

Routes in and out

Lima is connected by frequent international flights to major cities in Europe, the US and most major Latin American capitals. Entering or leaving Peru overland by road across the Bolivian, Chilean and Ecuadorian borders is easy. You can travel to and from Colombia and Brazil by boat along the Amazon River from Iquitos, and there are also several more remote Amazon border crossings with Brazil and Bolivia.

Peruvian books

John Hemming *Conquest of the Incas* (Pan). Compelling and authoritative account of how a ruthless band of Spanish adventurers managed to seize control of South America's most powerful and sophisticated empire.
Orin Starn, Carlos DeGregori and Robin Kirk (eds) *The Peru Reader: History, Politics, Culture* (Duke University Press). Excellent overview of Peru's history and culture, with excerpts from an extraordinary range of different writers.
Hugh Thomson *Cochineal Red* (Phoenix). The best travelogue on Peru in recent years, combining the search for lost forgotten Inca ruins with a broad overview of ancient Andean societies.
Mario Vargas Llosa *Conversation in the Cathedral* (Rayo). Arguably the greatest work of Peru's most celebrated novelist, an epic exploration of the culture of corruption told in his trademark non-sequential narrative style.

Peru online

An American in Lima Ⓦ www .americaninlima.com Amusing and well-observed expat blog covering Peruvian culture, cuisine, travel and daily life.
Andean Travel Web Ⓦ www.andean travelweb.com/peru Comprehensive English-language Peruvian travel site, with good information on all the main attractions, and links to all manner of useful sites including hotels and tour companies.
Go2Peru Ⓦ www.go2peru.com A detailed online guide to Peru run by the

National Chamber of Tourism, with links to all major tour operators and hotels.
iPeru Ⓦ**www.peru.info** Official tourist promotion site with information on everything from history and archeology to food and fiestas, as well as details on all the major attractions and practical travel advice.

Rumbos Ⓦ**www.rumbosperu.com** Peruvian environmental and travel magazine with good photos, travel articles, background information and practical tips on visiting a huge range of different sites.

Peruvian embassies and consulates

Australia
Peruvian Embassy, 40 Brisbane Ave, Level 2 Barton, Canberra, ACT 2600 ℡02/62737351, Ⓦwww.embaperu .org.au/

Canada
Peruvian Embassy, 130 Albert St, Suite 1901, Ottawa, ON. K1P 5G4, ℡613/ 238-1777, Ⓦwww.embassyofperu.ca/

New Zealand
Peruvian Embassy, Level Eight, Cigna House, 40 Mercer St, Wellington ℡04/499 8087, Ⓦwww.embassyofperu .org.nz/

South Africa
Peruvian Consulate, Brooklyn Gardens Building, Block A, 1st Floor, 235 Veale St, Corner Middel St, Nieuw Muckleneuk, 0181 Pretoria ℡0027/1234 68744

UK
Peruvian Embassy, 52 Sloane St, London SW1 9SP ℡202/4621081, Ⓦwww.peruembassy-uk.com/

US
Peruvian Embassy, 1700 Massachusetts Ave, NW, Washington DC 20036 ℡(202) 4621081, Ⓦwww .peruvianembassy.us/en.html.

Uruguay

Capital Montevideo	**Best time to go** September–April
Population 3.5 million	(summer)
Language Spanish	**Minimum daily budget** US$35
Currency Peso Uruguayo (U$)	
Climate Temperate, with long warm summers and mild winters	

Squeezed in between the vast expanses of Argentina and Brazil, diminutive Uruguay is usually overlooked by travellers to South America. It is, however, an oasis of stability in the fluctuating fortunes of the region, with moderate politics, an educated and tolerant population and a beguiling atmosphere of old-fashioned elegance reminiscent of neighbouring Argentina, whose neo-European culture Uruguay shares. There is no mass tourism in Uruguay and the country remains unspoilt and hospitable.

Given Uruguay's modest dimensions, its characterful capital, Montevideo, looms large in the national psyche – almost half the country's three-million-plus inhabitants live here, and the capital is very much the economic, cultural and political heart of the country. Not that Montevideo is Uruguay's only attraction; the country's alluring Atlantic coastline, centred on the ritzy resort of Punta del Este, also boasts more low-key seaside villages in which to loll on the beach and enjoy Uruguay's pleasantly Mediterranean climate. What really defines Uruguay, however, is its gaucho culture, which is even more ubiquitous and traditional than neighbouring Argentina's – you're still more likely to see farmhands wearing

bombachas (loose trousers), bandanas and felt hats than jeans. The colourful three-day "Fiesta de la Patria Gaucha", held in the town of Tacuarembó in late March, is a good place to see fine displays of gaucho horsemanship and other skills like horse-breaking and cattle herding.

Although parts of Montevideo aren't entirely safe at night, Uruguay is an otherwise safe place to travel, with reasonably priced accommodation and an efficient network of public transport.

Main attractions

● **Colonia del Sacramento** Founded by Portuguese settlers from Brazil in 1680, Colonia sits directly opposite Buenos Aires on the Río de la Plata. It's a charming town, Uruguay's prettiest, with whitewashed buildings, narrow cobbled streets and squares lined by plane trees, as well as the ruins of the seventeenth-century Convento de San Francisco and a nineteenth-century lighthouse, from where there are lovely views over the town.

● **Gaucho culture** Many Uruguayan estancias (ranches) offer comfortable homestays during which you can ride,

rope steers and learn about farm life. You might also be encouraged to join in with daily tasks performed by ranch hands like branding cattle, shearing sheep or milking cows, or be taken out for a ride in a traditional horse-drawn carriage.

● **Montevideo** Like nearby Buenos Aires, Montevideo's passions are tango, football and *maté*, although the city is more laid-back and relaxing than its brasher Argentine cousin. Along with elegant European-style coffeehouses and boulevards, the city also boasts a small colonial centre, the Ciudad Vieja, and one of the most atmospheric markets in South America, the Mercado del Puerto, housed in a large, nineteenth-century wrought-iron building and known for its delicious *parilla* (barbecues) – come here especially on Saturday afternoons to enjoy the grilled meat and mix with

the locals for whom it's a long-standing weekend tradition.

● **Punta del Este** On the Atlantic coast, 85km east of Montevideo, the glitzy seaside resort of Punta del Este is popular with wealthy and trendy Brazilians, Argentinians and, from December to February, European clubbers in search of winter sun. While Punta's beaches are broad and sandy, most visitors come for the best coastal nightlife south of Rio de Janeiro, with world-class DJs flown in from Europe and the US. Punta is far from cheap, though – costs are equivalent to those in the south of France.

Also recommended

● **Aguas Dulces** If you fancy a quiet beach holiday, head for the quaint fishing village of Aguas Dulces, 120km east of

Punta del Este, which has several good seafood restaurants and few tourists. The surrounding area has undeveloped sandy beaches, while 30km further north is the Parque Nacional Santa Teresa, which incorporates an eighteenth-century hilltop castle, pine and eucalyptus forests and marshes with abundant bird life.

● **Candombe** Montevideo's Barrio Sur is home to the country's colourful Afro-Uruguayan population, whose unique ceremonial form of music and dance, known as *candombe*, can be seen most weekends in the city's cabaret venues or, more authentically, outside on the barrio's Calle Carlos Gardel. As well as drumming and dancing, *candombe* events involve a fixed cast of characters including a matriarch, a medicine man and El Bastonero – a man with a magic wooden stick.

● **Dunes of Cabo Polonio** On the Atlantic coast 200km east of Montevideo, the Cabo Polonio offers one of Uruguay's wildest and most dramatic vistas, with a ten-kilometre stretch of shifting sand dunes, some of them reaching 30m in height, making for an invigorating coastal hike.

● **Las Termas** Located in the geothermically active eastern part of Uruguay, Las Termas is a series of natural hot spring resorts where you can relax in naturally heated pools or enjoy a hydro-massage. Particularly recommended is Termas del Daymán, 8km south of Salto and home to the first thermal aquapark in South America.

Routes in and out

There are several direct flights weekly from Madrid to Uruguay as well as regular flights from Miami via Brazil and Argentina to Montevideo. The easiest

way to reach the country is to fly directly to Buenos Aires from the US or Europe (London, Madrid and Amsterdam) and take the ferry across the Río de la Plata to Montevideo or Colonia. Alternatively, fly to São Paulo in Brazil and get one of several daily flights to Montevideo. There are a number of land crossings into Brazil – the most popular goes between Chuy at the northern end of Uruguay's Atlantic coast and twin city Chui in Brazil. There is also a land crossing to Argentina at Gualeguaychú, though this is less convenient than crossing the Río de la Plata.

Books

Mario Benedetti *Office Poems* (Host Publications). Reflections on the daily grind of middle-class Montevideo by the country's best-loved and frequently quoted poet.
Christopher Empson *The Far Horizons* (Rozenberg Publishers). Humorous memoirs of 30 years living among the gauchos in the early twentieth century.
William Henry Hudson *The Purple Land* (Dodo Press). Young Englishman goes native among the gauchos and guerillas of Uruguay in this intensely romantic nineteenth-century novel.

Uruguay online

Discover Uruguay Ⓦwww.discover uruguay.com Online travel agency set up by an expat Uruguayan with useful tourist information and essays on all things Uruguayan.
Uruguay Info Ⓦwww.uruguayinfo .com The enthusiastic website of two Germans living in Montevideo. Available in German and English with information on living in Uruguay, and features on culture, history and tourism and hundreds of photographs.

Uruguay Total ⓦ www.uruguaytotal
.com Uruguay's main internet portal,
with hundreds of links on business,
politics, the media and much more.

Uruguayan embassies and consulates

Australia
Embassy of Uruguay, PO Box 5058,
Kingston, ACT 2604 ☏02/6273 9100
Canada
Embassy of Uruguay, 130 Albert St,
Suite 1905, Ottawa, ON K10 5G4
☏613/234-2727
New Zealand
Embassy of Uruguay, c/o Kingett

Mitchell Ltd, Level 3, 79 Cambridge
Terrace, Christchurch 8051 ☏03/374
6774
South Africa
Embassy of Uruguay, 301 MB House,
3rd Floor, 1119 Burnett St, Hatfield
Square, PO Box 14818, Hatfield,
Pretoria 0102 ☏12-362 6521
UK
Embassy of Uruguay, 2nd Floor, 140
Brompton Rd, London, SW3 1HY
☏202/331-4219, ⓦwww.embassy
.org/uruguay
US
Consulate of Uruguay, 19131, I St (Eye
st, NW, Washington DC 20006 ☏(202)
3314219, ⓦwww.uruguay.org.

Venezuela

Capital Caracas	lowlands, cooler in the Andes
Population 27 million	**Best time to go** November–June
Languages Spanish, more than 20	(dry season)
minority indigenous languages	**Minimum daily budget** US$30
Currency Bolívar (B)	
Climate Hot and humid in the	

Venezuela is the fifth biggest country in South America and, like the continent's other Andean nations, encompasses a great variety of dramatic landscapes, from Andean peaks to the immense, wildlife-rich plains, swamps and rainforests of the Amazon and Orinoco basins. With almost three thousand kilometres of Caribbean coastline, Venezuela also boasts some glorious beaches (for example in Morrocoy or Mochima national parks) as well as numerous idyllic offshore islands surrounded by coral reefs. In addition, the wilderness hinterland is home to two of South America's most outstanding natural wonders: Angel Falls, the world's highest waterfall, with a drop of almost a kilometre; and the stunning, flat-topped sandstone mountains known as *tepuis* that rise almost vertically from the plains of the remote Gran Sabana.

Given these attractions, Venezuela receives surprisingly few visitors, other than the package tourists who fly in to enjoy the beach resort island of Margarita, and the smaller numbers who come specifically to see Angel Falls or visit less-developed parts of the Caribbean coast. Many budget travellers are put off by the country's relatively high costs, and by the visa requirement for travellers entering the country overland. As one of the world's biggest oil exporters, Venezuela has never really felt the need to promote its attractions abroad. This is a shame, as its splendid coastline and vast wilderness interior boast natural beauty to match anywhere else in Latin America, and good roads and other infrastructure make it easy to get away from the rather grim capital, Caracas.

In recent years, Venezuela's profile has increased for political reasons, with the rise of the radical left-wing president Hugo Chavez. In power since 1999, President Chavez is trying to transform Venezuela into a socialist society, but while a growing number of like-minded vistors come to see his revolution in action, others are put off by the political polarization it has provoked and the fears that he is edging towards dictatorship. Check the political situation before you go and be cautious about discussing politics in public.

Main attractions

● **Angel Falls** Set amid pristine rainforest inside the remote Parque Nacional Canaima in the southwest

of the country, the Angel Falls (Salto Angel, named after Jimmy Angel, the US bush pilot who stumbled across them in the 1930s) are Venezuela's most famous attraction. Plummeting almost 1km – around fifteen times the height of Niagara Falls – this is by far the highest waterfall in the world, an amazing spectacle made all the more alluring by its remote wilderness location. Getting to the falls is no easy matter: you have to fly into the village of Canaima, from where you can either fly over the falls in a light aircraft or travel to their foot by motorized canoe. This latter option is only possible during the June to December rainy season, which is in any case the best time to visit, since the high water levels mean that the falls are at their most spectacular.

● **Archipelago Los Roques** Situated some 160km off the mainland north of

Caracas, the Los Roques archipelago comprises a beautiful collection of coral atolls with white-sand beaches, fringed by extensive coral reefs. Protected as a national park, the islands support a great density and diversity of tropical marine life, making for fantastic snorkelling and diving. Nor are the waters crowded – the cost of reaching the islands by plane or yacht help keep visitor numbers low.

● **Gran Sabana** South of Angel Falls and set within the same massive Parque Nacional Canaima, the beautiful and remote Gran Sabana is a vast, rolling plateau covered with savannah grassland and tropical rainforest, from which rise over a hundred flat-topped mountains known as tepuis. Inhabited by scattered indigenous groups, the region is rich in wildlife, and the tops of the tepuis, where plant species have

▲ Angel Falls, Venezuela

evolved in isolation, are amongst the most unique natural habitats in Latin America. The largest of the tepuis is the 2810-metre Mount Roraima, which sits on the three-way border with Guyana and Brazil and can be climbed on a tough five- to six-day trek.

● **Mérida** Set at an altitude of 1640m within sight of Venezuela's highest mountain peaks, the friendly city of Mérida is the best base for exploring the Venezuelan Andes, which stretch for some 400km along the western side of the country. From the city you can take the world's longest and highest cable-car ride up to the 4765-metre summit of Pico Espejo for fabulous views of the mountains all around. Mérida is also home to a well-developed tour industry, which makes it easy to organize trekking, mountain biking, whitewater rafting and horseriding trips into the surrounding mountains, large areas of which are protected by Parque Nacional Sierra Nevada.

● **Parque Nacional Morrocoy** With its clear blue waters, near-deserted beaches and islands, and extensive coral reefs, Parque Nacional Morrocoy covers an idyllic stretch of the Caribbean coast west of Caracas, and is an excellent place for snorkelling, diving or just chilling out on the beach. It's best visited by taking day-trips by boat from the towns of Tucacas and Chichiriviche, though if you take your own camping equipment and supplies you can arrange to be dropped off on one of the deserted islands and enjoy a few days of blissful isolation.

Also recommended

● **Coro** The peaceful little port town of Coro, on the Caribbean coast about 180km west of Parque Nacional Morrocoy, was one of the first Spanish settlements in South America, and is home to the finest colonial architecture in Venezuela.

● **Isla de Margarita** The Isla de Margarita is Venezuela's biggest island and a major holiday resort, attracting large numbers of package tourists with its combination of beautiful beaches, modern hotel complexes and duty-free shopping. Despite the impact of mass tourism, however, the island's many beaches are so extensive that you can still find relatively peaceful stretches, especially if you avoid the main Venezuelan holiday periods (around Christmas and Easter), making it an excellent place to relax by the sea for a few days after some hard travelling elsewhere.

● **Orinoco Delta** The Orinoco Delta is a massive wetland region of swamp and rainforest where the waters of the mighty River Orinoco – the third biggest in South America – weave their way through an intricate system of waterways before reaching the sea. The delta supports a rich and varied range of wildlife, and is also home to the indigenous Warao, who reside in houses raised on stilts on many of the innumerable forested islands, and live largely by fishing from dugout canoes. You can visit this great wilderness on organized tours from the riverside town of Tucupita, staying in lodges on the delta.

Routes in and out

Caracas is a major regional hub for air travel, with regular flights from major cities in Europe and the United States, as well as most South American capitals. By land, there are four major cross-ings between Venezuela and Colombia, the easiest, safest and most scenic of which runs through the Andes between Cúcuta and San Antonio del Táchira. You can travel between Venezuela and Brazil along the recently opened road through the Gran Sabana, across the border at Santa Elena de Uairén and south to Boa Vista and Manaus in Brazil. There are no land crossings between Guyana and Venezuela; the only way to travel overland between the two is to go via Brazil. You can also enter and leave Venezuela by ferry between Isla Margarita and Trinidad and Tobago. Note that though you generally don't need a visa if you're flying into Venezuela, most nationalities do need one to enter the country overland, so check to make sure you can get one in a neighbouring country, or ideally pick one up before you leave home.

Venezuela books

Richard Gott *Hugo Chavez and the Boliviarian Revolution* (Latin America Bureau). Well-written account of the rise to power of Venezuela's charismatic and controversial president, by a veteran journalist who sympathizes with his revolutionary agenda.

John Lynch *Bolívar: a Life* (Yale University Press). Definitive English-language biography of the revered Venezuelan independence leader, which does well to separate the man from the myth.

Redmond O'Hanlon *In Trouble Again: A Journey between the Orinoco and the Amazon* (Penguin). Hilarious narrative of adventure in the depths of the Venezuelan rainforest.

Lisa St Aubin de Teran *The Hacienda* (Virago). Extraordinary personal memoir of an English child bride pitched into a life of isolation, cruelty and beauty on a remote Venezuelan coffee plantation.

Venezuela online

In Humboldt's footsteps ⓦwww .venezuelanodyssey.blogspot.com Entertaining blog by a British Venezuela fanatic with excellent information on Venezuelan food, music, culture and travel destinations.

Venezuela Analysis ⓦwww .venezuelanalysis.com Political news and comment on Venezuela from around the world, almost all of it from a pro-Chavez perspective – a useful antidote to the strong anti-Chavez bias in much of the media.

Venezuelan embassies and consulates

Australia
Embassy of Venezuela, 7 Culgoa Circuit O'Malley, Canberra, ACT 2606 ☎02/6290 2967, ⓦwww.venezuela -emb.org.au/

Canada
Embassy of Venezuela, 32 Range Rd, Ottawa, K1N 8J4, ☎613/235-5151

South Africa
Embassy of Venezuela, 474 Hatfield Gables South, 1st Floor, Suite 4, Hilda St, P O Box 11821, Hatfield, 0083, Pretoria ☎12-3626593

UK
Embassy of Venezuela, 1 Cromwell Rd, London SW7 2HR ☎020/7584 4206, ⓦwww.venezlon.demon.co.uk

US
Embassy of Venezuela, 1099 30th St, Washington, DC 20007 ☎(202) 3422214, ⓦwww.embavenez-us.org.

First-Time Latin America

Directory

1	Discount travel agents	299
2	Online booking agents	299
3	Specialist tour operators	300
4	Volunteer organizations	303
5	Health	303
6	Official advice on international trouble spots	304
7	Responsible tourism	305
8	Travel book and map stores	305
9	Online travel resources	306
10	Specialist Latin American resource centres	306
11	Travel equipment suppliers	307

Discount travel agents

Australia, New Zealand and South Africa

Backpackers World Travel Australia ℡1800/67-6763, New Zealand ℡0800/67-6763; Ⓦwww.backpackersworld.com.au

Flight Centres Australia ℡133 131 Ⓦwww.flightcentre.com.au, New Zealand ℡0800/24 35 44, Ⓦwww.flightcentre.co.nz, South Africa ℡0860/400727, Ⓦwww.flightcentre.co.za/

STA Travel Australia ℡134 782, Ⓦwww.statravel.com.au, New Zealand ℡0800/474 400, Ⓦwww.statravel.co.nz, South Africa ℡0861/781781, Ⓦwww.statravel.co.za/

Student Flights Australia ℡1800/046 462, Ⓦwww.studentflights.com.au

Trailfinders Australia ℡1300/780 212, Ⓦwww.trailfinders.com.au

UK

Apex Travel Ireland ℡01/241 8000, Ⓦwww.apextravel.ie

North South Travel UK ℡01245/608291, Ⓦwww.northsouthtravel.co.uk

STA Travel UK ℡0871/230 0040, Ⓦwww.statravel.co.uk

Trailfinders UK ℡0845/058 5858, Ⓦwww.trailfinders.com, Northern Ireland ℡028/9027 1888, Ireland ℡01/677 7888; Ⓦwww.trailfinders.ie

USIT Now Northern Ireland ℡028/ 9032 7111, Republic of Ireland ℡01/602 1906 Ⓦwww.usit.ie

US and Canada

Educational Travel Centre US ℡1-800/747-5551 or 608/256-5551, Ⓦedtrav.com

Flight Centre Canada ℡1-877/967-5302 Ⓦwww.flightcentre.ca

Liberty Travel US ℡1-888/271-1584 Ⓦww2.libertytravel.com

STA Travel US ℡1-800/781-4040, Ⓦwww.statravel.com

Travel Cuts Canada ℡1-866/246-9762, US ℡1-800/592-2887, Ⓦwww.travelcuts.com

Online booking agents

Cheap Flights

Ⓦwww.cheapflights.com.au (Australia)
Ⓦwww.cheapflights.ca (Canada)
Ⓦwww.cheapflights.co.za (South Africa)
Ⓦwww.cheapflights.co.uk (UK & Ireland)
Ⓦwww.cheapflights.com (US)

Cheap Tickets

Ⓦwww.cheaptickets.com (US)

Ebookers

Ⓦwww.ebookers.ie (Ireland)
Ⓦwww.ebookers.com (UK)

Expedia

Ⓦwww.expedia.com.au (Australia)
Ⓦwww.expedia.ca (Canada)
Ⓦwww.expedia.co.nz (New Zealand)
Ⓦwww.expedia.co.za (South Africa)
Ⓦwww.expedia.co.uk (UK)
Ⓦwww.expedia.com (US)

Skyscanners

Ⓦwww.skyscanners.net

Travelocity

Ⓦwww.zuji.com.au (Australia)
Ⓦwww.travelocity.ca (Canada)
Ⓦwww.zuji.co.nz (New Zealand)
Ⓦwww.travelocity.co.uk (UK)
Ⓦwww.travelocity.com (US)

www.roughguides.com

299

Specialist tour operators

Australia and New Zealand

Austral Tours Australia ☎03/9370 6621, ⓦwww.australtours.com. Central and South American specialists.

Australian Andean Adventures Australia ☎02/9299 9973, ⓦwww.andean adventures.com.au. Trekking specialist with mountain-climbing courses in Bolivia, Peru and Patagonia.

Latin Link Adventure New Zealand ☎0800/528 465, ⓦwww.latinlink.co.nz. Small organized tours to many regions within Latin America.

South American Travel Centre ☎1800/655051, ⓦwww.satc.com.au. Specialists in luxury, tailor-made tours to South and Central America and Cuba.

UK and Ireland

Condor Journeys and Adventures ☎01700/841 318, ⓦwww.condorjourneys -adventures.com. Imaginative ecotourism company with dozens of different themed tours.

Journey Latin America ☎020/8747 3108, ⓦwww.journeylatinamerica.co.uk. Long-established specialists in flights, packages and interesting tailor-made trips to Latin America. Also organize Spanish-language course holidays.

Last Frontiers ☎01296 653000, ⓦwww .lastfrontiers.com. Environmentally sensitive, specialist tour operator offering tailor-made itineraries for independent travellers in Latin America and Antarctica: riding, hiking and multi-activity – including scheduled departures.

Pura Aventura ☎0845/22 55 058, ⓦwww .pura-aventura.com. Challenging small-group adventure holidays with an emphasis on physical activity.

South America Safaris ☎020/8767 9136 ⓦwww.southamericansafaris.com. Budget camping trips (3–14 weeks) in purpose-built trucks.

US and Canada

Active South America ☎1-800/661-9073 ⓦwww.activesouthamerica.com. Outdoor and hiking specialists with hiking and biking trips to Costa Rica, Peru, Patagonia, Ecuador and the Galápagos Islands.

Far Horizons ☎1-800/552-4575, ⓦwww .farhorizons.com. Superb archeological trips to remote Maya, Inca and Easter Island sites led by renowned experts in the field.

Go South Adventures ☎1-866/393-0395, ⓦwww.go-south-adventures.com. Small group offering culturally sensitive adventure travel in South America with hiking and multi-activity tours.

Latin Trails ☎1-800/747-0567, ⓦwww .latintrails.com. Expert travel agency with 20 year's experience in Galápagos tours and Amazon travel.

Southern Explorations ☎1-877/784-5400, ⓦwww.southernexplorations.com. Specialists in private and small group tours (maxium 8) to South and Central America with a focus on sustainable tourism and personalized adventure travel.

www.roughguides.com

Volunteer organizations

There are hundreds of volunteer projects based in Latin America – the websites and books listed in Chapter 2 are a great place to start your research. Listed below are just a few more of the most ethical and responsible non-profit-making global voluntary organizations.

Australasian organizations

Australian Volunteers International ☎61/39279 1788, ⓦwww.ozvol.org.au. Postings for up to two years in Costa Rica, Guatemala, El Salvador and Nicaragua with shorter-term projects for younger volunteers.

Global Volunteer Network ☎04/569 9080, ⓦwww.volunteer.org.nz. Voluntary placements on community projects in Honduras, Costa Rica and Ecuador.

International Exchange Programs ☎0800/443 769, ⓦwww.iepnz.co.nz. A variety of work, teaching and study abroad programmes for Australasians wishing to go to Costa Rica or Peru.

Canadian Organizations

CADIP ☎613/231-4371 ⓦwww.cadip.org. Workcamps for volunteers in Brazil, Costa Rica, Mexico and Peru as well as longer-term volunteer placements.

CUSO-VSO ☎613/829-7445 ⓦwww.cuso.org. North American branch of international volunteer movement VSO with projects in Central America, Guyana and Peru.

UK organizations

British Trust for Conservation Volunteers (BTCV) ☎01302/388 883, ⓦwww2.btcv.org.uk. One of the largest environmental charities in Britain with a programme of international working holidays (as a paying volunteer) in many parts of Latin America.

Concordia ☎01273/422218, ⓦwww.concordia-iye.org.uk. Environmental, archeological and arts projects in Argentina, Brazil, Ecuador, Mexico and Peru are among some of the wide range offered for young people.

Peace Brigades International ☎0207/065 0775, ⓦwww.peacebrigades.org.uk. NGO dedicated to protecting human rights with placements accompanying human rights workers in trouble spots.

US organizations

Amigos de las Americas ☎1-800/231-7796, ⓦwww.amigoslink.org. Veteran non-profit organization placing young people in child health and other community schemes in Costa Rica, Honduras, Nicaragua and Panama.

Experiment in International Living ☎1-802/257-7751, ⓦwww.experiment international.org. Month-long community, environmental placements in half a dozen Latin American countries including Belize and Brazil.

Global Volunteers ☎1-800/487-1074, ⓦwww.globalvolunteers.org. Projects include working with children in Ecuador or on conservation in the Monteverde cloudforest in Costa Rica as well as others in Mexico and Peru.

Health

Australia, New Zealand and South Africa

Travellers' Medical and Vaccination Centres ☎1300/658 844 ⓦwww.tmvc.com.au. Lists vaccination centres throughout Australia, New Zealand and South Africa and provides general information on travel health. Excellent website.

UK and Ireland

Hospital for Tropical Diseases Travel Clinic Mortimer Market Centre, off Capper

St, London WC1E 6AU ☎020/7388 9600, ⓦwww.thehtd.org. The clinic is open Mon–Fri 9am–5pm by appointment or walk-in. A 20min consultation costs £15. A recorded health line (☎020/7950 59; 50p per min) gives advice on disease prevention and appropriate immunizations.

MASTA (Medical Advice Service for Travellers Abroad) ⓦwww.masta-travel-health.com. The largest network of private travel health clinics in the UK, with forty-five regional clinics, including in Scotland and Wales (check the website for nearest). A tailor-made travel health brief can be ordered online and costs £3.

Tropical Medical Bureau ☎1850/487 674, ⓦwww.tmb.ie. Branches throughout Dublin and rest of Ireland, offering all-in consultations covering everything from DVT to malaria prophylaxis.

US and Canada

American Society of Tropical Medicine and Hygiene ☎847/480-9592. ⓦwww.astmh.org. Society of tropical medical specialists with a comprehensive online directory of travel clinics.

Centers for Disease Control ☎1-800/232-4636, ⓦwww.cdc.gov. Publishes outbreak warnings, suggested inoculations, precautions and other background information for travellers. Excellent website and 24hr Travellers Hotline on ☎1-888/232-6348.

Public Health Agency of Canada ☎1-800/267-6788 ⓦwww.publichealth.gc.ca. Publishes a free booklet on travel health, *Well on Your Way* and has a list of travel clinics and lots of useful information on its website.

Travel health websites

Fit For Travel ⓦwww.fitfortravel.scot.nhs.uk. British National Health Service website carrying information about travel-related diseases and how to avoid them.

The International Society of Medicine ⓦwww.istm.org. The website of the International Society of Travel Medicine, with a full list of clinics specializing in international travel health.

Travel Health Online ⓦwww.tripprep.com. Travel Health Online provides an online-only comprehensive database of necessary vaccinations for most countries, as well as destination and medical service provider information.

World Health Organization ⓦwww.who.int. World Health Organization's website provides useful data on disease prevalence, prevention and current outbreak trends.

Official advice on international trouble spots

Australian Department of Foreign Affairs ☎1300/555 135, ⓦwww.dfat.gov.au

British Foreign and Commonwealth Office ☎0845/850 2829, ⓦwww.fco.gov.uk/en/

Canadian Department of Foreign Affairs ☎1-800/267-8370, ⓦwww.dfait-maeci.gc.ca

New Zealand Department of Foreign Affairs ☎04/439 8000, ⓦwww.mfat.govt.nz

US State Department Travel Advisory Service ☎202/512-1800, ⓦwww.travel.state.gov

South African Department of International Relations and Cooperation ☎12/3511000 ⓦwww.dfa.gov.za/

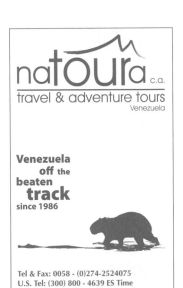
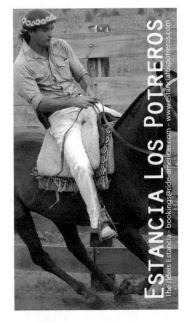
Responsible tourism

Global Exchange ⓦwww.globalexchange
.org. Not-for-profit organization that leads
"reality tours" to developing countries that
give participants the chance to learn about
the country while seeing it.

International Ecotourism Society
ⓦwww.ecotourism.org. Online factsheets
and reviews of eco-lodges and ecotour
operators.

Planeta ⓦwww.planeta.com Award-
winning clearing house with hundreds
of articles including official reports
on ecotourism in Latin America and

thousands of links to more general travel
websites.

Responsible Travel ⓦwww.responsible
travel.com. Website created by Body Shop
founder Anita Roddick, which reviews
hundreds of ecotours and accommodation
around the world.

Tourism Concern ⓦwww.tourism
concern.org.uk. Campaigns for the rights
of local people to be consulted in tourism
developments affecting their lives. Also
produces a quarterly magazine of news
and articles.

Travel book and map stores

Australia and New Zealand

Mapland 408 Centre Rd, Bentleigh,
Melbourne, Victoria 3204. ☏03/9557 8555,
ⓦwww.mapland.com.au

MapWorld 173 Gloucester St, Christchurch
☏0800/627 967, ⓦwww.mapworld.co.nz

Travel Bookshop 175 Liverpool St, Sydney
☏02/9261 8200, ⓦwww.travelbooks
.com.au

UK

Daunt Books 83 Marylebone High St, London W1M 3DE (and other London branches) ☎020/7224 2295, ⓦwww.dauntbooks.co.uk

Stanfords 12–14 Long Acre, London WC2E 9LP ☎020/7836 1321, ⓦwww.stanfords.co.uk

The Travel Bookshop 13–15 Blenheim Crescent, London W11 2EE ☎020/7229 5260, ⓦwww.thetravelbookshop.com.

US and Canada

Get Lost 1825 Market St, San Francisco, CA 94103 ☎415/437-0529, ⓦwww.getlostbooks.com

Longitude Books 115 W 30th St, #1206, New York, NY 10001 ☎1-800/342-2164, ⓦwww.longitudebooks.com

The Travel Bug Bookstore 3065 W Broadway, Vancouver V6K 2G9 ☎604/737-1122, ⓦwww.travelbugbooks.ca

World of Maps 1235 Wellington St, Ottawa, ON K1Y 3A3 ☎1-800/214-8524, ⓦwww.worldofmaps.com

Online travel resources

For country-specific websites, see the individual country profiles on pp.199–296. Websites for travel and online booking agents start on p.299, while travel health websites are listed on p.303.

ⓦwww1.lanic.utexas.edu The Latin American Network Information Centre, based at the University of Texas, is easily the best online resource on Latin America. Thousands of efficiently catalogued links to cultural, political and social issues among others.

ⓦwww.lata.org The Latin American Travel Association, based in London, is a non-profit organization that provides information on all aspects of travel to Latin America.

ⓦwww.latinamericalinks.com Comprehensive site aimed at travellers and featuring links on art, music, archeology, business etc as well as travel and tourism.

ⓦwww.latinworld.com Essays on all things Latin American.

ⓦwww.planeta.com Award-winning Latin American ecotourism clearing-house with links to other, lighter subjects.

ⓦwww.saexplorers.org Website of the South American Explorers' Club, based in Lima, Peru, which has general information on South America and a message board.

Specialist Latin American resource centres

The following places (most connected to academic institutions) run courses and lectures on Latin American themes. They also have specialist book collections and organize film showings and exhibitions – check their websites to find out about events.

Australia

Institute of Latin American Studies La Trobe University, Bundorra, Victoria 3083, Ⓦ www.latrobe.edu.au/history/las

Canada

Center for Research on Latin America and the Caribbean York University, 240 York Lanes, 4700 Keele St, Toronto, ON, M3J 1P3, Ⓦ www.yorku.ca/cerlac

Latin American Research Centre Social Sciences Building 004, 2500 University Drive NW, Calgary, Alberta T2N 1N4, Ⓦ larc.ucalgary.ca

UK

Canning House 2 Belgrave Square, London SW1X 8PJ, Ⓦ www.canninghouse .com

Centre of Latin American Studies (University of Cambridge) 17 Mill Lane, Cambridge CB3 9EF, Ⓦ www.latin -american.cam.ac.uk

Institute for the Study of the Americas (University of London) Senate House, Malet St, London WC1E 7HU, Ⓦ americas.sas .ac.uk

Latin America Bureau Ⓦ www.lab.org.uk

US

There are hundreds of Latin American resource centres in the US – these are some of the best.

Center for Latin American and Caribbean Studies 53 Washington Square South, Floor 4w, New York, NY 10012, Ⓦ www .nyu.edu/gsas/program/latin

Center for Latin American Studies University of California, 2334 Bowditch St, Berkeley, CA 94720, Ⓦ clas.berkeley.edu

Center for Latin American Studies ICC 484,Georgetown University 3700 O Street, NW Washington DC 20057-1026, Ⓦ clas .georgetown.edu

Latin American Network Information Center (LANIC) Teresa Lozano Long Institute of Latin American Studies, 1 University Station D0800, Austin, TX 78712, Ⓦ www.lanic.utexas.edu

Travel equipment suppliers

Australia, New Zealand and South Africa

Bivouac Ⓦ www.bivouac.co.nz

First Ascent Ⓦ www.firstascent.co.za

Mont Adventure Ⓦ www.mont.com.au

Mountain Designs Ⓦ www.mountain designs.com

Paddy Pallin Ⓦ www.paddypallin.com.au

UK

Blacks Ⓦ www.blacks.co.uk

Field and Trek Ⓦ www.fieldandtrek.com

Nomad Travel Ⓦ www.nomadtravel.co.uk

US and Canada

Mountain Equipment Co-op Ⓦ www.mec .ca

Mountain Gear Ⓦ www.mountaingear.com

Recreational Equipment Inc Ⓦ www.rei .com

Travel Medicine Ⓦ www.travmed.com

Final checklist

Documents
- Credit and debit cards
- Electronic ticket and flight details
- Guidebooks
- Insurance policy
- International driver's licence
- Maps
- Passport
- Phrasebook
- Phonecard
- Photocopies of vital documents
- Traveller's cheques

The bare essentials
- Backpack
- Clothes
- Daypack
- Fleece jacket
- Money belt
- Sarong
- Shoes
- Sun hat

Basic odds and ends
- Alarm clock
- Batteries
- Camera and battery charger
- Contact lens stuff/glasses
- Contraceptives
- First-aid kit

- Flashlight
- Mosquito repellent
- Padlock and chain
- Penknife
- Sunglasses
- Toiletries
- Towel
- USB memory stick
- Wallet

Other items worth considering
- Books
- Cigarette lighter
- Compass
- Earplugs
- Games
- Mosquito net
- iPod
- Notebook or journal and pens
- Photos/postcards of home
- Rain gear/umbrella
- Sewing kit
- Sheet sleeping bag
- Shortwave radio
- Sink plug
- String
- Water bottle, water purifier or purification tablets
- Waterproof money-holder

Book Aid
International
www.bookaid.org

Books change lives

Poverty and illiteracy go hand in hand. But in sub-Saharan Africa, books are a luxury few can afford. Many children leave school functionally illiterate, and adults often fall back into illiteracy in adulthood due to a lack of available reading material.

Book Aid International knows that books change lives.

Every year we send over half a million books to partners in 12 countries in sub-Saharan Africa, to stock libraries in schools, refugee camps, prisons, universities and communities. Literally millions of readers have access to books and information that could teach them new skills – from keeping chickens to getting a degree in Business Studies or learning how to protect against HIV/AIDS.

What can you do?

Join our Reverse Book Club and with your donation of only £6 a month, we can send 36 books every year to some of the poorest countries in the world. For every two pounds extra you can give, we can send another book!

Support Book Aid International today!

 Online. Go to our website at **www.bookaid.org**, and click on 'donate'

 By telephone. Start a Direct Debit or give a donation on your card by calling us on 020 7733 3577

Book Aid International is a charity and a limited company registered in England and Wales.
Charity No. 313869 Company No. 880754   39-41 Coldharbour Lane, Camberwell, London SE5 9NR
T +44 (0)20 7733 3577   F +44 (0)20 7978 8006   E info@bookaid.org   www.bookaid.org

Small print and

Index

A Rough Guide to Rough Guides

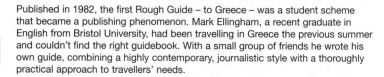

SMALL PRINT

Published in 1982, the first Rough Guide – to Greece – was a student scheme that became a publishing phenomenon. Mark Ellingham, a recent graduate in English from Bristol University, had been travelling in Greece the previous summer and couldn't find the right guidebook. With a small group of friends he wrote his own guide, combining a highly contemporary, journalistic style with a thoroughly practical approach to travellers' needs.

The immediate success of the book spawned a series that rapidly covered dozens of destinations. And, in addition to impecunious backpackers, Rough Guides soon acquired a much broader and older readership that relished the guides' wit and inquisitiveness as much as their enthusiastic, critical approach and value-for-money ethos.

These days, Rough Guides include recommendations from shoestring to luxury and cover more than 200 destinations around the globe, including almost every country in the Americas and Europe, more than half of Africa and most of Asia and Australasia. Our ever-growing team of authors and photographers is spread all over the world, particularly in Europe, the US and Australia.

In the early 1990s, Rough Guides branched out of travel, with the publication of Rough Guides to World Music, Classical Music and the Internet. All three have become benchmark titles in their fields, spearheading the publication of a wide range of books under the Rough Guide name.

Including the travel series, Rough Guides now number more than 350 titles, covering: phrasebooks, waterproof maps, music guides from Opera to Heavy Metal, reference works as diverse as Conspiracy Theories and Shakespeare, and popular culture books from iPods to Poker. Rough Guides also produce a series of more than 120 World Music CDs in partnership with World Music Network.

Visit www.roughguides.com to see our latest publications.

Rough Guide travel images are available for commercial licensing at www.roughguidespictures.com

Rough Guide credits

Text editor: Lucy Cowie
Layout: Anita Singh
Cartography: Maxine Repath
Picture editor: Sarah Cummins
Production: Rebecca Short
Proofreader: Karen Parker
Photographers: Sarah Cummins, Tim Draper, Roger d'Olivere Mapp, Suzanne Porter, Greg Roden
Editorial: Ruth Blackmore, Andy Turner, Keith Drew, Edward Aves, Alice Park, Lucy White, Jo Kirby, James Smart, Natasha Foges, Róisín Cameron, Emma Traynor, Emma Gibbs, Kathryn Lane, Monica Woods, Mani Ramaswamy, Harry Wilson, Amanda Howard, Lara Kavanagh, Alison Roberts, Joe Staines, Peter Buckley, Matthew Milton, Tracy Hopkins, Ruth Tidball; **Delhi** Madhavi Singh, Karen D'Souza, Lubna Shaheen
Design & Pictures: **London** Scott Stickland, Dan May, Diana Jarvis, Mark Thomas, Nicole Newman, Emily Taylor; **Delhi** Umesh Aggarwal, Ajay Verma, Jessica Subramanian, Ankur Guha, Pradeep Thapliyal, Sachin Tanwar, Nikhil Agarwal, Sachin Gupta
Production: Vicky Baldwin

Cartography: **London** Ed Wright, Katie Lloyd-Jones; **Delhi** Rajesh Chhibber, Ashutosh Bharti, Rajesh Mishra, Animesh Pathak, Jasbir Sandhu, Karobi Gogoi, Alakananda Roy, Swati Handoo, Deshpal Dabas
Online: **London** George Atwell, Faye Hellon, Jeanette Angell, Fergus Day, Justine Bright, Clare Bryson, Aine Fearon, Adrian Low, Ezgi Celebi, Amber Bloomfield; **Delhi** Amit Verma, Rahul Kumar, Narender Kumar, Ravi Yadav, Debojit Borah, Rakesh Kumar, Ganesh Sharma, Shisir Basumatari
Marketing & Publicity: **London** Liz Statham, Niki Hanmer, Louise Maher, Jess Carter, Vanessa Godden, Vivienne Watton, Anna Paynton, Rachel Sprackett, Laura Vipond, Vanessa McDonald; **New York** Katy Ball, Judi Powers, Nancy Lambert; **Delhi** Ragini Govind
Manager India: Punita Singh
Reference Director: Andrew Lockett
Operations Manager: Helen Atkinson
PA to Publishing Director: Nicola Henderson
Publishing Director: Martin Dunford
Commercial Manager: Gino Magnotta
Managing Director: John Duhigg

Publishing information

This third edition published February 2010 by
Rough Guides Ltd
80 Strand, London WC2R 0RL
14 Local Shopping Centre, Panchsheel Park, New Delhi 110017, India
Distributed by the Penguin Group
Penguin Books Ltd,
80 Strand, London WC2R 0RL
Penguin Group (USA)
375 Hudson Street, NY 10014, USA
Penguin Group (Australia)
250 Camberwell Road, Camberwell, Victoria 3124, Australia
Penguin Group (Canada)
195 Harry Walker Parkway N, Newmarket, ON, L3Y 7B3 Canada
Penguin Group (NZ)
67 Apollo Drive, Mairangi Bay, Auckland 1310, New Zealand
Cover concept by Peter Dyer.

Typeset in Bembo and Helvetica to an original design by Henry Iles.
Printed in Singapore
© Polly Rodger Brown and James Read 2010
Maps © Rough Guides
No part of this book may be reproduced in any form without permission from the publisher except for the quotation of brief passages in reviews.
320pp includes index
A catalogue record for this book is available from the British Library
ISBN: 978-1-84836-417-2
The publishers and authors have done their best to ensure the accuracy and currency of all the information in **The Rough Guide to First-Time Latin America**, however, they can accept no responsibility for any loss, injury, or inconvenience sustained by any traveller as a result of information or advice contained in the guide.

1   3   5   7   9   8   6   4   2

Help us update

We've gone to a lot of effort to ensure that the third edition of **The Rough Guide to First-Time Latin America** is accurate and up-to-date. However, things change – places get "discovered", opening hours are notoriously fickle, restaurants and rooms raise prices or lower standards. If you feel we've got it wrong or left something out, we'd like to know, and if you can remember the address, the price, the hours, the phone number, so much the better.

Please send your comments with the subject line "**Rough Guide First-Time Latin America Update**" to mail@roughguides.com. We'll credit all contributions and send a copy of the next edition (or any other Rough Guide if you prefer) for the very best emails.

Have your questions answered and tell others about your trip at www.roughguides.com

Acknowledgements

James Read: Thanks to everyone who's helped me on the road or shared in the adventures over the years. Special thanks and love as always to Emma, Freya and Iris. In fond memory of my compadre Coco.

Polly Rodger Brown: Thanks to Luis Maria Noya and his family particularly Patricia and Maxi for making my stay in Argentina such fun; to Alice

Warren for good times in Buenos Aires; to the crew of Aquidaban; to the Paraguayan Navy; to the taxi driver and Carlos who both rescued me in Sao Luis; to lovely Junior and Joao in Barrerinhas; to Stuart Sinclair, and above all to John Albert Duncan who keeps the home fires burning, always.

Readers' letters

Thanks to all the readers who have taken the time to write in with comments and suggestions (and apologies if we've inadvertently omitted or misspelt anyone's name):

Brendan Birkett, Caroline Trimm

Photo credits

Index

Map entries are in colour.

Country abbreviations		
Argentina .... Arg	Ecuador .... Ecu	Nicaragua .... Nic
Belize .... Bel	El Salvador .... ES	Panama .... Pan
Bolivia .... Bol	French Guiana .... FrG	Paraguay .... Par
Brazil .... Bra	Guatemala .... Gua	Peru .... Per
Chile .... Ch	Guyana .... Guy	Suriname .... Sur
Colombia .... Col	Honduras .... Hon	Uruguay .... Uru
Costa Rica .... CR	Mexico .... Mex	Venezuela .... Ven

A

accomodation 145–156
adventure sports 27
Aguas Dulces (Uru) 289
Ahuachapán (ES) 218
AIDS 172
airports 106–110
altitude 167
Amazon 22–23
  Bolivia 246
  Colombia 265
  Ecuador 270
  Peru 285
ancient civilizations
  34–38
Andes 23
Angel Falls (Ven) 292
antibiotics 157
Antigua (Gua) 220
archeology 34
Arequipa (Per) 283
Argentina 239–244
Argentina 241
  best time to go 239
  books 243
  climate 239
  costs 239
  embassies 244
  online 243
  routes in and out 243
Asunción (Par) 279
Atacama Desert (Ch) 260
Avenue of the Volcanoes
  (Ecu) 268
Ayacucho (Per) 285
Aztecs 36, 201
Azuero Peninsula (Pan)
  234
Atitlán Lake (Gua) 220

B

backpacks 93–96
Bahia (Bra) 254

Bahía de Navidad (Mex)
  204
Baja California (Mex) 205
Baños (Ecu) 270
Bartica (Guy) 275
Bay Islands (Hon) 225
Belize 207–210
Belize 209
  best time to go 207
  books 210
  climate 207
  costs 207
  embassies 210
  online 206
  routes in and out 210
Belize City 208
bicycles 142
birdwatching 31
boats 136
Bocas del Toro (Pan) 232
Bogotá (Col) 265
Bolivia 245–249
Bolivia 246
  best time to go 246
  books 249
  climate 246
  costs 246
  embassies 249
  online 249
  routes in and out 248
books 86–89
borders 44
Bosque Montecristo (ES)
  216
Brazil 250–256
Brazil 252–253
  best time to go 250
  books 254
  climate 250
  costs 250
  embassies 256
  online 256
  routes in and out 255
Buenos Aires (Arg) 240
buses 130–133, 137
bargaining 76
budgets 78
bungee jumping 28

C

Cabo Polonio (Uru) 290
Cajamarca (Per) 285
Cali (Col) 265
Campeche (Mex) 205
camping 153
Candombe (Uru) 290
Caparão, Parque Nacional
  (Bra) 255
Cancún (Mex) 20
car rental 139–141
Caracas (Ven) 22
Caracol (Bel) 207
Caribbean Sea 21, 204
Carnaval (Bra) 71, 254
Carnival 72
Carretera Austral (Ch)
  259
Cartagena (Col) 264
cash 159
Catamarca (Arg) 242
Caye Caulker (Bel) 208
Central America
  199–236
Central America 4
Cayenne (FrG) 273
Central Nature Reserve
  (Sur) 274
Central Valley (Ch) 260
Chachapoyas (Per) 285
chagas disease 159
Che Guevara trail (Bol)
  248
Chiapas (Mex) 205
Chichecastenango (Gua)
  222
Chichén Itzá (Mex) 20
Chiquitos (Bol) 248
Chihuahua (Mex) 205
Chile 257–262
Chile 258
  best time to go 257
  books 261
  climate 257

costs 257
embassies 262
online.............................. 262
routes in and out 261
Chiloé (Ch) 259
Chiriqui Highlands (Pan)
.... 234
Chocó (Col) 264
cholera 160
Ciudad Perdida (Col) 22
climate 66–70
climbing 27
clothes 97–99,
115
Coatepeque, Lago (ES)
.... 218
Colombia 263–267
Colombia 264
best time to go 263
books 267
climate 263
costs 263
embassies 267
online.............................. 266
routes in and out 266
Colonia de Sacramento
(Uru) 258
contraception 172
Copán (Hon) 225
Copper Canyon (Mex)
.... 205
Cordlillera Apaneca (ES)
.... 218
Cordillera Blanca (Per)
.... 284
Corn Islands (Nic) 229
Coro (Ven) 295
Coroico (Bol) 247
corruption 191
Costa Rica 211–215
Costa Rica 213
best time to go 211
books 214
climate 211
costs 211
embassies 215
online.............................. 214
routes in and out 214
Costa Verde (Bra) 254
Cotopaxi, Parque Nacional
(Ecu) 271
credit cards 79
crime 179–193
Cuenca (Ecu) 269
Cueva de los Manos
Pintadas (Arg) 242
Cusco (Per) 284
customs 106
Cuyabeno Reserve (Ecu)
.... 270

D

Darién Gap (Pan/Col) 32,
42, 234
Darién Parque Nacional
(Pan) 234
Day of the Dead (Mex)
.... 73, 202
dengue fever 160
Día de la Tradición (Arg) ... 73
diarrhoea 169
diving 28
documents 97
driving 43
drugs 191
dysentery 170

E

earthquakes 185
Easter Island (Ch) 261
eco-lodges 148
ecotourism 126
Ecuador 268–272
Ecuador 269
best time to go 268
books 272
climate 268
costs 268
embassies 272
online.............................. 272
routes in and out 271
e-mail 173
El Castillo (Nic) 229
El Salvador 216–219
El Salvador 217
best time to go 216
books 219
climate 216
costs 216
embassies 219
online.............................. 219
routes in and out 218
estancias 148, 280
Feria de Alasitas (Bol) 72
Fernando de Noronha (Bra)
.... 255
first aid kit 159
fiestas 70–73
film 89–92
flights 42, 48–52
buying a ticket 48–51
round the world 49
airpasses 51
flights, internal 127, 128
food and drink 121–123
food safety 168
football 255

footwear 99
French Guiana 273–277
French Guiana 274
best time to go 273
books 276
climate 273
costs 273
embassies 276
online.............................. 276
routes in and out 275

G

Galápagos Islands (Ecu)
.... 269
Garifuna 225
gauchos 288
gay travellers 114
Georgetown (Guy) 273
Giardia 169
Golfo de Fonseca (ES)
.... 216
Granada (Nic) 229
Gran Chaco (Par) 279
Gran Sabana (Ven) 293
gringos 117
Gringo Trail 24
Guanajuato (Mex) 202
Guatemala 220–224
Guatemala 221
best time to go 220
books 223
climate 220
costs 220
embassies 223
online.............................. 223
routes in and out 223
guerrillas 188
Guiana Space Centre (FrG)
.... 275
guidebooks 82, 305
Guyana 273–277
Guyana 274
best time to go 273
books 276
climate 273
costs 273
embassies 276
online.............................. 276
routes in and out 275

H

hammocks 153
hang-gliding 28
health 157–172, 303
heat, coping with 166
hepatitis 160

HIV...............................172
hitchhiking 143
homesickness...............111
homestays....................152
homophobia 190
homosexuality 114
Honduras.............224–227
Honduras 227
  best time to go.................224
  books.............................226
  climate...........................224
  costs..............................224
  embassies......................226
  online.............................226
  routes in and out............226
hotels 104, 145–156
Huaraz (Per)..................284
hurricanes....................186
hypothermia 166

I

Iberá, Reserva Natural (Arg)
....242
Iguazú Falls (Arg/Bra)
.............................240, 254
Iles du Salut (FrG).........274
immigration...................106
Incas 35, 284
Inca Trail (Per).........24, 284
indigenous culture 38–41
insurance.................52–54
internet 173
Inti Raymi (Per) 73
Iquitos (Per) 285
Isla del Sol (Bol)............247
Itaipú Dam (Par)............280
Iwokrama Rainforest
  Programme (Guy) 274
Ixil Triangle (Gua) 222

J

Jesuit missions (Bol).....248
Jesuit missions (Par) 280
jet lag...........................109

K

Kaietur Falls (Guy) 274
kayaking 28
kidnap...........................185
Kuelap (Per)..................285
Kuna Yala (Pan) 234

L

La Ceiba (Hon)..............225
Lake District (Arg).........240
Lake District (Ch)..........259
Lago Nicaragua (Nic)....230
Lago Titicaca (Per/Bol)
......................24, 247, 285
Lago de Yojoa (Hon).....225
Lagna San Rafael (Ch)
......................................259
Lamanai (Bel)................207
language, learning
.................................55–58
language schools 56–57
La Palma (ES)...............218
La Paz (Bol)...................247
Las Termas (Uru) 290
Lauca Parque Nacional (Ch)
....25
leishmaniasis 160
lesbian travellers...........114
Lethem (Guy) 275
Leticia (Col)...................265
Liberia (CR)...................212
Lima (Per) 286
Llanos (Ven) 32
lorries............................133
Los Glaciares Parque
  Nacional (Arg) 242
Los Mochis (Mex).........205
Los Roques archipelago
  (Ven)...........................293

M

Machalilla, Parque Nacional
  (Ecu)...........................270
Machu Picchu (Per) 284
magazines 85
mail...............................176
malaria.................162–165
Manu Biosphere Reserve
  (Per) 285
maps................43, 84, 305
Margarita (Ven) 295
Masaya (Nic).................230
Maya......35, 201, 207, 222,
225
media............................177
Mérida (Ven).................294
Mexico 201–206
Mexico 203
  best time to go.................201
  books 205
  climate............................201
  costs 201

  embassies......................206
  online.............................206
  routes in and out............205
Mexico City (Mex).........202
Minas Gerais (Bra)........255
money 74–81
money belts............96, 181
Montevideo (Uru)..........289
Morrocoy Parque Nacional
  (Ven)...........................295
Mosquitía (Nic) 225
mosquitoes 162–165
motorbikes 142
mountain biking......28, 247
mountaineering..............27
Mountain Pine Ridge Forest
  Reserve (Bel) 208

N

Nariz del Diablo (Ecu)
......................................271
national parks.................31
Nazca Lines (Per) 285
newspapers..................178
Nicaragua 228–231
Nicaragua.....................229
  best time to go.................228
  books 230
  climate............................228
  costs 228
  embassies......................231
  online.............................231
  routes in and out............230
Noel Kempff Mercado
  Parque Nacional (Bol)
......................................248

O

Oaxaca (Mex) 204
Ometepe (Nic) 230
Orinoco Delta (Ven) 295
Orosí (CR).....................212
Oruro Carnaval (Bol)....248
Osa Peninsula (CR) 211
Otavalo (Ecu)................270

P

Panama................232–236
Panama.........................233
  best time to go.................232
  books 235
  climate............................232
  costs 232

embassies 236
online.............................. 235
routes in and out.............. 235
Panama Canal 234
Panama City 234
Pantanal (Bra)............... 254
Paraguay 278–281
Paraguay 279
best time to go................. 278
books 280
climate............................ 278
costs 278
embassies 281
online.............................. 281
routes in and out.............. 280
Paramaribo (Sur) 275
parasites 170
passport 45,180
Patagonia (Ch/Arg) 26
Península Valdés (Arg)...242
Peru...................... 282–287
Peru............................... 283
best time to go................. 282
books 286
climate............................ 282
costs 282
embassies 287
online.............................. 286
routes in and out.............. 286
Petén (Gua) 31
photography 123, 197
Pico Bonito, Parque
   Nacional (Hon)...........225
Placencia (Bel)............... 208
Plages les Hattes (FrG)
   275
planes 128
Podocarpus, Parque
   Nacional (Ecu) 24
police 191
Popayán (Col) 266
Portobelo (Pan)............. 235
Potosí (Bol) 247
pot-holing 208
Puerto Maldonado (Per)
   285
Puerto Viejo de Talamanca
   (CR) 212
Punta del Este (Uru) 289

Q

Qoyllor Riti (Per) 72
Quebrada de Humahuaca
   (Arg) 242
Quito (Ecu).................... 270

R

rabies............................ 161
radio 178
rafting 28
Rapa Nui (Ch) 261
Rara Avis (CR) 213
religion 112
responsible tourism 124,
   305
Rio Bravo Conservation
   Area (Bel) 208
Rio de Janeiro (Bra)...... 254
Río Dulce (Gua) 222
Río Paraguay 280
Río Plátano Biophere
   Reserve (Hon)............ 225
Rurrenabaque (Bol) 247
Ruta de la Paz (ES) 218
Ruta Maya 20

S

Salta (Arg) 242
San Agustín (Col)..........265
San Andrés y Providencia
   (Col) 266
San Antonio de Areco (Arg)
   242
San Blas Archipelago (Pan)
   22
San Cristóbal de las Casas
   (Mex) 205
San Juan del Sur (Nic)
   230
San Pedro de Atacama (Ch)
   25
Santa Ana (ES) 218
Santa Elena Reserve (CR)
   212
Santiago (Ch)................ 257
schistosomiasis 161
scuba-diving.................... 28
safety and security
   .... 179–193, 95
Salar de Uyuni (Bol)......247
Salvador de Bahia (Bra)
   254
salsa 265
Semana Santa 71
Semuc Champey (Gua)
   221
sexism 113
sexual harassment 190
ships 44
Sierra de Agalta (Hon)...225

skiing 28, 261
snakes 170, 186
snorkelling 28
Solentiname (Nic) 230
Sololá (Gua)................. 221
South America 237–296
South America 5
Southern Cone 70
studying.......................... 59
Suchitoto (ES)............... 218
Sucre (Bol).................... 248
sunburn 165
sunscreen 165
surfing............................. 30
Suriname 273–277
Suriname....................... 274
best time to go................. 273
books 276
climate............................ 273
costs 273
embassies 276
online.............................. 276
routes in and out.............. 275
swimming 187

T

Tambopata-Candamo
   Reserve (Per) 285
Tayrona, Parque Nacional
   (Col) 265
taxis 138
teaching English 63
Tela (Hon)..................... 225
telephones........... 174–176
tetanus.......................... 161
theft.................... 180–184
Tierra del Fuego (Arg/Ch)
   243
Tikal (Gua) 222
Titicaca see Lago Titicaca
   285
Torres del Paine, Parque
   Nacional (Ch) 260
Tortuguero, Parque
   Nacional (CR).............212
tour operators............... 300
tours 144
trains.................... 134–137
transport............. 127–144
travel agents 51, 299
travellers' cheques 79
travel writing 197
trekking.................... 32–34
trucks............................ 133
Trujillo (Per).................. 286
Turrialba (CR)................ 213
typhoid 162

U

Uruguay 288–291
Uruguay 289
  best time to go 280
  books 290
  climate 280
  costs 280
  embassies 291
  online 290
  routes in and out 290
Ushuaia (Arg) 26
Uxmal (Mex) 20
Uyuni (Bol) 247

V

vaccinations 158
Valparaiso (Ch) 260
vegetarians 122
Venezuela 292–296
Venezuela 293
  best time to go 292
  books 296
  climate 292
  costs 292
  embassies 296
  online 296
  routes in and out 295
Vilcambamba (Ecu) 271
Virgen de Guadelupe (Mex)
  73
visas 45–47
VOIP 174
volcanoes 185, 266, 268
Volcán Arenal (CR) 212
Volcán Acaya (Gua) 222
Volcán Parinacota (Ch) ... 25
volunteering 60–61, 303

W

water 167
weather 66–70
websites 85, 306

wildlife 31
whale watching 205
whitewater rafting 28
working 62–64
World's Most Dangerous
  Road (Bol) 247

X

Xunantunich (Bel) 207

Y

Ybicuy, Parque Nacional
  (Par) 280
yellow fever 162
youth hostels 150
Yucatán Pennisula (Mex)
  .... 21, 202, 204
Yungas (Bol) 247

INDEX

So now we've told you about the things not to miss, the best places to stay, the top restaurants, the liveliest bars and the most spectacular sights, it only seems fair to tell you about the best travel insurance around

WorldNomads.com
keep travelling safely

Recommended by Rough Guides